CIMA

PRACTICE & REVISION KIT

Intermediate Paper 6

Financial Accounting

BPP Professional Education
January 2004

First edition 2001
Fourth edition January 2004

ISBN 0 7517 1505 0 (previous edition 0 7517 0280 3)

British Library Cataloguing-in-Publication Data
A catalogue record for this book
is available from the British Library

Published by

BPP Professional Education
Aldine House, Aldine Place
London W12 8AW

www.bpp.com

Printed in Great Britain by W M Print
45-47 Frederick Street
Walsall, West Midlands
WS2 9NE

We are grateful to the Chartered Institute of Management Accountants for permission to reproduce past examination questions. The answers to past examination questions have been prepared by BPP Professional Education.

CONTENTS

BPP)))
PROFESSIONAL EDUCATION

Contents

The headings in this checklist/index indicate the main topics of questions, but questions often cover several different topics.

Preparation questions, listed in italics, provide you with a firm foundation for attempts at exam-standard questions.

Questions set under the old syllabus *Financial Accounting* (FNA) paper are included because their style and content are similar to those which will appear in the Paper 6 exam.

Question and answer checklist

BPP
PROFESSIONAL EDUCATION

TOPIC INDEX

Listed below are the key Paper 6 syllabus topics and the numbers of the questions in this Kit covering these topics.

If you need to concentrate your practice and revision on certain topics or if you want to attempt all available questions that refer to a particular subject (be they preparation or exam-standard questions), you will find this index useful.

EFFECTIVE REVISION

What you must remember

Effective use of time as you approach the exam is very important. You must remember:

> **Believe in yourself**
> **Use time sensibly**

Believe in yourself

Are you cultivating the right attitude of mind? There is absolutely no reason why you should not pass this exam if you adopt the correct approach.

- **Be confident** – you've passed exams before, you can pass them again
- **Be calm** – plenty of adrenaline but no panicking
- **Be focused** – commit yourself to passing the exam

Use time sensibly

---

1 **How much study time do you have?** Remember that you must **eat, sleep,** and of course, **relax.**

2 **How will you split that available time between each subject?** A **revision timetable,** covering **what** and **how** you will revise, will help you organise your revision effectively.

3 **What is your learning style?** AM/PM? Little and often/long sessions? Evenings/weekends?

4 **Do you have quality study time?** Unplug the phone. Let everybody know that you're studying and shouldn't be disturbed.

5 **Are you taking regular breaks?** Most people absorb more if they do not attempt to study for long uninterrupted periods of time. A five minute break every hour (to make coffee, watch the news headlines) can make all the difference.

6 Are you **rewarding yourself** for your hard work? Are you leading a **healthy lifestyle**?

What to revise

Key topics

You need to spend most time on, and practise full questions on, **key topics**.

> Key topics
> - Recur regularly
> - Underpin whole paper
> - Appear often in compulsory questions
> - Discussed currently in press
> - Covered in recent articles by examiner
> - Shown as high priority in study material
> - Tipped by lecturer

Difficult areas

You may also still find certain areas of the syllabus difficult.

> Difficult areas
>
> - Areas you find dull or pointless
> - Subjects you highlighted as difficult when taking notes
> - Topics that gave you problems when you answered questions or reviewed the material

DON'T become depressed about these areas; instead do something about them.

- Build up your knowledge by **quick tests** such as the quick quizzes in your BPP Study Text.

- Work carefully through **numerical examples** and **questions** in the Text, and refer back to the Text if you struggle with computations in the Kit.

- **Note down weaknesses** that your answers to questions contained; you are less likely to make the same mistakes if you highlight where you went wrong.

Breadth of revision

Make sure your revision has sufficient **breadth**. You need to be able to answer all the compulsory questions and enough optional questions on the paper. On certain papers all major topics in the syllabus will be tested, through objective test questions or longer questions. On other papers it will be impossible to predict which topics will be examined in compulsory questions, which topics in optional questions.

Paper 6

In this paper do not spend all your revision practising the numerical techniques. 40% of the marks available will be for written sections of questions, so it is vital that you understand and can explain the principles behind the accounting practice.

How to revise

There are four main ways that you can revise a topic area.

Write it!
Read it!
Teach it!
Do it!

Effective revision

> **Write it!**

The Course Notes and the Study Text are too bulky for revision. You need a slimmed down set of notes that summarise the key points. Writing important points down will help you recall them, particularly if your notes are presented in a way that makes it easy for you to remember them.

> **Read it!**

You should read your notes or BPP Passcards actively, testing yourself by doing quick quizzes or writing summaries of what you have just read.

> **Teach it!**

Exams require you to show your understanding. Teaching what you are revising to another person helps you practise explaining topics. Teaching someone who will challenge your understanding, someone for example who will be taking the same exam as you, can help both of you.

> **Do it!**

Remember that you are revising in order to be able to answer questions in the exam. Answering questions will help you practise **technique** and **discipline**, which examiners emphasise over and over again can be crucial in passing or failing exams.

1   A bank of **objective test questions** is included for each syllabus area. Attempt all of these banks and use them as a **diagnostic tool**: if you get lots of them wrong go back to your BPP Study Text or look through the Paper 6 Passcards and do some revision. Additional guidance on how to tackle objective test questions is given on page (xxv). If you get the majority of the objective test questions correct, move on to any **preparation questions** included for the syllabus area. These provide you with a firm foundation from which to attempt exam-standard questions.

2   The more exam-standard questions you do, the more likely you are to pass the exam. At the very least, you should attempt the **key questions** that are highlighted from page (xiv) onwards.

3   You should produce **full answers** under **timed conditions,** and don't cheat by looking at the answer! Look back at your notes or at your BPP Study Text instead if you are really struggling. Produce answer plans if you are running short of time.

4   Always read the **Pass marks** in the answers. They are there to help you, and will show you which points in the answer are the most important.

5   **Don't get despondent** if you didn't do very well. Refer to the **topic index** and try another question that covers the same subject.

6   When you think you can successfully answer questions on the whole syllabus, attempt the **two mock exams** at the end of the Kit. You will get the most benefit by sitting them under strict exam conditions, so that you gain experience of the four vital exam processes.

- Selecting questions
- Deciding on the order in which to attempt them
- Managing your time
- Producing answers

BPP's *Learning to Learn Accountancy* book gives further invaluable advice on how to approach revision.

BPP has also produced other vital revision aids.

- **Passcards** – Provide you with clear topic summaries and exam tips
- **Success tapes** – Help you revise on the move
- **Videos** – Show you an overview of key topics and how they are related
- **MCQ cards** - Give you lots of practice in answering MCQs
- **i-Pass CDs** – Offer you tests of knowledge to be completed against the clock

You can purchase these products by completing the order form at the back of this Kit or by visiting www.bpp.com/cima.

DETAILED REVISION PLAN

The table below gives you **one possible approach** to your revision for *Financial Accounting*. There are of course many ways in which you can tackle the final stages of your study for this paper and this is just a **suggestion**: simply following it is no guarantee of success. You or your college may prefer an alternative but equally valid approach.

The BPP plan below, requires you to devote a **minimum of 45 hours** to revision of Paper 6. Any time you can spend over and above this should only increase your chances of success.

Suggested approach

1 For each section of the syllabus, **review** your **notes** and the relevant chapter summaries in the Paper 6 **Passcards**.

2 Then do the **key questions** for that section. These are **shaded** in the table below. Even if you are short of time you must attempt these questions if you want to pass the exam. Try to complete your answers without referring to our solutions.

3 For some questions we have suggested that you prepare **answer plans** rather than full solutions. This means that you should spend about 30% of the full time allowance on brainstorming the question and drawing up a list of points to be included in the answer.

4 Once you have worked through all of the syllabus sections attempt **mock exam 1** (the May 2003 paper) under strict exam conditions. Then, if you've got enough time, have a go at **mock exam 2** (the November 2003 paper), again under strict exam conditions.

Syllabus section	2004 Passcards chapters	Key questions in this kit	Comments	Done ☑
Regulation	1	1 2	These deal with the key issues included in FRS 18 which underpin accounts. Be prepared for a question in this area. Prepare full answers for both questions 1 and 2.	☐ ☐ ☐ ☐
		3	Basic knowledge on Companies Act accounts requirements which may well be tested. Materiality is a key notion which pervades accounting and audit work. Something that the examiner could slip in for a few valuable marks. Do an answer plan. True and fair is another popular topic.	☐
		4	Standards setting process has obvious appeal to an examiner. Gives you scope to discuss your 'favourite' FRSs. Answer plan.	☐
Financial statements	2 & 3	5	A mixed question. Worth reviewing the information relating to directors' emoluments.	☐
		7	A neat little question dealing with issues of application such as treatment of training costs and prior period bad debts. Also includes FRS10 on Goodwill. Prepare an answer plan but ensure you understand the suggested answer provided.	☐
		9	A good example of a standard published accounts question, the sort of thing that you are bound to meet in the exam.	☐

Syllabus section	2004 Passcards chapters	Key questions in this kit	Comments	Done ☑
		10, 11, 12,	All good examples of published accounts questions: do them if you feel you need the practice. Review how the tricky bits are done, eg NRV aspects in Q11.	☐
		13	EPS is a key topic which could appear in an FRS 3 context ratio question or as a stand alone question. Ensure you develop full answers. Identify and focus on the parts where you might be weak.	☐
Financial statements (contd)	2 & 3	17	This is a testing question covering many aspects of FRS 3 which could come up. You must know the proformas required by the question.	☐
		20	A useful written question covering discussive issues that could be examined. Worth developing an answer plan.	☐
	4	21	Cash flows statements is an obvious candidate for the paper. Practise it till you get it right. Supplement by using T accounts on tricky areas in other similar questions. You can score heavily on cash flow statements.	☐
Accounting standards	5 & 6	25	Key question on fixed assets. Practise it till you have perfected your answer.	☐
		26	Develop an answer plan. Think carefully about part (d).	☐
	7	27	Excellent and very relevant question on stock. Please develop a full answer and ensure you address the parts you may still be weak on.	☐
		28	Pilot question. Worth doing answer plan.	☐
		29	Long term contracts. A popular exam topic. Do this till you are confident that you can get it spot on. Remember individual amounts on one contract cannot be offset against another contract, eg debtor on contract A must be disclosed separately to an amount paid on account in contract B.	☐
	8	33	A recent and useful question, worth doing in full.	☐
	9	34	Part (a) deals with finance leases and substance over form. Part (b) covers statement of principles. Worth doing an answer plan.	☐
		35	A key question on HP accounting. Work through the question till you can get it right and make good time in the exams.	☐
	10	39	Develop an answer plan and review the suggested answer carefully.	☐
		40	This is a key question examining government grants. You must be able to respond properly to the three scenarios presented in part (b).	☐

Syllabus section	2004 Passcards chapters	Key questions in this kit	Comments	Done ☑
Accounting standards (contd)		41	FRS 8 can be a tricky area, but the actual question you get may be not so daunting. Have a go at doing a full answer to develop your confidence in this area.	☐
		42	This is a typical multi-standard question where you have to apply your theoretical knowledge of accounting standards to a spectrum of given scenarios. Do it and if necessary, redo the question, until you feel confident that you can crack a similar question in the exams.	☐
	11	43	Work through the question to develop a working knowledge for the exams. A written question can provide good marks.	☐ ☐
		45, 46	FRS12 is a popular exam topic: work through both questions with the answers ensuring you understand the principles and issues involved.	☐
		48	A practical question on FRS 8. Make a full attempt as it may appear again on a paper.	☐
		49, 51, 52, 53	The issue of shares and the repurchase of shares are popular topics with the examiner. Make sure that you can explain the principles and do the calculations.	☐
Performance	12	54, 58, 61, 65	These types of questions can usually give good marks. Work through these questions till you can do the necessary calculations quickly and accurately.	☐ ☐ ☐ ☐
			Practise the analysis and interpretation parts till you can make a series of coherent and mark worthy comments.	
		55, 56, 57, 59, 60, 62, 63, 64	Read through the answers to develop an overall awareness of the sorts of issues that could be examined.	☐
External audit	13	67	Mowbray Computers. This question tests your understanding of audit reports and their implications. Make sure you stick to the facts and avoid waffle.	☐
		68	A good question to build up your confidence in this area.	☐
			Don't be afraid to rework your answer till you can hit a high level of correctness.	

THE EXAM PAPER

Format of the paper (with effect from May 2003)

		Number of marks
Section A:	10 compulsory objective test questions	20
Section B:	One compulsory question	30
Section C:	Choose two out of four 25 mark questions	50
		100

Time allowed : 3 hours

A new examiner has been appointed with effect from May 2003. He has indicated that his ultimate intention is that the paper will be set in the proportions 60% computational and 40% written.

Analysis of past papers

The analysis below shows the topics which have been examined in the Pilot paper and the exams set up to November 2003. All these papers were set under the old format for the paper ie with no multiple choice questions.

November 2003

Section A

1   10 Multiple choice questions

Section B

2   Preparation of financial statements in a form suitable for publication and in accordance with current regulations.

Section C

3   Valuation of properties. External audit actions. Role of FRRP.
4   Analysis and interpretation of financial statements.
5   Treatment of brands and goodwill. Research and development costs. Government grants.
6   Preparation of cash flow statement. Explanation of usefulness of cash flow statements.

May 2003

Section A

1   10 Multiple choice questions

Section B

2   Preparation of financial statements in a form suitable for publication and in accordance with current regulations.

Section C

3   Finance leases, revision of useful economic life and initial recognition of tangible fixed assets
4   P/E ratio calculation. Accounting ratios and interpretation of accounts. Non-financial factors relating to a take-over target
5   *Statement of Principles,* characteristics of useful information, application of SOP to FRS 18, true and fair override
6   Post balance sheet events. Decomissioning costs.

Examiner's comments.

This was the first paper using the new format. Question one, multiple choice questions, was relatively well done by candidates. Question two was also relatively well done by candidates, although a large proportion was unable to read the question correctly and prepared detailed notes to the accounts as well as workings. Unfortunately some candidates seemed to rely almost entirely on questions 1 and 2 and made little attempt at the rest of the paper. The narrative sections of all questions were often ignored or the attempt was not adequate to achieve a pass on that section. Most candidates that made a reasonable attempt at section C of the paper achieved a pass.

November 2002

Section A

1   (a)   Preparation of financial statements in a form suitable for publications with notes
     (b)   Accounting treatment of sales
     (c)   Considerations of the external auditor in assessing accounting policies
     (d)   Disagreement in the auditor's report
2   Ratio analysis; substance over form; earnings per share

Section B (2 out of 4 questions)

3   Fixed assets, depreciation and FRS 15
4   Long term contracts
5   Accounting for the issue of shares; bonus issues; different types of share
6   FRS 12

Examiner's comments.

The narrative parts of all questions were often ignored, or the attempt was not adequate to achieve a pass on that part. Candidates should note that this paper assesses (among other things) candidates' understanding and application of accounting regulations and expects knowledge to be demonstrated through calculation and explanation or discussion.

May 2002

Section A

1   (a)   Preparation of financial statements in a form suitable for publication, including the reconciliation of movements in shareholders' funds, a statement of total recognised gains and losses and notes
     (b)   Main profitability ratios and reasons why they may have been distorted
         How the presentation of information in the financial statements helps the understanding of shareholders.
2   Preparation of a cash flow statement

Section B (2 out of 4 questions)

3   Accounting ratios. Limitation of the annual report as a basis for comparison of companies
4   Contingent liabilities and FRS 12
5   Financial Reporting Review Panel: role, disagreement over depreciation; role of the external auditor
6   Notes for taxation and deferred taxation and FRS 19

Examiner's comments.

As has previously been the case, the main problems were candidates' failure to read questions properly and therefore to produce the answers required, and carelessness, leading to avoidable errors.

Answers to the cash flow statement question were disappointing, although they should not present any problems to candidates at this level. The question on interpretation of accounts was well answered, and the examiner was impressed in question 1(b) with the ability of many candidates to apply common sense to a business or accounting situation.

November 2001

Section A

1   (a)   Preparation of financial statements in a form suitable for publication, with appropriate notes
    (b)   Statement of principles. Regulatory systems. Review of accounting policies. Relevance and reliability
2   Revaluation of fixed assets. Disclosures. Impact on accounting ratios and company position

Section B (2 out of 4 questions)

3   Accounting ratios. Assessment of management teams
4   Closing stocks and SSAP 9
5   Cash flow statements. Assessment of cash management efficiency
6   SSAP 13. Research costs. Development expenditure. True and fair override

Examiner's comments.

Candidates generally scored well on the published accounts question (Q1) although many made easily avoidable errors and some answers were badly structured.

It is often worth looking at a whole question before answering any of it, in order to gain a perspective on the whole issue. Thinking about one part can often provide clues and ideas to help with other parts.

A common error throughout was failure to address the precise requirements of questions. Candidates should try to avoid just memorising information; they need to be able to apply it to the specific question. There seemed to be a lack of understanding of some of the principles of accounting for stock.

May 2001

Section A

1   Preparation of profit and loss account and balance sheet. EPS and FRS 14
2   Deferred tax. The auditor's report and their duties

Section B (2 out of 4 questions)

3   Working capital cycle
4   Related party disclosures
5   Purchase of own shares by a company
6   Leases, ratios and gearing

Examiner's comments.

Candidates generally scored well on the published accounts question (Q1) although many made easily avoidable errors and some answers were badly structured.

Students must ensure that they address the actual requirements of the question and avoid regurgitating prepared answers or padding.

Generally, written questions must demonstrate a good commercial awareness, in a real world sense.

The exam paper

Pilot paper

Section A

1   Preparation of a published profit and loss account, balance sheet and notes to the accounts
2   Revaluation of fixed assets. Depreciation. Investment properties

Section B (2 out of 4 questions)

3   Calculation of ratios and explanation of a company's performance
4   Calculation and discussion of the disclosure of long-term contracts
5   Explanation of SSAP 21 and the Statement of Principles
6   Explanation and preparation of the pensions note as per SSAP 24

EXAM TECHNIQUE

Passing professional examinations is half about having the knowledge, and half about doing yourself full justice in the examination. You must have the right approach at the following times.

> **Before the exam**
>
> **Your time in the exam hall**

Before the exam

1   Set at least one **alarm** (or get an alarm call) for a morning exam.

2   Have **something to eat** but beware of eating too much; you may feel sleepy if your system is digesting a large meal.

3   Allow plenty of **time to get to the exam hall**; have your route worked out in advance and listen to news bulletins to check for potential travel problems.

4   **Don't forget** pens, pencils, rulers, erasers, watch. Also make sure you remember **entrance documentation** and **evidence of identity**.

5   Put **new batteries** into your calculator and take a spare set (or a spare calculator).

6   **Avoid discussion** about the exam with other candidates outside the exam hall.

Your time in the exam hall

1   *Read the instructions (the 'rubric') on the front of the exam paper carefully*

Check that the exam format hasn't changed. Examiners' reports often remark on the number of students who attempt too few - or too many - questions, or who attempt the wrong number of questions from different parts of the paper.

2   *Select questions carefully*

Read through the paper once, underlining the key words in the question and jotting down the most important points.   Select the optional questions that you feel you can answer best. You should base your selection on:

- The **topics** covered
- The **requirements of the whole question** (see page (xxvi) for the guidance on what the examiner means)
- How easy it will be to **apply the requirements** to the details you are given
- The availability of **easy marks**

Make sure that you are planning to answer the **right number of questions,** all the compulsory questions plus the correct number of optional questions.

3   *Plan your attack carefully*

Consider the **order** in which you are going to tackle questions. It is a good idea to start with your best question to boost your morale and get some easy marks 'in the bag'.

4   *Check the time allocation for each question*

Each mark carries with it a **time allocation** of 1.8 minutes (including time for selecting and reading questions, and checking answers). A 25 mark question therefore should be selected, completed and checked in 45 minutes. When time is up, you **must** go on to the next question or part. Going even one minute over the time allowed brings you a lot closer to failure.

5   *Read the question carefully and plan your answer*

Read through the question again very carefully when you come to answer it. Plan your answer taking into account how the answer should be **structured**, what the **format** should be and **how long** it should take.

Confirm before you start writing that your plan makes **sense**, covers **all relevant points** and does not include **irrelevant material.** Two minutes of planning plus eight minutes of writing is virtually certain to earn you more marks than ten minutes of writing.

6   *Answer the question set*

Particularly with written answers, make sure you **answer the question set**, and not the question you would have preferred to have been set.

7   *Gain the easy marks*

Include the obvious if it answers the question and don't try to produce the perfect answer.

Don't get bogged down in small parts of questions. If you find a part of a question difficult, get on with the rest of the question. If you are having problems with something, the chances are that everyone else is too.

8   *Produce an answer in the correct format*

The examiner will **state in the requirements** the format in which the question should be answered, for example in a report or memorandum.

9   *Follow the examiner's instructions*

You will **annoy** the examiner if you ignore him or her.

10   *Lay out your numerical computations and use workings correctly*

Make sure the layout fits the **type of question** and is in a style the examiner likes. Show all your **workings** clearly and explain what they mean. **Cross reference** them to your solution. This will help the examiner to follow your method (this is of particular importance where there may be several possible answers).

11   *Present a tidy paper*

You are a professional, and it should show in the **presentation of your work**. Students are penalised for poor presentation and so you should make sure that you write legibly, label diagrams clearly and lay out your work neatly. Markers of scripts each have hundreds of papers to mark; a badly written scrawl is unlikely to receive the same attention as a neat and well laid out paper.

12   *Stay until the end of the exam*

Use any spare time **checking and rechecking** your script. This includes checking:

* You have **filled out** the **candidate details correctly.**
* Question parts and workings are **labelled clearly.**
* Aids to navigation such as **headers and underlining** are used effectively.
* **Spelling, grammar** and **arithmetic** are correct.

13   *Don't discuss an exam with other candidates afterwards*

There's nothing more you can do about it so why discuss it?

14 ***Don't worry if you feel you have performed badly in the exam***

It is more than likely that the other candidates will have found the exam difficult too. Don't forget that there is a competitive element in these exams. As soon as you get up to leave the exam hall, *forget* **that exam** and think about the next - or, if it is the last one, celebrate!

> BPP's *Learning to Learn Accountancy* book gives further invaluable advice on how to approach the day of the exam.

BPP
PROFESSIONAL EDUCATION

TACKLING MULTIPLE CHOICE QUESTIONS

The MCQs in your exam contain four possible answers. You have to **choose the option that best answers the question**. The three incorrect options are called distracters. There is a skill in answering MCQs quickly and correctly. By practising MCQs you can develop this skill, giving yourself a better chance of passing the exam.

You may wish to follow the approach outlined below, or you may prefer to adapt it.

Step 1.   Skim read all the MCQs and identify which appear to be the easier questions.

Step 2.   Work out **how long** you should allocate to each MCQ bearing in mind the number of marks available and any guidance the examiner has given about how long they should take in total. Also remember that the examiner will not expect you to spend an equal amount of time on each MCQ; some can be answered instantly but others will take time to work out.

Step 3.   Attempt each question – **starting with the easier questions** identified in Step 1. Read the question thoroughly. You may prefer to work out the answer before looking at the options, or you may prefer to look at the options at the beginning. Adopt the method that works best for you.

You may find that you recognise a question when you sit the exam. Be aware that the detail and/or requirement may be different. If the question seems familiar, read the requirement and options carefully – do not assume that it is identical.

Step 4.   Read the four options and see if one matches your own answer. Be careful with numerical questions, as the distracters are designed to match answers that incorporate **common errors**. Check that your calculation is correct. Have you followed the requirement exactly? Have you included every stage of the calculation?

Step 5.   You may find that none of the options matches your answer.

- Re-read the question to ensure that you understand it and are answering the requirement

- Eliminate any obviously wrong answers

- Consider which of the remaining answers is the most likely to be correct and select that option

Step 6.   If you are still unsure, make a note and continue to the next question. Likewise if you are nowhere near working out which option is correct, leave the question and come back to it later.

Step 7.   Revisit unanswered questions. When you come back to a question after a break, you often find you can answer it correctly straightaway. If you are still unsure, have a guess. You are not penalised for incorrect answers, so **never leave a question unanswered!**

TACKLING OBJECTIVE TEST QUESTIONS

What is an objective test question?

An objective test (**OT**) question is made up of some form of **stimulus**, usually a question, and a **requirement** to do something.

(a) Filling in a blank or blanks in a sentence

(b) Listing items in rank order

(c) Stating a definition

(d) Identifying a key issue, term or figure

(e) Calculating a specific figure

(f) Completing gaps in a set of data where the relevant numbers can be calculated from the information given

(g) Identifying points/zones/ranges/areas on graphs or diagrams

(h) Matching items or statements

(i) Stating whether statements are true or false

(j) Writing brief (in a specified number of words) explanations to the data given

(k) Deleting incorrect items

(l) Choosing right words from a number of options

CIMA guidance

CIMA has offered the following **guidance** about OT questions in the exam which you should remember if any OTs are set.

- **Only your answers will be marked,** not workings or any justifications.

- If you **exceed a specified limit on the number of words** you can use in an answer, you will **not be awarded any marks**.

- If you make **more than one attempt** at a question, clearly **cross through** any answers that you do not want to submit. If you don't do this, only your first answer will be marked.

We strongly suggest that you take note of the guidance given above if you have to answer OT questions in the exam.

WHAT THE EXAMINER MEANS

The table below has been prepared by CIMA to help you interpret exam questions.

The verbs used in questions indicate which key skills you will be using to answer them, and therefore the depth your answer should have, and how you should use the information you are given in the question.

Learning objective	Verbs used	Definition	Examples in the Kit
1 Knowledge What you are expected to know	• List	• Make a list of	Q48
	• State	• Express, fully or clearly, the details of/facts of	Q16
	• Define	• Give the exact meaning of	Q20(a)
2 Comprehension What you are expected to understand	• Describe	• Communicate the key features of	Q3
	• Distinguish	• Highlight the differences between	Q1
	• Explain	• Make clear or intelligible/state the meaning of	Q4
	• Identify	• Recognise, establish or select after consideration	Q18(a)
	• Illustrate	• Use an example to describe or explain something	
3 Application Can you apply your knowledge?	• Apply	• To put to practical use	
	• Calculate/compute	• To ascertain or reckon mathematically	Q37(a)
	• Demonstrate	• To prove the certainty or to exhibit by practical means	
	• Prepare	• To make or get ready for use	Q8
	• Reconcile	• To make or prove consistent/compatible	Q17(d)
	• Solve	• Find an answer to	
	• Tabulate	• Arrange in a table	
4 Analysis Can you analyse the detail of what you have learned?	• Analyse	• Examine in detail the structure of	Q64
	• Categorise	• Place into a defined class or division	
	• Compare and contrast	• Show the similarities and/or differences between	
	• Construct	• To build up or complete	
	• Discuss	• To examine in detail by argument	Q23(b)(c)
	• Interpret	• To translate into intelligible or familiar terms	
	• Produce	• To create or bring into existence	

Learning objective	Verbs used	Definition	Examples in the Kit
5 Evaluation Can you use your learning to evaluate, make decisions or recommendations?	• Advise • Evaluate • Recommend	• To counsel, inform or notify • To appraise or assess the value of • To advise on a course of action	 Q57(d) Q63(e)

BPP
PROFESSIONAL EDUCATION

CURRENT ISSUES

The 2003 edition of the BPP text for CIMA Paper 6, Financial Accounting, is fully up to date for examinable material at the date of its publication.

No further examinable material relevant to this paper has been published since then.

USEFUL WEBSITES

The websites below provide additional sources of information of relevance to your studies for *Financial Accounting.*

- **www.bpp.com**

  The website of the BPP group. Links with BPP Publishing and BPP Accountancy Courses with details of products and services that can help you achieve your professional qualification.

- **www.cimaglobal.com**

  CIMA's own website. Includes Student section

- **www.accountingweb.com**

  A US site with articles on current accounting related issues. The site is searchable by accounting topic.

- **www.ft.com**

  The site of The Financial Times. Excellent business search facility.

- **www.economist.com**

  The site of The Economist. Another good business search facility.

- **www.asb.org.uk**

  The official Accounting Standards Board website.

SYLLABUS MINDMAP

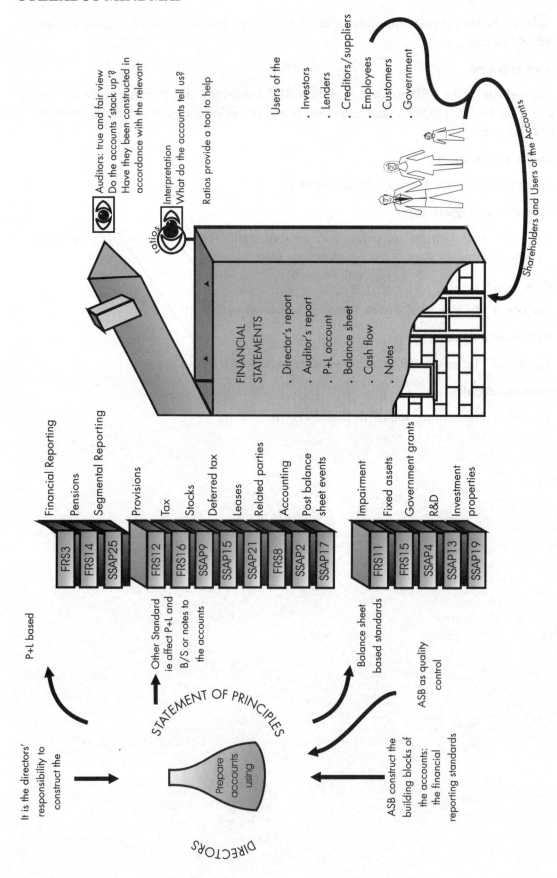

Questions

2

> **REGULATION**
>
> The objective test questions and questions 1 to 4 cover regulation, the subject of Part A of the BPP Study Text for Paper 6.

OBJECTIVE TEST QUESTIONS

1   Which accounting concepts are identified in FRS 18 Accounting Policies as playing a pervasive role in financial statements?

   A   Prudence and accruals.
   B   Going concern and accruals. ⁄
   C   Prudence and going concern.
   D   Going concern, accruals, consistency and prudence.

2   What is the function of the Financial Reporting Review Panel (FRRP)?

   A   To review financial reporting standards (FRSs) to identify any necessary changes.

   B   To investigate material departures from the requirements of the Companies Act 1985 and accounting standards in company financial statements ⁄

   C   To provide guidance to the Accounting Standards Board on policy and to arrange finance for the standard setting process.

   D   To promote harmonisation of UK accounting standards (FRSs) with international accounting standards (IASs)

3   Which of the following characteristics of financial information contribute to reliability, according to the Accounting Standards Board's Statement of Principles for Financial Reporting?

   1   Neutrality   ⁄
   2   Completeness ⁄
   3   Prudence   ⁄
   4   Consistency

   A   All four characteristics
   B   1, 2 and 3 only
   C   1, 2 and 4 only
   D   3 and 4 only

4   The Accounting Standard's Board's (ASB's) Statement of Principles defines liabilities as:

   A   Amounts owed to a third party
   B   Obligations to transfer economic benefits as a result of past transactions or events ⁄
   C   Expenditure that has been incurred but not yet charged to the profit and loss account
   D   Obligations that may arise in the future

5   Which of the following statements about the provisions of the Companies Act 1985 (CA 1985) are true?

   1   A public company's financial statements must include a chairman's report.

   2   A public's company's directors' report must disclose details of the company's policy on the payment of creditors.

   3   A company has six months from its balance sheet date to lodge its accounts with the Registrar of Companies

   4   A company may disregard a provision of the CA 1985 if this is necessary for the financial statements to give a true and fair view.

   A   1, 2, 3 and 4.
   B   2, 3 and 4 only
   C   1 and 3 only.
   D   2 and 4 only

6   Which of the following best explains the prudence concept as described in the ASB's Statement of Principles for Financial Reporting and FRS 18 Accounting Policies?

   A   Ensuring that financial information is free from material error.

   B   Ensuring at all times that assets and gains are understated and liabilities and losses are overstated.

   C   The inclusion of a degree of caution in the exercise of judgements in conditions of uncertainty.

   D   Recognition of revenue and profits only when realised, with provision made for all known liabilities and losses.

If you struggled with these objective test questions, go back to your BPP Study Text for this paper and revise Chapter 1 before you tackle the written questions on regulation.

---

1   PREPARATION QUESTION: ACCOUNTING POLICIES AND ESTIMATION TECHNIQUES

FRS 18 *Accounting policies* distinguishes between accounting policies and estimation techniques and the accounting for changes in each is very different.

Required

(a) Distinguish between accounting policies and estimation techniques, as defined by FRS 18 and state the differences in accounting for a change in accounting policy and a change in an estimation technique.

(b) For items (i) to (v) below, state in each case whether the proposed changes represent changes in accounting policies or estimation techniques, giving brief reasons.

   (i)   **Depreciation of vehicles**

   (1) An entity has previously depreciated vehicles using the reducing balance method at 40% per year. It now proposes to depreciate vehicles using the straight-line method over five years, since it believes this better reflects the pattern of consumption of economic benefits.

   (2) As in (1), an entity has previously depreciated vehicles using the reducing balance method at 40% per year and now proposes to depreciate vehicles using the straight-line method over five years. In addition, it has previously recorded the depreciation charge within cost of sales, but now proposes to include it within administrative expenses.

   (ii) **Classification of overheads**

   An entity has previously shown certain overheads within cost of sales. It now proposes to show those overheads within administrative expenses.

   (iii) **Indirect overheads recorded in the value of stock**

   A manufacturing entity has three indirect cost centres (A, B and C). It has previously assessed that the indirect costs attributable to production are 30% of A and 40% of B. Having reassessed the nature of those cost centres' activities, it now assesses that the indirect costs attributable to production are 25% of A, 40% of B and 10% of C.

   (iv) **Capitalised finance costs**

   An entity has previously charged to the profit and loss account interest incurred in connection with the construction of tangible fixed assets. It now proposes to capitalise such interest, as permitted by FRS 15 *Tangible fixed assets*, since it believes this better reflects the cost of constructing those assets.

   (v)   **Provisions**

   An entity has previously measured a particular provision on an undiscounted basis, in accordance with FRS 12 *Provisions, contingent liabilities and contingent assets*, as the effect of discounting was not material.

   However, this year it has revised upwards its estimates of future cash flows associated with the provision and, as a result, the effect of discounting is now material. FRS 12 therefore requires it to report the provision at the discounted amount.

2   PREPARATION QUESTION: SELECTING ACCOUNTING POLICIES

FRS 18 suggests that selection of appropriate accounting policies should be judged against the following objectives:

(a) Relevance
(b) Reliability
(c) Comparability
(d) Understandability

Required

Explain the meaning of the above terminology within the context of FRS 18.

3   COMPANIES ACT 1985 REQUIREMENTS (5/95 amended)   *45 mins*

The Companies Act 1985 requires that the profit and loss account and balance sheet should be laid out in prescribed formats. These statements should also be supplemented by a number of further disclosures, which are usually presented in the form of notes to the profit and loss account and the balance sheet.

Required

(a) Explain how the requirement to present the profit and loss account and balance sheet in prescribed formats helps the readers of financial statements.   **7 Marks**

(b) Briefly describe *two* notes to the financial statements which are typically found in a set of published financial statements and which are provided in response to Companies Act disclosure requirements. Explain why this information is useful to the readers of financial statements.   **8 Marks**

(c) True and fair accounts should be free from material error or misstatement. Explain what is meant by materiality in this context.   **5 Marks**

(d) Explain what is meant by financial statements showing a true and fair view.   **5 Marks**

Total Marks = 25

4   ACCOUNTING STANDARDS (11/00 amended)   *45 mins*

One of your friends has recently decided to invest in some quoted securities. He is, however, concerned that the companies in which he is interested may have inflated their share prices by publishing misleading financial statements. He is aware that the accountancy profession has established a standard setting body, but has read that this organisation is subject to a number of influences.

Required

(a) Explain how the Accounting Standards Board (ASB) goes about setting a Financial Reporting Standard (FRS). Explain how the process could be influenced by the preparers of financial statements.   **8 Marks**

(b) Explain the procedures which must be followed if a company's directors and auditors consider that the application of the requirements of an accounting standard would give a misleading impression.   **7 Marks**

(c) Explain why it can be difficult for the directors to discharge the duty to present a true and fair view.   **5 Marks**

(d) Briefly describe two Financial Reporting Standards issued by the Accounting Standards Board which help to ensure that companies do not overstate assets or gains or understate liabilities or losses.

5 Marks

Total Marks = 25

FINANCIAL STATEMENTS

The objective test questions and questions 5 to 26 cover financial statements, the subject of Part B of
the BPP Study Text for Paper 6.

OBJECTIVE TEST QUESTIONS

1   The Companies Act 1985 lays down detailed requirements about company financial
    statements.

    Which of these statements about these requirements are correct? (Assume in all cases that
    material figures exist for every item referred to.)

    1   The total of all fixed assets may be shown in the balance sheet, with an analysis into
        tangible assets, intangible assets and investments shown by note.

    2   If a company holds its own shares, they must be shown in the balance sheet as a
        deduction from called up share capital.

    3   Debenture loans could appear under the heading 'Creditors: amounts falling due
        within one year'

    4   Details of movements in all fixed assets must be shown by note.

    5   A note must give an analysis of stocks into raw materials, work in progress and
        finished goods.

    6   Details of movements in reserves must be shown by note.

    A   All the statements are correct.
    B   3, 4, 5 and 6 only.
    C   1, 3, 4 and 5 only.
    D   1, 2, and 6 only.

2   Which, if any, of the following statements about limited companies are correct?

    1   Public companies must lodge their accounts with the Registrar of Companies within
        six months of the end of their accounting reference period.

    2   Private companies must deliver copies of their accounts to their members but are not
        required to lodge them with the Registrar of Companies.

    3   The accounting records of a company must be open to inspection by a member of the
        company at all times.

    A   None of the statements above.
    B   1 and 2 only are correct.
    C   2 and 3 only are correct.
    D   1 and 3 only are correct

3   A company qualifies as 'small' under the Companies Act 1985 if it meets two out of three
    criteria as to turnover, balance sheet totals and number of employees.

Which of the following correctly states the limits?

	Turnover not exceeding	Balance sheet total not exceeding £	Number of employees not exceeding £
A	£5.6m	£11.2m	50
B	£5.6m	£11.2m	250
C	£1.4m	£2.8m	50
D	£2.8m	£1.4m	50

4 Which of the following statements about company financial statements are true?

1 The statement of total recognised gains and losses must not include unrealised gains.

2 A company qualifying as 'small' as defined in the Companies Act 1985 does not normally need to file a profit and loss account with the Registrar of Companies.

3 Investments may appear in the balance sheet as either fixed assets or current assets.

4 When a revalued asset is sold, the revaluation surplus may be transferred from revaluation reserve to profit and loss account reserve in the balance sheet.

A 2, 3 and 4
B 3 and 4
C 1 and 2
D 1 and 4

5 Which of the following constitutes a change of accounting policy according to FRS 18 Accounting Policies?

1 A change in the basis of valuing stock.

2 A change in depreciation method.

3 Charging depreciation in cost of sales when it has previously been charged in administrative expenses.

4 A change from an undiscounted basis to a discounted basis in reporting deferred tax.

A 1, 2 and 4.
B 2, 3 and 4.
C 1, 3 and 4.
D 1, 2 and 3.

6 Which of the following items must appear in the directors' report of a company, if applicable?

1 Recommended dividend
2 Details of political and charitable donations if they together total more than £200.
3 Names of the directors of the company.
4 Principal activities of the company
5 Details of the company's policy as regards the payment of creditors.

A All of the items must be covered.
B 1, 3 and 4 only
C 3 and 4 only.
D 1, 3 and 5 only.

7   Which of the following items would qualify for treatment as an extraordinary item according to FRS 3 Reporting Financial Performance, if material?

1   Profit or loss on the sale of part of the entity.
2   Profit or loss on disposal of fixed assets.
3   Abnormal charges for bad debts and write-offs of stock and work in progress.
4   Settlement of insurance claims.

A   All four items.
B   1 and 4 only.
C   1, 2 and 3 only
D   None of the items.

8   FRS 3 Reporting Financial Performance identifies three types of exceptional item which must be shown separately on the face of the profit and loss account.

Which of the following items qualify for this treatment?

1   Profits or losses on the sale or termination of an operation. ✓

2   Settlement of insurance claims.

3   Expropriation of assets.

4   An earthquake or other natural disaster.

5   Profits or losses on non-routine disposals of fixed assets.

6   Costs of a fundamental reorganisation altering the nature and focus of the entity's operations. ✓

A   1, 3 and 4.
B   2, 3 and 6.
C   1, 5 and 6.
D   2, 4 and 5.

9   Which of these items may appear in a company's statement of total recognised gains and losses, according to FRS 3 Reporting Financial Performance?

1   Profit for the financial year
2   Dividends paid and proposed.
3   Unrealised revaluation gains and losses. ✓
4   Prior year adjustments ✓
5   New share capital subscribed.

A   1, 2 and 5 only.
B   1, 2, 3 and 4
C   1, 3 and 4 only
D   All five items

10 Which trading companies does SSAP 25 Segmental Reporting apply to?

1 All companies.

2 All public companies.

3 Private companies qualifying as medium-sized under Companies Act 1985.

4 Private companies exceeding ten times the medium-sized company limits in Companies Act 1985.

A 1 only.
B 2 only.
C 2 and 3.
D 2 and 4.

11 Which of the following correctly states the calculation of the main earning per share (EPS) figure as required by FRS14?

A Profit after interest and before tax divided by the weighted average of ordinary shares in issue during the period.

B Profit for the financial year less preference dividends divided by the weighted average number of ordinary shares in issue during the period.

C Profit for the financial year less preference dividends divided by the number of ordinary shares in issue at the end of period.

D Profit for the financial year before charging extraordinary items less preference dividends divided by the weighted average number of shares in issue during the period.

12 Which of the following events may cause a company to restate its earnings per share (EPS) for the previous year in the comparative figures for the current year?

1 A bonus issue of ordinary shares in the current year.
2 A rights issue of ordinary shares in the current year.
3 An issue of shares at full market price in the current year.
4 A change in accounting policy.

A 2, 3 and 4 only.
B 1, 2 and 4 only.
C 1, 2 and 3 only.
D 1 and 4 only.

13 An extract from BJ plc's profit and loss account for the year ending 31 December 20X2 is given below.

	£
Profit before tax	756,000
Corporation tax	224,000
Profit after tax	532,000
Dividends	248,000
Retained profit	284,000

The company's issued share capital is made up of 1,000,000 50 pence ordinary shares and £800,000 of £1 6% preference shares.

What is the basic earnings per share for the year?

A   48.4 pence
B   53.2 pence
C   70.8 pence
D   75.6 pence

(14) Q plc has issued share capital of 10,000,000 ordinary shares of 50p each at 31 December 20X6.

On 1 April 20X7 the company made a rights issue of 2,000,000 shares at £1 each. The market price of the shares immediately before the issue was £1.24.

The company's earnings for 20X7 were £1,158,000.

What is Q plc's earnings per share for 20X7 in pence to two places of decimals?

A   9.65p
B   10.07p
C   10.14p
D   10.00p

Handwritten notes (left margin): Actual cum Rights / TERP / 1·24 / 1·20 / 5 @ 1·24 = 6·2 / 1 @ £1 / 6 / 72 / TERP = 1·2

Handwritten notes (right): 31. Dec X6 10,000,000 time 3/12   Bonus fraction 1·24/1·2
1. Ap X7 12,000,000 9/12   2583,333·3 / 11,58'3333·3

15   Which of the following could be classified as potential ordinary shares according to FRS 14 Earnings per Share?

1   Share capital authorised but not yet issued.
2   Convertible loan stock. ✓
3   Shares issued by way of a bonus issue. ✓
4   Convertible preference shares

A   1 only
B   2 and 4 only.
C   2, 3 and 4
D   All four items.

(16) A company's capital structure throughout 20X5 consists of:

2m ordinary shares of 50p each.
£1m 8% convertible loan stock.

The loan stock may be converted to ordinary shares in 20X8 at the rate of 1 ordinary share for every £2 of loan stock.   *500,000 shares*

The company's profit after tax in 20X5 was £500,000.
The tax rate is 30%.

Handwritten notes (left margin): Earnings + interest saved net of tax / 1,000,000 x 8% x 70% / + 500,000 / Shares = Basic + new shares on conversion

What is the company's fully diluted earnings per share (EPS) for 20X5, to one place of decimals?

A   27.8p
B   23.2p
C   22.2p
D   20.0p

Handwritten: £ 556,000 / 2,500,000

17   On 1 March 2001 G plc had 800,000 £1 ordinary shares in issue. On 1 June 2001 the company made a 1 for 4 rights issue at an issue price of £1.80. On 1 June 2001 the market value of G plc's shares was £2.20.

The reported profits for the year ended 28 February 2002 were £8,800,000 and the earnings per share for the year ended 28 February 2001 was 9.8 pence per share.

What figures would appear in the profit and loss account for the year ending 28 February 2002 for earnings per share?

	30 June 2002	*30 June 2001*
A	8.8 pence	9.4 pence
B	8.8 pence	9.8 pence
C	9.2 pence	9.4 pence
D	9.2 pence	9.8 pence

18   The following is an extract from a cash flow statement prepared by a trainee accountant:

Reconciliation of operating profit to net cash flow from operating activities.

	£000
Operating profit	3,840
Depreciation and amortisation	(1,060)
Loss on sale of building	210
Increase in stocks	(490)
Decrease in creditors	290
Net cash inflow from operating activities	2,790

↑stocks ∴ pay more ∴ cf↓

Which of the following criticisms of this extract are correct?

1   Depreciation and amortisation should have been added, not deducted. ✓
2   Loss on sale of building should have been deducted, not added.
3   Increase in stocks should have been added, not deducted.
4   Decrease in creditors should have been deducted, not added. ✓

A   1 and 4.
B   2 and 3.
C   1 and 3.
D   2 and 4.

19   In the year ended 31 December 20X4 a company sold some plant which had cost £100,000 for £20,000. At the time of sale the net book value of the plant was £18,000.

Which of the following correctly states the treatment of the transaction in the company's cash flow statement?

	Proceeds of sale	*Profit on sale*
A	Cash inflow under Financing	Deducted from profit in calculating cash flow from operations.
B	Cash inflow under Capital Expenditure ✓	Added to profit in calculating cash flow from operations.
C	Cash inflow under Financing	Added to profit in calculating cash flow from operations.
D	Cash inflow under Capital Expenditure ✓	Deducted from profit in calculating cash flow from operations. ✓

20   Which of the following items should *not* appear in a company's cash flow statement?

      1   Proposed dividends.
      2   Dividends received.
      3   Bonus issue of shares.
      4   Surplus on revaluation of a fixed asset.
      5   Proceeds of sale of an investment not connected with the company's trading activities.

      A   1, 2, 3 and 5.
      B   3 and 4 only.
      C   1, 3 and 4.
      D   2 and 5.

21   Which, if any, of the following statements about cash flow statements are correct according to FRS1 Cash Flow Statements?

      1   The direct and indirect methods produce different figures for operating cash flow.

      2   In calculating operating cash flow using the indirect method, an increase in stock is added to operating profit.

      3   Figures shown in the cash flow statement should include value added tax.

      4   The final figure in the cash flow statement is the increase or decrease in cash and cash equivalents.

      A   1 and 4
      B   2 and 3
      C   2 only
      D   None of the statements is correct.

22   A company's balance sheets at 31 December 20X4 and 20X5 included the following items:

	Balance sheets at	
	31.12.X5	31.12.X4
	£000	£000
Current liabilities		
Taxation	840	760
Proposed dividend	360	300
Profit and loss account		
(total retained profit)	1,660	1,470

The company paid no interest or interim dividends during these years, and the tax provision of £760,000 in the 20X4 balance sheet was the amount paid in 20X5. Using this information, what is the company's operating profit for 20X5 for inclusion in its cash flow statement?

      A   £190,000
      B   £1,390,000
      C   £1,250,000
      D   £1,660,000

23   The balance sheets of R plc at 31 December 20X3 and 20X4 included these figures:

	31 December	
	20X3	20X4
	£m	£m
Fixed assets – cost	40	50
Accumulated depreciation	(10)	(14)
	30	36

14

The profit and loss account for the year ended 31 December 20X4 showed the following figures

Depreciation charge for year	£6m
Loss on sales of fixed assets	£1m

The company purchased new fixed assets costing £16m during the year.

What figure should appear in the company's cash flow statement for 20X4 for receipts from the sale of fixed assets?

A   £3m

B   £5m

C   £4m

D   The figure cannot be calculated from the information provided.

(handwritten working)
FA
Bal b/d 40 | loss sale tru
Dep 6 | Dep 6
additions 16 | c/d 50
56 | 56

24   The final figure in a cash flow statement is the increase or decrease in cash in the period.

Which of the following items are included in this cash movement?

1   Cash at bank

2   Overdraft at bank

3   Deposits repayable within 24 hours

4   Current asset investments readily convertible into known amounts of cash and which can be sold without disrupting the company's business.

A   All four items

B   1, 2 and 3 only.

C   1 and 2 only

D   1 and 3 only

25   Which of the following should appear in a cash flow statement under the heading Returns on Investment and Servicing of Finance, according to FRS 1 Cash Flow Statements?

1   Dividends paid on preference shares.

2   Interest capitalised as part of the cost of a fixed asset.

3   The interest element of finance lease rental payments.

A   All three items

B   1 and 2 only

C   1 and 3 only

D   2 and 3 only

> If you struggled with these objective test questions, go back to your BPP Study Text for this paper and revise Chapters 2 to 4 before you tackle the written questions on financial statements.

5   PREPARATION QUESTION: PUBLISHED ACCOUNTS

XYZ plc is a listed company which manufactures in the United Kingdom. It is primarily involved in the production and marketing of crystal glassware, and in the manufacture and installation of kitchen and bedroom furniture.

Crystal glassware accounts for 60% of the company's sales turnover and contributes 45% of the trading profits. 70% of glassware sales is exported and provides 50% of the glassware trading profits.

For the year ended 31 March 20X5, trading profits, before interest charges and taxation, amounted to £1.6 million on a sales turnover of £28 million.

Details of the company's directors and of their shareholdings are as follows.

The number of ordinary shares held in XYZ plc at 31 March 20X5 were Director A (Chairman), 30,720; Director B, 21,200; Director C, nil; Director D, 800; Director E, 750 and Director F, 4,200. Directors A and F acquired 1,800 and 2,300 shares respectively during the year ended 31 March 20X5, but no change had occurred in the holdings of the other directors.

During the year fees received by Directors A and E amounted to £15,000 and £8,000 respectively. Other emoluments received by Directors B, C, D and F amounted to £47,000, £28,400, £22,300 and £21,500 respectively. The company paid £37,600 during the year in respect of directors' pension contributions.

Required

From the above narrative and information, state which of the items you would expect to find in the annual report and accounts of the company, prepared in accordance with the Companies Acts; indicate where each item would appear; and show, by computation where necessary, how the information for each item would be presented.

Approaching the question

1   Be sure to read the question carefully. It tests your knowledge of the Companies Act 1985, not of SSAPs, FRSs or Stock Exchange regulations.

2   There are no 'red herrings' in this question! Each piece of information is important and belongs somewhere.

3   The information in the question is presented in an unstructured way; you must identify headings and sub-headings which help you to structure your answer.

4   A good technique would be to jot down next to each item in the question where it would appear and whether a computation is necessary. This should enable you to approach your answer in a logical fashion.

6   PREPARATION QUESTION: DISCONTINUED OPERATIONS

The following data relates to Pinguo Ltd for the year ended December 20X4.

* Pinguo Ltd's profit for the financial year was £2,290,000

* Land was revalued at market value of £3,000,000. Its book value had been £2,000,000.

Required

(a)   Prepare a statement of total recognised gains and losses for Pinguo Ltd for the year ended 31 December 20X4.

(b) FRS 3 *Reporting financial performance* requires separate disclosure of the results of continuing operations, acquisitions and discontinued operations.

  (i)   Explain what is meant, in FRS 3, by 'acquisitions' and 'discontinued operations'.

  (ii)   Why is it useful to distinguish between the three types of operations for financial reporting purposes?

7   U PLC (FAC, 11/94 amended)   *45 mins*

The managers of U plc are in the process of preparing the company's annual report. They have listed the following material problems which will have to be resolved before the financial statements can be finalised.

(a) *Plant and machinery*

During the year, the company carried out a major overhaul of its plant and machinery. The directors are of the opinion that, because the company receives expenditure in maintaining its plant and machinery to a high standard, it should no longer be depreciated. **4 Marks**

(b) *Bad debt from previous year*

The company had to write off as bad a debt which had appeared in the balance sheet of the previous year. The directors are of the opinion that this should be treated as a prior period adjustment rather than showing the write-off as part of bad debts incurred during the current year. **4 Marks**

(c) *Training costs*

The company organised a series of training courses for all members of its sales staff. The directors are of the opinion that the company will benefit from this investment for several years to come and have proposed that the cost of the courses should be capitalised and written off over five years. **4 Marks**

(d) *Government grant*

A grant was received towards the cost of renovating the company's factory. The directors claim that they would have invested in this work even if the grant had not been available. They are, therefore, of the opinion that the grant is merely a source of revenue and so should be treated as income for the current year. **4 Marks**

(e) *Revaluation*

The company owns two buildings, the factory and the head office. According to a recent valuation the head office is now worth £100,000 more than its book value whereas the factory, due to the need for renovation, is worth £50,000 less than its book value. Due to the impending renovation the directors propose only to revalue the head office in the financial statements. **5 Marks**

(f) *Goodwill*

During the year, the company purchased a controlling interest in another company. This involved a payment for goodwill. The directors are keen to carry this asset forward indefinitely on the grounds that the goodwill will increase in value over time. **4 Marks**

Required

Explain why the directors' proposed treatments would be incorrect in each of the above cases and also explain how each should be accounted for. You should refer to accounting standards where appropriate. **Total Marks = 25**

8   **P LTD (FAC, 5/94 amended)**   *45 mins*

The following information has been extracted from the accounting records of P Ltd.

TRIAL BALANCE AS AT 31 MARCH 20X4

	£'000	£'000
Sales		5,000
Cost of sales	1,350	
Dividends received		210
Administration	490	
Distribution	370	
Interest payable	170	
Application and allotment		300
Taxation	25	
Interim dividend	170	
Tangible fixed assets	4,250	
Short-term investments	2,700	
Stock	114	
Debtors	418	
Bank	12	
Creditors		136
Long term loans (repayable 20Y2)		1,200
Share capital		1,500
Share premium		800
Profit and loss		923
	10,069	10,069

handwritten: under Dr.: ~~over~~ Provision · Audit fee

(a)   Interest on the long term loans of £30,000 relating to the year ended 31 March 20X4 has not yet been paid or accounted for.

(b)   The balance on the application and allotment account represents money received from the issue of 200,000 £1 shares at a premium of 20 pence per share. This offer was oversubscribed. The shares were allotted on 28 March 20X4. Applicants received four fully-paid shares for every five applied for, and surplus payments were refunded in April 20X4. No entries had been made in the accounting records in respect of the allotments by 31 March 20X4.

(c)   On 31 March 20X4 the directors decided to revalue the buildings to £3.8 million. The buildings originally cost £3 million and had a net book value at 31 March 20X4 of £2.6 million. *handwritten: (2 1.2 × 1.250 = 5.450)*

(e)   During the year, the company paid a final dividend of £240,000 in respect of the year ended 31 March 20X3. This was in addition to the interim dividend paid on 1 September 20X3 in respect of the year ended 31 March 20X4. The balance on the taxation account comprises the balance remaining from the settlement of the estimated corporation tax charge for the year ended 31 March 20X3.

(f)   The depreciation charge for the year was £850,000 and is included in cost of sales and administration. *handwritten: already.*

(g)   The corporation tax charge for the year has been estimated at £470,000 and the directors wish to set up a deferred tax provision of £56,000.

(h)   The directors have proposed a final dividend of £270,000.

(i)   The audit fee of £200,000 has not yet been accounted for. *handwritten: admin*

Required

Prepare a profit and loss account and balance sheet for the year ended 31 March 20X4. These should be in a form suitable for publication.

Your answer should include any notes intended for publication and these should be distinguished from workings.

You are *not* required to prepare a note on accounting policies.   **25 Marks**

9   CONFECTIONERY ETC (5/02 amended)   *54 mins*

J plc is a large company which is listed on its national stock exchange. It has been going through a period of rapid change in response to shareholder pressures and also adverse comment in the financial press. The company's latest trial balance at 31 March 20X4 is as follows.

J PLC
TRIAL BALANCE AT 31 MARCH 20X4

	£ million	£ million
Operating activities		
Administrative expenses	60	
Cost of sales – clothing *Disconhnued*	140	
Cost of sales – confectionery	40	
Cost of sales – games software	60	
Distribution costs	45	
Sales – clothing *Dis conhnued*		250
Sales – confectionery		100
Sales – games software		300
	345	650
Other activities		
Bank	9	
Creditors		16
Debtors	54	
Deferred tax		(10)
Finance charges on leases	(6)	
Finance leases		40
Interest	(31)	
Loans (repayable 20Y2)		300
Profit and loss		29
Reorganisation costs	30	
Revaluation reserve		35
Share capital (£1 shares – fully paid)		400
Share premium		200
Stock at 31 March 20X4	30	
Tangible fixed assets	1,170	
Taxation *under provision*	(5)	
	1,680	1,680

(handwritten workings: 31 +6 = 37 ... Alredy 4 ... 33)

(i)   J plc stopped manufacturing clothing during the year. The closure of this operation was completed during the year and so no further reorganisation costs are expected to arise in respect of this.

(ii)   J plc expanded the games software operation during the year. Substantial amounts were spent on the recruitment of new staff, the organisation of a new factory for manufacturing games discs and cartridges and the conversion of the company's old clothing shops into games shops. Prior to this expansion, the company's games software operation was very much smaller and did not have any of its own manufacturing capacity.

(iii) Reorganisation costs are made up as follows.

	£ million
Loss on disposal of clothing factory	11
Redundancy and other costs of closure	9
Reorganisation of games software	10
	30

(iv) During the year ended 31 March 20X4, J plc sold its clothing factories, which had a book value of £205 million, for £194 million. This loss on disposal was included in the total for reorganisation costs. ✓

(v) Administrative expenses and distribution costs can be allocated as follows.

	Administration	*Distribution*
	%	%
Clothing	20	20
Confectionery	50	40
Games software	30	40

(vi) During the year ended 31 March 20X4, J plc acquired £821 million of new tangible fixed assets, primarily the factory and equipment for the manufacture of games software. Some of this was financed by borrowing. Finance leases worth £48 million and £200 million of long-term loans were taken out.

(vii) The finance leases outstanding at 31 March 20X4 include £10 million that will be payable within twelve months. The remainder will be repaid within five years.

(viii) During the year ended 31 March 20X4 J plc charged a total of £90 million depreciation on its tangible fixed assets.

(ix) The balance on the revaluation reserve represents the effects of the revaluation in previous years of the property used in the company's confectionery interests. A revaluation of these properties on 31 March 20X4 increased their values by a further £100 million. The adjustments required to incorporate this revaluation in the accounting records have not yet been made.

(x) The figure in the trial balance for interest includes £4 million spent on finance for the construction of the new factory. The directors have decided to capitalise these finance charges.

(xi) On 30 June 20X4 the company issued 100 million shares for £1.60 each by means of a rights issue. The market price of the shares immediately before the rights issue was £1.80.

(xii) The balance on the taxation account represents the balance remaining after settling the tax charge for the year ended 31 March 20X4. The directors have estimated the tax charge for the year ended 31 March 20X4 at £42 million. The provision for deferred tax is to be increased to £16 million.

(xiii) J plc has not paid a dividend for several years and the directors do not intend to pay one in the immediate future.

Required:

(a) Prepare the profit and loss account for J plc for the year to 31 March 20X4 and a balance sheet at that date, in a form suitable for publication and in accordance with all current regulations.

> Notes to the financial statements are not required, but all workings must be clearly shown. DO NOT prepare a statement of accounting policies or a statement of total recognised gains and losses or a SSAP 25 segmented analysis.

20 Marks

(b) Prepare a reconciliation of movements in shareholders' funds for J plc for the year ended 31 March 20X4.   **5 Marks**

(c) Calculate J plc's earnings per share for the year ended 31 March 20X4.   **5 Marks**

Total Marks = 30

10   SHOPPING CENTRES (5/97, amended)   *54 mins*

L plc operates several large shopping centres across the country. These centres are located on the outskirts of major towns and cities; each centre has at least three major retail stores which belong to L plc. The company advertises heavily, both on national television and on regional radio stations.

The company rents out smaller shops in each of its centres. The tenants pay rent and are also required to contribute to the costs of advertising. Both rents and contributions to advertising are paid in advance.

L plc has recently commissioned an advertising campaign. This will be broadcast over a two-year period commencing at the end of June 20X7. The company has paid the consultants who designed the campaign, and has purchased most of the television and radio advertising time in advance. L plc's marketing experts expect that the advertising campaign will help to build customer loyalty and will continue to attract income for anything up to three years after the end of the campaign.

L plc has invoiced its tenants for 40% of the cost of the campaign. The invoices were sent out just prior to the end of the current financial year. Given that L plc has effectively 'sold' this advertising, the company's managing director is in favour of treating the £800,000 invoiced as turnover for the year ended 31 March 20X7.

The following summarised trial balance has been extracted from the books of L plc.

TRIAL BALANCE AT 31 MARCH 20X7

	£'000	£'000
Retail sales		25,000 ✗
Cost of retail sales	16,250 ✗	
Administration expenses	250 ✗	
Distribution costs (excluding advertising campaign)	500 ✗	
Advertising campaign	D. 2,000	
Rental income		1,500 ✗ other income
Advertising charges to tenants		800 – accruals
Balances recoverable from tenants for advertising	D. 800	
Interest paid	350 ✗	
✗ Corporation tax underprovided for year to 31 March 20X6	30 ✗	
✗ Fixed assets: cost or valuation	27,000 ✗	
✗ Fixed assets: depreciation		4,200 ✗
✓ Revaluation reserve		8,000 ✗ revaluations
Stock at 31 March 20X7	850 ✗	
Bank	700 ✗	
Trade creditors		1,800 ✗
Long-term loans		2,300 ✗
Share capital		4,000
Retained profits		1,130
	48,730	48,730

(i) The company revalued its land during the year. This was the first time that such a revaluation had taken place. The land had cost £9 million and had not been depreciated. The valuation was conducted by Valier and Co, a firm of Chartered Surveyors.

(ii) During the year the company spent £11 million on new fixed assets. These replaced assets which had originally cost £4 million. Those assets were sold for £1.8 million, including a gain on disposal of £300,000. The gain has been included under the appropriate cost headings on the trial balance.

(iii) Depreciation of £3.7 million has been charged during the year and is included under the appropriate cost headings on the trial balance.

21

(iv) The directors have proposed a final dividend of £750,000 for the year ended 31 March 20X7.

(v) Corporation tax for the year has been estimated at £2.1 million.

Required

(a) Prepare L plc's profit and loss account for the year ended 31 March 20X7, statement of total recognised gains and losses and balance sheet at that date.

> These should be in a form suitable for publication *and* should include the notes to the financial statements (insofar as is possible given the information provided).
>
> You are *not* required to provide a statement of accounting policies *or* to calculate the company's earnings per share.

(handwritten in margin: which notes add value?)

25 Marks

(b) Explain whether or not you agree with the managing director's argument that the proportion of advertising billed to tenants has been sold and can, therefore, be included in turnover for the year ended 31 March 20X7. State any assumptions made.

5 Marks
Total Marks = 30

11   ELECTRONIC COMPONENTS (11/02 amended)   *54 mins*

M plc manufactures components for sale to the electronics industry. The following trial balance has been extracted from the company's financial records:

M PLC
TRIAL BALANCE AT 30 SEPTEMBER 20X4

	£ million	£ million
Administrative expenses	64	
Bank	98	
Cost of sales	1,142	
Deferred tax		291
Disposal of plant and machinery	11	
Distribution costs	148	
Dividend – interim paid	300	
Interest	72	
Loans (repayable 20Z0)		1,618
Plant and machinery – cost	794	
Plant and machinery – depreciation to date		324
Premises – cost	4,456	
Premises – depreciation to date		811
Retained profit brought forward		1,132
Share capital		600
Stock at 30 September 20X4	45	
Taxation		37
Trade creditors		327
Trade debtors	980	
Turnover		2,970
	8,110	8,110

(handwritten annotations: "Disposal" near Disposal of plant and machinery; "B/ at begin" and "B at end" near Plant and machinery cost; "Dep begin" near depreciation)

(i) M plc is a quoted company. Authorised share capital is 800 million shares of £1.00. Issued share capital is 600 million shares of £1.00, fully paid.

(ii) Plant and machinery which had cost £125 million and had been depreciated by £78 million was sold during the year. New plant and machinery was purchased for £160 million. These transactions have been included in the above figures. There were no other transactions involving fixed assets.

(iii) Depreciation for the year has still to be charged as follows.

Premises	2% of cost
Plant and machinery	25% reducing balance

A whole year's depreciation is charged in the year of acquisition and none in the year of disposal.

(iv) The trial balance figure for stock is calculated on the following basis.

	Purchase price £ million	Attributable manufacturing overheads £ million	Attributable non-manufacturing overheads £ million	Total cost £ million	Net realisable value £ million
Current stock	26	7	3	36	51
Obsolete stock	6	2	1	9	5
Total				45	56

Total cost is lower than total net realisable value and so the directors have valued the stock at £45 million. The external auditors have refused to accept this valuation, arguing that it is inconsistent with the requirements of SSAP 9 *Stocks and long-term contracts*. M plc's directors have agreed to correct the stock figure to bring it into line with SSAP 9.

(v) The directors have estimated the tax charge for the year at £120 million. The balance on the taxation account is the amount remaining after settling the liability for the year ended 30 September 20X3.

(vi) The provision for deferred tax has arisen from the timing differences arising from accelerated capital allowances on the company's tangible fixed assets. The tax written-down value of tangible fixed assets at 30 September 20X4 was £2,985 million. It is estimated that tax will be paid at a rate of 30% when these timing differences reverse.

(vii) The directors propose a final dividend of £150 million.

Required:

(a) Prepare the profit and loss account for M plc for the year to 30 September 20X4 and a balance sheet at that date, in a form suitable for publication and in accordance with current regulations.

> Notes to the financial statements are NOT required, but all workings must be clearly shown. DO NOT prepare a statement of accounting policies, a statement of total recognised gains and losses, or a reconciliation of movements in shareholders' funds.

20 Marks

(b) Calculate M plc's earnings per share for the year ended 30 September 20X4.   **3 Marks**

(c) M plc's external auditors disagreed with the company's treatment of the closing stock value. If M plc had not changed the closing stock value explain how this would have been reflected in the auditor's report on the financial statements.   **4 Marks**

(d) Explain how the concept of neutrality affects the preparation of financial statements.

3 Marks

Total Marks = 30

12 RADAR EQUIPMENT (5/99, amended) *54 mins*

T plc manufactures radar equipment for military and civil aircraft. The company's latest trial balance at 31 December 20X8 is as follows:

	£'000	£'000
Administration costs	800	
Bank overdraft		700
Debtors	2,000	
Factory - cost	18,000	
Factory - depreciation		1,800
Factory running costs	1,200	
Loan interest	1,680	
Long -term loans		12,000
Machinery - costs	13,000	
Machinery - depreciation		8,000
Manufacturing wages	1,300	
Opening stock - parts and materials	400	
Opening stock - work-in-progress	900	
Profit and loss account		380
Purchases - parts and materials	2,300	
Research and development	5,300	
Sales		10,000
Sales salaries	600	
Share capital		15,000
Trade creditors		600
Trade fair	1,000	
	48,480	48,480

(i) Stock was counted at 31 December 20X8. Closing stocks of parts and materials were valued at £520,000 and closing stocks of work-in-progress were valued at £710,000. There are no stocks of finished goods because all production is for specific customer orders and goods are usually shipped as soon as they are completed.

(ii) No depreciation has been charged for the year ended 31 December 20X8. The company depreciates the factory at 2% of cost per annum and all machinery at 25% per annum on the reducing balance basis.

(iii) The balance on the research and development account is made up as follows:

	£
Opening balance (development costs brought forward)	2,100,000
Purchase of laboratory calibration equipment	600,000
Long-range radar project	900,000
Wide-angle microwave project	1,700,000
	5,300,000

The opening balance comprises expenditure on new products which have just been introduced to the market. The company has decided that these costs should be written off over ten years, starting with the year ended 31 December 20X8. T plc has a policy of capitalising all development costs which meet the criteria laid down by SSAP 13.

The new calibrating equipment is used in the company's research laboratory. It is used to ensure that the measurement devices used during experiments are properly adjusted. The long-range radar project is intended to adapt existing military radar technology for civilian air traffic control purposes. The company has built a successful prototype and has had strong expressions of interest from a number of potential customers. It is almost certain that the company will start to sell this product early in the year 20Y0 and that it will make a profit.

The wide-angle microwave project is an attempt to apply some theoretical concepts to create a new radar system for use in military aircraft. Initial experiments have been promising, but there is little immediate prospect of a saleable product because the transmitter is far too large and heavy to install in an aeroplane.

(iv) During the year the company spent £1,000,000 in order to exhibit its product range at a major trade fair. This was the first time that T plc has attended such an event. No orders have been received as a direct result of this fair, although the sales director has argued that contacts were made which will generate sales over the next few years.

(v)   T plc has made losses for tax purposes for several years. It does not expect to pay any tax for the year ended 31 December 20X8.

(vi) The directors do not plan to pay any dividends for the year ended 31 December 20X8.

Required

(a) Prepare T plc's profit and loss account for the year ended 31 December 20X8 and its balance sheet at that date.

> These should be in a form suitable for publication and should be accompanied by notes as far as you are able to prepare these from the information provided.
>
> Do not prepare a statement of accounting policies, a statement of total recognised gains and losses, a reconciliation of movements in shareholders' funds or a calculation of earnings per share.

20 Marks

(b) (i)   Explain how each of the following items should be treated in T plc's financial statements.

Research and development:

1	New calibrating equipment purchased for laboratory	**2 Marks**
2	Long-range radar project	**3 Marks**
3	Wide-angle microwave project	**2 Marks**

(ii) Explain how the costs associated with the trade fair should be treated in T plc's financial statements.   **3 Marks**

Total Marks = 30

13   **MANUFACTURING (5/01 amended)**   *54 mins*

G plc is a large manufacturing company. It is listed on its national stock exchange. The company's shares are widely held by a very large number of individual shareholders and its activities are heavily reported in the business press.

G plc's trial balance at 31 December 20X2 is shown below.

	£m	£m
Administrative expenses	130	
Bank	10	
Cost of sales	240	
Deferred taxation		200
Dividend – interim paid	40	
Intangible fixed assets – net book value	1,900	
Interest	95	
Long-term loans		1,100
Profit and loss account		1,875
Sales		1,000
Selling and distribution costs	100	
Share capital		500
Share premium		400
Stock at 31 December 20X2	110	
Tangible fixed assets – net book value	2,400	
Taxation		10
Trade creditors		30
Trade debtors	90	
	5,115	5,115

Notes

(handwritten: not paid yet – to B/S under <1yr)

(handwritten right margin: over dr under. 10 over provision)

(a) The directors estimate the tax charge on the year's profits at £120 million. The balance on the taxation account represents the balance remaining after settling the amount due for the year ended 31 December 20X1.

(b) The balance on the provision for deferred taxation should be increased to £280 million which represents a provision for all known deferred tax liabilities at the balance sheet date.

(c) The directors have proposed a final dividend of £60 million. ✓

(d) G plc's share capital is made up of £1 shares, all of which are fully paid up. The company issued 100 million shares on 28 February 20X2. These were sold for their full market price of £1.40 per share. This sale has been included in the figures shown in the trial balance. *(handwritten: do nothing except put in note)*

(e) A major customer went into liquidation on 16 January 20X3, owing G plc £8 million. G plc's directors are of the opinion that this amount is material. *(handwritten: – AFTER CLOSING)*

(f) A member of the public was seriously injured on 24 January 20X3, while using one of G plc's products, and has lodged a claim for substantial damages. The company lawyer is of the opinion that the company will have to pay £2 million in compensation. G plc's directors are of the opinion that this amount is material.

(handwritten: FRS12 cont. liabilities → non adjusting. SSAP 17 PBB events)

Required

(a) Prepare G plc's profit and loss account for the year ended 31 December 20X2 and its balance sheet at that date.

> These should be in a form suitable for publication and should be accompanied by notes as far as you are able to prepare these from the information provided.
>
> Do **not** prepare a statement of accounting policies, a statement of total recognised gains and losses, a reconciliation of movements in shareholders' funds or calculate earnings per share.

20 Marks

(handwritten left margin: If I get OS purchases etc need to work out Share)

(handwritten left margin: Increase provision more. P&L. £ on B/S)

(handwritten left margin: Share cap = 500 £1 shares 100m sold mkt price £1·40)

(handwritten left margin: Dist costs + trade debtors)

(handwritten bottom: – Operating π – Tax – Dividends. – Creditors <1yr – Deferred Tax. – Cap & Reserves notes)

(b) (i)   Calculate G plc's earnings per share (EPS) in accordance with the requirements of FRS 14 *Earnings per share*.   **4 Marks**

(ii)   It has been suggested that the EPS ratio is unique in that its calculation is the subject of detailed Accounting Standards. Explain why it has been necessary to provide such detailed guidance on the calculation of EPS.   **6 Marks**

Total Marks = 30

14   PROTECTIVE CLOTHING (11/01 amended)   *54 mins*

L plc manufactures protective clothing and overalls for sale to specialist retailers. The following trial balance has been extracted from the company's financial records.

L plc – Trial balance at 30 June 20X1

	£ million	£ million
Administration salaries	22	
Bank	45	
Cost of goods sold	208	
Distribution costs	51	
Dividend	96	
Fixtures, fittings, tools and equipment – cost	46	
Fixtures, fittings, tools and equipment – depreciation		14
Interest paid	5	
Land and buildings – cost	534	
Land and buildings – depreciation		178
Loans (repayable 20Y5)		76
New process (University of Newtown)	8	
Plant and machinery – cost	282	
Plant and machinery – depreciation		99
Retained profit brought forward		38
Share capital		100
Share premium		60
Stock at 30 June 20X1	16	
Taxation		10
Trade creditors		13
Trade debtors	57	
Turnover		755
Warranties		27
	1,370	1,370

Notes

(a)   The company gives a three-year warranty on all of its products. The balance on the warranties account represents the provision for future warranty costs as estimated at 30 June 20X0. The balance at 30 June 20X1 should be modified to £35 million.

(b)   The directors have decided to change their method for charging depreciation on fixtures, fittings, tools and equipment. Previously, they had not depreciated certain categories of equipment on the grounds that this was a common industry practice. The directors have, however, decided that it would give a fairer presentation of the results of the business if depreciation was charged on all fixtures, fittings, tools and equipment. The figures in the trial balance are based on the old policy. If the company had used the new policy instead, it would have had a balance at 30 June 20X0 of £26 million on the fixtures, fittings, tools and equipment depreciation account instead of the £14 million currently shown.

(c)   Plant and machinery which had cost £42 million was sold at its book value of £23 million during the year. New plant and machinery was purchased for £55 million.

These transactions have been included in the above figures. There were no other transactions involving fixed assets.

(d) Depreciation for the year has still to be charged as follows:

Land and buildings	2% of cost
Fixtures, fittings, tools and equipment	25% reducing balance
Plant and machinery	25% reducing balance

A whole year's depreciation is charged in the year of acquisition and none in the year of disposal.

(e) During the year, the company paid £8 million to the University of Newtown for work on a new process to make the company's clothing more durable. A new fabric has been produced, but this tends to cause a severe allergic reaction to wearers. The company is working to overcome this problem before test marketing can begin.

(f) The directors have estimated the tax charge for the year at £30 million. The balance on the taxation account is the amount remaining after settling the liability for the year ended 30 June 20X0.

(g) The directors propose a final dividend of £80 million.

(h) L plc is a quoted company. Authorised share capital is 200 million shares of £1. Issued share capital is 100 million shares of £1, fully paid. This includes 40 million shares that were issued on 31 March 20X1 for a total consideration of £65 million.

Required

(a) Prepare L plc's profit and loss account for the year ended 30 June 20X1 and its balance sheet at that date. These should be in a form suitable for publication and should be accompanied by notes as far as you are able to prepare these from the information provided.

Do **not** prepare a statement of accounting policies, a statement of total recognised gains and losses, a reconciliation of movements in shareholders' funds.   **25 Marks**

(b) L plc's finance director has been re-reading the Accounting Standard's Board Statement of Principles for Financial Reporting (SoP) with a view to amending the company's accounting policies if they do not reflect best practice. The company's policy of providing for future warranty costs raises some concerns with respect to the need to provide information which is both relevant and reliable. The finance director is concerned that this estimated balance might not be sufficiently reliable to include in the financial statements.

Required

Explain why there may be a conflict between relevance and reliability. Your answer should refer to the issues affecting the relevance and reliability of the provision for future warranty costs.   **5 Marks**

Total Marks = 30

15   **COSMETICS** (5/96, amended)   *54 mins*

D plc has been involved in three lines of business: the operation of a chain of retail pharmacies; the manufacture and sale of cosmetics; and the manufacture and sale of a skin-care ointment. The following summarised trial balance has been extracted from the books of D plc.

TRIAL BALANCE AS AT 31 MARCH 20X6

	£'000	£'000
Retail sales		4,700
Cost of retail sales	1,645	
Cosmetic sales		7,300
Cost of cosmetic sales	3,285	
Ointment sales		1,600
Cost of ointment sales	880	
Administration expenses	1,900	
Distribution costs	1,600	
Closure costs	920	
Taxation	100	
Dividends	1,200	
Fixed assets: cost	7,700	
Fixed assets: depreciation		1,600
Stock at 31 March 20X6	411	
Trade debtors	240	
Bank	27	
Trade creditors		310
Deferred taxation		600
Share capital		3,500
Retained profits		298
	19,908	19,908

(a) The company closed down its ointment factory during the year. This involved expenses totalling £920,000.

(b) Most sales of cosmetics and ointments were to external customers on normal credit terms. There is no need for any adjustment in respect of sales to the retail segment of D plc or in respect of any closing stocks held by D plc's retail segment.

(c) Administration costs should be split between retailing, cosmetics and ointment in the ratio 5:3:2. Distribution costs should be split in the ratio 3:1:1.

(d) The balance on the taxation account comprises a balance of £100,000 left after the final settlement of the corporation tax liability for the year ended 31 March 20X5.

(e) The company expects to receive tax relief of £240,000 on the costs incurred in closing the ointment factory. Corporation tax on the operating profits for the year has been estimated at £1,020,000.

(f) The provision for deferred taxation is to be increased by £90,000.

(g) The directors have proposed a final dividend of £1,000,000.

(h) Four users of the company's skin-care ointment claim to have been injured by it. D plc's lawyers are contesting this claim, but they are uncertain whether any damages will have to be paid. The plaintiffs' lawyers are claiming damages totalling £750,000.

Required

Prepare a profit and loss account and balance sheet for D plc. These should be in a form suitable for publication (insofar as is possible given the information provided).

You should assume that D plc is required to publish the segmental information required by SSAP 25 *Segmental reporting.* **30 Marks**

16   **PREPARATION QUESTION: FRS 3 SITUATIONS**

(a)   Alison Ltd manufactures and sells cash registers. The new managing director has carried out a thorough assessment of the company, and has decided that it would profit the company to contract out the manufacturing process. The company duly ceased production before the year end but continued selling to the same customer list, supplied by the new subcontractors.

Required

State whether the cessation of production constitutes a 'discontinued activity' under FRS 3.

(b)   During an accounting period Barry Ltd closed one of its two equipment hire shops. The staff of the closed shop were made redundant. All the stock and equipment from the closed shop were transferred to the shop which remained open. No significant loss of revenue or change in customer base were anticipated.

Required

State whether the closure constitutes a material reduction in operating facilities.

(c)   On 23 September 20X3, the board of directors of Catherine plc decided to close a loss making operation. The company's year end is 30 September 20X3 and at that date the following estimates were made about the operation in question.

Time required to effect closure	1 year
Loss in that year	£3.1m
Fixed assets: net book value	£2.3m
recoverable on closure	£1.8m

On 30 September 20X3 the closure plans had not yet been implemented and the decision had not been announced.

Required

State which costs should be provided for at 30 September 20X3.

Approaching the question

1   Questions on FRS 3 are unlikely to be very complicated at this level and may be written questions like this.

2   It is the *application* of this standard to various situations which is important - you cannot simply 'rote learn' the provisions of FRS 3, you must also understand them.

17   **DIVERSIFIED (Specimen paper)**   *45 mins*

D plc is a diversified company which has operated in four main areas for many years. Each of these activities has usually contributed approximately one quarter of the company's annual operating profit.

During the year ended 31 December 20X3, the company disposed of its glass-making division and reorganised the other three divisions. These changes involved large numbers of redundancies.

The company's chief accountant has prepared the following summary.

ANALYSIS OF COSTS AND REVENUES, YEAR ENDED 31 DECEMBER 20X3

	Glassmaking	*Other divisions*
	£'000	£'000
Turnover	150	820
Operating expenses	(98)	(470)
Redundancies	(100)	(30)
Fees associated with closure/reorganisation	(27)	(12)
Losses on disposal of fixed assets	(78)	(19)

The company also incurred interest charges of £37,000 during the year.

The tax charge for the year has been estimated at £24,000.

The directors have proposed a dividend of £30,000.

The company financed the closure and reorganisation by means of a share issue which raised £180,000. Shareholders' funds at the beginning of the year were made up as follows.

	£'000
Share capital (including share premium)	400
Revaluation reserve	160
Profit and loss	670
	1,230

The balance on the revaluation reserve arose when the company valued the properties used in its retail division. In view of recent developments, it has been decided that this reserve should be reduced to £90,000.

The depreciation charge for the year was £84,000. If the properties had not been revalued the depreciation charge for the year would have been £75,000.

Required

(a) 'The objective of [Financial Reporting Standard 3] is to require reporting entities ... to highlight a range of important components of financial performance to aid users in understanding the performance achieved by a reporting entity in a period and to assist them in forming a basis for their assessment of future results and cash flows.' (FRS 3, paragraph 1)

'A layered format is to be used for the profit and loss account to highlight a number of important components of financial performance:

(i)   Results of continuing operations

(ii)   Results of discontinued operations

(iii)   Profits or losses on the sale or termination of an operation, costs of a fundamental reorganisation or restructuring and profits or losses on the disposal of fixed assets

(iv)   Extraordinary items.'   (FRS 3, Summary, paragraph (b))

Explain why each of the above components is needed in order to assess a business's future results and cash flows.   **10 Marks**

(b) Prepare an outline profit and loss account for the year ended 31 December 20X3 for D plc in a form suitable for publication.   **6 Marks**

(c) Prepare the statement of total recognised gains and losses for the year.   **2 Marks**

(d) Prepare a reconciliation of movements in shareholders' funds for D plc in accordance with the requirements of FRS 3.   **4 Marks**

(e) Prepare the note of historical cost profits and losses.   **3 Marks**

Total Marks = 25

BPP
PROFESSIONAL EDUCATION

18   FRS 3 PROFITS: T PLC (11/00)   *45 mins*

The following statements were extracted from T plc's latest annual report.

PROFIT AND LOSS ACCOUNT FOR THE YEAR ENDED 31 MARCH 20X5

	Note	£'000	£'000
Turnover			
Continuing operations			1,700
Discontinued operations			250
			1,950
Operating profit	1		
Continuing operations			200
Discontinued operations			17
			217
Profit on disposal of fixed assets	2	8	
Net profit before taxation on sale or			
termination of operations	2	32	
Interest payable and similar charges		(51)	
			(11)
Profit before taxation			206
Taxation			(29)
Profit after taxation			177
Dividends			(40)
			137

STATEMENT OF TOTAL RECOGNISED GAINS AND LOSSES

	£'000
Profit for the year	177
Unrealised gain on fixed assets	120
Total recognised gains since the last annual report	297

RECONCILIATION OF MOVEMENT IN SHAREHOLDERS' FUNDS

	£'000
Recognised gains relating to the year	297
Dividends	(40)
Shares issued	500
	757

Notes

1   *Profit before taxation on ordinary activities*

	Continuing operations £'000	Discontinued operations £'000	Total £'000
Turnover	1,700	250	1,950
Cost of sales	(1,100)	(200)	(1,300)
	600	50	650
Distribution costs	(50)	(5)	(55)
Administration expenses	(350)	(28)	(378)
	200	17	217
Interest payable and similar charges	(43)	(8)	(51)
	157	9	166
Exceptional items	8	22	30
	165	31	196

2   *Exceptional items*

	£'000
Continuing operations	
Profit on disposal of fixed assets	8
Discontinued operations	
Net profit before taxation on sale or termination of operations	32
Taxation	(10)
Net profit after taxation on sale or termination of operations	22

(a)   It has been suggested that FRS 3 has structured the profit and loss account so that there is no single profit figure. This enables readers to derive different performance measures for different purposes.

Required

Using T plc's profit and loss account as an illustration, identify three profit figures which could be used to measure the company's performance and explain how each might be useful to the shareholders.   **10 Marks**

(b)   The profit and loss account is supplemented by a statement of total recognised gains and losses and a reconciliation of movement in shareholders' funds.

Required

Explain the purpose of these statements, using T plc as an illustration.   **5 Marks**

(c)   Explain how the directors of T plc would determine the company's distributable profits.   **5 Marks**

(d)   At the company's annual general meeting one of the shareholders complained that the dividend of £40,000 seemed small in comparison to the total recognised gains for the year of £297,000.

Required

Explain why it is unlikely that the company could distribute the full amount of total recognised gains as a dividend.   **5 Marks**

Total Marks = 25

19   **WHOLESALING COMPANY** (5/98 amended)   *45 mins*

H plc is a wholesaling company with a retained profit for the year to 31 March 20X8 of £109,000.

During the year ending 31 March 20X8 a purchase system fraud was discovered. The purchasing office supervisor admitted that he had been conducting a fraud since September 20X6. He had stolen approximately £35,000 during the year ended 31 March 20X7 and a further £25,000 during the period from April to September 20X7. He claimed that all of the money stolen had been spent. He refused to provide any evidence to support these estimates and would say nothing further about the fraud. The company dismissed him for gross misconduct, but did not inform the police or pursue repayment of the £60,000 stolen.

The directors have decided to treat the cost of the fraud committed during the year ended 31 March 20X8 as an exceptional item.

The company's external auditors have been informed and they have advised that the amounts stolen are material.

(a) Explain why FRS 3 requires exceptional items and prior period adjustments to be disclosed in the financial statements. (You may find it helpful to refer to the formal definitions of these terms, which are given below.)   **6 Marks**

(b) In addition to treating this year's losses through fraud as an exceptional expense, the directors decided to treat last year's losses as a prior period adjustment.

Explain whether you agree with the directors' decision to treat this year's losses through fraud as an exceptional expense and last year's losses as a prior year adjustment.   **7 Marks**

(c) It has been suggested that almost nothing can be treated as an extraordinary item. Explain whether you agree with this. Explain why the Accounting Standards Board (ASB) would have wished to make it difficult to treat an expense as extraordinary.

   5 Marks

(d) FRS 3 requires the publication of a statement of total recognised gains and losses and also a note of historical cost profits and losses. Explain why these statements might be helpful to readers.   **7 Marks**

Exceptional items

Material items which derive from events or transactions that fall within the ordinary activities of the reporting entity and which individually or, if of a similar type, in aggregate, need to be disclosed by virtue of their size or incidence if the financial statements are to give a true and fair view.

Extraordinary items

Material items possessing a high degree of abnormality which arise from events or transactions that fall outside the ordinary activities of the reporting entity and which are not expected to recur. They do not include exceptional items nor do they include prior period items merely because they relate to a prior period.

Prior period adjustments

Material adjustments applicable to prior periods arising from changes in accounting policies or from the correction of fundamental errors. They do not include normal recurring adjustments or corrections of accounting estimates made in prior periods.

   Total Marks = 25

20   **KING CASH** (5/96 adapted)   *45 mins*

It has been suggested that 'cash is king' and that readers of a company's accounts should pay more attention to information concerning its cash flows and balances than to its profits and other assets. It is argued that cash is more difficult to manipulate than profit and that cash flows are more important.

Required

(a) Define what is meant by the term 'cash'.   **5 Marks**

(b) Explain whether you agree with the suggestion that cash flows and balances are more difficult to manipulate than profit and non-cash assets.   **8 Marks**

(c) Explain why it might be dangerous to concentrate on cash to the exclusion of profit when analysing a set of financial statements.   **7 Marks**

(d) Explain how a cash flow statement provides useful information for users of the financial statements over and above the information in the profit and loss account and balance sheet.   **5 Marks**

   Total Marks = 25

21   M PLC (5/02)

M plc's balance sheets at the end of the current year were as follows.

BALANCE SHEET

	31 March 20X4		31 March 20X3	
	£ million	£ million	£ million	£ million
Fixed assets				
Tangible assets		644		462
Current assets				
Stock	19		16	
Trade debtors	37		30	
Bank	12		15	
	68		61	
Creditors: amounts due within one year				
Trade creditors	(9)		(6)	
Finance leases	(2)		(1)ˣ	
Proposed dividend	(7)		(5)	
Taxation	(24)		(16)	
	42		28	
Net current assets		26		33
		670		495
Creditors: amounts due after one year				
Finance leases	(26)		(10)ˣ	
Loans	(110)		(175) ˣ	
Provisions for liabilities and charges		(136)		(185)
Deferred tax		(20)		(10)
		514		300
Capital and reserves				
Share capital		300		200
Share premium		40		10
Revaluation reserve		135		80
Profit and loss		39		10
		514		300

(handwritten: deferred tax in P&L; Retained π 29)

You are also given the following information:

(handwritten: → note 1. & fixed asset)

(a) The depreciation charge for the year was £42 million. Fixed assets with a net book value of £64 million were disposed of at a loss of £8 million.

(handwritten: Fixed asset, Cap expend. → Nt 1, fixed asset)

(b) The tax charge for the year was £48 million.

(c) Interest payable in the year was made up of £15 million of loan interest and £3 million of finance lease charges. A further £4 million of loan interest has been capitalised as part of the cost of a new factory being built. *(handwritten: Fixed asset.)*

(d) An interim dividend of £4 million was paid during the year. *(handwritten: — + last yrs proposed = 9)*

(e) Finance leases of £26 million were taken out during the year. *(handwritten: Fixed asset)*

(handwritten: have asset + liability. New asset)

Required:

(handwritten: LT financing.)

Prepare M plc's cash flow statement for the year ended 31 March 20X4 in the form prescribed by FRS 1 *Cash Flow Statements*. Your answer should include the notes and other disclosures required by FRS 1.

25 Marks

(handwritten working: Tax — Paid / deferred tax c/d / Bal c/d X / X | bal b/d / deferred tax b/d / P+L / X)

22   T PLC I (11/01 AMENDED)   *45 mins*

The following information has been extracted from the draft financial statements of T plc.

T PLC
PROFIT AND LOSS ACCOUNT FOR THE YEAR ENDED 30 SEPTEMBER 20X1

	£'000
Sales	15,000
Cost of sales	(9,000)
	6,000
Other operating expenses	(2,400)
	3,600
Interest	(24)
Profit before taxation	3,576
Taxation	(1,040)
Dividends	(1,100)
	1,436
Balance brought forward	4,400
	5,836

T PLC
BALANCE SHEETS AT 30 SEPTEMBER

	20X1		20X0	
	£'000	£'000	£'000	£'000
Fixed assets		18,160		14,500
Current assets:				
Stock	1,600		1,100	
Debtors	1,500		800	
Bank	150		1,200	
	3,250		3,100	
Current liabilities:				
Creditors	(700)		(800)	
Proposed dividend	(700)		(600)	
Taxation	(1,040)		(685)	
	(2,440)		(2,085)	
Net current assets		810		1,015
		18,970		15,515
Long-term loans		(1,700)		(2,900)
		17,270		12,615
Deferred tax		(600)		(400)
		16,670		12,215
Ordinary share capital		2,500		2,000
Share premium		8,334		5,815
Profit and loss		5,836		4,400
		16,670		12,215

FIXED ASSETS

	Land and buildings £'000	Plant and machinery £'000	Total £'000	
Cost				
30 September 20X0	8,400	10,800	19,200	
Additions	2,800	5,200	8,000	
Disposals	-	(2,600)	(2,600)	+
30 September 20X1	11,200	13,400	24,600	
Depreciation				
30 September 20X0	1,300	3,400	4,700	
Disposals	-	(900)	(900)	+
Charge for year	240	2,400	2,640	—>
30 September 20X1	1,540	4,900	6,440	
Net book value				
30 September 20X1	9,660	8,500	18,160	
30 September 20X0	7,100	7,400	14,500	

Plant and machinery was sold during the year for £730,000.

Required

(a) Prepare T plc's cash flow statement and associated notes for the year ended 30 September 20X1. These should be in a form suitable for publication.   **15 Marks**

After the publication of the balance sheet at 30 September 20X0, the directors of T plc were criticised for holding too much cash. The annual report for the year ended 30 September 20X1 claims that the company has managed its cash more effectively.

(b) Explain whether T plc's cash management appears to have been any more effective this year.   **5 Marks**

(c) Calculate the gearing ratio (including deferred tax as part of long term loans) for each of the two years. What are the arguments for and against including deferred tax in the gearing ratio?   **5 Marks**

Total Marks = 25

23   CASH FLOW ISSUES

(a) The starting point for the cash flow statement is the net cash flow from operating activities. There are two methods of arriving at this figure: the direct method and the indirect method.

Required

(i)   Describe the difference between the direct method and the indirect method.

(ii) Explain why FRS 1, cash flow statements, requires entities to use the indirect method but permits entities to make additional disclosures using the direct method.   **6 Marks**

(b) It is often said that because cash flow statements eliminate the accruals impact, it is less susceptible to window dressing and manipulation, than conventional profit and loss accounts.

Required

(i)   Outline the benefits to users of financial statements afforded by cash flow statements eliminating the accruals basis of accounting.

(ii) Discuss whether cash flow statements minimise the impacts of window dressing. Give examples to support your case.   **10 Marks**

(c) Some business people believe that controlling cash flow is a more important objective than focusing on profit in managing a business effectively.

Required

Discuss the role of cash flow as compared to profit from the perspective of a businessperson trying to manage a business. **6 Marks**

(d) The role of the *Reconciliation of Net Cash Flow to Movement in Net Debt* is not always that clear to users of financial statements.

Required

Explain the usefulness of the *Reconciliation of Net Cash Flow to Movement in Net Debt* to readers of a cash flow statement. **3 Marks**

Total Marks = 25

> **ACCOUNTING STANDARDS**
>
> The objective test questions and questions 27 to 53 cover accounting standards, the subject of Part C of the BPP Study Text for Paper 6.

OBJECTIVE TEST QUESTIONS

1   According to FRS 15 Tangible Fixed Assets, which, if any, of the following statements about depreciation are correct?

   1   The main purpose of depreciation is to reflect the fall in value of an asset in the balance sheet over its useful life.

   2   When an asset is revalued, depreciation relating to the revaluation surplus should be debited to the revaluation reserve rather than the profit and loss account.

   3   Provision for depreciation ensures that there are funds available to replace an asset when this becomes necessary, though in times of inflation additional amounts may need to be set aside.

   4   A change in depreciation method constitutes a change in accounting policy and must be accounted for as such.

   A   1 and 4
   B   2 and 3.
   C   4 only
   D   None of the statements is correct.

2   FRS 15 Tangible Fixed Assets contains rules relating to the capitalisation of interest costs incurred in constructing a tangible fixed asset.

   Which of the following statements about these rules are correct?

   1   If borrowings are not specific to a particular project, interest on expenditure on that project cannot be capitalised.

   2   The aggregate amount of interest capitalised must be disclosed in the company's financial statements.

   3   Capitalisation of interest must cease when the fixed asset concerned is ready for use.

   4   If a company adopts a policy of capitalising interest costs on the construction of fixed assets, it must apply that policy to all qualifying construction projects.

   A   1, 2 and 3 only.
   B   2 and 3 only.
   C   1 and 4 only.
   D   2, 3 and 4 only.

3   FRS 11 Impairment of Fixed Assets and Goodwill requires impairment to be measured by comparing the carrying value of the asset with its recoverable amount.

   Which of the following is the correct definition of recoverable amount according to FRS 11?

   A   Net realisable value.
   B   Value in use.
   C   The lower of net realisable value and value in use.
   D   The higher of net realisable value and value in use.

4   On 1 April 2000 a company purchased new plant for its factory at a cost of £800,000. The plant is expected to have a useful economic life of five years. On the same day the company received a Government grant for 15% of the cost of the plant. The company uses the deferred credit method of accounting for government grants.

What is the credit to the profit and loss account for the year ending 31 March 2002 and the balance on the government grant deferred income account at that date?

	P&L credit	Deferred income balance
A	£24,000	£72,000
B	£24,000	£96,000
C	£120,000	£72,000
D	£120,000	£96,000

120,000

5   Which of the following statements about FRS 11 Impairment of Fixed Assets and Goodwill are correct?

1   Fixed assets and goodwill must be checked annually for evidence of impairment.

2   An impairment loss must be recognised immediately in the profit and loss account, except that all or part of a loss on a revalued asset may be recognised in the statement of total recognised gains and losses.

3   If individual assets cannot be tested for impairment, it may be necessary to test a group of assets as a unit.

A   1, and 2 only
B   1 and 3 only
C   2 and 3 only
D   1, 2 and 3

6   Which of the following statements about SSAP 19 Investment Properties are correct?

1   Investment properties do not require depreciation, but should be carried in the balance sheet at current open market value, re-assessed every year.

2   Increases in the value of investment properties should be taken to an investment revaluation reserve.

3   Decreases in the value of investment properties are debited to investment revaluation reserve, but no debit balance on the reserve account is allowed.

4   A debit balance on the investment revaluation reserve is allowed if the deficit in the revaluation of an investment property is temporary.

A   1, and 3 only.
B   2 and 3 only.
C   2 and 4 only.
D   1, 2 and 4 only.

7   A company's balance sheet includes the following items under the heading of Intangible assets:

		£m	£m
1	Development costs		4
2	Trade marks at cost less amortisation		2
③	Purchased goodwill (cost £3 million)	4	
④	Internally developed goodwill at valuation	3	
		7	
5	Negative goodwill	(2)	5

Which of these items should <u>not</u> be included as shown, according to the Companies Act 1985 and FRS 10 Goodwill and Intangible Assets?

A   1 and 4.
B   2 and 3.   *Internally developed not shown*
C   3 and 4.   *Purchased shouldn't be valued upwards!*
D   3, 4 and 5.

8   Which of these statements about goodwill are correct, according to FRS 10 Goodwill and Intangible Assets?

1   Negative goodwill should be shown on the balance sheet as a deduction from positive goodwill.

2   FRS10 allows goodwill to be written off immediately against reserves as an alternative to capitalisation and amortisation.

3   As a business grows, purchased goodwill may be revalued upwards to reflect that growth.

4   Internally developed brands must not be capitalised.

A   1 and 4
B   2 and 3
C   3 and 4
D   1 and 2

9   Negative goodwill might be recognised in the balance sheet:

A   By a company making heavy losses

B   By a company whose goodwill is eliminated by a major adverse event

C   By a company acquiring another company at a price below the fair value of that company's net assets.

D   In none of these circumstances.

10   Which of the following statements about methods of valuing investments for balance sheet purposes are correct?

1   Fixed asset investments are initially valued at cost, but may be revalued upwards to market value.

2   Readily marketable current asset investments are included at current market value.

3   Current asset investments that are not readily marketable should be included at the lower of cost and net realisable value.

4   An increase or decrease in the market value of readily marketable current asset investments should be taken to the profit and loss account.

41

A   All four statements are correct.

B   1, 2 and 4 only.

C   1 and 3 only.

D   2, 3 and 4 only.

11   Which of the following items should be included in arriving at the cost of a stock of finished goods held by a manufacturing company, according to SSAP 9 Stocks and Long-term Contracts?

1   Carriage inwards on raw materials delivered to factory.

2   Carriage outwards on goods delivered to customers.

3   Factory supervisors' salaries.

4   Factory heating and lighting.

5   Cost of abnormally high idle time in the factory.

6   Import duties on raw materials.

A   1, 3, 4 and 6.

B   1, 2, 4 ,5 and 6.

C   3, 4 and 6.

D   2, 3 and 5.

12   Which of the following statements about SSAP 9 Stocks and Long-term Contracts are correct?

1   Production overheads should be included in cost on the basis of a company's actual level of activity in the period

2   In arriving at the net realisable value of stock, trade discounts and settlement discounts must be deducted.

3   In accounting for long-term contracts, the whole of an expected loss on completion should be provided for as soon as it is seen to be likely to arise.

4   It is permitted to value finished goods stock at materials plus labour cost only, without adding production overheads.

A   1 only

B   2 only

C   3 only

D   None of them

13   The following details relate to a long-term contract at 31 December 20X3:

	£
Contract price	400,000
At 31 December 20X3:	
Costs to date	230,000
Work certified to date	300,000
Progress payments received	280,000
Estimated costs to completion	60,000

What figures should be included for this contract in the accounts at 31 December 20X3, according to SSAP9 Stocks and Long-term Contracts?

	Profit and loss account			Balance sheet Stocks-long-term contracts
	Turnover	*Costs*	*Debtors*	*contracts*
	£	£	£	£
A	300,000	230,000	20,000	-
B	300,000	217,500	20,000	12,500
C	280,000	230,000	-	-
D	280,000	217,500		12,500

14   On what basis should dividends receivable and payable be shown in financial statements?

A   Both should be shown at the actual amount receivable or payable.

B   Dividends receivable should be 'grossed up' for related tax credits but dividends payable should be shown at the actual amount payable.

C   Dividends receivable should be shown at the actual amount receivable but dividends payable should be 'grossed up' for related tax credits.

D   Both should be shown grossed up for related tax credits

15   Which of the following is an example of a permanent timing difference for deferred tax purposes?

A   Entertaining expenses
B   Accelerated capital allowances
C   Interest payments
D   Provisions

16   Which of the following statements about deferred tax are correct?

1   FRS 19 Deferred tax requires provision for deferred tax to the extent that it is probable that a liability or asset will crystallise.

2   FRS19 requires deferred tax balances to be discounted, using the post-tax yield to maturity on government bonds with similar maturity dates to the deferred tax liabilities or assets

3   Deferred tax liabilities are required by the Companies Act 1985 to be shown in the balance sheet, under the heading of 'Provision for liabilities and charges'.

4   All deferred tax recognised in the profit and loss account should be included within the heading 'tax on profit or loss on ordinary activities', except for deferred tax relating to extraordinary items.

A   1, and 2 and 3 only
B   1, 2 and 4 only
C   3 and 4 only
D   All the statements are correct

17   In accounting for deferred tax, which of the following items can give rise to timing differences?

    1   Differences between depreciation and tax capital allowances
    2   Expenses charged in the profit and loss account but disallowed for tax
    3   Revaluation of a fixed asset
    4   Unrelieved tax losses

    A   1, 3 and 4 only
    B   1 and 2 only
    C   3 and 4 only
    D   All four items

18   At 1 January 20X4, Q plc had a credit balance of £400,000 on its deferred tax account, all attributable to accelerated capital allowances.

During the year ending 31 December 20X4, the company made a trading loss of £300,000 after providing depreciation of £80,000. Capital allowances amounted to £200,000. The company is trading profitably again in 20X5 and expects to make a profit of £500,000 in that year. The company's tax rate should be taken as 20%.

What figure should appear in Q plc's balance sheet at 31 December 20X4 for deferred tax?

    A   £364,000
    B   £220,000
    C   £424,000
    D   None of these figures

19   A company leases some plant on 1 January 20X4. The cash price of the plant is £9,000, and the company leases it for four years, paying four annual instalments of £3,000 beginning on 31 December 20X4.

The company uses the sum of the digits method (Rule of 78) to allocate interest.

What is the interest charge for the year ended 31 December 20X5?

    A   £900
    B   £600
    C   £1,000
    D   £750

20   A company leases some plant on 1 January 20X4. The cash price is £9,000, and the company leases it for four years, paying four annual instalments of £3,000, beginning on 1 January 20X4.

The company uses the sum of the digits method to allocate interest.

What is the interest charge for the year ended 31 December 20X5?

    A   £750
    B   £500
    C   £900
    D   £1,000

21 A dealer receives motor vehicles from the manufacturer on a consignment basis.

Which one or more of the following are indications that the cars should be accounted for as stock of the dealer, at the time of delivery from the manufacturer?

1 The dealer has the right to return the cars to the manufacturer without penalty.
2 The dealer bears the risk of obsolescence.
3 The price paid by the dealer is based on the price when the dealer sells the vehicle.
4 The manufacturer has the right to require the dealer to return the stock.

A 1, 3 and 4
B 2 only
C 1 and 3
D 2 and 4

22 A company sells a building for £1,000,000.

Which of the following conditions attached to the sale would suggest that the transaction should be accounted for as a loan and not a sale?

1 The company has undertaken to buy back the building in five years' time.

2 The company retains the right to determine the future use of the building.

3 The company will bear the risk of changes in value of the asset because the original purchase price will be adjusted retrospectively to reflect variations in the value of the building.

A 1 and 2 only
B 1 and 3 only
C 2 and 3 only
D All three conditions.

23 Which of the following events after the balance sheet date would normally be classified as *adjusting*, according to SSAP 17 Accounting for Post Balance Sheet Events?

1 Destruction of a major fixed asset
2 Issue of shares or debentures
3 Discovery of error or fraud
4 Evidence of permanent diminution in value of a property as at the balance sheet date.
5 Purchases and sales of fixed assets

A 1, 2 and 5 only
B 3 and 4 only
C 3, 4 and 5 only
D 1, 3 and 4 only

24   Which of the following events after the balance sheet date would normally be classified as *non-adjusting*, according to SSAP 17 *Accounting for post balance sheet events*?

1   Opening new trading operations
2   Sale of stock held at the balance sheet date for less than cost
3   Insolvency of a debtor
4   Strikes or other labour disputes
5   Nationalisation or other government action.

A   2 and 3 only
B   1, 2 and 3 only
C   2, 3, 4 and 5 only
D   1, 4 and 5 only

25   Which of the following statements about FRS 12 *Provisions, contingent liabilities and contingent assets* are correct?

1   Provisions should be made for constructive obligations (those arising through a company's pattern of past practice) as well as for obligations enforceable by law.

2   Discounting may be used when estimating the amount of a provision if the effect is material.

3   A restructuring provision must include the estimated costs of retraining or relocating continuing staff.

4   A restructuring provision may only be made when a company has a detailed plan for the reconstruction and a firm intention to carry it out.

A   All four statements are correct
B   1, 2 and 4 only
C   1, 3 and 4 only
D   2, 3 and 4 only

26   Which of the following criteria must be present in order for a company to recognise a provision?

1   There is a present obligation as a result of past events

2   It is probable that a transfer of economic benefits will be required to settle the obligation

3   A reliable estimate of the obligation can be made

A   All three criteria must be present
B   1 and 2 only
C   1 and 3 only
D   2 and 3 only

27   FRS 12 *Provisions, contingent liabilities and contingent assets* governs the recognition of contingent items. Which of the following statements about contingencies, if any, are correct according to FRS 12?

1   A contingent liability must be disclosed by note if it is probable that an obligation will arise and its amount can be estimated reliably.

2   A contingent asset must be disclosed by note if it is probable that it will arise.

3   An entity should not recognise a contingent liability

A   None of the statements is correct
B   1 and 2
C   2 and 3
D   All of the statements are correct

28   Q plc is currently defending two legal actions:

Case (i). A competitor is suing Q plc for £3,000,000, claiming that Q plc has copied its patented processes and infringed its copyright. Q plc is contesting the claim on the basis that it developed its own superior processes. Q plc's lawyers have advised the directors of Q plc that there is not really a case to answer and there is only a remote possibility of Q plc losing.

Case (ii). A customer is suing for £1,000,000, claiming that Q plc's products damaged their electronic equipment. Q plc is contesting the claim. Lawyers have advised Q plc's directors that the case is still at a very early stage and it is difficult to predict the outcome. At the moment, the most accurate estimate by the lawyers is that there is slightly less than a 50 per cent chance of the case succeeding.

What should Q plc put into their financial statements for these claims?

A   Make a provision for £1,000,000 for case (ii) and disclose details of case (i)
B   Make a provision for £1,000,000 for case (ii) and make no disclosure for case (i)
C   Make no provisions but disclose details of case (ii)
D   Make no provisions but disclose details of both cases

29   In 20X8 a company made the following expenditure

	£m
Cost of factory development (being depreciated over ten years)	3.6
Training costs	0.8
Relocation costs	0.4

Government grants of 20 per cent of all these costs were received in 20X8.

What total amount should be credited to the company's profit and loss account for 20X8 in respect of the grants received?

A   £960,000
B   £312,000
C   £600,000
D   None of these figures

30   Which of the following are normally held to be weaknesses of historical cost accounting (HCA)?

1   HCA maintains financial capital but does not maintain physical capital

2   Provision of depreciation based on historical cost tends to result in profit being overstated

3   Holding gains on trading stock are included in profit

A   1 and 2 only
B   1 and 3 only
C   All three are weaknesses of HCA
D   2 and 3 only

31   A company made an issue of 100,000 ordinary shares of 50p at £1.10 each. The cash received was correctly recorded in the cash book but the whole amount was entered into ordinary share capital account.

Which of the following journal entries will correct the error made in recording the issue?

		Debit £	Credit £
A	Share capital account	10,000	
	Share premium account		10,000
B	Cash	60,000	
	Share premium account		60,000
C	Share capital account	60,000	
	Share premium account		60,000
D	Share premium account	60,000	
	Share capital account		60,000

32   A company issued 1,000,000 £1 shares at £1.50 each payable as follows:

On application (including premium)	70p
On allotment	30p
First and final call	50p

All monies were received except for the call due from a holder of 10,000 shares. These shares were subsequently forfeited and reissued at £1.60 per share.

What *total* will be credited to share premium account as a result of this issue?

A   £501,000
B   £506,000
C   £511,000
D   None of the above.

33   A company has forfeited shares for non-payment of any calls (including application and allotment), but has not yet reissued them.

How, if at all, will the forfeited shares be shown in the company's balance sheet?

A   As a deduction from called up share capital
B   As a current asset investment in own shares
C   As a current asset under debtors
D   No item appears in the balance sheet for the shares

34   Which of the following statements about company distributions are correct?

1   A company with a qualified audit report on its most recent financial statements is not allowed to pay a dividend unless the auditors confirm that it is in order for it to do so.

2   In determining distributable profit, both public and private companies must allow for unrealised profits and losses.

3   When fixed assets have been revalued, only depreciation relating to the original cost of the assets needs to be deducted in calculating distributable profit.

A   1 and 3 only
B   1 and 2 only
C   2 and 3 only
D   All three statements are correct

35   Which of the following are permitted uses for a private company's share premium account, according to the Companies Act 1985?

1   Issuing fully paid bonus shares
2   Being repaid to members as part of a reduction of share capital authorised by the court
3   Writing off preliminary expenses of company formation
4   Writing off subsequent share issue expenses

A   1, 2 and 3 only
B   1, 3 and 4 only
C   2, 3 and 4 only
D   All four are permitted

36   The balance sheet of B plc is as follows:

	£
Called up share capital (shares of £1 each, fully paid)	300,000
Share premium account	60,000
Profit and loss account	160,000
	520,000
Sundry net assets	520,000

The company is to buy 40,000 of its shares on the open market for £90,000. The shares were originally issued at £1.20 per share.

What balance will remain on the company's profit and loss account after the correct recording of the share purchase?

A   £120,000
B   £78,000
C   £130,000
D   £70,000

37   A Limited's balance sheet is as follows:

	£
Called up share capital	
Ordinary shares of £1 each, fully paid	280,000
Profit and loss account	80,000
	360,000
Sundry net assets	360,000

The company is to buy 50,000 of its own shares at £2 each.

What, if any, is the amount of the permissible capital payment in this share purchase?

A   A permissible capital payment does not arise because A Limited is a private company.
B   £20,000
C   £30,000
D   £50,000

38   Z Ltd has 500,000 50 pence ordinary shares in issue and makes a 1 for 5 bonus issue. Before the bonus issue the capital and reserves of Z Ltd are as follows:

	£
Ordinary share capital	250,000
Share premium	30,000
Profit and loss account	180,000

After the bonus issue the share capital and reserves of Z Ltd will be made up of:

		£
A	Ordinary share capital	350,000
	Share premium	30,000
	Profit and loss account	180,000
B	Ordinary share capital	300,000
	Share premium	-
	Profit and loss account	180,000
C	Ordinary share capital	300,000
	Share premium	-
	Profit and loss account	160,000
D	Ordinary share capital	350,000
	Share premium	-
	Profit and loss account	110,000

39   The balance sheet of X plc at 31 December 20X5 is shown below:

	£m
Called up share capital	
ordinary shares of 50p each, fully paid	10
Profit and loss account	3
	13
Sundry net assets	13

At this date X plc purchased 1,000,000 of its own ordinary shares at par. 300,000 £1 preference shares were issued at £1.20 each to help finance the purchase.

What balance should appear on the company's capital redemption reserve account when these transactions have been correctly recorded?

A   £140,000
B   £200,000
C   £500,000
D   None of these figures

40   FRS 8 Related Party Transactions governs disclosures required for transactions between a company and parties deemed to be related to it.

Which of the following parties will normally be held to be related parties of a company?

1   Its associates and joint ventures
2   A shareholder with 10 per cent of the company's voting rights
3   Its directors
4   Close family of the company's directors
5   Providers of finance to the company
6   A customer or supplier with whom the company has a significant volume of business

A   All of the parties listed
B   1, 2, 3 and 4 only
C   1, 3 and 4 only
D   3, 5 and 6 only

> If you struggled with these objective test questions, go back to your BPP Study Text for this paper and revise Chapters 5 to 11 before you tackle the written questions on accounting standards.

24   PREPARATION QUESTION: HENHAO

> *Depreciation* is the measure of the wearing out, consumption or other reduction in the useful economic life of a fixed asset whether arising from use, effluxion of time or obsolescence through technological or market changes.

The following is an extract from Henhao plc's draft balance sheet and notes to the accounts for the year ended 31 December 20X0.

	£
Land and buildings	
At cost at 31.12.X0 (note 10)	100,000
Accumulated depreciation	10,000

Note 10. Land and buildings

The market value of the land and buildings is £1,500,000.

The land element cost £50,000 and the buildings are being depreciated on the straight line basis at 2%.

Required

(a) Amend the above draft extract so that it complies with FRS 15 *Tangible Fixed Assets*.

(b) Write a brief note addressed to the directors explaining the concept of depreciation as it applies to land and buildings.

(c) Explain why a building owned for its investment potential should be accounted for differently from one which is occupied by its owners.

25   T PLC II (Pilot paper amended)   *54 mins*

T plc is a quoted company which owns a large number of hotels throughout the UK. During the year ending 31 December 20X0 the company's external auditors expressed some concern that a large proportion of the hotels were several years old and yet none had ever been professionally revalued. The directors were unsure whether there was a material difference between the market valuations and net book values, and commissioned a valuation on three of the company's oldest hotels in order to see whether a more detailed valuation might prove useful.

	Original cost	*Depreciation to 31.12. X0*	*Market value at 31.12. X0*	*Estimated useful life at 31.12.X0*
	£'000	£'000	£'000	Years
Hotel A	800	180	1,300	50
Hotel B	700	120	850	30
Hotel C	1,000	140	650	40

The hotels are depreciated at 2% per annum on cost.

During the year ended 31 December 20X1 the directors are planning to start a major programme of repairs and refurbishment on the company's hotels. Over a five-year period the buildings will be checked to ensure that they are structurally sound, and they will be repaired whenever necessary.

Preliminary investigations suggest that some of the hotels will not achieve their expected useful lives if the company does not invest in this preventative maintenance. The company will also redecorate the hotels and replace most of the furniture in the bedrooms and restaurants. The redecoration will create a new corporate image for all of T plc's hotels that will improve the company's marketing and promotion.

The directors are keen to evaluate the effects of the revaluation of the hotels. They have asked for some further analyses and reports.

Required

(a) (i) Calculate the effects of the revaluation on the depreciation charge on the three hotels for the year ended 31 December 20X1, assuming that a full year's depreciation is charged on the revalued amounts.   **3 Marks**

   (ii) Calculate the balance which would appear on the revaluation reserve in respect of the revalued hotels.   **2 Marks**

   The directors regard the company's hotels as assets which generate both income and capital gains. Two of the hotels which were valued are appreciating in value. The company has sold hotels in the past in order to realise such gains.

   (iii) Explain whether it would be feasible for the directors to justify charging no depreciation, on the grounds that their hotels tend to increase in value or are held as investment properties. Your answer should refer to accounting concepts and to relevant accounting standards.   **6 Marks**

   (iv) The directors are keen to capitalise the costs of the programme of repairs and refurbishment. Describe the factors which will have to be considered in deciding whether this will be acceptable from an accounting point of view. Your answer should refer to accounting concepts and to the relevant accounting standards as appropriate.   **5 Marks**

(b) One of T plc's directors believes that the company should not have revalued the hotels just because of the external auditors' concerns. He has suggested that the finance director should withhold the results of the valuation from the auditor until the board has had an opportunity to consider its implications. The information should be released only if the directors decide to incorporate the results in the financial statements. The finance director is unhappy with this suggestion because he is concerned that it might lead to a qualified audit report.

Required

   (i) Describe the external auditors' responsibilities with respect to the financial statements.   **7 Marks**

   (ii) Explain what is meant by a 'qualified' audit report and describe the differences between a 'qualified' and an 'unqualified' report.   **7 Marks**

   Total Marks = 30

26   B PLC (11/01 amended)   *45 mins*

The directors of B plc have commissioned an independent valuation of the land and buildings at 30 June 20X1. The findings from this report are summarised below.

	Cost £m	Depreciation to date £m	Valuation £m	Comments
Factory A	250	70	160	This factory has been well maintained, but is located in an area where industrial property prices have been depressed by market conditions.
Factory B	150	60	120	This factory is in an area that has benefited from growth in the local economy driving up property prices.
Factory C	134	48	40	This factory has been badly maintained for several years and its valuation reflects the deterioration that has arisen because of this.
	534	178		

B plc has never revalued its land and buildings. The directors are unsure whether they should adopt a policy of doing so. They are concerned that FRS 15 *Tangible fixed assets* has an 'all or nothing' approach which would impose a duty on them to maintain up-to-date valuations in the balance sheet for all land and buildings into the indefinite future. They are also concerned that the introduction of current values will make the accounting ratios based on their balance sheet appear less attractive to shareholders and other users of the financial statements.

Required

(a) Explain why FRS 15 requires those companies who revalue fixed assets to revalue all of the assets in the relevant classes and why these valuations must be kept up to date.

7 Marks

(b) Explain whether it is logical for FRS 15 to offer companies a choice between showing all assets in a class at either cost less depreciation or at valuation. **4 Marks**

(c) Calculate the figures that would appear in B plc's financial statements in respect of land and buildings if the company opts to show the factories at their valuation. You should indicate where these figures would appear, but do **not** prepare any detailed notes in a form suitable for disclosure. **6 Marks**

(d) Explain how the revaluation of fixed assets is likely to affect key accounting ratios and explain whether these changes are likely to make the company appear stronger or weaker. **8 Marks**

Total Marks = 25

27 **S LTD (FAC, 5/92 amended)** *45 mins*

S Ltd is a manufacturing company. It held its annual stock count on 31 March 20X2, the company's year end. The accounts department is currently working its way through the stock sheets placing a value on the physical stocks. The company has had a difficult year and profits are likely to be lower than in the previous year.

Raw materials

Stocks of raw materials are valued at cost. The finance director has suggested that the cost has been understated in previous years because the company has not taken the costs of delivery or insurance into account. These can be substantial in the case of imported goods. It has been proposed that these costs be taken into account in the valuation of closing stocks of raw materials.

Work in progress

The cost of work in progress includes an element of overheads. The following table of figures has been prepared in order to assist in the calculation of the overhead absorption.

Fixed costs	£
Factory rent, rates and insurance	150,000
Administration expenses	240,000
Factory security	110,000

Variable costs	£
Factory heat, light and power	300,000
Sales commissions and selling costs	120,000
Depreciation of machinery	200,000
Depreciation of delivery vehicles	70,000

Overheads are usually absorbed on the basis of labour hours. The stock sheets suggest that 500 labour hours have been included in work in progress. A total of 70,000 hours have been worked by production staff during the year. This figure is, however, much lower than the normal figure of 95,000 hours.

Finished goods

Finished goods have already been valued at £400,000. This figure includes some obsolete stocks which cost £70,000 to produce, but which are likely to be sold at a scrap value of £500. There are also several batches of a new product which will be launched early in the new financial year. These cost £90,000 to manufacture. Independent market research suggests that it is very likely that the new product will be sold for considerably more than this. If, however, the launch is unsuccessful, the new product will have to be sold as scrap for £1,000. The finance director has said that the aggregate net realisable value of all closing stocks of finished goods is at least £500,000 and so there is no need to worry about the obsolete and new stock products.

Required

(a) Explain the general SSAP 9 rule as to the valuation of stocks and the reason why this rule exists. **2 Marks**

(b) (i) Explain whether the costs of delivery and insurance should be included in the valuation of raw materials. **3 Marks**

(ii) Assuming that the change is made, state how the change should be accounted for. **3 Marks**

(c) (i) Explain how SSAP 9 requires overheads to be treated in the valuation of closing stocks. **4 Marks**

(ii) Calculate the value of overheads to be absorbed to S Ltd's closing stock of work in progress. **3 Marks**

(d) (i) Explain whether the valuation of closing stocks at the lower of cost and net realisable value should be done on an item-by-item basis or on the basis of the aggregate cost of all items as compared with their aggregate net realisable value. **3 Marks**

(ii) State how you would value the obsolete items and the new product line, giving reasons for your valuation in each case. **4 Marks**

(e) Suppose that the new product is launched in May 20X2 (before the financial statements are approved by the directors) and the launch is unsuccessful. What effect, if any, would this have on the financial statements for the year ended 31 March 20X2?

3 Marks

Total Marks = 25

28   C PLC (Pilot Paper)   *45 mins*

C plc is a civil engineering company. It started work on two long-term projects during the year ended 31 December 20X0. The following figures relate to those projects at the balance sheet date.

	Maryhill bypass £'000	Rottenrow Centre £'000
Contract price	9,000	8,000
Costs incurred to date	1,400	2,900
Estimated costs to completion	5,600	5,200
Value of work certified to date	2,800	3,000
Cash received from contractee	2,600	3,400

An old mineshaft has been discovered under the site for the Rottenrow Centre and the costs of dealing with this have been taken into account in the calculation of estimated costs to completion. C plc's lawyers are reasonably confident that the customer will have to bear the additional costs which will be incurred in stabilising the land. If negotiations are successful then the contract price will increase to £10m.

C plc recognises turnover and profits on long-term contracts on the basis of work certified to date.

Required

(a) Calculate the figures which would appear in C plc's financial statements in respect of these two projects.

14 Marks

(b) It has been suggested that profit on long-term contracts should not be recognised until the contract is completed. Briefly explain whether you believe that this suggestion would improve the quality of financial reporting for long-term contracts.

6 Marks

(c) The commercial director is unhappy about a loss being shown on the Rottenrow Centre contract as when the contract price is increased it will be profitable. He argues that £10m should be used as the contract price. Write a brief note to the director explaining the accounting for the Rottenrow Centre.

5 Marks

Total Marks = 25

29   QUAN PLC   *54 mins*

Quan plc designs and installs computer systems for large companies and government organisations. Most of the company's sales involve several months of activity and some contracts can take up to two years to complete.

The company's trial balance at 30 September 20X8 was as follows.

	£'000	£'000
Contract A - Costs incurred to date	1,200	
Contract B - Costs incurred to date	3,100	
Contract A - Invoiced to client		2,000
Contract B - Invoiced to client		3,000
Contract A - Amount due from client	200 *receivable*	
Contract B - Amount due from client	300	
Turnover		14,000
Cost of sales	7,700	
Administration expenses	2,200	
Distribution costs	1,400	
Dividends received		480
Taxation	500 *under provision*	
Dividends	1,200	
Fixed assets - cost	7,500	
Fixed assets - depreciation		1,300
Fixed asset investments	2,500	
Stock at 30 September 20X8	560 +120	
Trade debtors	1,160	
Bank	40	
Trade creditors		380
Share capital		5,500
Retained profits		2,900
	29,560	29,560

Notes

(i) The figures for turnover and cost of sales relate to work done during the year ended 30 September 20X8, excluding all transactions relating to Contracts A and B.

(ii) Quan plc recognises turnover and profit on long-term contracts on the basis of the proportion of total contract price invoiced to customers. All anticipated losses are recognised as soon as they are foreseen. The company's standard contract usually permits customers to withhold 10% of the invoiced value of work done until the system has been installed and agreed to be satisfactory.

(iii) Contract A commenced during the year ended 30 September 20X8. The contract has a total value of £5 million. Quan plc anticipates that it will spend a further £1.5 million in order to complete this contract.

(iv) Contract B also commenced during the year ended 30 September 20X8. The contract has an agreed total value of £4 million. There have been some problems with this project which were not anticipated when the contract was drafted. Quan plc expects to spend a further £1.2 million in order to complete the contract. This includes £800,000 of additional costs which relate to the unforeseen problems. Quan plc's lawyers are currently attempting to negotiate a revised contract price of £4.8 million, although the customer is insistent that the system be completed for the original price. Quan plc's lawyers are 'reasonably confident' that they can make the customer pay for the additional costs. There is no possibility of these negotiations being completed before the financial statements have to be finalised.

(v) The balance on the taxation account is the amount remaining after the settlement of the liability for the year ended 30 September 20X7.

(vi) The directors have estimated the tax charge for the year at £740,000.

(vii) The directors have proposed a dividend of £700,000.

(a) Quan plc's finance director has made the point to the board that the company should account for Contract B on the assumption that its eventual selling price will be £4 million and not the £4.8 million that the company is seeking from the customer, even though there is a strong possibility that the higher amount will be obtained.

    (i) It has been suggested that there can be considerable inconsistency between companies in the manner in which they recognise profits on partly-completed long-term contracts.

        Explain why this might be, and explain why SSAP 9 permits the anticipation of such profits, despite the accounting problems which this may cause.   **5 Marks**

    (ii) Explain why, for accounting purposes, Quan plc should assume that Contract B will be sold for £4 million.   **3 Marks**

(b) Prepare Quan plc's profit and loss account for the year ended 30 September 20X8 and its balance sheet at that date. These should be in a form suitable for publication and should be accompanied by notes as far as you are able to prepare these from the information provided.

Do not prepare a statement of accounting policies, a statement of total recognised gains and losses, a reconciliation of movements in shareholders' funds or calculate earnings per share.   **22 Marks**

Total Marks = 30

30   S PLC 1 (11/02)   *45 mins*

S plc is a shipbuilder which is currently working on two contracts.

	Deep sea fishing boat	*Small passenger ferry*
	£'000	£'000
Contract price (fixed)	3,000	5,000
Date work commenced	1 October 20X1	1 October 20X2
Proportion of work completed during year ended 30 September 20X2	30%	Nil
	£'000	£'000
Invoiced to customer during year ended 30 September 20X2	900	Nil
Cash received from customer during year ended 30 September 20X2	800	Nil
Costs incurred during year ended 30 September 20X2	650	Nil
Estimated cost to complete at 30 September 20X2	1,300	
Proportion of work completed during year ended 30 September 20X3	25%	45%
	£'000	£'000
Invoiced to customer during year ended 30 September 20X3	750	2,250
Cash received from customer during year ended 30 September 20X3	700	2,250
Costs incurred during year ended 30 September 20X3	580	1,900
Estimated cost to complete at 30 September 20X3	790	3,400

S plc recognises turnover and profit on long-term contracts in relation to the proportion of work completed.

Required

(a)   Calculate the figures that will appear in S plc's profit and loss account for the year ended 30 September 20X3 and its balance sheet at that date in respect of each of these contracts.   **14 Marks**

The Accounting Standards Board's Statement of Principles for Financial Reporting (SoP) effectively defines losses on individual transactions in such a way that they are associated with increases in liabilities or decreases in assets. Liabilities are defined as 'obligations of an entity to transfer economic benefits as a result of past transactions or events'.

(b)   Explain how the definition of losses contained in the SoP could be used to justify the requirement of SSAP 9 – *Stocks and Long-term Contracts* to recognise losses in full on long-term contracts as soon as they can be foreseen.   **6 Marks**

(c)   Explain how the booking of attributable profit under long-term contract accounting is compatible with the desirable feature of prudence as envisaged by FRS 18, *Accounting Policies*.   **5 Marks**

Total Marks = 25

31   PREPARATION QUESTION: PATEL LIMITED

Patel Limited has previously reported deferred tax on an undiscounted basis. However, it appears that the norm in its particular industry is to report deferred tax on a discounted basis. The finance director believes that for reasons of comparability, the company should adopt the normal industry policy.

Required

Explain whether the proposed change represents a change in accounting policy or in estimation technique. State your reasons.

32   TAXATION (5/01 amended)   *45 mins*

(a)   Identify the main disclosures required in financial statements relating to deferred taxation and explain why each is necessary. Explain the basis on which deferred tax balances must now be calculated according to FRS 19.   **10 Marks**

(b)   Identify the main requirements of FRS 16 *Current tax*?   **5 Marks**

(c)   (i)   Identify the external auditor's duties with respect of the disclosure of specific items in the financial statements, such as those in respect of deferred taxation or current tax.

Do **not** describe any of the detailed audit tests that the auditor would conduct.

5 Marks

(ii)   Explain how the audit report would be affected by any disagreement over the disclosures made.   **5 Marks**

Total Marks = 25

33   H PLC (5/02)   *45 mins*

H plc is a major manufacturing company. According to the company's records, timing differences of £2.00 million had arisen at 30 April 20X4 because of differences between the carrying amount of tangible fixed assets and their tax base. These had arisen because H plc had exercised its right to claim accelerated tax relief in the earlier years of the asset lives.

At 30 April 20X3, the timing differences attributable to tangible fixed assets were £2.30 million.

The corporation tax rate has been 30% in the past. On 30 April 20X4, the directors of H plc were advised that the rate of taxation would decrease to 28% by the time that the timing differences on the tangible fixed assets reversed.

The estimated corporation tax charge for the year ended 30 April 20X4 was £400,000. The estimated charge for the year ended 30 April 20X3 was agreed with the Revenue and settled without adjustment.

Required:

(a) Prepare the notes in respect of current taxation and deferred tax as they would appear in the financial statements of H plc for the year ended 30 April 20X4. (Your answer should be expressed in £ million and you should work to two decimal places.) **7 Marks**

(b) FRS 19 *Deferred Tax* requires companies to publish a reconciliation of the current tax charge reported in the profit and loss account to the charge that would result from applying the standard rate of tax to the profit on ordinary activities before tax. Explain why this reconciliation is helpful to the readers of financial statements. **6 Marks**

(c) Explain the role of the Financial Reporting Review Panel (FRRP). **7 Marks**

(d) Explain whether the FRRP's role could be left to the external auditor. **5 Marks**

Total Marks = 25

---

34   STATEMENT OF PRINCIPLES/SSAP 21 *45 mins*

The following definitions have been taken from the Accounting Standards Board's *Draft Statement of Principles*.

- 'Assets are rights or other access to future economic benefits controlled by an entity as a result of past transactions or events.'

- 'Liabilities are obligations of an entity to transfer economic benefits as a result of past transactions or events.'

SSAP 21 *Leases and hire purchase contracts* requires lessees to capitalise finance leases in their financial statements.

Required

(a) Explain how SSAP 21's treatment of finance leases applies the definitions of assets and liabilities. **10 Marks**

(b) Identify the disclosure requirements of SSAP 21 with regard to finance leases?

5 Marks

(c) Explain how the *Statement of Principles* assists in the standard-setting process.

10 Marks

Total Marks = 25

35   Q HP (5/94 adapted) *45 mins*

Q Ltd, a vehicle dealership, has recently started to sell vans on hire purchase terms. The company made its first hire purchase sale on 1 October 20X2. The van had cost Q Ltd £10,000. Its cash selling price would have been £12,560. Instead Q Ltd asked for a deposit of £3,400 and four half-yearly instalments of £2,700 each. This is equivalent to an interest rate of 7% per half-year on the outstanding balance. The van has a useful economic life of 5 years.

The person responsible for maintaining Q Ltd's records has recorded this sale by debiting HP debtors and crediting sales with the total amount receivable from the customer: £14,200.

Required

(a) Explain why Q Ltd's treatment of this sale is in breach of relevant key accounting concepts.   **7 Marks**

(b) Prepare extracts from Q Ltd's profit and loss accounts for the year ended 31 March 20X3 and 31 March 20X4 and the balance sheets at those dates, to show how the sale should be accounted for.   **9 Marks**

(c) Legally, goods sold by hire purchase do not become the property of the buyer until the final payment has been made. Explain why purchasers still show goods which are being purchased under hire purchase terms as assets in their balance sheets.   **4 Marks**

(d) Prepare extracts from the purchaser's profit and loss accounts for the year ended 31 March 20X3 and 31 March 20X4 and the balance sheet at those dates.   **5 Marks**

Total Marks = 25

36   HIRE PURCHASE (11/90 adapted)   *45 mins*

DBD Ltd has bought three computers since 20X7. All are subject to hire purchase agreements with the vendor, XF plc.

Data relating to the computers are as follows.

	Computer A	*Computer B*	*Computer C*
Date of purchase	30 June 20X7	31 March 20X8	31 March 20X9
Cash price	£8,000	£6,000	£6,000
Deposit	£1,040	£720	£720
Total interest	£1,920	£1,320	£800
Number of quarterly instalments	12	12	8

The hire purchase agreements state that the first quarterly instalment is due three months after the date of purchase.

It is DBD Ltd's policy to assume that hire purchase interest accrues evenly over the life of the agreement and to credit the total hire purchase price to the vendor at the date of purchase. A hire purchase interest account is maintained.

Depreciation of computers is at 20% per annum on the written-down value. A full year's depreciation is charged against profit in the year of purchase.

DBD Ltd's financial year ends on 31 December. The company has no other computers.

Required

(a) Show the relevant entries in the following accounts for the financial years ended 31 December 20X7, 31 December 20X8 and 31 December 20X9:

(i)   The asset account for computers   **3 Marks**
(ii) Provision for depreciation on computers   **3 Marks**
(iii) XF plc's account   **7 Marks**
(iv) Hire purchase interest suspense account   **4 Marks**

(b) SSAP 21 requires that when calculating the present value of a finance lease, the interest rate implicit in the lease should be used.

Describe in your own words the definition of interest rate implicit in a lease.   **3 Marks**

(c) Show the total HP interest charge to the profit and loss account for each of the three years if the sum of the digits method is used to allocate the total interest.   **5 Marks**

Total Marks = 25

37   T LTD (11/96 amended)   *54 mins*

T Ltd entered into a leasing agreement with Lessor plc on 1 October 20X5. This involved a specialised piece of manufacturing machinery which was purchased by Lessor plc to T Ltd's specifications. The contract involves an annual payment in arrears of £1,200,000 for five years.

At the start of the lease with Lessor plc the present value of the minimum lease payments was calculated in accordance with the rules contained in SSAP 21 and found to be £4,100,000. The fair value of the machinery at the commencement of the contract was £4,680,000.

T Ltd is responsible for the maintenance of the machinery and is required to insure it against accidental damage. The machinery would normally be expected to have a useful economic life of approximately seven years. T Ltd depreciates its tangible fixed assets on the straight line basis.

The lease has been classified as an operating lease in the draft accounts for the year ended 30 September 20X6.

You are reminded that Statement of Standard Accounting Practice 21 contains the following definitions:

A *finance lease* is a lease that transfers substantially all the risks and rewards of ownership to the lessee. It should be presumed that such a transfer of risks and rewards occurs if, at the inception of a lease, the present value of the minimum lease payments, including any initial payment, amounts to substantially all (normally 90 per cent or more) of the fair value of the leased asset.

An *operating lease* is a lease other than a finance lease.

The SSAP also requires lessees to adopt the following accounting practice:

*   A finance lease should be recorded in the balance sheet of a lessee as an asset and as an obligation to pay future rentals. At the inception of the lease the sum to be recorded both as an asset and as a liability should be the present value of the minimum lease payments, derived by discounting them at the interest rate implicit in the lease.

*   An asset leased under a finance lease should be depreciated over the shorter of the lease term and its useful life.

*   The rental under an operating lease should be charged on a straight-line basis over the lease term.

(a) (i)   Explain whether you agree with T Ltd's decision to classify its lease agreement with Lessor plc as an operating lease.   **4 Marks**

(ii) Assuming that the lease agreement is to be treated as a finance lease instead of an operating lease, with an implied interest rate of 14.2% per annum, calculate the following figures relating to the leased asset:

- Finance charge for the year ended 30 September 20X6
- Depreciation charge for the year ended 30 September 20X6
- Fixed asset at 30 September 20X6
- Current liabilities at 30 September 20X6
- Long-term liabilities at 30 September 20X6   **10 Marks**

(iii) Assume that Lessor plc paid £3,900,000 for the machinery. Its year end is also 30 September. Show how it would treat the lease in its profit and loss account for the year to 30 September 20X6 and in its balance sheet at that date. Assume that Lessor plc treats the lease as a finance lease and that it uses an interest rate of 14.2%.   **5 Marks**

(b) Several weeks before T Ltd's year end, the company's finance director forecast profit before tax and interest for the year at £4,600,000, long-term liabilities at £4,000,000 and equity at £10,500,000. These forecasts assumed that the lease agreement would be treated as an operating lease.

The finance director was keen to forecast the company's return on capital employed and gearing. She was particularly concerned that the gearing ratio should be satisfactory.

Required

(i) Explain why the gearing ratio is an important measure of stability.   **3 Marks**

(ii) Calculate the forecast return on capital employed and gearing ratios, using the estimated figures prepared by the finance director.   **2 Marks**

(iii) (1) Explain whether *each* of the ratios calculated in (ii) above would increase or decrease if the lease were classified as a finance lease.

You are not required to recalculate the actual ratios.   **3 Marks**

(2) Explain whether the adjusted ratios described in (iii) (1) would be more or less relevant to internal planning and management decisions than those which you calculated in (ii)   **3 Marks**

Total Marks = 30

38   S PLC 2 (5/01 amended)   *45 mins*

S plc is a large manufacturing company. The company needs to purchase a major piece of equipment which is vital to the production process. S plc does not have sufficient cash available to buy this equipment. It cannot raise the necessary finance by issuing shares because it would not be cost-effective to have a share issue of the amount involved. The directors are also unwilling to borrow because the company already has a very high level of debt in its balance sheet.

C Bank has offered to lease the equipment to S plc. The bank has proposed a finance package in which S plc would take the equipment on a two-year lease. The intention is that S plc will take out a second two-year lease at the conclusion of the initial period and a third at the conclusion of that one. By that time the equipment will have reached the end of its useful life.

C Bank will not require S plc to commit itself in writing to the two secondary lease periods. Instead, S plc will agree in writing to refurbish the equipment to a brand new condition before returning it to C Bank. This condition will, however, be waived if the lease is subsequently extended to a total of six years or more. Once the equipment is used, it would be prohibitively expensive to refurbish it.

BPP PROFESSIONAL EDUCATION

S plc's directors are very interested in the arrangement proposed by C Bank. They believe that each of the two-year contracts could be accounted for as an operating lease because each covers only a fraction of the equipment's expected useful life.

Required

(a) Explain how the decision to treat the lease as an operating lease rather than a finance lease would affect S plc's profit and loss account, balance sheet and any accounting ratios based on these.   **6 Marks**

(b) Explain how the financial statements of C Bank would be affected if the lease is treated as an operating lease rather than a finance lease.   **5 Marks**

(c) Explain whether S plc should account for the proposed lease as an operating lease or as a finance lease.   **4 Marks**

(d) The relationship between debt and equity in a company's balance sheet is often referred to as the gearing ratio. Explain why companies are often keen to minimise the gearing ratio.   **5 Marks**

(e) It has been suggested that the rules governing the preparation of financial statements leave some scope for the preparers of financial statements to influence the profit figure or balance sheet position. Explain whether you agree with this suggestion.   **5 Marks**

Total Marks = 25

39   PREPARATION QUESTION: RESEARCH AND DEVELOPMENT

> Research and development expenditure means expenditure falling into one or more of the following broad categories (except to the extent that it relates to locating or exploiting oil, gas or mineral deposits or is reimbursable by third parties either directly or under the terms of a firm contract to develop and manufacture at an agreed price calculated to reimburse both elements of expenditure).
>
> (a) *Pure (or basic) research*: experimental or theoretical work undertaken primarily to acquire new scientific or technical knowledge for its own sake rather than directed towards any specific aim or application.
>
> (b) *Applied research*: original or critical investigation undertaken in order to gain new scientific or technical knowledge and directed towards a specific practical aim or objective.
>
> (c) *Development*: use of scientific or technical knowledge in order to produce new or substantially improved materials, devices, products or services, to install new processes or systems prior to the commencement of commercial production or commercial applications, or to improving substantially those already produced or installed.
>
> *SSAP 13, Paragraph 21*

Required

(a) Explain why it is considered necessary to distinguish between applied research and development expenditure and how this distinction affects the accounting treatment.

(b) State whether the following items are included within the SSAP 13 definition of research and development, and give your reasons:

   (i)   Market research
   (ii)   Testing of pre-production prototypes
   (iii) Operational research
   (iv)   Testing in search of process alternatives

40   PREPARATION QUESTION: GOVERNMENT GRANTS

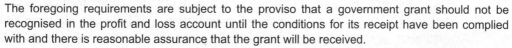

> Subject to paragraph 24 of this statement, government grants should be recognised in the profit and loss account so as to match them with the expenditure towards which they are intended to contribute. In the absence of persuasive evidence to the contrary, government grants should be assumed to contribute towards the expenditure that is the basis for their payment. To the extent that grants are made as a contribution towards specific expenditure on fixed assets, they should be recognised over the expected useful economic life of the related assets. Grants made to give immediate financial support or assistance to an enterprise or to reimburse costs previously incurred should be recognised in the profit and loss account of the period in which they become receivable. Grants made to finance the general activities of an enterprise over a specific period or to compensate for a loss of current or future income should be recognised in the profit and loss account of the period in respect of which they are paid.
>
> The foregoing requirements are subject to the proviso that a government grant should not be recognised in the profit and loss account until the conditions for its receipt have been complied with and there is reasonable assurance that the grant will be received.
>
> *SSAP 4, Paragraphs 23, 24*

Required

(a)   Explain how the requirements of SSAP 4 *Accounting for government grants* are consistent with the two concepts of the going concern assumption and accruals which underlie the preparation of financial statements in terms of FRS 18.

(b)   Describe how the grant-related aspects of the following events should be accounted for with respect to a limited company.

    (i)   A grant of 20% towards the cost of a fixed asset, the economic life of which is estimated to be 10 years, and which is financed by a five year loan.

    (ii)   A grant towards revenue expenditure in one year, on the condition that if certain requirements were not met in the next five years, all or part of the grant might be repayable.

    (iii)   A grant towards consultancy costs to design and install a standard costing system.

41   PREPARATION QUESTION: ACE (FRS 8)

FRS 8 *Related party disclosures* was issued in October 1995. Prior to its existence, there were specific requirements for related party disclosures contained in the 1985 Companies Act.

Required

Explain why related party disclosures are needed and why FRS 8 was considered necessary given the existing requirements of the 1985 Companies Act.

42   VARIOUS: D PLC (5/93)   *45 mins*

D plc is a large paper manufacturing company. The company's finance director is working on the published accounts for the year ended 31 March 20X3. The chief accountant has prepared the following list of problems which will have to be resolved before the statements can be finalised.

(a) *Post balance sheet events (SSAP 17)*

A fire broke out at the company's Westown factory on 4 April 20X3. This has destroyed the factory's administration block. Many of the costs incurred as a result of this fire are uninsured.

A major customer went into liquidation on 27 April 20X3. The customer's balance at 31 March 20X3 remains unpaid. The receiver has intimated that unsecured creditors will receive very little compensation, if any.   **5 Marks**

(b) *Possible investment property (SSAP 19)*

The company decided to take advantage of depressed property prices and purchased a new office building in the centre of Westville. This was purchased with the intention of the building being resold at a profit within five years. In the meantime, the company is using the property to house the administrative staff from the Westown factory until such time as their own offices can be repaired. It is anticipated that this will take at least nine months. The managing director has suggested that the building should not be depreciated.   **3 Marks**

(c) *Possible development expenditure (SSAP 13)*

The company paid the engineering department at Northtown University a large sum of money to design a new pulping process which will enable the use of cheaper raw materials. This process has been successfully tested in the University's laboratories and is almost certain to be introduced at D plc's pulping plant within the next few months.

The company paid a substantial amount to the University's biology department to develop a new species of tree which could grow more quickly and therefore enable the company's forests to generate more wood for paper manufacturing. The project met with some success in that a new tree was developed. Unfortunately, it was prone to disease and the cost of the chemical sprays needed to keep the wood healthy rendered the tree uneconomic.   **6 Marks**

(d) *Possible contingent liabilities (FRS 12)*

One of the company's employees was injured during the year. He had been operating a piece of machinery which had been known to have a faulty guard. The company's lawyers have advised that the employee has a very strong case, but will be unable to estimate likely financial damages until further medical evidence becomes available.

One of the company's customers is claiming compensation for losses sustained as a result of a delayed delivery. The customer had ordered a batch of cut sheets with the intention of producing leaflets to promote a special offer. There was a delay in supplying the paper and the leaflets could not be prepared in time. The company's lawyers have advised that there was no specific agreement to supply the goods in time for this promotion and, furthermore, that it would be almost impossible to attribute the failure of the special offer to the delay in the supply of the paper.   **6 Marks**

(e) *Convertible debentures (FRS 4)*

On 1 April 20X2 the company issued £500,000 of convertible 4% debentures, incurring issue costs of £15,000. In the opinion of the directors, the terms of the conversion are such that it is virtually certain that the debentures will eventually be converted into ordinary shares of the company.   **5 Marks**

Required

Explain how each of these matters should be dealt with in the published accounts for the year ended 31 March 20X3 in the light of the accounting standards referred to above. You should assume that the amounts involved are material in every case.

Total Marks = 25

43   V PLC (11/97 amended)   *54 mins*

V plc imports electronic goods and sells them to large retail organisations. Almost half the company's sales occur during the months of October and November.

(a) The following information was discovered after the first draft of the financial statements for the year ended 30 September 20X7 was prepared, but before the statements had been finalised and approved by the board of directors.

    (1) The company's computer network was installed during the year ended 30 September 20X6. It was technically advanced at the time of installation and was expected to operate reliably for at least ten years. V plc's directors have, however, discovered that the company's main competitors have installed newer technology which provides them with more detailed planning and marketing information. V plc might be forced to replace its computers within the next twelve months. It is unlikely that the existing system could be sold for much more than its scrap value.

    (2) A loan of £500,000 was taken out during September 20X7 to pay for the additional stocks which were purchased in advance of the seasonal increase in sales. While the loan was formally repayable in the year 20Y2, the loan agreement provided that the company could repay it at any time without penalty. V plc actually repaid the loan in full at the end of October 20X7.

    (3) Closing stocks include £100,000 for a large quantity of a newly-developed electronic machine. This machine has had disappointing reviews from computer magazines, and initial sales have been slow.

    (4) V plc introduced a new warranty service during the year ended 30 September 20X7. The retailers who sell V plc's products offer their customers a three-year warranty on all high-value purchases in return for a fee. The retailer keeps part of the fee as a commission and passes the balance to V plc. The company's share of these fees has been included in the sales figure for the year. V plc has had to replace very few items under the warranty scheme this year, although the company's technical staff expect that most items which are likely to fail will do so during the final year of the warranty period. It is difficult to estimate the likely costs of replacing defective goods under the warranty scheme, although V plc is confident that these costs will not exceed the fees received.

Required

Explain how EACH of the four matters (a) to (d) above is likely to affect the company's annual accounts. Describe the additional information that you would require before finalising the treatment of these matters.   **16 Marks**

(b) At 30 September 20X7, V plc had 1,000,000 £1 ordinary shares in issue. At that date, the company was in the process of issuing 200,000 new shares with a nominal value of £1.00 each and had received £110,000 from applicants for the new share issue.

These shares were allotted during October 20X7. The total issue price was £1.40 per share. Applicants were asked to pay £0.50 per share on application.

During October the directors returned a total of £10,000 to those applicants who had requested fewer than 500 shares each. On the same date, 200,000 shares were allotted to successful applicants.

The successful applicants were asked to pay a further £0.60 per share. This sum included the share premium. This first call was to be paid in full by the end of November 20X7 or the share would be forfeited. A total of £118,800 was received by the deadline. One shareholder failed to pay the £1,200 due on an allocation of 2,000 shares.

The 2,000 forfeited shares were reissued in December 20X7. They were sold for £900 and treated as £0.70 paid.

Required

(i)   Open the relevant accounts (including the ordinary share capital and share premium accounts) and enter the above transactions.   **10 Marks**

(ii)   Assuming that there are no further transactions in respect of share capital, show how the balances in the various accounts in (i) above would appear in V plc's balance sheet at 30 September 20X8.   **4 Marks**

Total Marks = 30

44   H PLC I (11/01 amended)   *45 mins*

H plc is a major electronics company. It spends a substantial amount of money on research and development. The company has a policy of capitalising development expenditure, but writes off pure and applied research expenditure immediately in accordance with the requirements of SSAP 13 *Research and development*.

The company's latest annual report included a page of voluntary disclosures about the effectiveness of the company's research programme. This indicated that the company's prosperity depended on the development of new products and that this could be a very long process. In order to maintain its technical lead, the company often funded academic research studies into theoretical areas, some of which led to breakthroughs which H plc was able to patent and develop into new product ideas. The company claimed that the money spent in this way was a good investment because for every twenty unsuccessful projects there was usually at least one valuable discovery which generated enough profit to cover the whole cost of the research activities. Unfortunately, it was impossible to tell in advance which projects would succeed in this way.

A shareholder expressed dismay at H plc's policy of writing off research costs in this manner. He felt that this was unduly pessimistic given that the company earned a good return from its research activities. He felt that the company should invoke the Accounting Standards Board's true and fair override and capitalise all research costs.

Required

(a)   Explain why it might be justifiable for H plc to capitalise its research costs.   **5 Marks**

(b)   Explain why SSAP 13 imposes a rigid set of rules which prevent the capitalisation of all research expenditure and make it difficult to capitalise development expenditure.

5 Marks

(c)   Explain whether the requirements of SSAP 13 are likely to discourage companies such as H plc from investing in research activities.   **5 Marks**

(d)   Describe the advantages and disadvantages of offering companies the option of a true and fair override in preparing financial statements.   **5 Marks**

(e)   A company's accounting treatment of development expenditure depends upon its accounting policy in this area. Identify the main requirements of FRS 18 *Accounting policies* regarding choice of accounting policies.   **5 Marks**

Total Marks = 25

45   L PLC (5/02 amended)   *45 mins*

L plc sells gaming cards to retailers, who then resell them to the general public. Customers who buy these cards scratch off a panel to reveal whether they have won a cash prize. There are several different ranges of cards, each of which offers a different range of prizes.

Prize-winners send their winning cards to L plc and are paid by cheque. If the prize is major, then the prize-winner is required to telephone L plc to register the claim and then send the winning card to a special address for separate handling.

All cards are printed and packaged under conditions of high security. Special printing techniques make it easy for L plc to identify forged claims and it is unusual for customers to make false claims. Large claims are, however, checked using a special chemical process that takes several days to take effect.

The directors are currently finalising their financial statements for the year ended 31 March 2002. They are unsure about how to deal with the following items.

(i)   A packaging error on a batch of 'Chance' cards meant that there were too many major prize cards in several boxes. L plc recalled the batch from retailers, but it was too late to prevent many of the defective cards being sold. The company is being flooded with claims. L plc's lawyers have advised that the claims are valid and must be paid. It has proved impossible to determine the likely level of claims that will be made in respect of this error because it will take several weeks to establish the success of the recall and the number of defective cards.

(ii) A prize-winner has registered a claim for a £200,000 prize from a 'Lotto' card. The financial statements will be finalised before the card can be processed and checked.

(iii) A claim has been received for £100,000 from a 'Winner' card. The maximum prize offered for this game is £90,000 and so the most likely explanation is that the card has been forged. The police are investigating the claim, but this will not be resolved before the financial statements are finalised. Once the police investigation has concluded, L plc will make a final check to ensure that the card is not the result of a printing error.

(iv) The company received claims totalling £300,000 during the year from a batch of bogus 'Happy' cards that had been forged by a retailer in Newtown. The police have prosecuted the retailer and he has recently been sent to prison. The directors of L plc have decided to pay customers who bought these cards 50% of the amount claimed as a goodwill gesture. They have not, however, informed the lucky prize-winners of this yet.

Required:

(a) Identify the appropriate accounting treatment of each of the claims against L plc in respect of (i) to (iv) above. Your answer should have due regard to the requirements of FRS 12 *Provisions, contingent liabilities and contingent assets.*

                                    3 marks for each of (i) to (iv) = 12 Marks

(b) It has been suggested that readers of financial statements do not always pay sufficient attention to contingent liabilities even though they may have serious implications for the future of the company.

(i)   Explain why insufficient attention might be paid to contingent liabilities.   **4 Marks**

(ii) Explain how FRS 12 prevents companies from treating as contingent liabilities those liabilities that should be recognised in the balance sheet.   **4 Marks**

(c) Explain how the presentation of information in a set of financial statements helps shareholders to obtain a balanced understanding of the ways that wealth has been created by a company on their behalf.

5 Marks

Total Marks = 25

46   FRS 12 (11/02 amended)   *45 mins*

(a) FRS 12 *Provisions, Contingent Liabilities and Contingent Assets* requires contingencies to be classified as remote, possible, probable and virtually certain. Each of these categories should then be treated differently, depending on whether it is an asset or a liability.

Required:

Explain why FRS 12 classifies contingencies in this manner.   **5 Marks**

(b) The chief accountant of Z plc, a construction company, is finalising the work on the financial statements for the year ended 31 October 20X3. She has prepared a list of all of the matters that might require some adjustment or disclosure under the requirements of FRS 12.

negligence – our fault, legal obligation

Provision for £100k

(i) A customer has lodged a claim against Z plc for repairs to an office block built by the company. The roof leaks and it appears that this is due to negligence in construction. Z plc is negotiating with the customer and will probably have to pay for repairs that will cost approximately £100,000.

Get nothing ∴ no provision as not a chance would get anything. no disclosure

obligation probabilities

(ii) The roof in (i) above was installed by a subcontractor employed by Z plc. Z plc's lawyers are confident that the company would have a strong claim to recover the whole of any costs from the subcontractor. The chief accountant has obtained the subcontractor's latest financial statements. The subcontractor appears to be almost insolvent with few assets.

increase provision by £40k

(iii) Whenever Z plc finishes a project, it gives customers a period of three months to notify any construction defects. These are repaired immediately. The balance sheet at 31 October 20X2 carried a provision of £80,000 for future repairs. The estimated cost of repairs to completed contracts as at 31 October 20X3 is £120,000.

Asset could disclose then if receive then bal sheet post event SSAP 17

(iv) During the year ended 31 October 20X3, Z plc lodged a claim against a large firm of electrical engineers which had delayed the completion of a contract. The engineering company's directors have agreed in principle to pay Z plc £30,000 compensation. Z plc's chief accountant is confident that this amount will be received before the end of December 20X3.

do nothing

(v) An architect has lodged a claim against Z plc for the loss of a laptop computer during a site visit. He alleges that the company did not take sufficient care to secure the site office and that this led to the computer being stolen while he inspected the project. He is claiming for consequential losses of £90,000 for the value of the vital files that were on the computer. Z plc's lawyers have indicated that the company might have to pay a trivial sum in compensation for the computer hardware. There is almost no likelihood that the court would award damages for the lost files because the architect should have copied them.

Required:

Explain how each of the contingencies (i) to (v) above should have been accounted for. Assume that all amounts stated are material.

3 marks for each of (i) to (v) = 15 marks

(c)   The following notes relate to VJ Ltd.

(i)   VJ Ltd's largest customer, Acme plc, placed an order during September 20X2 for all of the goods that it is likely to require during the year ending 30 September 20X3. VJ Ltd invoiced Acme plc for these goods during September 20X2. A total of £800 million was debited to debtors and credited to sales in respect of this invoice. A provision for £300 million was created in respect of the estimated cost of manufacturing the invoiced goods.

(ii)   Acme plc agreed to place the order referred to in note (i) above only after receiving a number of written assurances from VJ Ltd's directors. The goods themselves will be delivered at times and in quantities decided by Acme plc. Acme plc will pay for the goods in accordance with VJ Ltd's normal credit terms after delivery. Acme plc can cancel the order without penalty at any time and any remaining balance on the invoice will be cancelled immediately.

The Accounting Standards Board's Statement of Principles for Financial Reporting effectively defines profits on individual transactions in terms of increases in net assets.

This means that profits are normally associated with an increase in the value of assets, where assets are defined as 'rights or other access to future economic benefits controlled by an entity as a result of past transactions or events'.

Required

Explain whether VJ Ltd is justified in treating the transaction described in notes (i) and (ii) above as a sale.   **5 Marks**

Total Marks = 25

47   AIMS OF ASB (5/96 amended)   *45 mins*

(a)   One of the aims of the Accounting Standards Board (ASB) is to establish and improve the standards of financial accounting for the benefits of users of financial information.

Required

Explain how the following accounting standards make it easier for the users of financial information to make sensible decisions about the performance and position of a company.

(i)   FRS 3 *Reporting financial performance*   **5 Marks**
(ii)   SSAP 25 *Segmental reporting*   **5 Marks**
(iii) FRS 12 *Provisions, contingent liabilities and contingent assets*   **5 Marks**

(b)   SSAP 17 defines adjusting events as post balance sheet events which provide additional evidence of conditions existing at the balance sheet date. If they materially affect the amounts to be included, they need to be reflected in the financial statements.

Non-adjusting events are events which arise after the balance sheet date and concern conditions which did not exist at that time. Consequently they do not result in changes in amounts in financial statements. They may, however, be of such materiality that their disclosure is required by way of notes to ensure that financial statements are not misleading.

Required

Give five examples of adjusting events and five examples of non-adjusting events.

10 Marks

Total Marks = 25

71

48   NEWCARS PLC (5/01 amended)   *45 mins*

Newcars plc is a vehicle dealership; it sells both new and good quality second-hand cars. The company is large and has a large number of shareholders. The only large block of shares is held by Arthur, who owns 25% of Newcars plc. Arthur is a member of Newcars plc's board of directors and he takes a keen interest in the day-to-day management of the company.

Arthur also owns 25% of Oldcars plc. Oldcars plc sells inexpensive second-hand cars which tend to be either relatively old or have a high mileage. Arthur is also a member of the board of directors of Oldcars plc.

Apart from Arthur, Newcars plc and Oldcars plc have no shareholders in common. The only thing that they have in common, apart from Arthur's interest in each, is that Newcars plc sells a large number of cars to Oldcars plc. This usually happens when a customer of Newcars plc has traded in a car that is too old to be sold from Newcars plc's showroom. Most of these cars are immediately resold to Oldcars plc and go into Oldcar plc's normal trading stock. These sales account for approximately 5% of Newcars plc's turnover. Oldcars plc acquires approximately 20% of its cars from Newcars plc.

Required

(a) Explain whether Newcars plc and Oldcars plc are related parties in terms of the requirements of FRS 8 *Related party disclosures*. List any additional information that you would require before making a final decision.   **7 Marks**

(b) Assuming that Newcars plc and Oldcars plc are related parties, describe the related parties' disclosures that would have to be made in the companies' financial statements in respect of the sale and purchase of cars between the two companies.   **6 Marks**

(c) Explain why it is necessary to disclose such information in respect of transactions involving related parties.   **7 Marks**

(d) In general terms, explain the problems that an external auditor might have in determining what are material related party transactions.   **5 Marks**

Total Marks = 25

49   PREPARATION QUESTION: ISSUE OF SHARES

On 30 March 20X4 the directors of Rudolph Ltd allotted 150,000 ordinary shares of £1 each at a premium of 30p payable as follows.

On application	20p
On allotment	40p (including premium)
First call	35p
Second call	35p

Amounts due on application were received on 23 March and amounts due on allotment were received on 5 April. The calls were made on 30 April and 25 June.

The first and second calls were not met on 10,000 shares and these were forfeited on 31 July, but all other amounts due were received on 4 May and 29 June for the first and second calls respectively.

You are required to prepare journal entries to record the foregoing transactions in the books of Rudolph Ltd for the year ended 31 August 20X4.

Approaching the question

1   This is a specialised question but straightforward if you bear in mind the following points.

2   *Application* is where potential shareholders apply for shares in the company and send cash to cover the amount applied for.

3   *Allotment* is when the company allocates shares to the successful applicants and returns cash to unsuccessful applicants.

4   A *call* is where the purchase price is payable in instalments. The company will 'call' for instalments.

5   If a shareholder fails to pay a call, his shares may be *forfeited* without the need to return the money he has paid. These forfeited shares may then be *reissued* to other shareholders.

6   Cash received is recorded initially in application, allotment and call accounts.

50   PREPARATION QUESTION: PURCHASE OF OWN SHARES

In recent years several large listed companies have purchased their own ordinary shares.

You are required to:

(a) Summarise the accounting requirements for a public listed company when it purchases its own shares.

(b) Give six advantages of a company purchasing its own shares.

Guidance notes

1   You may be asked these requirements as part of a larger question.
2   The advantages of such arrangements are important - otherwise why would companies bother?

51   PREPARATION QUESTION: PURCHASE OF OWN SHARES (CALCULATION)

Gregory Ltd is a small privately-owned company. The draft balance sheet for the current year is as follows.

DRAFT BALANCE SHEET OF GREGORY LIMITED
AS AT 31 DECEMBER 20X2

	£	£
Fixed assets		65,000
Net current assets (ex cash)	81,250	
Cash	16,250	
		97,500
		162,500
£1 ordinary shares		82,500
£1 6.5% preference shares (redeemable)		40,000
Share premium account		25,000
Profit and loss account		15,000
		162,500

The terms of the redemption of the preference shares are that such shares may be redeemed at a premium of 9%. The preference dividend is paid to date and the shares were originally issued at par (no premium). The company has decided to redeem the shares now, with funding from an agreed £32,500 overdraft and a new issue of 15,000 ordinary shares at a premium of 50p per share.

The managing director, who is also the majority shareholder, is worried that the transaction will not be allowed under Companies Act 1985 (as amended by CA 1989) because the capital of the company will be reduced.

Required

Assuming that the capital reduction can proceed, show the draft balance sheet of Gregory Ltd after it has been carried out.

---

52   H PLC II (5/01 amended)   *45 mins*

H plc was established in 19W6 to develop advanced computer software. The company was established with the financial backing of B Bank. B Bank invested £2 million in H plc's share capital, buying 2 million £1 shares at par. The agreement was that B Bank would leave this investment in place for five years. At the end of that period, H plc would buy the shares back from B Bank at a price that reflected the company's success during that period.

An independent accountant advised that B Bank's 2 million shares in H plc were worth £4.5 million. The shares were repurchased on 30 April 20X1 for that amount.

H plc's balance sheet immediately before the repurchase was as follows.

H plc
Balance sheet at 30 April 20X1 (before share repurchase)

	£ million
Net assets	18.0
Share capital	7.0
Profit and loss	11.0
	18.0

The net assets figure includes £8.0 million cash.

Required

(a) Prepare H plc's balance sheet as it would appear immediately after the share repurchase.   **5 Marks**

(b) When a company repurchases its shares, it must normally make a transfer from its profit and loss account to its capital redemption reserve (CRR). It has been suggested that this transfer is necessary to protect the company's lenders. Explain how the transfer to the CRR protects the interests of lenders when a company repurchases its shares.   **10 Marks**

(c) Explain why companies are permitted to buy back their own shares.   **5 Marks**

(d) Explain why companies might wish to buy back their own shares.   **5 Marks**

Total Marks = 25

---

53   CAPITAL TRANSACTIONS (11/02 amended)   *45 mins*

(a) W plc is an expanding company. The directors decided to offer 1 million new £1.00 ordinary shares for sale at an issue price of £1.20 per share. At that time, the company had balances of £4 million on share capital and £1.25 million on share premium.

Applicants were required to pay £0.25 per share with their application. Applications were received for 2.1 million shares.

The directors rejected a number of smaller applications for a total of 100,000 shares. The remainder of the applicants were each allotted one share for every two applied for, deemed £0.50 per share paid.

Applicants were asked to pay £0.40 per share on allotment, which was deemed to include the share premium. One applicant holding 2,000 shares did not pay this instalment by the due date and the shares were forfeited.

The forfeited shares were reissued for £0.60 per share and were thereafter treated as having the same rights as the other shares in the issue.

A final call was made for the remaining £0.30 per share. All shareholders paid the final call by the due date.

Required:

Prepare the following accounts.

(i)   Share capital

(ii)   Share premium

(iii)   Application and allotment

(iv)   Investment in own shares

(v)   Call   **8 Marks**

(b) X plc is a listed company which is considering a bonus issue of new shares, financed out of distributable profits.

Required:

Identify the effects that this issue would have on the company's capital structure. Your answer should explain how the bonus issue would affect the interests of the company's shareholders and creditors.   **6 Marks**

(c) The share capital section of some balance sheets is complicated by the fact that it is possible to issue a range of different types of share, some of which are more like loan instruments than ordinary shares.

Required:

Explain why certain types of share capital should be classified separately.   **6 Marks**

(d) The Companies Act is more flexible in its rules regarding the redemption of shares where the company is private.

Required

Explain the provisions whereby private companies may redeem their own shares out of capital.   **5 Marks**

Total Marks = 25

PERFORMANCE

The objective test questions and questions 54 to 64 cover performance, the subject of Part D of the BPP Study Text for Paper 6.

OBJECTIVE TEST QUESTIONS

1   How is the length of a trading company's working capital cycle normally calculated, assuming all sales and purchases are made on credit?

A   The average time from purchase of goods for sale to receipt of cash on sale of these goods.

B   Collection period for debtors plus stock turnover period minus collection period for creditors

C   Stock turnover period plus collection period for creditors minus collection period for debtors

D   Collection period for debtors plus stock turnover period plus collection period for creditors.

2   Which, if any, of the following statements about a company's accounting liquidity ratios are likely to be true?

1   The higher a company's current ratio is the more efficiently it is operating

2   A high gearing ratio suggests that a company's financial position is more secure than that of a company with a low gearing ratio.

3   If a company revalues its fixed assets, its gearing ratio will be reduced.

4   If a company treats leases as operating leases rather than finance leases its gearing ratio will be increased.

A   None of these statements
B   3 only
C   1 and 4
D   2 and 3

The following information is relevant for questions 3 to 6

The summarised financial statements of a company, ignoring taxation, are shown below:

PROFIT AND LOSS ACCOUNT

	£m
Operating profit	30
Interest paid	(6)
	24
Dividends paid and proposed	(12)
	12

BALANCE SHEET

	£m
Fixed assets	140
Net current assets	160
	300
Less: Loan capital	(120)
	180
Ordinary share capital	100
Share premium account	36 ✓
Revaluation reserve	8 ✓
Profit and loss account	36 ✓
	180

3   Which of the following correctly expresses the gearing ratio of the company?

    A   120/100 = 120%

    B   180/120 = 150%

    C   180/300 = 60%

    D   120/300 = 40%

Prior charge capital / total capital = loan cap / TALCL

4   What is the company's return on owners' equity?

    A $30/180 = 16^2/_3\%$

    B $12/180 = 6^2/_3\%$

    C   24/100 = 24%

    D $24/180 = 13^1/_3\%$

ROE = PAT / SF   24 / 180

5   What is the company's return on capital employed?

    A   30/300 = 10%

    B   24/300 = 8%

    C $30/180 = 16^2/_3\%$

    D   12/300 = 4%

ROCE = PBIT / TALCL   30 / 300

6   What is the company's dividend cover?

    A   15 times

    B $2^1/_2$ times

    C   2 times

    D   3 times

EPS = PAT - pref / No shares   24 / 100

Div cover = EPS / Div per ord share   24/12

The following information relates to questions 7 and 8

The summarised financial statements of a listed company as at 31 December 20X4 are shown below:

PROFIT AND LOSS ACCOUNT

	£m	£m
Operating profit		60
Interest paid		(10)
		50
Taxation		(15)
		35
Dividends paid and proposed		
Preference	3	
Ordinary	17	(20)
Retained profit		15

BPP
PROFESSIONAL EDUCATION

BALANCE SHEET

	£m
Share capital	
Ordinary share capital (shares of 50p each)	200
6% preference shares (shares of £1 each)	50
Profit and loss account	200
	450
Sundry net assets	450
	450

The price of the company's ordinary shares at 31 December 20X4 was 300p per share. There were no changes in the company's share capital during the year.

7   What is the company's earnings per share to one place of decimals?

   A   8.0p
   B   16.0p
   C   8.8p
   D   4.3p

8   What is the company's price/earnings ratio to one place of decimals?

   A   6.0
   B   9.4
   C   8.6
   D   37.5

> If you struggled with these objective test questions, go back to your BPP Study Text for this paper and revise Chapter 12 before you tackle the written questions on performance.

54   PREPARATION QUESTION: OVERTRADING

When a business has insufficient resources, particularly of a liquid nature, to maintain its existing level of operation, it may be said to be in a position of *overtrading*.

This situation may arise through internal mis-management, or through external factors, or a combination of both.

You are required to identify and explain briefly the ways in which such a situation may arise. Your answer should deal with:

(a)   Those factors internal to the business
(b)   Those factors external to the business

Approaching the question

1   In most examination questions on interpretation of accounts you will be given a set of accounts and/or ratios and asked to calculate ratios and interpret them, perhaps with some specific aim in view.

2   This preparation question is about one specific situation which may arise, namely overtrading. If you can show in answering the question that you are aware of the symptoms of overtrading, you will know what signs to look for in a conventional interpretation of accounts question.

3   Part (b) of this question can be answered using thought and common sense rather than text book knowledge.

55   PREPARATION QUESTION: ANN NAIDU

Ann Naidu wishes to invest some money in one of two private companies. She has obtained the latest management accounts for Blue Ltd and Red Ltd prepared for internal purposes. She has asked you to help her assess the relative profitability of the two companies. The management accounts of the companies are shown below.

SUMMARY PROFIT AND LOSS ACCOUNTS
YEAR ENDED 31 DECEMBER 20X4

	Blue Limited	Red Limited
	£'000	£'000
Turnover	11,522	5,854
Cost of sales	(4,724)	(1,932)
Gross profit	6,798	3,922
Distribution costs	(1,844)	(936)
Administrative expenses	(2,074)	(878)
Operating profit	2,880	2,108
Interest paid and similar charges	(304)	(80)
Profit on ordinary activities before taxation	2,576	2,028
Tax on profit on ordinary activities	(618)	(486)
Profit for the financial year	1,958	1,542
Dividends	(624)	(282)
Retained profit for the year	1,334	1,260

SUMMARY BALANCE SHEET AS AT 30 SEPTEMBER 20X4

	Blue Limited		Red Limited	
	£'000	£'000	£'000	£'000
Fixed assets		12,376		5,450
Current assets	3,044		2,204	
Current liabilities	(2,030)		(1,090)	
Net current assets		1,014		1,114
Long term loan		(3,800)		(1,000)
		9,590		5,564

79

The management reports show the following ratios.

	Blue Limited	Red Limited
Return on capital employed	21.5%	32.1%
Gross profit margin	59.0%	67.0%
Net profit percentage	25.0%	36.0%
Earnings per share	47p	82p

Required

(a) Prepare a report for Ann Naidu that

  (i) Briefly explains the meaning of each ratio

  (ii) Uses each ratio to assess the relative profitability of the companies

  (iii) Concludes, with reasons, which company is the more profitable

(b) Ratio analysis is a useful tool in analysing and interpreting financial statements. Outline the key practical limitations of ratio analysis.

56 RATIOS: T PLC (11/97 adapted) *45 mins*

You are the assistant accountant of T plc. The company's computerised accounting package produced a monthly profit statement and balance sheet. The chief accountant uses these to prepare a summarised report on the company's performance and financial position, and presents this to the board of directors.

You have been asked to prepare the report for the month of October 20X7. The statements are shown below:

PROFIT AND LOSS ACCOUNTS FOR THE MONTH OF:

	October 20X7 £'000	September 20X7 £'000
Sales	900	700
Cost of goods sold	(368)	(175)
	532	525
Other operating costs	(240)	(250)
Net profit	292	275

BALANCE SHEETS AT THE END OF:

	October 20X7 £'000	£'000	September 20X7 £'000	£'000
Fixed assets		1,898		1,500
Stock	32		220	
Debtors	1,010		720	
Bank			12	
	1,042		952	
Creditors	(185)		(360)	
Bank	(371)		-	
Working capital		486		592
		2,384		2,092
Share capital		1,000		1,000
Profit and loss		1,384		1,092
		2,384		2,092

You have been given the following additional information.

(a) During October the company paid £400,000 for a new piece of machinery purchased during the month. This was financed by a bank overdraft as a temporary measure. The company will receive the proceeds of a £400,000 long-term loan during December 20X7.

(b) The sales figure for October includes £200,000 for sales made to a charity at cost price. Apart from supporting the charity's work, this sale generated some valuable publicity for the company. The stock was all purchased during September 20X7.

(c) The report should include the following ratios based on the October and September figures:

GP
———
Turnover   700 $\frac{532}{700}$

(i)   Gross profit ratio percentage
(ii)   Current ratio
(iii) Debtors turnover in days
(iv)   Creditors turnover in days
(v)   Stock turnover in days
(vi)   Return on capital employed

These should all allow for the effects of the unusual transactions described in (a) and (b) above. Stock was worth £37,000 at the beginning of September 20X7.

(d) The managing director has suggested calculating the return on capital employed as part of the monthly reporting package. The chief accountant does not believe that it would be useful to calculate this ratio for a period as short as one month.

Required

(a) Calculate the ratios listed in (c) above. These should take the matters described in (a) and (b) into account. Briefly explain any adjustments you have made to the figures shown in the summarised financial statements.   **17 Marks**

(b) Explain why it might be argued that a return on capital employed (ROCE) ratio based on monthly statements might not be particularly useful.   **3 Marks**

(c) Prepare an analysis of the cashflow for the month of October 20X7, using the direct method, for management purposes.   **5 Marks**

Total Marks = 25

57   **PERFORMANCE INDICATORS** (5/96 adapted)   *45 mins*

H plc manufactures vehicle parts. The company sells its products to a number of independent distributors who resell the goods to garages and other retail outlets in their areas. H plc has a policy of having only one distributor in any given geographical area. Distributors are selected mainly on the basis of financial viability. H plc is keen to avoid the disruption of sales and loss of credibility associated with the collapse of a distributor.

The company is currently trying to choose between two companies which have applied to be its sole distributor in Geetown, a new sales area.

The applicants have supplied the following information.

	Applicant X			*Applicant Y*		
	20X3	*20X4*	*20X5*	*20X3*	*20X4*	*20X5*
Sales (£'000)	1,280	1,600	2,000	1,805	1,900	2,000
Gross profit %	22	20	18	23	22	24
Return on capital employed %	8	12	16	14	15	16
Current ratio	1.7:1	1.9:1	2.1:1	1.7:1	1.65:1	1.7:1
Quick ratio	1.4:1	1.1:1	0.9:1	0.9:1	0.9:1	0.9:1
Gearing %	15	21	28	29	30	27

Required

(a) Explain why trends in accounting ratios could provide a more useful insight than the latest figures taken on their own.   **4 Marks**

(b) Using the information provided above, explain which of the companies appears to be the safer choice for the role of distributor. **11 Marks**

(c) Often ratio analysis on its own is not sufficient for interpreting accounts meaningfully. Identify what other information should be reviewed. **5 Marks**

(d) Comparison of two companies using ratio analysis can be distorted if the companies have different accounting policies. Using examples of two different accounting policies explain the effect on return on capital employed and gearing. **5 Marks**

Total Marks = 25

58   BENCHMARKING: CUTLERS (Specimen paper amended)   *45 mins*

B is the managing director of CE Ltd, a small, family-owned company which manufactures cutlery. His company belongs to a trade association which publishes a monthly magazine. The latest issue of the magazine contains a very brief article based on the analysis of the accounting statements published by the 40 companies which manufacture this type of product. This contains the following table.

	Average for all companies in the industry	
Return on shareholders' equity	33%	26%
Return on total capital employed	29%	19%
Gross profit percentage	30%	20%
Current ratio	1.9:1	1.5:1
Stock turnover	37 days	38.5
Debtors turnover	41 days	49 days
Gearing – (debt/capital employed)	40%	35%

CE Ltd's latest financial statements are as follows.

PROFIT AND LOSS ACCOUNT FOR THE YEAR ENDED 31 OCTOBER 20X3

$Roe = \dfrac{Pbefore\ tax}{SF} \quad \dfrac{110}{424}$

	£'000	£'000
Sales		900
Cost of goods sold		720
Gross profit		180
Selling and administrative expenses	55	
Interest	15	
		70
Net profit		110

$ROCE = \dfrac{PBIT}{TALCC\ SF + CT\ debt} \quad \dfrac{110}{574}$

BALANCE SHEET AS AT 31 OCTOBER 20X3

$\dfrac{GP}{Turnover} \quad \dfrac{180}{900}$

$Stock\ T = \dfrac{COS}{Stock} \quad \dfrac{720}{96}$

$\dfrac{120}{900} =$

	£'000	£'000
Fixed assets		500
Current assets		
Stock	96	
Debtors	120	
Bank	5	
	221	
Current liabilities		
Creditors	(147)	
		74
		574
Long-term liabilities		
10% debentures		150
		424
Share capital		100
Reserves		324
		424

221
147

150
424 + 150

Required

(a) Calculate *each* of the ratios listed in the magazine article, using CE Ltd's financial statements, and comment briefly on CE Ltd's performance in comparison to the industrial averages. **12 Marks**

(b) Explain *four* reasons why it could be misleading to compare CE Ltd's ratios with those taken from the article. **13 Marks**

Total Marks = 25

59 INHERITANCE: BUSINESS STRATEGY (Pilot paper amended) *45 mins*

Your friend inherited a small manufacturing company during 19X9. At the beginning of 20X0 he appointed a full-time managing director to run the company on his behalf. The new managing director has made a number of changes to the company's business strategy. Your friend has very little business experience, and is concerned that the new director's changes have not been particularly beneficial.

The profit and loss accounts for the years ended 31 December 19X9 and 20X0 are shown below, along with the balance sheets at those dates.

Profit and loss accounts for the year ended 31 December

	19X9	20X0
	£'000	£'000
Sales	2,700	8,400
Cost of sales	(1,080)	(5,040)
Gross profit	1,620	3,360
Selling expenses	(450)	(810)
Bad debts	(54)	(420)
Depreciation	(174)	(624)
Interest	(36)	(576)
Net profit	906	930
Balance brought forward	981	1,887
	1,887	2,817

Balance sheets as at 31 December

	19X9		20X0	
	£'000	£'000	£'000	£'000
Fixed assets				
Factory		1,350		1,323
Machinery		1,470		5,289
		2,820		6,612
Current assets				
Stock	90		714	
Debtors	249		1,749	
Bank	36		-	
	375		2,463	
Current liabilities				
Creditors	(108)		(525)	
Bank	-		(33)	
	(108)		(558)	
Working capital		267		1,905
		3,087		8,517
Borrowings		(300)		(4,800)
		2,787		3,717
Share capital		900		900
Profit and loss		1,887		2,817
		2,787		3,717

Required

(a) List and explain four major changes which the new managing director has made to the running of the company and explain whether each has been beneficial. You should support your answer with appropriate ratios. **20 Marks**

(b) Explain why it might be misleading to evaluate the effects of the changes after just one year. **5 Marks**

Total Marks = 25

60   REDUCING OVERDRAFT: LINDA PLC   *45 mins*

The directors of Linda plc are keen to reduce the company's bank overdraft by at least £600,000. They believe that this could be accomplished by better management of the company's trade debtors.

In January 20X7 one of the company's junior managers submitted a suggestion to the board that the company should offer trade debtors a 2% discount if they pay for purchases made during March 20X7 before the end of that month. He estimated that 40% of the company's customers would take advantage of such an offer, thereby reducing the bank overdraft at the balance sheet date and reducing the debtors' turnover in days. The board rejected this suggestion, partly because of the cost of the discount but mainly because it would make the financial accounts misleading and therefore the external auditors might qualify the audit report.

The following information has been extracted from the financial statements for the year ended 31 March 20X7.

Cash sales	£12.0 million
Credit sales	£14.0 million
Trade debtors	£2.2 million
Bank overdraft	£800,000

All sales occur evenly throughout the year.

Required

(a) Calculate the debtors' turnover (in days) from the above figures. **2 Marks**

(b) Calculate a target debtors' turnover (in days) necessary to reduce Linda plc's trade debtors by £600,000. **3 Marks**

(c) Calculate the estimated debtors' balance and overdraft which would have been outstanding if the board had accepted the manager's suggestion. **5 Marks**

(d) Explain why the manager's proposal would have rendered the financial statements misleading *and* explain how the effects of the discount would have had to be accounted for. **5 Marks**

(e) Explain how the directors of Linda plc could avoid a qualified audit report if the managers' proposal were adopted. **5 Marks**

(f) Cashflow statements; state what characteristics of business performance such statements help to assess. **5 Marks**

Total Marks = 25

84

61   K PLC (05/02)   *45 mins*

K plc sells branded consumer products direct to the general public. The company has a policy of comparing its annual report with those of its two main competitors – Pricecut Ltd and Bigstore plc. The directors of K plc try to identify ways in which they might use their competitors' ideas in order to improve their own performance.

The summary financial statements of the three companies are shown below.

PROFIT AND LOSS ACCOUNTS
FOR THE YEAR ENDED 30 APRIL 20X4

	K plc £'000	*Pricecut Ltd* £'000	*Bigstore plc* £'000
Sales	5,000	4,000	11,000
Cost of goods sold	(1,500)	(2,000)	(2,750)
Advertising	(400)	(480)	(880)
Sales staff	(350)	(400)	(880)
Other expenses	(600)	(160)	(1,430)
Net profit	2,150	960	5,060

BALANCE SHEETS AT 30 APRIL 20X4

	K plc £'000	*Pricecut Ltd* £'000	*Bigstore plc* £'000
Tangible fixed assets	5,000	1,300	8,000
Current assets			
Stock	123	99	286
Bank	10	3	17
	133	102	303
Current liabilities			
Creditors	(115)	(82)	(286)
Net current assets	18	20	17
Total assets les current liabilities	5,018	1,320	8,017
Share capital and reserves	5,018	1,320	8,017

Required:

(a)   Identify the main differences between K plc's business practices and those of Pricecut Ltd and Bigstore plc, using ratios as appropriate to support your answer.   **15 Marks**

(b)   Describe the limitations of the annual report as a basis for the comparison of companies in the manner suggested by the directors of K plc.   **5 Marks**

(c)   One of the companies may have made major investments in tangible fixed assets during the year. Identify the main profitability ratios that are likely to be adversely affected by this and explain why each is likely to be distorted.   **5 Marks**

Total Marks = 25

62   J PLC (11/00 amended)   *54 mins*

(a)   J plc operates in the canned foods industry which is currently undergoing dynamic change in consumer tastes as well as production technology. The directors of J plc have been talking about discontinuing various product lines or areas of the business and exploring the possibility of going into others.

Required

(i)   Set out and explain the criteria for classification of discontinued operations for the purposes of FRS 3.   **6 Marks**

(ii)   Describe how users of accounts can benefit from the disclosures on discontinued operations.   **3 Marks**

(b) The expansion plans of the directors of J plc include purchasing another company in their industry. They have narrowed the choice down to two similarly-sized companies, both of which have suitable locations and production facilities. The directors of J plc have decided that their best strategy is to identify the company which has the weaker management team. The directors believe that should make it easier to negotiate a lower price from the existing shareholders.

The summary financial statements of the two companies under consideration are as follows:

	A Ltd	B Ltd
	£'000	£'000
Operating profit	170	140
Interest	(32)	(29)
	138	111
	£'000	£'000
Fixed assets	470	940
Net current assets	20	50
	490	990
Loans	(200)	(223)
	290	767
Share capital	70	65
Revaluation reserve	0	450
Profit and loss account	220	252
	290	767

B Ltd's revaluation reserve arose when it revalued its factory premises five years ago. The depreciation charge has been increased by £14,000 per annum for each of the last five years because of this. The two companies own similar fixed assets which are of a similar age. Most of the difference between the book values is attributable to the fact that B Ltd has revalued while A Ltd has not.

Required

(i)   Calculate, for each of the two companies:

   (1) Return on total capital employed   **2 Marks**
   (2) Return on shareholders' equity   **2 Marks**
   (3) Gearing.   **2 Marks**

   You should use the above figures, without making any adjustments for the effects of B Ltd's revaluation.

(ii) Restate B Ltd's profit figure and balance sheet to make the figures comparable with those of A Ltd, and recalculate the ratios in (i) (1), (2) and (3) using your revised figures.   **6 Marks**

(iii) Explain which of the two companies appears to be the better managed. Your answer should make use of the ratios calculated in (i) and (ii) above and of any other information which can be obtained from the figures given in the summary financial statements for A Ltd and B Ltd.   **5 Marks**

(iv) Explain how the revaluation of B Ltd's fixed assets affected the ratio analysis, and explain why a company might wish to revalue its fixed assets.   **4 Marks**

Total Marks = 30

63   Q LTD I (5/01 amended)   *45 mins*

Q Ltd is a small company which distributes spare parts to the motor trade. The company has been experiencing cash flow problems recently, and the directors have decided to examine the working capital cycle with a view to seeing whether they can release some cash through better working capital management.

The company has a very steady level of sales and purchases throughout the year. Credit sales were £3,600,000 during the year ended 30 April 20X1 and credit purchases were £2,400,000. Trade debtors and creditors at 30 April 20X1 were £630,000 and £200,000 respectively. The company's stock figure has been approximately £480,000 throughout the year.

The directors are of the opinion that careful credit management could reduce debtors turnover to 40 days. The company could reduce stocks by 30% without adversely affecting sales. Trade creditors would be prepared to wait up to 50 days for payment.

Required

(a) (i)   Calculate Q Ltd's working capital cycle in days, using the figures relating to transactions for the year ended 30 April 20X1 and the balances outstanding at that date.

     (ii) Calculate the working capital cycle in days, based on the directors' hypothetical figures.   **7 Marks**

(b) Explain why it is important for companies to monitor their working capital cycles, using the figures calculated in part (a) above to illustrate your explanation.   **5 Marks**

(c) Calculate the amount of cash that would be released if Q Ltd implemented the new stock control and credit management policies suggested by management.   **3 Marks**

(d) Describe the main difficulties that will have to be overcome in order to put the directors' new policies into practice.   **5 Marks**

(e) Suggest any other methods by which the directors might seek to overcome their cash flow problems.   **5 Marks**

Total Marks = 25

64   Q LTD II (11/01 amended)   *45 mins*

Q Ltd is a major public company that operates a number of hotels across the country. It has a policy of expanding by buying established independent hotels and converting these to the Q plc brand. The company has a policy of selecting hotels for acquisition on the basis of gross profit percentage and general profitability. Gross profit percentage is important because a high margin suggests that the hotel is in a location that is popular with business travellers, who tend to pay a higher rate than tourists. General profitability is important because Q plc has discovered that the success of a hotel is often attributable to the quality of its management team. Q plc has a policy of offering the existing managers an attractive salary package to retain their services after the takeover.

Q plc is choosing between two hotels in Aytoun. Both hotels are of a similar size and offer similar facilities. Both operate as independent companies. Both are available for purchase. Their latest annual reports are summarised below.

PROFIT AND LOSS ACCOUNTS

	Hotel A year ended 31 March 20X1		Hotel B year ended 31 August 20X1	
	£'000	£'000	£'000	£'000
Room hire				
Receipts	900		800	
Housekeeping staff costs	(180)		(136)	
Depreciation	(197)		(243)	
Other costs	(45)		(56)	
Room hire gross profit		478		365
Bar and restaurant				
Receipts	400		450	
Food and drink	(80)		(104)	
Kitchen and waiting staff	(60)		(81)	
Depreciation	(47)		(68)	
Other costs	(32)		(40)	
Bar and restaurant gross profit		181		157
Total gross profit		659		522
Management salaries	(162)		(88)	
Other operating costs	(8)		(13)	
		(170)		(101)
Operating profit		489		421
Interest		(10)		(90)
Net profit		479		331
Tax		(144)		(107)
Profit after tax		335		224

BALANCE SHEETS

	Hotel A at 31 March 20X1		Hotel B at 31 August 20X1	
	£'000	£'000	£'000	£'000
Tangible fixed assets				
Premises		2,200		1,800
Furniture and fittings		700		900
Kitchen equipment		100		200
		3,000		2,900
Current assets				
Bar and restaurant stock	3		6	
Debtors	45		40	
Bank	7		5	
	55		51	
Current liabilities	(153)		(113)	
Net current liabilities		(98)		(62)
Bar and restaurant gross profit		2,902		2,838
Long-term loans		(200)		(1,000)
		2,702		1,838
Share capital		1,500		1,000
Profit and loss		1,202		838
		2,702		1,838

Both balance sheets include the current year's tax charge in current liabilities.

Identical accounting policies have been used to prepare both sets of financial statements.

Required

(a) Analyse the profitability and efficiency of both companies and identify the one which appears most profitable. You should support your analysis with appropriate ratios.

12 Marks

(b) Explain the problems associated with identifying the better management team using ratios applied to these financial statements. **8 Marks**

(c) Comment on any figures or ratios that appear unusual either in the context of the hotel industry or in comparing the two hotels. **5 Marks**

Total Marks = 25

65 P PLC (11/02) *45 mins*

Some of P plc's shareholders have complained that the company was less profitable last year than its main competitor Q plc. The profit and loss accounts of P plc and its main competitor Q plc for the year ended 30 September 20X4 and their balance sheets at that date are summarised below.

PROFIT AND LOSS ACCOUNTS
FOR THE YEAR ENDED 30 SEPTEMBER 20X4

	P plc		Q plc	
	£ million	£ million	£ million	£ million
Turnover		1,845		2,978
Cost of sales		(758)		(1,310)
Gross profit		1,087		1,668
Distribution costs	(136)		(273)	
Administration expenses	(61)		(51)	
		(197)		(324)
Operating profit		890		1,344
Interest		(104)		(101)
		786		1,243
Taxation		(69)		(78)
		717		1,165
Dividends		(400)		(600)
		317		565
Balance brought forward		415		833
Balance carried forward		732		1,398
Earnings per share		119 pence		42 pence

BALANCE SHEETS AT 30 SEPTEMBER 20X4

	P plc		Q plc	
	£ million	£ million	£ million	£ million
Fixed assets				
Tangible assets		4,002		4,380
Current assets				
Stock	42		74	
Trade debtors	180		293	
Bank	113		118	
	335		485	
Creditors: amounts due within one year	(292)		(317)	
Net current assets		43		168
		4,045		4,548
Creditors: amounts due after one year				
Loans		(2,022)		(2,200)
		2,023		2,348
Provisions for liabilities and charges				
Deferred tax		(291)		(250)
		1,732		2,098
Share capital				
P plc = £1.00 shares/Q plc = 25p shares)		600		700
Revaluation reserve		400		
Profit and loss		732		1,398
		1,732		2,098

BPP PROFESSIONAL EDUCATION

Required

(a) Compare the profitability of P plc and Q plc for the year ended 30 September 20X4. Identify any specific areas in which P plc should investigate its performance relative to that of Q plc.   **9 Marks**

(b) The managing director has asked for an explanation of the earnings per share ration (EPS). Explain the purpose and limitations of the EPS ratio, using P plc and Q plc as examples.   **6 Marks**

(c) Explain why it might not always be meaningful to compare the performance of two companies using their financial statements.   **5 Marks**

(d) Suggest what additional documents, reports or information might be useful in reviewing the performance of companies.   **5 Marks**

Total Marks = 25

EXTERNAL AUDIT

The objective test questions and questions 65 - 68 cover external audit, the subject of Part E of the BPP Study Text for Paper 6.

OBJECTIVE TEST QUESTIONS

1   Which of these statements about auditors are correct?

    1   The auditors of a large company are likely to place emphasis on checking the operation of the company's systems of internal control.

    2   The prevention and detection of fraud are primarily the responsibility of a company's directors. ✓

    3   Although the auditors' report does not cover the directors' report, they should nevertheless review it to ensure that it does not conflict with the information in the financial statements. ✓

    A   All three statements are correct
    B   1 and 2 only
    C   1 and 3 only
    D   2 and 3 only

2   Which of the following are statutory rights of the auditors of a limited company?

    1   Right of access to the company's records at all times ✓

    2   Right to attend all meetings of directors

    3   Right to attend all general meetings of the company ✓

    4   Right to obtain any information and explanations they think necessary for their audit from the company's officers. ✓

    A   All four are statutory rights

    B   1, 2 and 3 only

    C   1, 3 and 4 only

    D   1, 2 and 4 only

3   Which of the following are covered by the auditor's report?

    1   Cash flow statement
    2   Statement of total recognised gains and losses
    3   Notes to the profit and loss account and balance sheet

    A   All three are covered.
    B   1 and 2 only
    C   2 and 3 only
    D   1 and 3 only

4   A company's auditors find insufficient evidence to substantiate the company's cash sales, which are material in amount.

What form of qualification of the audit report would normally be appropriate in this situation?

A   Qualified opinion – disagreement
B   Qualified opinion – limitation on auditors' work
C   Disclaimer of opinion
D   Qualified opinion – adverse opinion

5   A company's accounting records were largely destroyed by fire shortly after the balance sheet date. As a result the financial statements contain a number of figures based on estimates.

What form of qualification of the audit report would be appropriate in this situation?

A   Qualified opinion – disagreement
B   Qualified opinion – limitations on auditors' work
C   Disclaimer of opinion
D   Qualified opinion – adverse opinion

6   An auditor forms the opinion that a company's trade debtors are overstated by a material amount because of the company's failure to provide for a debt due from a company that has ceased trading.

What form of qualification of the audit report would normally be appropriate in this case?

A   Qualified opinion – disagreement
B   Qualified opinion – limitation on auditors' work
C   Disclaimer of opinion
D   Qualified opinion – adverse opinion

7   Which of the following is *not* implied by an unqualified audit report?

A   The accounts are in agreement with the records and returns.
B   Proper accounting records have been kept by the company.
C   No fraudulent activities have taken place during the period.
D   There is consistency between the accounts and the directors' report.

8   Which of the following matters are covered by the auditors' report?

1   Whether the company has kept proper accounting records

2   Whether the accounts are in agreement with the accounting records.

3   Whether details of directors' remuneration and benefits have been correctly disclosed in the financial statements

4   Whether details of loans to directors have been correctly disclosed in the financial statements.

A   1 and 2 only
B   1, 2 and 3 only
C   3 and 4 only
D   All four matters are covered

> If you struggled with these objective test questions, go back to your BPP Study Text for this paper and revise Chapter 13 before you tackle the written questions on external audit.

66   PREPARATION QUESTION: REPORTING

(a)   Suggest two sets of circumstances in which the auditors may qualify their report owing to inherent uncertainty.

(b)   Suggest four types of circumstances in which the auditors include an emphasis of matter paragraph because of inherent uncertainty.

Approaching the question

1   You should be able to answer this question easily if you have taken in the material in your study text.

2   Be careful in part (a). There are very few realistic circumstances where the auditors cannot find audit evidence to support the financial statements.

3   It is useful to have to hand examples of each type of qualification, to introduce in general answers on qualifications of audit reports.

67   MOWBRAY COMPUTERS   *45 mins*

You are carrying out the audit of Mowbray Computers Ltd for the year ended 30 April 20X4. The company assembles microcomputers from components purchased from the Far East and sells them to retailers, and to individuals and businesses by mail order. In the current year, there has been a recession and strong competition which has resulted in a fall in sales and the gross profit margin. This had led to a trading loss and the company experiencing going concern problems.

Required

(a)   Describe the factors which indicate that a company may not be a going concern. Your list should include all factors, and not just those which apply to Mowbray Computers Ltd.   **17 Marks**

(b)   Consider the form of audit report (ie qualified or unqualified) you would use on Mowbray Computers Ltd's financial statements, if you conclude that the company is experiencing serious going concern problems, in the following two situations:

   (i)   You conclude that the financial statements give sufficient disclosure of the going concern problems.

   (ii)   There is no disclosure of the going concern problems in the financial statements and you believe there is a serious risk that the company will fail in the foreseeable future.   **8 Marks**

In each case you should say how the audit report will differ from an unqualified audit report (ie example 1 of SAS 600 *Auditors' reports on financial statements*).

Total Marks = 25

68   AUDIT REPORTS   *45 mins*

Auditing Standard 600 *Auditor's reports on financial statements*, issued in May 1993, introduced the extended audit report and changes in the form of qualified reports.

Your firm is the auditor of the following two companies, and you have been asked to consider the form of qualified or unqualified audit report which should be given.

(a)   Gamston Burgers plc has a loss-making branch and it has included fixed assets relating to this branch at £710,000 after deducting a provision for impairment in value of £250,000. The directors believe that if operating changes are made and economic conditions improve, there is a reasonable probability of the branch trading satisfactorily, which will result in the current value of tangible fixed assets exceeding £710,000. However, under the current circumstances, the directors consider the extent of any impairment in value to be uncertain. You have obtained all the evidence you would have reasonably expected to be available.

If trading conditions do not improve, your audit investigations have concluded that the branch will have to close. If the branch closes, the tangible fixed assets will be worthless, as the property is leased and the cost of moving any tangible fixed assets will be more than their net realisable value. If the tangible fixed assets are worthless, you have concluded that the effect will be material, but it will not result in the financial statements being misleading.

(b) Keyworth Supermarket Limited sells good to the general public and customers pay in cash or by cheque. Your audit tests reveal that controls over cash takings and custody of the stock are weak, and you have not been able to obtain sufficient evidence to quantify the effect of any misappropriation of stock or cash takings. You have concluded that:

   (i)   If the uncertainty relates to all the company's sales, it could result in the financial statements being misleading

   (ii) And if the uncertainty relates to only the sale of fresh fruit and vegetables, which comprise 10% of the company's sales, it will have a material effect on the financial statements but it will not result in them being misleading.

Required

(a) Describe the duties of an auditor.   **5 Marks**

(b) List and briefly describe the contents of an unqualified audit report.   **8 Marks**

(c) Consider and describe the form of an unqualified or qualified audit report you would give in each of the following situations:

   (i)   On Gamston Burgers plc's financial statements if you agree with the directors' statements about the uncertainty relating to the value of the tangible fixed assets of the branch.

   (ii) On Gamston Burgers plc's financial statements if you have come to the conclusion that trading conditions will not improve and the company will close the branch. Thus, the tangible fixed assets will be worthless

   (iii) On Keyworth Supermarket Ltd's financial statements if the uncertainty about the misappropriation of stock and cash takings relates to *all* the company's sales

   (iv) On Keyworth Supermarket Ltd's financial statements if the uncertainty about the misappropriation of stock and cash takings relates only to the sale of fresh fruit and vegetables which comprise 10% of the company's sales.   **12 Marks**

Total Marks = 25

69   AUDIT REPORTING   *45 mins*

(a) State four types of situation where auditors are required by the Companies Act to report by exception.   **3 Marks**

(b) In November 20X3, the head office of Theta Ltd was damaged by a fire. Many of the company's accounting records were destroyed before the audit for the year ended 31 January 20X4 took place. The company's financial accountant has prepared financial statements for the year ended 31 January 20X4 on the basis of estimates and the information he has been able to salvage. You have completed the audit of these financial statements.

Required

(i)   Explain what would be contained in the 'basis of opinion' and 'opinion' paragraphs of the auditors' report which you would issue on the financial statements of Theta Ltd for the year ended 31 January 20X4.   **6 Marks**

(ii)   Explain the reasons for your audit opinion.   **4 Marks**

(iii) Explain and distinguish between the following forms of qualified audit opinion:

   (1) Disagreement
   (2) Disclaimer
   (3) Adverse opinion   **7 Marks**

(c) Describe the legal rights of an external auditor.   **5 Marks**

Total Marks = 25

Answers

REGULATION

OBJECTIVE TEST ANSWERS: REGULATION

1   B

2   B

3   B

4   B

5   D   1   There is no legal requirement to produce a chairman's report

        3   A company has seven months from its balance sheet date to lodge its accounts with the Registrar.

6   C

1   PREPARATION QUESTION: ACCOUNTING POLICIES AND ESTIMATION TECHNIQUES

(a)   **Accounting policies** are defined by FRS 18 as those principles, bases, conventions, rules and practices applied by an entity that specify how the effects of transactions and other events are to be reflected in its financial statements through recognising, selecting measurement bases for, and presenting assets, liabilities, gains, losses and changes to shareholders' funds. Accounting policies by definition do not include estimation techniques.

Accounting policies define the **process** whereby transactions and other events are reflected in financial statements. For example, an accounting policy for a particular type of expenditure may specify whether an asset or a loss is to be recognised; the basis on which it is to be measured; and where in the profit and loss account or balance sheet it is to be presented.

Estimation techniques are the methods adopted by an entity to arrive at estimated monetary amounts, corresponding to the **measurement bases** selected, for assets, liabilities, gains, losses and changes to shareholders' funds.

Estimation techniques implement the measurement aspects of accounting policies. An accounting policy will specify the basis on which an item is to be measured; where there is uncertainty over the monetary amount corresponding to that basis, the amount will be arrived at by using an estimation technique.

The **distinction is important** because changes in accounting policy are accounted for as **prior period adjustments,** whereas the effects of changes in estimation techniques are taken through the current year profit and loss account.

Tutor's hint. The situations in (b) are taken directly from FRS 18, which has a short checklist to determine whether the change is due to an accounting policy or just an estimation technique. To summarise the results of this for each part of (b):

Does this involve a change to:	(i) (1)	(i) (2)	(ii)	(iii)	(iv)	(v)
Recognition?	×	×	×	×	✓	×
Presentation?	×	✓	✓	×	✓	×
Measurement basis?	×	×	×	×	×	×

(b)   **Accounting policy or estimation technique**

   (i)   **Depreciation**

        (1)   Vehicles are being recognised and presented in the same way as before, and using the same, historical cost measurement basis. The only change is to the

estimation technique used to measure the unexpired portion of each vehicle's economic benefits. This is **not a change of accounting policy**. (Note that this point is also made in FRS 15 *Tangible fixed assets*.)

(2) This accounting change involves both a change to presentation and a change of estimation technique, as in (i) (1) above. As the method of presentation has changed, the former is a change of accounting policy but the latter is not. The two changes must therefore be **accounted for separately**. No change is made to the amount of depreciation charged in earlier periods, but the profit and loss account for the preceding period is restated to move the depreciation charge from cost of sales to administrative expenses.

(ii) **Overheads**

Although there is no change to the recognition and measurement of costs, they are being presented differently. This is therefore a **change of accounting policy**.

(iii) **Indirect overheads in stock valuation**

Directly attributable costs, once estimated, must be treated as part of an asset as they continue to be and always have been. Accordingly there is no change to recognition. In addition, both stocks and overheads continue to be presented in the same way and measured on the same basis (stocks are measured at the amount of directly attributable historical costs). This is a **change of estimation technique**.

(iv) **Finance costs**

The transaction whose effects are being reflected is the incurring of directly attributable finance costs. That transaction is still being measured in the same way, but there is a change to recognition, in that it is now being recognised as (part of) an asset rather than as an expense. (FRS 18 states that where accounting standards allow a choice over what is to be recognised, that choice is a matter of accounting policy.) There is also, consequently, a change to the presentation of the transaction in the balance sheet and the profit and loss account. This is a **change of accounting policy**.

(v) **Provisions**

FRS 12 requires entities to report provisions at the best estimate of the expenditure required to settle the present obligation at the balance sheet date. Where that estimate is based on future cash flows, it is permissible to use undiscounted amounts only where the effect of the time value of money is not material. In such circumstances, the use of undiscounted future cash flows is, in effect, an estimation technique for arriving at the present value. Therefore this is **not a change in accounting policy**.

2   **PREPARATION QUESTION: SELECTING ACCOUNTING POLICIES**

The appropriateness of a company's accounting policies should be judged against the objectives of relevance, reliability, comparability and understandability. These objectives are discussed individually below, but in practice should be considered together within the context of a company's particular circumstances.

(a) **Relevance**

(i) The overall objectives of a company's financial statements are to:

- Provide **information** about its **financial performance** and **financial position**

- Be useful for **assessing** the **stewardship** of management

- Be useful for making **economic decisions**.

(ii) The criteria for **assessing the relevance** of financial information include:

- The **ability to influence the economic decisions** of users
- **Timeliness** to influence those decisions
- **Predictive or confirmatory value** or both.

(iii) In identifying the most appropriate accounting policy, an entity will consider which measurement basis is most relevant and how to present information in the most relevant way.

(b) **Reliability**

Financial information is reliable if the following apply:

(i) Can be depended upon by users to **represent faithfully** what it purports to represent and therefore **reflects the substance of the transactions** and other events that have taken place

(ii) Is **free from deliberate or systematic bias** (ie it is **neutral**)

(iii) Is **complete** within the **bounds of materiality**

(iv) Under **conditions of uncertainty**, it has been **prudently prepared** (ie a degree of caution has been applied in exercising judgement and making the necessary estimates).

Prudence and uncertainty

(i) In practice, there may be circumstances where there is **uncertainty**, either about the existence of assets, liabilities, gains, losses and changes to shareholders' funds, or about the amount at which they should be measured. **Prudence** requires that accounting polices take account of such uncertainty in **recognising and measuring** those assets, liabilities, gains, losses and changes to shareholders' funds.

(ii) FRS 18 specifies that in conditions of **uncertainty**, more **confirmatory evidence** should be obtained about the **existence** of an asset or gain than about the existence of a liability or loss, and a **greater reliability** needed in the **measurement** of assets and gains than for liabilities and losses.

(iii) **However, it is not necessary to exercise prudence where there is no uncertainty. Nor is it appropriate to use prudence as a reason for, for example, creating excessive provisions, deliberately understating assets or gains, or deliberately overstating liabilities or losses, because that would mean that the financial statements are not neutral and therefore not reliable.**

(iv) The above definition of prudence is subtly different from the definition of prudence under the now defunct SSAP 2 which focused on ensuring that revenues and profits are recognised only when realised and losses and liabilities are recognised as soon as these are foreseen. FRS 18 does not refer to matching. Under the old SSAP 2 regime, if there was a conflict between accruals and prudence, prudence took precedence.

(v)   Under FRS 18, conflict may arise between two aspects of reliability, namely neutrality and prudence. **Neutrality involves freedom from deliberate or systematic bias.** On the other hand, **prudence is a potentially biased concept that seeks to ensure that, under conditions of uncertainty, gains and assets are not overstated and losses and liabilities are not understated.**

(vi) In the selection of accounting policies, the competing demands of neutrality and prudence are reconciled by finding a balance that ensures that the **deliberate and systematic understatement of assets and gains and overstatement of liabilities and losses do not occur.**

(c) **Comparability**

Information in a company's financial statements gains greatly in usefulness if it can be **compared** with **similar information** about the company for some other period or point in time, and with similar information about other entities.

Comparability can usually be achieved through a combination of **consistency** and **disclosure**.

(d) **Understandability**

Information provided by financial statements needs to be capable of being understood by users having a reasonable knowledge of business and economic activities and accounting and a willingness to study with reasonable diligence the information provided. Appropriate accounting policies will result in financial information being presented in a way that enables its significance to be perceived by such users.

Balancing the different objectives

There can be tensions between relevance, reliability, comparability and understandability. In particular, sometimes the accounting policy that is most relevant to a particular entity's circumstances is not the most reliable, and vice versa.

Where there is conflict between the various objectives, the most appropriate accounting policy will usually be that which is the **most relevant of those that are reliable.**

3   COMPANIES ACT 1985 REQUIREMENTS

> **Pass marks.** This was a discussion of the Companies Act requirements. Any two notes required by the Companies Act could be discussed in part (b). The CIMA suggested answer looks at guarantees and financial commitments, and the analysis of directors' remuneration.
>
> This question tests your ability to describe the problems faced by the readers of financial statements. This is an important issue because there would be very little point in publishing statements if they could not be understood. Furthermore, the ability to put oneself in the position of a reader will make it easier to prepare useful financial statements.
>
> Remember it is impossible to give a great deal of credit for an answer which made no real attempt to address the question. This question was on the Companies Act, not accounting standards.
>
> Use headings which show that you are addressing the question and help the marker to give you marks.

(a) **Helpfulness of prescribed formats**

(i)   There are many **different types of readers** of financial statements, for example shareholders, creditors, lenders who are likely to have different requirements from the financial statements.

(ii) By prescribing the format for these statements, the Companies Act 1985 ensures that the **information** given by different companies will be **relevant, reliable and comparable**. Anyone who is prepared to develop a knowledge of the basic formats should be able to **understand** the financial statements and to **compare** different companies' results.

(iii) The prescribed formats also help to ensure that accounts are **consistent from one year to the next**. Results can be compared over a period of time, not just for one company but also **with other companies**.

If there were **no set format**, companies could prepare their accounts in whatever manner they wished. This would render comparisons, such as **performance ratios, difficult if not meaningless**.

(b) **Notes to the financial statements**

Two notes required by the Companies Act 1985 are an analysis of debtors and details of related party transactions.

Analysis of debtors

(i) This is between trade debtors, other debtors and prepayments. Readers can use the trade debtors figures to analyse the number of debtor days outstanding at the year end. This can indicate whether the company is having difficulties in collecting its debts.

(iii) The Companies Act also requires further disclosure of any debtor due over one year after the balance sheet date. This is very important in determining the company's liquidity ratio. If a large amount of debtors is not due for more than one year, the company may have difficulty in meeting payments to its creditors.

Related party transactions

(i) The disclosure of related party transactions required by the Companies Act is between the company and its directors (or persons connected to the directors).

(ii) These transactions include loans and credit transactions. This is particularly important to readers of the accounts, as it can reveal forms of otherwise hidden remuneration. A director could have a large loan from the company at a low rate of interest. Not only would the director be receiving an additional form of remuneration, via the low interest rate, but the company would not be receiving a good return on its asset.

(iii) These transactions could have an impact on various performance ratios, such as return on capital. This is because the interest received in the profit and loss account will be lower than a commercial rate. In addition, if the loan is for a long period of time, this would tie up assets that could otherwise be used for business purposes.

(c) **Materiality**

Materiality refers to the **significance** or **importance** of a particular item or matter in the context of financial statements as a whole.

An item or matter is material if its **omission** or **misstatement** would significantly **influence** the **decision** of a **reasonable user** of the financial statements.

Materiality may be considered in the context of any individual primary statement within the financial statements or any individual item included in them.

Some accountants may use '**materiality guidelines**' (ie pre-set limits), but ultimately decisions about materiality involve **professional judgement**.

Materiality refers not only to monetary amounts, but also to the way accounting information is presented in financial statements, eg the profit figure may be fairly stated, but certain assets and liabilities which should be disclosed separately have been misstated by being netted off against each other, ie **materiality is both quantitative and qualitative**.

Certain items such as directors' remuneration are subject to specific disclosure requirements **irrespective of materiality**.

In practice, a **combined evaluation** of the impact of **individual errors** must be performed. A number of individually immaterial errors may in **aggregate** have a **material impact on the company's accounts**.

(d) **True and fair view**

There is no statutory or other regulatory definition of a true and fair view however its rather complex meaning has been developed over time. It is possible to consider truth and fairness individually but the final meaning of the phrase requires consideration of the term in its **entirety**.

Truth

If financial statements are said to show a **true view** then the figures shown should be **reliable, relevant** and as **accurate** as possible given the estimates that have to be made in their preparation.

Fairness

Fairness, in terms of financial statements, can be thought of in two ways. On one hand the presentation in the financial statements is **plain, distinct** and **understandable**. On the other the financial statements are **free from any bias**, impartial, just and equitable.

True and fair

Taken together the meaning of true and fair has grown to mean that financial statements are prepared **in accordance with generally accepted accounting principles.** This means that they accord with the requirements of the Companies Act and accounting standards. The financial statements should also be prepared on a **consistent basis** and should be **understandable** and **not misleading**.

4   ACCOUNTING STANDARDS

> **Pass marks**. This question represented easy marks - you should be well aware of the UK standard-setting process, as well as the way the true and fair concept can be used to override accounting standards.
>
> Remember that it is pointless including irrelevant material - better to spend the time on a question you can answer in full.
>
> Identify headings and subheadings that help you plan your response and show the marker that you have addressed the question properly.

(a) **Standard setting process**

(i)   **Topic/issue selection**

Topics that become the subject of FRSs are identified by the ASB from its own research or from external sources, including submissions from interested parties.

When a topic is identified, the technical staff of the ASB (headed by a full-time technical director) undertake a programme of research and consultation. This involves consideration of and consultation on:

- the relevant conceptual issues,

- existing pronouncements and practice in the UK, overseas and internationally and

- the economic, legal and practical implications

of the introduction of particular accounting requirements.

(ii) **Procedure to an FRS**

When the issues have been identified and debated by the Board, a discussion draft is normally produced and circulated to parties who have registered their interest. The purpose of this document is to form a **basis for discussion** with parties particularly affected by, or having knowledge of, the issues raised in the proposals.

An exposure draft of an accounting standard (a Financial Reporting Exposure Draft or FRED) **is then published** to allow an opportunity for all interested parties to comment on the proposals and for the Board to gauge the appropriateness and level of acceptance of those proposals.

(iii) **Influence of preparers**

It is at this point that **the process could be influenced by the preparers of financial statements in general.** However, it should also be remembered that the Board itself consists of members from a wide constituency of preparers and users of accounts. It is therefore much harder than it used to be for preparers of accounts, or even groups of them, to influence the outcome of a decision on a standard.

(iv) **Board approval**

The exposure draft is refined in the light of feedback resulting from the period of public exposure. A majority of two thirds of the Board is required to approve the new standard. Such standards are issued on the Board's own authority and are subject to legal backing.

(b) **True and fair view – procedures for directors and auditors**

In those exceptional (ie *very* rare) circumstances where a company's directors and auditors consider that the application of the requirements of an accounting standard would give a misleading impression, the requirements of the standard should be departed from to the extent necessary to give a true and fair view. In such cases informed and unbiased judgement should be used to devise an appropriate alternative treatment, which should be consistent with the economic and commercial characteristics of the circumstances concerned.

Particulars of any material departure from an accounting standard, the reasons for the departure and its financial effects should be disclosed in the financial statements. The disclosure made should be equivalent to that given in respect of departures from specific accounting provisions of companies legislation.

Review Panel

It should be noted here that the **Financial Reporting Review Panel has the power to insist** (through the courts if necessary) **on the revision of 'defective' accounts where it feels that departure from an accounting standard was not justified.** The directors would be forced to pay costs in such circumstances, and the auditors could also be disciplined for failure to qualify the audit report for non-compliance with the standard.

(c) **The difficulty of presenting a true and fair view**

The **over-riding principle** of the Companies Act is that the financial statements of limited companies must show a true and fair view. However, the term 'true and fair' is **not legally defined** in legislation or accounting standards and is therefore **open to interpretation**. Because acceptable accounting practice evolves over time, **the meaning of 'true and fair' changes over time**. The Companies Act requires directors to present 'a true and fair view', rather than '*the* true and fair view'.

In practice, financial statements that **comply with the requirements of the Companies Acts and of accounting standards** normally give a true and fair view. However, there are still many occasions on which **judgement** is required. For example, to account for a tangible fixed asset, preparers of financial statements must estimate its useful economic life and select an appropriate method of depreciation. Where there is a choice of acceptable accounting policies, directors are expected to **select the most appropriate** one for the company's circumstances, having regard to the objectives of relevance, reliability, comparability and understandability. In selecting accounting policies, they may have to **strike a balance** between these objectives where they conflict.

In addition, there are still areas, such as revenue recognition, which are **not covered by any accounting standard.**

Financial statements are used by many different groups of people, each with their own perspectives and requirements. It is possible that the meaning of 'true and fair' may depend upon the expectations of the user.

(d) **Two financial reporting standards**

FRS 5, *Reporting the substance of transactions*, was issued with the objective of ensuring that entities reported the **commercial substance** of their transactions and that the commercial effect of the transactions, and any resulting assets, liabilities, gains or losses should be faithfully represented in the financial statements. The aim of the standard is to ensure that all true assets and liabilities of the entity are shown on the balance sheet according to their commercial substance rather than their strict legal form. In some cases this may mean that assets and liabilities which at one time were excluded from the balance sheet must now be shown on the balance sheet.

FRS 12, *Provisions, contingent liabilities and contingent assets*, states that **a provision is a liability of uncertain timing or amount.** According to FRS 12 a provision should only be recognised when an entity has a legal or constructive **obligation** as a result of **a past event**, it is probable that a **transfer of economic benefits** will be required to settle the obligation and a **reliable estimate** can be made of the amount of the obligation. Unless these conditions are met, no provision should be recognised. This has meant that companies cannot manipulate their profits, as has happened in the past, by setting up a provision in a year of high profits to be released to the profit and loss account at a later date when profits are lower.

Tutorial note. Other areas that could have been discussed include impairment under FRS 11 or full provision for deferred tax under FRS 19.

FINANCIAL STATEMENTS

OBJECTIVE TEST ANSWERS: FINANCIAL STATEMENTS

1   B

2   A   1   Public companies must lodge their accounts with the Registrar within seven months of the end of their accounting reference period

      2   Private companies are required to lodge their accounts with the Registrar

      3   Accounts must be kept at the registered office but they are normally only open to inspection by officers of the company.

3   D

4   A   1   The statement of total recognised gains and losses shows all gains and losses for the year - the realised gains and losses from the profit and loss account and any unrealised gains and losses such as revaluation surpluses/deficits.

5   C

6   A

7   D

8   C

9   C

10   D

11   B

12   B

13   A   Profit after preference dividend (£532,000 – £48,000) = £484,000

$$\text{EPS} = \frac{£484,000}{1,000,000} = 48.4 \text{ pence}$$

14   D   A   £1,158,000/12m = 9.65

         B $(^3/_{12} \times 10m) + (^9/_{12} \times 12m)$ =   11,500,000
             £1,158,000/11,500,000   =   10.07p

         C $(^3/_{12} \times 10m \times 120/124) + (^9/_{12} \times 12m)$ =   11,419,354
             £1,158,000/11,419,354   =   10.14p

         D   Ex rights price

	£
10m × £1.24	12.4
2m × £1.00	2.0
12m	14.4

             14.4/12   =   £1.20

             $(^3/_{12} \times 10m \times 124/120) + (^9/_{12} \times 12m) = 11,583,333$

             EPS = £1,158,000/11,583,333 = 10.00p

15   B

16   C   A   £500,000 +(£80,000 – 30%)/2,000,000
         B   (£500,000 + £80,000)/2,500,000
         C   (£500,000 + [£80,000 – 30%])/2,500,000
         D   £500,000/2,500,000

17   The correct answer is C.

Theoretical ex-rights price

	£
4 shares @ £2.20	8.80
1 share @ £1.80	1.80
5 shares @ £2.12	10.60

Current year EPS - number of shares

800,000 × 3/12 × 2.20/2.12	207,547
1,000,000 × 9/12	750,000
	957,547

$$\text{EPS 28 February 20X2} = \frac{£8,800,000}{957,547}$$

$$= 9.2 \text{ pence}$$

$$\text{EPS 28 February 20X1} = 9.8 \times 2.12/2.20$$

$$= 9.4 \text{ pence}$$

18   A

19   D

20   C

21   D

22   B   A   £1,660,000 – £1,470,000
B   £1,660,000 + £840,000 + £360,000 – £1,470,000
C   £1,660,000 + £760,000 + £300,000 – £1,470,000
D   –

23   A

FIXED ASSETS – COST

	£m		£m
Opening balance	40	Transfer disposal	6
Cash	16		
		Closing balance	50
	56		56

FIXED ASSETS ACCUMULATED DEPRECIATION

	£m		£m
		Opening balance	10
Transfer disposal	2		
		Profit and loss account	6
Closing balance	14		
	16		16

FIXED ASSETS – DISPOSAL

	£m		£m
Transfer cost	6	Transfer depreciation	2
		Loss on sale	1
		Proceeds of sale (balancing figure)	3
	6		6

A   As above
B   As above but with loss £1m on wrong side of disposal account
C   As above but with loss on sale omitted (written down value 6-2 taken)

24   B

25   A

5   PREPARATION QUESTION: PUBLISHED ACCOUNTS

(a)   Directors' report

The directors' report must contain a statement of the principal activities of the company, for example:

> 'The principal activities of the company are the production and marketing of crystal glassware, and the manufacture and installation of kitchen and bedroom furniture.'

(b)   Segmental information

A note to the accounts must disclose segmental information, being the split of turnover and profit before taxation between classes of business, and the split of turnover between geographical markets.

One possible lay-out would be as follows.

	Turnover 20X5 £m	Turnover 20X4 £m	Profit before taxation 20X5 £m	Profit before taxation 20X4 £m
Class of business				
Crystal glassware	16.80	X	0.72	X
Kitchen and bedroom furniture	11.20	X	0.88	X
	28.00	X	1.60	X
Geographical market				
United Kingdom	16.24	X		
Overseas	11.76	X		
	28.00	X		

(c)   Turnover

'**Turnover**' is preceded by an Arabic number on each of the statutory profit and loss account formats, so the figure **may either be disclosed on the face of the profit and loss account itself, or in a note to the accounts**.

(d)   Profits before interest and taxation

There is no requirement to disclose profits before interest and taxation. Instead the requirement is to disclose profit on ordinary activities before taxation (after interest) on the face of the profit and loss account.

(e)   Directors details

The directors' report must **disclose the names of persons who were directors at any time in the period under review, and also the interests in shares or debentures** of group companies at the beginning of the period (or date of appointment if later) and the end of the period must be given for each person who is a director at the end of the period. (This information may instead be given in the notes to the accounts.)

	Ordinary shares held in XYZ Ltd	
Director	*31 March 20X5*	*31 March 20X4*
A	30,720	28,920
B	21,200	21,200
C	-	-
D	800	800
E	750	750
F	4,200	1,900

(f) **Directors' emoluments**

The following **information** must be **given by note** in respect of directors' emoluments:

(i) Aggregate emoluments
(ii) Gains made on exercise of share options
(iii) Amounts receivable under long term incentive schemes
(iv) Company pension contributions
(v) Compensation for loss of office
(vi) Sums paid to third parties for directors' services

Where the aggregate amount (i) to (iii) above is greater than £200,000 the following information must be given about the emoluments of the highest paid director:

(i) Aggregate emoluments (including gains made on exercise of share options and amounts receivable under long term incentive schemes):

(ii) Company pension contributions;

(iii) Accrued pensions.

For XYZ plc

	£
Directors' emoluments	
Aggregate emoluments	142,200
Pension contributions	37,600
	179,800

6 PREPARATION QUESTION: DISCONTINUED OPERATIONS

(a) PINGUO LIMITED
STATEMENT OF TOTAL RECOGNISED GAINS AND LOSSES
FOR THE YEAR ENDED 31 DECEMBER 20X4

	£'000
Profit for the financial year	2,290
Unrealised surplus on revaluation of properties	1,000
Total gains and losses recognised since last annual report	3,290

(b) (i) An acquisition is an operation of the reporting entity that is **acquired during the period.**

A discontinued operation is one which meets **four conditions.**

(1) The **sale** or **termination** must be **completed** before the earlier of **three months** after the year end or the **date** the **financial statements are approved.**

(2) The **former activity** must have **ceased permanently**.

(3) The sale or termination has a **material effect** on the **nature** and **focus** of the entity's **operations** and represents a **material reduction** in its **operating facilities**.

(4) The assets, liabilities, results of operations and activities are **clearly distinguishable**.

(ii) The distinction between acquisitions, continuing operations and discontinued operations enables the user of accounts to make a **better judgement** of the **company's performance**, both **past and future**.

For example, if a company did not appear to be very profitable, but the profit and loss account thus analysed showed that a poor performing division had been

110

closed during the year, a user might be able to **predict** more favourable results for the **future**.

Equally, if good performance is due to an acquisition, this needs to be shown separately, rather than merged with the rest of the company's results.

Furthermore an acquisition must be ignored when comparing this year's results with those of previous years, so that **like is compared with like.**

7   U PLC

> **Pass marks**. The various parts of this question cover well-established accounting practice. Try to explain the accounting treatment succinctly, and refer directly to the relevant accounting standard.

(a) **Plant and machinery**

FRS 15 states that:

(i)   tangible fixed assets **should be depreciated over their useful economic lives;** and

(ii)   **subsequent expenditure** (for example, to maintain the asset in working order) **does not remove the need to charge depreciation.**

All fixed assets except land have **finite useful economic lives**. On very rare occasions, certain assets (such as heritage properties) are maintained to a high standard and their economic lives may be extended so that any depreciation charge is immaterial. This clearly does not apply here.

However, the overhaul has probably **extended the useful economic life** of the plant and machinery and:

(i)   the expenditure should be **capitalised** as part of the cost of the plant; and

(ii)   the useful economic life of the plant should be reviewed and the carrying amount should be **depreciated over its revised remaining economic life.**

(b) **Bad debt from previous year**

(i)   **FRS 3 defines prior period adjustments as material adjustments applying to prior periods arising from changes in accounting policies or from the correction of fundamental errors.**

(ii)   The bad debt does not meet this definition and so cannot be treated as a prior period adjustment. It is merely a current year charge arising from the correction of an accounting estimate (in this case the bad debt provision) made in the previous year.

(c) **Training costs**

(i)   **Training costs are not specifically dealt with in any accounting standard. However, SSAP 13**, which **deals with research and development**, allows development costs to be carried forward only where future benefits will arise and where they relate to a clearly defined project.

(ii)   In this case there is **no specific benefit** against which the training costs can be linked, just an expectation that it will lead to enhanced performance. Given this **uncertainty**, it would **not** be **prudent** to **carry forward** these costs and they should be **written off** as incurred.

(d) **Government grant**

SSAP 4 requires that where grants are **made as a contribution towards specific expenditure on fixed assets,** the grant should be treated as deferred income which is credited to the profit and loss account by instalments over the expected useful economic life of the related asset on a basis that is consistent with the depreciation policy.

(e) **Revaluation**

FRS 15 allows the **revaluation** of tangible fixed assets but states that this must apply to **all assets in that class of fixed asset.** Therefore the directors cannot revalue the head office building and not the factory building. Either both should remain at historic cost in the balance sheet or both buildings should be revalued.

(f) **Goodwill**

(i) FRS 10 does not allow purchased goodwill to be carried forward indefinitely.

(ii) FRS 10 specifies purchased goodwill should be treated as an intangible asset and written off over its useful economic life. There is a rebuttable presumption that this will not exceed 20 years.

8 **P LTD**

> **Pass marks**. This is a very common examination area. Candidates who are methodical and give well-laid out solutions should do well.
>
> It is not time-efficient to produce 'blank' notes where no information is provided in the question.

P LIMITED
PROFIT AND LOSS ACCOUNT FOR THE YEAR ENDED 31 MARCH 20X4

	Notes	£'000	£'000
Sales			5,000
Cost of sales			1,350
Gross profit			3,650
Distribution costs		370	
Administrative expenses (490 + 200)		690	
			1,060
Operating profit	1		2,590
Income from investments		210	
Interest payable (170 + 30)	2	(200)	
			10
Profit on ordinary activities before taxation			2,600
Taxation	3		551
Profit for the financial year			2,049
Dividends	4		440
Profit retained for the financial year			1,609

P LIMITED
BALANCE SHEET AS AT 31 MARCH 20X4

	Notes	£'000	£'000
Fixed assets			
Tangible			5,450
Current assets			
Investments		2,700	
Stock		114	
Debtors		418	
Cash		12	
		3,244	
Creditors: amounts due within one year	5	1,166	
Net current assets			2,078
Total assets less current liabilities			7,528
Creditors: amounts due after more than one year	6		1,200
Provision for liabilities and charges	7		56
			6,272
Capital and reserves			
Share capital	8		1,700
Share premium	9		840
Revaluation reserve	9		1,200
Profit and loss	9		2,532
			6,272

NOTES TO THE ACCOUNTS

1   *Operating profit*

	£'000
Operating profit is stated after charging:	
Depreciation	850
Audit fee	200

2   *Interest payable and similar charges*

	£'000
Loans not wholly repayable within five years	200

3   *Tax on profit on ordinary activities*

	£'000
Based on profit for the year	
Corporation tax	470
Corporation tax under-provided in previous years	25
Deferred tax	56
	551

4   *Dividends*

		£'000
Ordinary:	interim paid	170
	final proposed	270
		440

5   *Creditors: amounts due within one year*

	£'000
Trade creditors	136
Current corporation tax	470
Proposed final dividend	270
Due on the allotment of shares	60
Accruals (200 + 30)	230
	1,166

6   *Creditors: amounts due after more than one year*

	£'000
Loans not wholly repayable within five years	
Loan at X% per annum wholly repayable in 20Y2	1,200

7   *Provision for liabilities and charges*
      Deferred tax   £'000
      At 1 April 20X3   -
      Provided in the year   56
      At 31 March 20X4   56

8   *Share capital*   *Authorised*   *Allotted, called up and*
                                                                  fully paid
      Ordinary shares of £1 each   X   1,700,000

On 28 March 20X4 200,000 ordinary shares were issued at £1.20. The offer was over-subscribed and applicants received four fully-paid shares for every five applied for. Surplus allotment monies received of £60,000 are included in creditors.

9   *Reserves*   *Share premium*   *Profit and loss*
                                  accounts   *Revaluation*   *account*
                                   £'000   £'000   £'000
      At 1 April 20X4   800   -   923
      Arising on the issue of shares 40
      Revaluation in the year   1,200
      Retained profit for the year   1,609
                                   840   1,200   2,532

> *Tutorial note.* Normally the profit and loss account, balance sheet and notes would show comparative figures.

Working

1   *Excess allotment monies*
                                                                         £'000
      Allotment monies received   300
      Shares issued at 20p premium (200,000 × £1.20)   (240)
      Excess monies   60

9   CONFECTIONERY ETC

> **Pass marks.** The examiner commented that the key to this question is familiarity with the format of the statements. Working through the CA presentation requirements in a methodical manner produces a clear set of financial statements and workings. This is a very predictable question, of a type that appears in most diets. It is possible to improve both speed and accuracy in this type of question through practice and more practice.
>
> Sometimes you will be asked for notes to the financial statements whereas at other times you need not produce notes. Please make sure you read the question requirements very carefully.

J PLC
PROFIT AND LOSS ACCOUNT
FOR THE YEAR ENDING 31 MARCH 20X4

	Continuing operations £ million	Discontinued operations £ million	Total £ million
Turnover (W1)	400	250	650
Cost of sales (W2)	(100)	(140)	(240)
Gross profit	300	110	410
Distribution costs (W3)	(36)	(9)	(45)
Administrative expenses (W4)	(48)	(12)	(60)
Operating profit	216	89	305
Reorganisation costs	(10)		(10)
Loss on sale of property (W5)		(11)	(11)
Costs of closure (W5)		(9)	(9)
Profit before interest	206	69	275
Interest payable (W6)			(33)
Profit before tax			242
Taxation (W7)			(53)
Profit for the year			189
Balance brought forward			29
Balance carried forward			218
Earnings per share (W8)			50.1 pence

J PLC
BALANCE SHEET AS AT 31 MARCH 20X4

	£ million	£ million
Fixed assets		
Tangible assets (W9)		1,274
Current assets		
Stock	30	
Debtors	54	
Bank	9	
	93	
Creditors: amounts falling due within one year		
Creditors	16	
Taxation	42	
Finance leases (W10)	10	
	68	
Net current assets		25
		1,299
Creditors: amounts falling due after more than one year		
Loans	300	
Finance leases (W10)	30	
		(330)
Provisions for liabilities and charges		
Deferred tax (W11)		(16)
		953
Capital and reserves		
Share capital (W12)		400
Share premium (W12)		200
Revaluation reserve (W13)		135
Profit and loss account		218
		953

J PLC
RECONCILIATION OF MOVEMENT IN SHAREHOLDERS FUNDS

	£ million
Profit for the financial year	189
Other recognised gains and losses in the year	100
New share capital subscribed (100 x £1.60)	160
Net addition to shareholders funds	449
Opening shareholders' funds (300 + 140 + 35 + 29)	504
Closing shareholders' funds	953

Workings

1   *Turnover*

		£ million
Continuing -	confectionery	100
	games software	300
		400
Discontinued - clothing		250
Total		650

2   *Cost of sales*

		£ million
Continuing -	confectionery	40
	games software	60
		100
Discontinued - clothing		140
Total		240

3   *Distribution costs*

		£ million
Continuing -	confectionery (40%)	18
	games software (40%)	18
		36
Discontinued - clothing (20%)		9
		45

4   *Administrative expenses*

		£ million
Continuing -	confectionery (50%)	30
	games software (30%)	18
		48
Discontinued - clothing (20%)		12
		60

5   This is in respect of clothing operation closed during the year.

6   *Interest payable*

	£ million
Interest per TB	31
Finance lease charges	6
	37
Interest capitalised	(4)
	33

7   *Taxation*

	£ million
Current year tax charge	42
Underprovision in previous year	5
Deferred tax	6
	53

8   *Earnings per share*

Theoretical ex-rights price:

3 shares	@ £1.80	£5.40
1 share	@ £1.60	£1.60
4 shares	@ £1.75	£7.00

Bonus element of share issue $= \dfrac{£1.80}{£1.75}$

	Million
Number of shares	
Before issue -	
$300 \times 1.80/1.75 \times 3/12$	77
After issue	
$400 \times 9/12$	300
	377

$$EPS = \frac{£189}{377}$$

$$= 50.1 \text{ pence}$$

9   *Tangible fixed assets*

	£ million
Per TB	1,170
Capitalised interest	4
Revaluation	100
	1,274

10   *Finance leases*

	£ million
Payable within one year	10
Payable between one and five years	30
	40

11   *Deferred tax*

	£ million
Balance at 1 April 2001	10
Charge for the year	6
Balance at 31 March 2002	16

12   *Share capital and share premium*

	Share capital £ million	*Share premium* £ million
Balance at 1 April 2001	300	140
Issued during the year	100	60
Balance at 31 March 2002	400	200

13   *Revaluation reserve*

	£ million
Balance at 1 April 2001	35
Revaluation during the year	100
Balance at 31 March 2002	135

10 SHOPPING CENTRES

> **Pass marks**. This question required the preparation of financial statements from trial balance. Such questions are set very regularly. You must distinguish notes to the accounts from workings. The best way do to this is to study the published financial statements of one or two limited companies.
>
> Do not provide a statement of accounting policies, this is not required by the question. It would not be penalised but it would not be rewarded either. However you do need a statement of total recognised gains and losses.

(a) L PLC
PROFIT AND LOSS ACCOUNT
FOR THE YEAR ENDED 31 MARCH 20X7

	Notes	£'000	£'000
Turnover	1		25,000
Cost of sales			(16,250)
Gross profit			8,750
Distribution costs		500	
Administration expenses		250	
			(750)
			8,000
Other operating income			1,500
Operating profit			9,500
Interest payable	2		(350)
Profit on ordinary activities before taxation			9,150
Tax on profit on ordinary activities	3		(2,130)
			7,020
Dividends	4		(750)
Retained profit for the year			6,270

L PLC
BALANCE SHEET AS AT 31 MARCH 20X7

	Notes	£'000	£'000
Fixed assets			
Tangible assets	5		22,800
Current assets			
Stock		850	
Debtors	6	2,800	
Bank		700	
		4,350	
Creditors: amounts falling due within one year	7	(4,650)	
Net current liabilities			(300)
			22,500
Creditors: amounts falling due after more than one year			
Loans			(2,300)
Accruals and deferred income			(800)
			19,400
Capital and reserves			
Called up share capital			4,000
Revaluation reserve	8		8,000
Profit and loss account	8		7,400
			19,400

L PLC
STATEMENT OF TOTAL RECOGNISED GAINS AND LOSSES

	£'000
Profit for the year	7,020
Unrealised surplus on revaluation	8,000
Total recognised gains	15,020

Notes to the accounts

1   *Turnover*

Turnover represents the amounts derived from the provision of goods and services which fall within the company's ordinary activities, stated net of value added tax.

2   *Interest payable*

	£'000
Loans not wholly payable within 5 years	350

3   *Tax on profit on ordinary activities*

	£'000
Based on profit for year:	
Corporation tax	2,100
Corporation tax underprovided in previous years	30
	2,130

4   *Dividends*

	£'000
Equity dividends on ordinary shares	
Final proposed	750

5   *Tangible fixed assets*

	Freehold land £'000	Other £'000	Total £'000
Cost/valuation			
At 1 April 20X6	9,000	3,000	12,000
Additions		11,000	11,000
Revaluations	8,000		8,000
Disposals		(4,000)	(4,000)
At 31 March 20X7	17,000	10,000	27,000
Accumulated depreciation			
At 1 April 20X6	-	3,000	3,000
Charge for year	-	3,700	3,700
Disposals	-	(2,500)	(2,500)
At 31 March 20X7	-	4,200	4,200
Net book value			
At 31 March 20X7	17,000	5,800	22,800
At 1 April 20X6	9,000	Nil	9,000

The land was revalued at £17m during the year by Valier & Co, a firm of Chartered Surveyors. The historic cost of the land included at revaluation is £9m.

6   *Debtors*

	£'000
Trade debtors	800
Prepayments	2,000
	2,800

Included in prepayments are amounts due in more than one year of £1,200,000.

7   *Creditors: amounts falling due within one year*

	£'000
Trade creditors	1,800
Dividends payable	750
Corporation tax payable	2,100
	4,650

8   *Reserves*

	Revaluation reserve £'000	*Profit and loss account* £'000
At 1 April 20X6	-	1,130
Revaluation of land	8,000	
Retained profit for year		6,270
At 31 March 20X7	8,000	7,400

Pass marks. There is no single correct answer to part (b). There is no particular accounting standard that directly covers the issue. Marks will be awarded for the quality of arguments.

(b) **Treatment of advertising billings**

I do not agree with the managing director's argument that the proportion of advertising billed to tenants can be included in turnover for the year ended 31 March 20X7. The actual advertising will only commence in June 20X7 and run for two years.

Financial statements, except for cash flow statements should be prepared on an **accruals basis**. This means that credits or charges should be reflected in the profit and loss account in the period in which they occur rather than in the period in which any amounts involved are received or paid. In this scenario, neither L Limited or its tenants have accrued any benefits in terms of advertisements for their money.

The recognition, measurement and presentation of an event/transaction should correspond closely to the impact of the event/transaction. **Prudence** requires that any **uncertainty** in the recognition and measurement of gains and losses should be taken into consideration. Under FRS 18, any uncertainty should be addressed by reviewing confirmatory evidence. In this case, there seems to be little uncertainty involved because L plc should be entitled to advertising recovery once the advertisements are made public.

It should be noted the recoveries made from tenants are unlikely to represent turnover of L plc, whose principle activity is the management of shopping centres. As the question says, the recoveries are contributions to the cost of advertising.

11   **ELECTRONIC COMPONENTS**

Pass marks. Read the question carefully to ensure whether notes to the financial statements are **required or not**.

(a) **M PLC**
PROFIT AND LOSS ACCOUNT
FOR THE YEAR ENDED 30 SEPTEMBER 20X4

	£m	£m
Turnover		2,970
Cost of sales (W1)		(1,267)
Gross profit		1,703
Distribution costs		(148)
Administrative expenses (W2)		(153)
Operating profit		1,402
Loss on sale of fixed assets		(11)
Profit on ordinary activities before interest		1,391
Interest payable		(72)
Profit on ordinary activities before taxation		1,319
Tax on profit on ordinary activities (W3)		(69)
Profit on ordinary activities after taxation		1,250
Dividends paid and proposed (W4)		(450)
Retained profit for the financial year		800
Retained profit at beginning of financial year		1,132
Retained profit at end of financial year		1,932
Earnings per ordinary share		208 pence

BALANCE SHEET AS AT 30 SEPTEMBER 20X4

	£m	£m
Tangible fixed assets (W5)		3,908
Current assets		
Stock (W6)	38	
Debtors	980	
Bank	98	
	1,116	
Creditors: amounts falling due within one year (W7)	(597)	
Net current assets		519
Total assets less current liabilities		4,427
Creditors: amounts falling due after		
more than one year (20Z0 loan)		(1,618)
		2,809
Provision for liabilities and charges (W8)		(277)
		2,532
Capital and reserves		
Called up share capital		600
Retained profit		1,932
		2,532

Workings

1   *Cost of sales*

	£m
Per TB	1,142
Adjustment re-NRV of stock (45 – 38)(W6))	7
Depreciation of plant and machinery	
(794 - 324) × 25%	118
	1,267

2   *Administrative expense*

	£m
Per TB	64
Depreciation of premises (£4,456 × 2%)	89
	153

3   *Taxation*

Current tax

	£m
UK corporation tax charge for the year	120
Adjustment in respect of prior periods	(37)
	83

Deferred tax

Origination and reversal of timing differences (W9)	(14)
	69

4   *Dividends*

	£m
Interim paid (50p)	300
Final proposed (25p) (W7)	150
	450

5   *Tangible fixed assets*

	Land and buildings £m	Plant and machinery £m	Total £m
Cost			
At 1 October 20X1	4,456	759	5,215
Additions	-	160	160
Disposals	-	(125)	(125)
At 30 September 20X2	4,456	794	5,250
Depreciation			
At 1 October 20X1	811	402	1,213
Charge for the year (W1) (W3)	89	118	207
On disposals	-	(78)	(78)
At 30 September 20X2	900	442	1,342
Net book value at 1 October 20X1	3,645	357	4,002
Net book value at 30 September 20X2	3,556	352	3,908

6   *Closing stock*

	Purchase price £m	Attributable production overheads £m	Total relevant cost £m	Net realisable value £m	Lower of costs and net realisable value £m
Current stock	26	7	33	51	33
Obsolete stock	6	2	8	5	5
Total					38

7   *Creditors: amounts falling due within one year*

	£m
Trade creditors	327
Corporation tax (W3)	120
Proposed dividend (W4)	150
	597

8   *Provision for liabilities and charges*

	£m
Capital allowances in excess of depreciation:	
Balance at 1 October 20X1	291
Decrease for year (W9)	(14)
Balance at 30 September 20X2	277

9   *Deferred tax*

	£m
Net book value of fixed assets	
Plant and machinery (794 – 324 – 118) (W1)	352
Premises (4,456 – 811 – 89) (W2)	3,556
	3,908
Tax written down value	2,985
Accelerated capital allowances	923
Deferred tax balance required 923 × 30% (W8)	277
Deferred tax balance in TB	291
Decrease in deferred tax balance (W8)	14

(b) **Earnings per share**

$$\frac{£1,250,000}{600,000 \text{ shares}} = 208\text{p/share}$$

(c) **Audit report**

(i) **Disagreement – Accounts impact fundamental**

If the directors of M plc had not changed their treatment of the closing stock to value each line of stock at the lower of cost and net realisable value rather than at the total lower value then there would **potentially** be a **position of disagreement** between the auditors and the directors. In the case of a disagreement if the auditors felt that the matter was **fundamental** to the **financial statements** then they would issue an **adverse opinion**.

(ii) **Disagreement – Accounts impact material but not fundamental**

Alternatively if they felt that the area of **disagreement** was **material but not fundamental** then they would issue an 'except for' opinion. This would require an additional paragraph in the auditors opinion stating that **except for** the treatment of the closing stock the financial statements give a **true and fair view**.

(iii) **Materiality test**

This type of qualified report would only be issued if the auditors assessed that the matter was **material**. In this case the adjustment of £4million might not appear to be material in the **context of a retained profit** of £803 million. However, the auditors may have felt that it was material in the **context of the stock valuation** of £45 million, being almost 10% of the correct valuation figure. If it was considered to be material then an except for report as described above would be issued.

(d) **Neutrality**

(i) Information provided by financial statements must be neutral, ie **free from** deliberate or systematic **bias**

(ii) Financial information is not neutral if it has been selected or presented in such a way as to influence the making of a decision or judgement in order to achieve a predetermined result or outcome

(iii) Neutrality militates against setting up of hidden reserves and **excessive provisions**

(iv) One of the criteria for financial information being **reliable** is neutrality

12 **RADAR EQUIPMENT**

> **Pass marks.** Watch the treatment of R&D expenditure and the trade fair costs. As this is a manufacturing company all factory related costs appear in cost of sales.
>
> The only way in which to prepare for a published accounts question is to practice on as many examples as possible from past papers and similar sources. This type of question offers any reasonably prepared candidate an opportunity to score a very high mark and it is foolish to throw away marks through carelessness or poor preparation.
>
> It would be worthwhile doing part (b) before attempting the published accounts in part (a). Always read through the entire question before starting.

(a) T PLC
PROFIT AND LOSS ACCOUNT FOR THE YEAR ENDED 31 DECEMBER 20X8

	Notes	£'000
Turnover		10,000
Cost of sales (W1)		(8,540)
Gross profit		1,460
Selling and distribution costs (W2)		(1,600)
Administration costs		(800)
Operating loss	1	(940)
Interest payable		(1,680)
Loss for the financial year		(2,620)
Retained profits b/fwd		380
Retained losses c/fwd		(2,240)

T PLC
BALANCE SHEET AT 31 DECEMBER 20X8

	Notes	£'000	£'000
Fixed assets			
Intangible fixed assets	2		2,790
Tangible fixed assets	3		20,040
			22,830
Current assets			
Stock	4	1,230	
Debtors		2,000	
		3,230	
Creditors: amounts falling due within one year	5	(1,300)	
Net current assets			1,930
			24,760
Creditors: amount falling due after more one years			(12,000)
			12,760
Share capital and reserves			
Called up share capital			15,000
Profit and loss account			(2,240)
			12,760

T PLC

NOTES TO THE FINANCIAL STATEMENTS

1 *Operating loss*

The operating loss is stated after charging	£'000
Depreciation (W1)	1,760
Staff costs (600 + 1,300)	1,900
Research expenditure written off	1,700
Amortisation of capitalised development costs	210
Exceptional item	1,000

The exceptional item consists of the costs incurred in exhibiting the company's product range at a major trade fair.

2   *Intangible fixed assets*

	Cost £'000	Amortisation £'000	Net Book Value £'000
Development expenditure:			
At 1 January 20X8	2,100	-	2,100
Additions	900	-	900
Charge for the year	-	(210)	(210)
At 31 December 20X8	3,000	(210)	2,790

The company has capitalised these development costs in order to match them with expected future revenues. The development costs brought forward are being written off over ten years. The costs incurred during the year are not yet being amortised, as the products are not yet commercially available.

3   *Tangible fixed assets*

	Land and buildings £'000	Plant and machinery £'000	Total £'000
Cost			
At 1 January 20X8	18,000	13,000	31,000
Additions	-	600	600
At 31 December 20X8	18,000	13,600	31,600
Accumulated depreciation			
At 1 January 20X8	1,800	8,000	9,800
Charge for the year	360	1,400	1,760
At 31 December 20X8	2,160	9,400	11,560
Net book value at 31 December 20X8	15,840	4,200	20,040
Net book value at 1 January 20X8	16,200	5,000	21,200

4   *Stocks*

	£'000
Raw materials	520
Work in progress	710
	1,230

5   *Creditors: amounts falling due within one year*

	£'000
Trade creditors	600
Bank overdraft	700
	1,300

Workings

1   *Cost of sales*

		£'000
Opening stock	- parts and materials	400
	- WIP	900
Purchases		2,300
		3,600
Closing stock	- parts and materials	(520)
	- WIP	(710)
		2,370
Depreciation	- factory (2% × 18,000)	360
	- machinery (25% × (13,600 – 8,000))	1,400
Factory running costs		1,200
Manufacturing wages		1,300
Research cost written off		1,700
Amortisation of development costs (10% × 2,100)		210
		8,540

125

£'000

2 *Selling and distribution costs*

Sales salaries   600
Trade fair costs   1,000
                                                                _____
                                                                1,600
                                                                _____

(b)

> **Pass marks.** This question is the key to the published accounts in part (b). At the very least, you should have thought through this treatment before attempting part (a) and I would recommend doing this part **before** attempting part (a). It always pays to read through all of the questions connected to the scenario before attempting any of the answers.
>
> An unacceptable approach to this question is to use acronyms such as 'DEFER' or 'SECTOR' as the answer itself, eg by stating that 'the project meets the SECTOR criteria' without any elaboration. **The reciting of memory aids such as this does nothing to demonstrate any understanding and will rarely earn any marks in this paper.** Information should be used as the basis for a discussion of the issues in the scenario.

(i)   **Accounting treatment**

(1)   **New calibrating equipment purchased for the laboratory**

This is used to ensure that measurement devices used in experiments are properly adjusted. As such, this equipment is not used solely for research and development projects. Furthermore, the equipment can be used in any project and so is not specifically identifiable with any one project. In these circumstances, the equipment should be treated as a tangible fixed asset and depreciated in the same way as existing plant and machinery.

(2)   **Long-range radar**

This project is nearing completion. A successful prototype has been built and there is definite commercial interest. Market research suggests that when the product goes on sale early in 20Y0, it will make a profit. The project, therefore, satisfies the requirements of SSAP 13 and so the costs can be deferred to future periods. As the company's policy is to defer such development costs, they should be included in intangible fixed assets. No amortisation should be charged until commercial production commences.

(3)   **Wide-angle microwave**

This project is in its early stages. However the transmitter currently being used is not a viable commercial product due to its size and weight. Therefore, the future viability of this project is uncertain. According to the criteria in SSAP 13, this expenditure is applied research and should be written off to the profit and loss account as incurred.

(ii)   **Costs of the trade fair**

At £1,000,000, this is considered as material. In addition this is the first time that the company has attended such an event. Although no sales were generated at the time of the fair, it is likely that the contacts made could generate future sales.

There is no specific accounting standard dealing with this type of expenditure, nor is its treatment laid down in the Companies Acts. In such circumstances, the concepts of accruals outlined in FRS 18 should be considered. On the basis of the accruals concept, costs should be written off in the year to which they relate, rather than in the year any cash is paid. As the trade fair has not yet produced any income, it could be argued that the costs should be carried forward.

However, as there is uncertainty that the costs will actually generate any income in the future, the notion of prudence suggests that the costs should be written off immediately.

The expenditure of £1,000,000 is material and by virtue of its size would need disclosure to sustain the true and fair view given by the financial statements. Hence, the expense needs to be disclosed as an exceptional item in the notes to the accounts.

13 MANUFACTURING

> **Pass marks**. Part (a) is a straightforward published accounts question with no real complications. Set out your proformas and use notes rather than workings for items such as tax and dividends.

(a) PROFIT AND LOSS ACCOUNT FOR THE YEAR ENDED 31 DECEMBER 20X0

	Notes	£m	£m
Turnover			1,000
Cost of sales			240
Gross profit			760
Distribution costs (W1)	1	108	
Administration expenses		130	
			238
Operating profit			522
Interest payable and similar charges			95
Profit on ordinary activities before taxation			427
Taxation	2		190
Profit on ordinary activities after taxation			237
Dividends	3		100
Retained profit for the financial year			137

BALANCE SHEET AS AT 31 DECEMBER 20X0

	Notes	£m	£m
Fixed assets			
Intangible assets			1,900
Tangible assets			2,400
			4,300
Current assets			
Stock		110	
Trade debtors (W1)		82	
Bank		10	
		202	
Creditors: amounts due within one year			
Trade creditors		30	
Taxation		120	
Proposed dividend		60	
		210	
Net current liabilities			8
			4,292
Creditors: amounts due after more than one year			
Loans			1,100
			3,192
Provision for liabilities and charges			
Deferred taxation	4		280
			2,912
Share capital	5		500
Share premium	5		400
Profit and loss account	6		2,012
			2,912

Notes

1   *Distribution costs*

Included in distribution costs is an exceptional bad debt write off of £8 million.

2   *Taxation*

	£m
Corporation tax charge	120
Over provision in previous year	(10)
Increase in provision for deferred tax	80
	190

3   *Dividends*

	£m
Interim dividend paid	40
Final dividend proposed	60
	100

4   *Deferred taxation*

	£m
Balance at 31 December 19W9	200
Increase in provision	80
	280

5   *Share capital and share premium*

	Share capital £m	Share premium £m
Balance at 31 December 19W9	400	360
Issued during the year	100	40
Balance at 31 December 20X0	500	400

6   *Profit and loss account*

	£m
Retained profits at 31 December 19W9	1,875
Retained profit for the financial year	137
Retained profits at 31 December 20X0	2,012

7   *Post balance sheet event*

A damages claim was lodged against the company after the year end for the sum of £2 million. This matter has now been placed in the hands of the company's legal advisors who are of the opinion that this sum will have to be paid in compensation.

Workings

1   *Distribution costs and trade debtors*

	Distribution costs £m	Trade debtors £m
Per trial balance	100	90
Write off of bad debt	8	(8)
	108	82

> **Pass marks**. The EPS calculation is a standard one but you must think carefully about, and plan, your answer to part (ii).

(b)   (i)   **FRS 14 – EPS calculation**

	Jan – Feb	Mar – Dec
Shares	400m	500m
Days	60	306

Weighted average number of shares $= (400m \times \dfrac{60}{366}) + (500m \times \dfrac{306}{366})$

$= 484$ million

Earnings after taxation but before dividends $= £237$ million

Earnings per share $= \dfrac{£237m}{484m}$

$= 49.0$ pence

(ii) **Need for guidance**

(1) In practice, EPS is a key figure used in **capital markets. Market analysts** use it widely in their assessment of a company's performance and in their reports to clients regarding the buying or selling of shares in the company.

(2) EPS is also used in the calculation of the **price/earnings ratio** of a company which is **published information**.

(3) The **P/E ratio** is itself widely **used by analysts** and **investors** to **relate** the company's **current share price to the accounting earnings**.

In the past many companies have attempted to manipulate EPS in order to show the company in a more favourable light.

Because EPS is so important in the capital markets, either as a figure on its own, or as part of the calculation of the price/earnings ratio, it is **essential** that the figure is **calculated precisely**.

FRS 14 was therefore introduced to provide **guidance** on the precise method of **calculating EPS**. This means that the EPS and the price/earnings ratios of companies are:

- **comparable over time**; and
- **comparable between companies**.

Without such regulation EPS would be less useful because its precise calculation could not be guaranteed to be without distortion.

In achieving **uniformity of calculation**, FRS 14 has helped to overcome several practical problems.

(1) Determining the **number of shares** to be used in the **calculation** where a company has **issued shares during the year**

(2) Determining how many **shares** were **in issue** during the year depending upon whether they were issued at **full market price**, at a **discount** in a **rights** issue or as a **bonus issue**.

14 PROTECTIVE CLOTHING

Pass marks. The examiner commented that generally candidates scored well in this question. Many marks were, however, lost through easily avoidable errors, and a significant minority of answers were badly structured.

(a) L PLC PROFIT AND LOSS ACCOUNT FOR THE YEAR ENDED 30 JUNE 20X1

	Notes	£ m
Turnover		755
Cost of sales (W1)		262
Gross profit		493
Distribution costs (W1)		51
Administrative expenses (W1)		46
Interest payable and similar charges		5
Profit on ordinary activities before taxation	1	391
Tax on profit on ordinary activities	2	20
Profit for the financial year		371
Dividends paid and proposed	3	176
Profit for the financial year		195
Profit and loss account b/f (W2)	4	26
Profit and loss account c/f		221

L PLC BALANCE SHEET AS AT 30 JUNE 20X1

	Notes	£ m	£ m
Fixed assets:			
Tangible assets	5		497
Current assets:			
Stocks		16	
Debtors		57	
Bank		45	
		118	
Creditors: amounts falling due within one year			
	6	123	
Net current liabilities			5
Total assets less current liabilities			492
Creditors: amounts falling due after more than one year	7		76
Provisions for liabilities and charges	8		35
			381
Capital and reserves			
Called up share capital	9		100
Share premium	9		60
Profit and loss account			221
			381

Notes to the accounts

1   *Profit before tax*

Profit before tax is stated after charging

	£m
Depreciation (11 + 5 + 46)	62

2   *Taxation*

	£m
Tax on profit for the year	30
Overprovision in previous year	(10)
	20

3   *Dividends*

	£m
Dividend paid	96
Dividend proposed	80
	176

4   *Prior period adjustment*

During the current year there has been a change of accounting policy. Previously, certain categories of equipment were not depreciated. However, the directors have decided that these assets will now be depreciated. This change in policy would have resulted in the accumulated depreciation of equipment being £12 million higher than shown in the last financial statements. This has been treated as a prior period adjustment and the opening profit and loss account balance has been reduced by £12 million.

5   *Tangible fixed assets*

	Land and buildings £m	Fixtures and fittings £m	Plant and machinery £m	Total £m
Cost				
At 1 July 20X0	534	46	269	849
Additions	-	-	55	55
Disposals	-	-	(42)	(42)
At 30 June 20X1	534	46	282	862
Accumulated depreciation				
At 1 July 20X0	178	14	118	310
Prior period adjustment	-	12	-	12
Provision for year	11	5	46	62
Disposals	-	-	(19)	(19)
At 30 June 20X1	189	31	145	365
Net book amount:				
At 1 July 20X0	356	20	151	527
At 30 June 20X1	345	15	137	497

6   *Creditors: amounts falling due within one year*

	£m
Trade creditors	13
Taxation and social security	30
Proposed dividends	80
	123

7   *Creditors: amounts falling due after more than one year*

	£m
Long term loan	76

This amount is repayable in 20Y5.

8   *Provision for liabilities and charges*

	£m
Warranties:	
At 1 July 20X0	27
Profit and loss account charge	8
At 30 June 20X1	35

9   *Called up share capital and reserves*

	£1 ordinary share capital £m	Share premium £m	Profit and loss account £m
At 1 July 20X0	60	35	38
Prior period adjustment	-	-	(12)
Shares issued	40	25	-
Profit for the financial year	-	-	195
At 30 June 20X1	100	60	221

The authorised share capital is 200 million shares of £1.

> **Pass marks**. The marking scheme for this question allocated the marks almost equally among the profit and loss account, the balance sheet and the notes to the accounts. Make sure that you don't overlook the notes and concentrate exclusively on the other documents. The examiner commented that one failing was that candidates confused notes and workings: you should keep them separate from the outset. Set up a proforma for the notes to the accounts that you will need, and set up a workings sheet on a different page.

Workings

1

	Cost of goods sold £m	Administrative expenses £m	Distribution costs £m
Per trial balance	208	22	51
Warranties	8		
Research costs		8	
Depreciation:			
Land and buildings			
534 × 2%		11	
Fixtures and fittings			
(46 – 26) × 25%		5	
Plant and machinery			
(282 – 99) × 25%	46		
	262	46	51

2   *Profit and loss account b/f*

	£m
Per trial balance	38
Less prior period adjustment (26 – 14)	(12)
	35

This is treated as a prior period adjustment as it is a change in accounting policy from charging no depreciation on certain items to a policy of charging depreciation.

> **Pass marks**. In part (a) you needed to recognise that the change in depreciation method is a change of accounting policy and therefore a prior period adjustment. Part (b) requires some thought and planning, not just definitions of relevance and reliability.

(b) **Relevance and reliability – future warranty costs**

The SoP defines **relevant information** as being information that has the ability to influence the **economic decisions** of users and is provided in time to influence those decisions. However, decision making processes and information are often dependent on the quality of **future oriented projections**.

Reliable information is defined as information which can be depended upon to **represent faithfully** what it purports to represent, is free from deliberate or systematic bias and material error and under conditions of uncertainty a degree of caution has been applied in exercising the necessary judgements. Generally, reliable information is based on **past events**.

Therefore there can sometimes be **tension** between **relevance** and **reliability**. The problem with the provision for future warranty costs is that there is uncertainty as to how much the warranties will cost in the future.

The future cost of warranties is certainly **relevant information** as these costs are likely to be incurred, they are **material** and therefore they are **likely** to **influence** the **economic decisions of users**.

However, there is a problem regarding the **reliability** of the provision as the **amount** has to be **estimated,** as the warranty cost cannot be known for certain. L plc should have some view from **past experience** as to how much these warranties are likely to cost, and provided that the estimate of the provision has been made with a **degree of caution**, the **relevance** of the provision **should outweigh** the **reliability problem**.

Where there is **tension** between **relevance** and **reliability** the **SoP** states that the **approach** taken should be the one that **results in the relevance of the information being maximised**.

It might also be worth noting that the approach recommended by **FRS 18**, when determining **accounting policies**, is to take the **route of going for the most relevant of those that are reliable**.

> **Pass marks**. The examiner said that many candidates failed even to distinguish the qualities of relevance and reliability which are little different in their accounting context from in their normal English usage. You should always think carefully when defining and explaining and make sure that you understand the definitions yourself before committing them to paper.

15 COSMETICS

> **Pass marks**. Questions of this type are quite common. Lay out the proforma P & L account and balance sheet, leaving plenty of space; then fill in the numbers in order, adding the relevant notes as you progress. Remember that you need the SSAP 25 disclosures.
>
> Common pitfalls include a lack of knowledge of the disclosure requirements of FRS 3 and an inability to account for corporation tax or for contingencies.

D PLC
PROFIT AND LOSS ACCOUNT
FOR THE YEAR ENDED 31 MARCH 20X6

	Note	Continuing operations £'000	Discontinued operations £'000	Total £'000
Turnover	1	12,000	1,600	13,600
Cost of sales		4,930	880	5,810
		7,070	720	7,790
Net operating expenses				
Administration		1,520	380	1,900
Distribution		1,280	320	1,600
		2,800	700	3,500
Operating profit		4,270	20	4,290
Loss on termination of operations	2			(920)
Profit on ordinary activities before taxation				3,370
Taxation	3			(970)
Profit for the financial year				2,400
Dividends	4			(2,200)
Retained profit for the year				200

STATEMENT OF TOTAL RECOGNISED GAINS AND LOSSES

	£'000
Profit attributable to members of the company	2,400

D PLC
BALANCE SHEET OF D PLC AT 31 MARCH 20X6

	Note	£'000	£'000
Fixed assets	5		6,100
Current assets			
Stock		411	
Debtors		240	
Bank		27	
		678	
Creditors: amounts due in less than one year	6	(2,090)	
Net current liabilities			(1,412)
			4,688
Provision for liabilities and charges			
Deferred taxation	7		(690)
			3,998
Capital and reserves			
Issued share capital			3,500
Profit and loss account	8		498
	9		3,998

NOTES TO ACCOUNTS

1   *Turnover and segmental analysis*

Turnover represents the amounts derived from the provision of goods and services which fall within the group's ordinary activities, stated net of value added tax.

The company operates in two lines of business, the operation of a retail pharmacy and the manufacture and sale of cosmetics. A third area of business, the manufacture and sale of skin care ointment, was discontinued during the year.

	Pharmacy £'000	Cosmetics £'000	Ointment £'000	Total £'000
Turnover				
Continuing operations	4,700	7,300		12,000
Discounted operations			1,600	1,600
	4,700	7,300	1,600	13,600
Profit				
Continuing operations	1,145	3,125		4,270
Discontinued operations			20	20
	1,145	3,125	20	4,290
Non-operating exceptional items				(920)
Profit on ordinary activities before taxation				3,370

2   *Exceptional item*

	£'000
Loss on termination of skincare operations	920
Tax relief thereon	(240)
	680

3   *Tax on profit on ordinary activities*

	£'000
Based on the profit for the year	
Corporation tax	1,020
Deferred taxation	90
	1,110
Corporation tax underprovided in previous years	100
	1,210
Tax relief on loss on termination of operations	(240)
	970

4   *Dividends*

	£'000

		Answers	Notes
	Equity dividends		
	Interim paid	1,200	
	Final proposed	1,000	
		2,200	

5 *Tangible fixed assets*

	£'000
Cost at 31 March 20X6	7,700
Depreciation at 31 March 20X6	1,600
NBV at 31 March 20X6	6,100

6 *Creditors: amounts due in less than one year*

	£'000
Trade creditors	310
Current corporation tax (1,020 – 240)	780
Dividends payable	1,000
	2,090

7 *Provisions for liabilities and charges*

	£'000
Deferred taxation	
At 1 April 20X5	600
Arising during year	90
At 31 March 20X6	690

8 *Profit and loss account*

	£'000
At 1 April 20X5	298
Retained for year	200
At 31 March 20X6	498

9 *Reconciliation of shareholders' funds*

	£'000
Total recognised gains and losses	2,400
Dividends	(2,200)
Total movements during the year	200
Shareholders' funds at 1 April 20X5	3,798
Shareholders' funds at 31 March 20X6	3,998

10 *Contingencies*

Four users of the company's skin-care ointment have made a claim against the company for damages of £750,000 for alleged injury caused by the ointment. No provision has been made in these financial statements, as the directors believe that the company is not liable. The action will be contested.

Workings

1 *Tax liability*

	£'000
Corporation tax provision	1,020
Tax relief on closure costs	(240)
	780

2 *Profit split*

	Pharmacy	Cosmetics	Total
	£'000	£'000	£'000
Turnover	4,700	7,300	12,000
Cost of sales	1,645	3,285	4,930
	3,055	4,015	7,070
Net operating expenses			
Administration (5:3)	950	570	1,520
Distribution (3:1)	960	320	1,280

	1,145	3,125	4,270

16 PREPARATION QUESTION: FRS 3 SITUATIONS

(a) (i) **Discontinued operations**. Operations may only be treated as discontinued if they are sold/terminated and meet certain conditions. One of these conditions is that the termination has a material affect on the nature and focus of operations of the enterprise.

   A cessation of manufacturing, as given in this situation, **does not necessarily meet this condition.**

   (ii) The purpose of manufacturing the cash registers was ultimately the creation of profit through sales to customers.

   (iii) Contracting out production enables the company to be more cost effective and does not have a material impact on ultimate purpose. The cessation of manufacturing does not constitute a discontinued activity in this case.

(b) (i) A further condition for treating an activity as discontinued is that the termination is **expected to lead to a material reduction in turnover in a continuing market.**

   (ii) The cost of the closures would be charged in arriving at operating profits and, if material, should be disclosed separately; but there is no significant loss of revenue or change in customer base or material effect on the nature and focus of the reporting entity's operations. The operations of the closed shop are therefore not discontinued.

(c) As **the company is not demonstrably committed to the closure,** the only provision required is the £0.5m to reduce the fixed assets to their recoverable amount. This provision will be classed as continuing operations as the operations have not yet been discontinued.

17 DIVERSIFIED

> **Pass marks**. You should be completely familiar with FRS 3's requirements.

(a) Each of these components is needed in order to assess a business's future results and cash flows for the following reasons.

   (i) **Results of continuing operations**

   These results include those of acquisitions and they give a strong indication of how the business will perform in the future, as these are the results which might recur. By excluding discontinued operations, the readers of the accounts are not misled about likely future performance.

(ii) **Results of discontinued operations**

These results are obviously not going to recur in future, but they do indicate the overall strategy of the business and they therefore indicate likely future events. This is particularly true of large conglomerates which buy and sell businesses constantly; it is, in fact, their trade.

(iii) **Profits or losses on the sale or termination of an operation, etc**

These costs are specific exceptional items which FRS 3 requires to be disclosed on the face of the profit and loss account. The impact of such figures will not recur and so should be shown separately from operating results. They do indicate significant policy decisions or changes in policy on the part of the company and they may therefore indicate future performance.

(iv) **Extraordinary items**

Such items are very rare; the FRS 3 description precludes most trading items as such items must show a high degree of abnormality. Once again, such items are unlikely to recur and so should be shown separately but, depending on the nature of such items, they may have an impact on future events and so they should be disclosed fully to the users of the accounts.

(b) D PLC
PROFIT AND LOSS ACCOUNT
FOR THE YEAR ENDED 31 DECEMBER 20X3

	Continuing operations £'000	Discontinued operations £'000	Total £'000
Turnover	820	150	970
Operating expenses	(470)	(98)	(568)
Operating profit	350	52	402
Costs of closure and reorganisation	(42)	(127)	(169)
Loss on disposal of fixed assets	(19)	(78)	(97)
Profit on ordinary activities before interest	289	(153)	136
Interest payable			(37)
Profit on ordinary activities before taxation			99
Tax on profit on ordinary activities			(24)
Profit on ordinary activities after taxation			75
Dividends			(30)
Retained profit for the financial year			45

(c) STATEMENT OF TOTAL RECOGNISED GAINS AND LOSSES

	£'000
Profit for the financial year	75
Unrealised loss on revaluation of properties	(70)
Total recognised gains and losses for the year	5

(d) RECONCILIATION OF MOVEMENTS IN SHAREHOLDERS' FUNDS

	£'000
Profit for the financial year	75
Dividends	(30)
	45
New share capital subscribed	180
Unrealised loss on revaluation of properties	(70)
Net addition to shareholders funds	155
Opening shareholders' funds	1,230
Closing shareholders' funds	1,385

137

(e) NOTE OF HISTORICAL COST PROFITS AND LOSSES

	£'000
Reported profit on ordinary activities before taxation	99
Difference between historical cost depreciation and actual depreciation charge (84 – 75)	9
Historical cost profit before taxation	108
Historical cost profit retained for the year (45 + 9)	54

18 FRS 3 PROFITS: T PLC

> **Pass marks**. FRS 3 is a very popular exam topic, reflecting its importance in financial reporting. The answer given here is probably longer than you would be expected to give in an exam; this is for tutorial purposes. You should concentrate on the points in bold font.
>
> If you are given figures in a question, always try to bring them in to the answer if it is appropriate to do so. It is also a good idea to use the company or business name, eg T plc's profit and loss account … This shows the examiner that you are applying what you know and focusing on the specific scenario given, rather than merely churning out general points you have learnt.
>
> Do not be disheartened if you did not make all the points that are made in the model answer. For example the last couple of lines in (a)(ii) would be a prizewinner point.

(a) **FRS 3 – profits**

FRS 3 requires that the profit and loss account should be analysed between continuing operations, acquisitions, and discontinued operations to the level of operating profit.

T plc's profit and loss account and related note show a number of profit figures; of which three - profit from continuing operations, profit from discontinued operations and total profit after tax - may be useful to the shareholders of T plc in the following ways.

(i) **Profit from continuing operations**

Profit from continuing operations (for T plc, £200,000) **will demonstrate to the shareholders the level of profit that has been generated from operations that will be on-going,** ie those that will continue to earn profits for the company in subsequent years.

It will enable them to make an assessment of future performance and allow them to make like-for-like comparisons in subsequent years.

This figure will itself change over time as operations are acquired or divested, so that year-on-year figures and comparatives must be analysed carefully.

Profits may of course rise or fall for many different reasons, even where the underlying operations remain the same.

(ii) **Profit from discontinued operations**

Operating profit from discontinued operations is £17,000 in the case of T plc. Discontinued operations as defined by FRS 3 are those which have ceased permanently, ie they will make no future contribution to the results of the company.

Separate identification allows shareholders to assess the effect of terminating this portion of the company's activities and the contribution they made to the company's results. The shareholders can also assess the impact of selling or closing those operations on the results of the business as a whole.

T plc's overall gross profit margin was 33% (650/1,950 × 100%), but this has been depressed by the lower gross profit margin on discontinued operations of 20% (50/250 × 100%). Shareholders might therefore expect T plc's gross profit margin to be higher in future.

(iii) **Total profit after tax**

Total profit from the combined types of operation after tax is the figure that the shareholders are most familiar with. It reports the overall result for the year from all activities and in the case of T plc is £177,000. It is **important to shareholders as it represents what they could receive on distribution, *or* what is retained in reserves, adding capital value to their investment.**

(b) **Statement of total recognised gains and losses**

This statement must include all gains and losses generated during the period. It will **include all unrealised gains and losses as well as those realised gains and losses which have already been recognised in the profit and loss account.** For example, the unrealised gain on fixed assets of £120,000 cannot be taken to the profit and loss account until realised, but it can be shown here to give shareholders important information about the state of the business.

Transactions with shareholders (including the payment of dividends) and goodwill write-offs on acquisitions are excluded from this statement.

Reconciliation of movement in shareholders' funds

This reconciliation, as one would expect, reconciles the opening and closing totals of shareholders' funds, ie it shows changes to a company's capital.

It includes, as well as the items in the statement of total recognised gains and losses, other changes in shareholders' funds (eg dividends, new share capital subscribed) which are **important in understanding the change in the financial position of the company over the year** and which are given prominence by this statement.

In the case of T plc, reconciling items include both dividends and shares issued, which have respectively decreased and increased shareholders' funds.

(c) The rules regarding the distributable profits of a Public Limited Company come from the Companies Act 1985. No distribution by a public company may reduce the company's net assets below the value of its called-up share capital and its undistributable reserves. The effect of this is that the amount of distributable profit is **accumulated realised profits less accumulated realised losses less accumulated unrealised losses.**

(d) **Companies Act and other legal restrictions**

Total recognised gains for the year of £297,000 includes £120,000 of unrealised gains arising on fixed assets. **The Companies Act 1985 does not allow unrealised gains to be distributed by way of dividend.** Hence the realised profits for the year available for distribution are only £177,000. The dividend of £40,000 represents a distribution of 22.6% of this figure.

There may also be other legal restrictions because of T plc's status as a public company.

Liquidity

The company may not have enough ready cash to pay the entire profit as a dividend. In any case, **paying a high dividend which leaves the company short of cash may affect its operating ability,** both on a short-term basis (paying current liabilities when due) and in the long term (acquiring assets or new businesses, or repaying debt).

Share price effects

It is recognised as **more appropriate to pay stable, steadily rising dividends**; a company's share price can be adversely affected if dividends rise and fall erratically.

19   WHOLESALING COMPANY

> **Pass marks**. In this question you not only have to know the requirements of FRS 3 but also to understand the rationale behind its introduction.

(a)   **Reasons for FRS 3 disclosures**

FRS 3 represents an attempt by the ASB to improve the quality of financial information provided to shareholders and to restrict the way companies can manipulate figures.

(i)   **Exceptional items**

The required treatment of exceptional items reflects these FRS 3 objectives. Exceptional items must be disclosed separately in order to draw them to the attention of users of the financial statements. Highlighting such transactions gives users a better picture of the company's profitability and progress for the year. FRS 3 also requires that three specific exceptional items should be shown on the face of the profit and loss account:

- profits (losses on sales) termination of an operation
- costs of reorganisation
- profit/loss on sale of fixed assets

(ii)   **Prior period adjustments**

Prior period adjustments were introduced to facilitate consistency in the preparation of financial statements.

If material errors are discovered in the prior year accounts, the comparative figures should be restated in order to restore the validity of the true and fair view. In addition, should a change in accounting policy give rise to financial statements that are inconsistent with those of the previous year, the comparative figures should be restated for the sake of consistency.

(b)   **Directors' decision**

By definition, for this year's losses from fraud to be treated as an exceptional item they must be so material that failure to disclose them would mean that the financial statements no longer gave a true and fair view.

Losses of £25,000 represent 23% of retained profit for the year and are considered material by the auditors. **The directors are therefore correct in treating the losses as an exceptional item.**

Note that even if the losses are not considered sufficiently material to treat as an exceptional item, the directors should disclose them separately by way of a note to the accounts. This is in keeping with the spirit of FRS3, which aims to improve the quality of information provided in the accounts.

Last year's losses of £35,000 are also considered material by the auditors. However, the losses do not represent a fundamental accounting error or a change in accounting policy, and therefore should not be treated as a prior period adjustment. Nonetheless, the directors should disclose the loss on the grounds that a comparative figure for this year's loss should be given.

(c)   **Extraordinary items**

In FRS3 the ASB stresses that extraordinary items are extremely rare. The Chairman of the ASB has suggested by way of example that 'if the Martians landed and destroyed a company's factory, that could be treated as an extraordinary item!' On these grounds, very little can be treated as an extraordinary item.

Because extraordinary items come 'below the line', companies could improve their reported pre-tax profits simply by treating expenses as extraordinary. The rationale behind the ASB's decision to make it difficult to treat an expense as extraordinary therefore centres on the desire to prevent companies from manipulating their results in this way.

(d)   **Role of STRGL**

The statement of total recognised gains and losses is helpful to readers because it **expands the information required in public accounts.** It summarises all gains and losses occurring during the period, both realised and unrealised, and enables the user to consider these when assessing the overall performance of the company. Without the statement the user might not have complete information, as some gains and losses are taken directly to reserves.

The note of historical cost profits and losses applies when the company uses alternative accounting rules as regards revaluation of assets. It clearly illustrates to the user any material deviation between

(i)   The profit figure per the profit and loss account

(ii)   The profit figure that would have arisen had historical costs been used.

This **assists the user in comparing the results of companies which revalue their assets against those of companies which do not.**

20   KING CASH

> **Pass marks**. With this type of question, which is fairly 'open ended', it is important to plan your answer before you start writing, particularly in order to avoid confusing the three parts of the question.

(a)   **Definition of cash**

Cash in hand and deposits repayable on demand with any qualifying financial institution less overdrafts from any qualifying financial institution repayable on demand.

Deposits are repayable on demand if they can be withdrawn at any time without notice and without penalty or if a maturity or period of notice of not more than 24 hours or one working day has been agreed.

Cash includes cash in hand and deposits denominated in foreign currencies.

(b)   **Manipulation**

(i)   **Profit**

Profit for a particular financial period can be manipulated **by means of adjustments made to income and/or expenditure which are perfectly allowable or even required under existing accountancy rules.**

Take, for example, a provision for warranty costs. Prudence requires that such a provision be made for such costs as are likely to arise. However, the accounting

BPP
PROFESSIONAL EDUCATION

bases and estimation techniques used in determining the level of provision needed are very subjective and hence can be used to manipulate profit levels.

(ii) **Non cash assets**

Non-cash asset values can also be manipulated by means of valuation or provisions determined subjectively. Examples of these are provisions for doubtful debts, valuation of work in progress and the estimation of useful lives of fixed assets (and hence the relevant depreciation charge). These valuations or provisions affect the asset in question and also affect profit.

(iii) **Cash manipulation**

There may be some scope to manipulate cash, eg by holding back payments to creditors at the year end to enhance bank balances. However, there is **not the opportunity to use subjective provisions or valuations to amend the amount of cash that a company has.**

The level of cash is an absolute amount supported by evidence from a third party eg bank statements. It does not deteriorate (ie a £10 note is worth £10, not £9) and hence requires no provision to be made against it.

(c) **Focus on cash**

(i) **Role of cash**

Cash indicates the level of *liquidity* of the company at the date of the financial statements. The cash flow statement shows the inflows and outflows of cash over the accounting period. Cash is likely to be generated from the company's operations and some from other sources eg the issue of shares, sales of fixed assets. **Profitable companies may fail because of their failure to generate cash, but companies which do not make profits will cease to make cash and will also fail.**

(ii) **Profit and performance**

The profit that a company generates is a measure of its *performance* over the period from its business activities. This profit is subject to manipulation as discussed above, however it is **an indication of the success or otherwise of the company in the long term.**

(iii) **Cash vs profit**

A company might be performing poorly but be showing good cash balances. This could be done by selling off assets or issuing loans which generate cash without doing anything to improve its trading performance. **Managers who concentrate on increasing cash flows or maintaining positive cash balances may fail in maximising *profits* for shareholders.**

(iv) **Working capital management**

To go further, **companies should not hold large cash balances unless interest rates are high**. Rather, the funds should be invested in assets and working capital, which should be managed to produce a better return (ie profit) than only interest on cash balances. **Good working capital management should ensure enough cash is available to meet day-to-day running expenses** (plus an amount for contingencies perhaps).

Summary

Therefore, it is necessary to use both indicators when looking at financial statements.

Profit should be used to measure performance. Cash is used to indicate a company's liquidity (can it meet its debts as and when they fall due) and also via the cash flow statement to show how cash has been generated through various sources and whether it has been invested or retained.

(d) The profit and loss account shows the amount of profit that has been made during the period and comparison of the opening and closing balance sheet will determine the amount of any increase or decrease in cash in the period.

It is the cash flow statement however which shows users of the financial statements **why** there has been an increase or decrease in cash and this is information that cannot be found elsewhere in the financial statements. The cash flow statements starts with the amount of **cash** that has been **generated from the operations** of the business and then shows the amounts of cash that have been received or paid for interest, tax, capital investment, dividends, short term investments and longer term financing. Under accruals accounting this information cannot be easily determined from the balance sheet and profit and loss account.

This additional information provides users with insights into the **financial adaptability** of the company and can give them an indication of the **future prospects** of the company.

21   M PLC

> **Pass marks**. The examiner commented that the answers to this question were disappointing, as cash flow statements should not present problems at this level. Many answers demonstrated little familiarity with the format of the statement and its disclosures.
>
> This is the sort of question that can provide easy marks if well mastered through constant practice.

BPP
PROFESSIONAL EDUCATION

M PLC

CASH FLOW STATEMENT FOR THE YEAR ENDING 31 MARCH 20X4

Reconciliation of operating profit to net cash inflow from operating activities

	£ million	£ million
Operating profit (W1)		106
Depreciation		42
Loss on sale of fixed assets		8
Increase in stocks (19 - 16)		(3)
Increase in debtors (37 - 30)		(7)
Increase in creditors (9 - 6)		3
Net cash inflow from operating activities		149
Net cash inflow from operating activities		149
Returns on investment and servicing of finance		
Loan interest (15 + 4)	(19)	
Finance lease charges	(3)	
		(22)
Taxation (W2)		(30)
Capital expenditure		
Payments to acquire fixed assets (W3)	(203)	
Proceeds from sale of fixed assets (64 -8)	56	
		(147)
Equity dividends paid (5 + 4)		(9)
Net cash outflow before financing		(59)
Financing		
Issue of shares (300 + 40 - 200 + 10)	130	
Loan repayments (175 - 110)	(65)	
Capital element of finance lease rentals (W4)	(9)	
		56
Decrease in cash		(3)

Reconciliation of net cash flow to movement in net debt (Note)

	£ million	£ million
Decrease in cash	(3)	
Cash outflow from repayment of debt	65	
Cash outflow from repayment of finance leases	9	
Change in net debt		71
New finance leases		(26)
Net debt at 1 April 20X3 (1 + 10 + 175 - 15)		(171)
Net debt at 31 March 20X4 (2 + 26 + 110 - 12)		(126)

Note: Analysis of changes in net debt

	At 1 April 20X3 £ million	Cash flows £ million	Other non-cash changes £ million	At 31 March 20X4 £ million
Cash at bank	15	(3)		12
Loans	(175)	65		(110)
Finance leases	(11)	9	(26)	(28)
	(171)	71	(26)	(126)

Workings

1   *Operating profit*

	£ million
Increase in profit and loss account (39 - 10)	29
Add back: tax charge	48
dividend (4 + 7)	11
interest payable (15 + 3)	18
Operating profit	106

2   *Taxation*

TAXATION ACCOUNT

	£ million		£ million
Cash paid (bal fig)	30	Opening balance current	16
Closing balance current	24	Opening balance deferred	10
Closing balance deferred	20	Profit and loss	48
	74		74

3   *Fixed assets*

FIXED ASSETS AT NBV

	£ million		£ million
Opening balance	462	Depreciation	42
Interest capitalised	4	Disposal	64
Finance lease assets	26		
Revaluation (135 – 80)	55		
Cash paid for additions(bal fig)	203	Closing balance	644
	750		750

4   *Finance leases*

OBLIGATIONS UNDER FINANCE LEASES

	£ million		£ million
Cash paid (bal fig)	9	Opening balance (1 + 10)	11
Closing balance (2 + 26)	28	Fixed assets	26
	37		37

22   T PLC

> **Pass marks**. The examiner commented that this question was popular and was generally answered well. He advised that the key to this kind of question is familiarity with the format and the disclosure requirements, and the best way to achieve this is through practice. Most errors were of detail, for example failure to calculate the amount of tax paid during the year correctly.

(a)   T CASH FLOW STATEMENT FOR THE YEAR ENDED 30 SEPTEMBER 20X1

Reconciliation of operating profit to net cash inflow from operating activities

	£'000	£'000
Operating profit		3,600
Depreciation		2,640
Loss on disposal (2,600 – 900 – 730)		970
Increase in stock (1,600 – 1,100)		(500)
Increase in debtors (1,500 – 800)		(700)
Decrease in creditors (800 – 700)		(100)
Net cash flow from operating activities		5,910

CASH FLOW STATEMENT

Net cash flow from operating activities		5,910
Returns on investment and servicing of finance		
Interest paid		(24)
Taxation		
Tax paid (W1)		(485)
Capital expenditure		
Purchase of fixed assets	(8,000)	
Proceeds of sale of fixed assets	730	
		(7,270)
		(1,869)

Equity dividends paid

Dividend paid (W2)		(1,000)
		(2,869)

Financing

Repayment of loans	(1,200)	
Issue of shares		
(2,500 + 8,334 – 2,000 – 5,815)	3,019	
		1,819
Decrease in cash (1,200 – 150)		(1,050)

Reconciliation of net cash flow to movement in net debt

Decrease in cash in the period	(1,050)	
Cash used to redeem loan	1,200	
Change in net debt		150
Net debt at 1 October 2000 (2,900 – 1,200)		(1,700)
Net debt at 30 September 2001 (1,700 – 150)		(1,550)

Analysis of changes in net debt

	At 1 October 20X0 £'000	Cash flows £'000	At 30 September 20X1 £'000
Cash at bank	1,200	(1,050)	150
Debt	(2,900)	1,200	(1,700)
Total	(1,700)	150	(1,550)

Workings

1   *Tax paid*

Tax

	£'000		£'000
Cash flow (bal fig)	485	Opening balance – current	685
Closing balance - current	1,040	Opening balance - deferred	400
Closing balance - deferred	600	P&L	1,040
	2,125		2,125

2   *Dividend paid*

Dividend

	£'000		£'000
Cash paid (bal fig)	1000	Opening balance	600
Closing balance	700	P&L	1,100
	1,700		1,700

Pass marks. The examiner commented that many candidates made little or no attempt at this part of the question. This could have been because candidates spent too long on part (a) or because they chose the question on the basis of part (a) without appreciating the requirements of part (b).

The only common error was to argue that cash had been mismanaged simply because the balance had declined. The preamble to the question implied that the balance had been reduced by a deliberate policy of the directors.

(b)   At the end of last year T plc did have a large cash balance. The main elements of T plc's cash management this year have been to use that cash to repay some of the outstanding loans. However, due to a huge investment in fixed assets the company has had to raise funds by a share issue.

It could be argued that equity funds are more expensive than loan capital and therefore the loan should not have been repaid simply to be replaced by additional equity funds. However if the loan was due for repayment during the year the company would have had no choice, although a further loan could have been taken out to replace it.

T plc has also chosen to pay an interim dividend of £400,000 as well as the non-discretionary payments of tax and interest.

(c)

		20X1	20X0

$$\text{Gearing ratio} = \frac{\text{Long term loans}}{\text{Shareholders' funds} + \text{long term loans}} \qquad \frac{1,700 + 600}{18,970} = 12\% \qquad \frac{2,900 + 400}{15,515} = 21\%$$

The argument for including the deferred tax balance as part of long term loans is that technically the deferred tax balance represents additional corporation tax that is **due to be paid** in future as a result of originating timing differences such as capital allowances exceeding depreciation charges. However it can also be argued that in a **going concern** business the deferred tax balance will always remain as the company constantly replaces its fixed assets and therefore the likelihood of eventual repayment of the tax balance is small.

It can also be argued that deferred tax is very different in nature to other forms of long-term capital. Deferred tax is a long term creditor balance but unlike loans, debentures or preference shares it is not a conscious element of the **financing** of the business.

The gearing ratio is an indicator to users of the financial statements of the level of **risk** of a business. This includes the risk of the company not being able to service its finance by paying interest on its loans and replacing the loans with other finance when the term of the loan is over. These are not problems that have to be faced with deferred tax as there is no interest to be paid and the balance does not have to be replaced with a substitute at any time in the future.

23 CASH FLOW ISSUES

(a) (i) **Methods of arriving at net cash flow from operating activities**

- The **direct method** lists and totals the **actual operating cash flows** of an entity: cash received from customers less cash paid to suppliers and cash paid to and on behalf of employees.

- The **indirect method adjusts operating profit for non-cash items** such as depreciation, and movements in working capital (normally stocks, debtors and creditors). These adjustments are shown in the note reconciling operating profit to net cash flow from operating activities, as required by FRS 1.

(ii) **Why FRS 1 requires the indirect method**

The reconciliation note helps users of the financial statements to understand the **difference between profit and cash flow**. It also shows the movements on the individual items within working capital. This enables users to see **how successful or otherwise the entity has been in managing stocks, debtors and creditors in order to generate cash**. For example, it may highlight a situation where an increase in trade debtors has turned a high operating profit into a net outflow of cash. This information is important, because it can **alert users to potential liquidity problems.**

However, the direct method can also provide useful information. By showing the actual cash flows it **enables users to see how the company generates and uses cash in its operations**. The disadvantage of the direct method is that for many entities the practical problems of providing the information outweigh the benefits to users. For this reason its use is optional.

(b) (i)   **Benefits of eliminating impact of accruals basis of accounting**

- The effects of **provisions** are **excluded**.

- It may be easier to **compare** the cash flows of **different companies** instead of profits. This avoids the impact of different **accounting policies** and **estimation techniques,** but not the implications of different **business practices** eg one hotel may employ its own in-house cleaners whereas another hotel may contract out its cleaning tasks. This may be useful information to management in making effective operating decisions.

- A review of the cash flow statement can give an idea of **where the money is coming from**. Is the company generating enough cash from **operating activities**? Or does the company have to rely on **borrowings** and **sales of fixed assets**?

- Cash flow statements **avoid** the consequences of **revaluations** of fixed assets.

- Cash flow statements provide information that helps in the assessment of **liquidity, solvency** and **financial adaptability**.

- Eliminating the impact of accruals highlights the role of cash. The **survival** of a business depends on its **ability to generate cash** to meet its liabilities.

(ii)   **Potential for window dressing**

Cash flow statements can themselves be susceptible to **window dressing/manipulation**.

- **Holding back** on **payments** to make the cash flow look better.

- **Selling off assets, borrowing** more money or **issuing new shares** can be used to cover for lack of cash flow from operations.

- Making a **special effort** to **collect debtors** before the period end.

- **Transactions** themselves can be arranged in a **cash flow advantageous manner** eg lease or hire an asset to spread payments rather than one-off acquisitions.

Because of the above, it may be helpful to **review** the **cash flow** from the **various sources against** the **liabilities** shown in the **balance sheet**. For example, is the level of cash flow from operations adequate to cover current liabilities?

(c) **Business management implications**

Cash flow statements and a proper understanding of the cash flows of a business can play a key role in the effective management of a business.

- Cash management is an important part of **business survival**. A business can be profitable but will hit trouble if it lacks **cash to pay its debts**.

- Cash flow statements could deliver more accurate **messages to shareholders and employees**. There may be profits but perhaps not the cash for high dividends or optimistic wage claims. Stakeholders expectations can therefore be managed better.

- Cautious focus on cash may lead businesses to be **commercially risk averse** and **not maximise profitability**.

- **Idle cash** is unlikely to provide as profitable returns as compared to those that can be earned on good commercial activities or projects.

- Acquisitions of **fixed assets** may adversely affect cash flow, but are nevertheless **important for long term growth** of a business.

- Profit is good measure of commercial performance whereas cash provides information on financial adaptability and liquidity. **In the long-term, positive cash flow will depend on the business being profitable.**

(d) **Usefulness to readers**

Net debt is made up of the **borrowings** of the company, less **cash** and **liquid resources**. The net debt or net funds shows the overall **liquidity** of the company which is not a figure that is shown anywhere else in the financial statements.

- The reconciliation of net cash flow to movement in net debt shows not only the overall net debts/funds position but also how that position has been arrived at by bringing together changes in borrowings, investment or disinvestment in liquid resources and increases or decreases in cash.

- This adds to the information available to the users of the financial statements in assessing the **financial position and adaptability** of the company.

ACCOUNTING STANDARDS

OBJECTIVE TEST ANSWERS: ACCOUNTING STANDARDS

1   D

2   D

3   D

4   The correct answer is A.

Profit and loss account credit	=	(£800,000 × 15%)/5 years
	=	£24,000
Balance on deferred income	=	£120,000 - (2 × £24,000)
	=	£72,000

5   D

6   D

7   C   Purchased goodwill should not be revalued upwards.

Internally generated goodwill should not be recognised in the financial statements.

8   A

9   C

10   A

11   A

12   C   1   Production overheads should be included in cost on the basis of normal budgeted activity level

2   The net realisable value is after deducting trade discounts but not settlement discounts

4   Production overheads should be included in cost.

13   B   A   As in question
B   As in question, but costs 300/400 × £290,000 = £217,500
C   As in question
D   As in question but costs as in B.

14   A

15   A

16   C   1   This is a description of the partial provision method whereas FRS 19 requires full provision for deferred tax

2   FRS allows discounting but does not require it.

17   A

			£	
18	A		400,000	
		£300,000 × 20%	60,000	loss
			340,000	
		(£200,000 − £80,000) × 20%	24,000	depreciation/CAs
			364,000	
	B		400,000	
			300,000	loss
			100,000	
			120,000	depreciation/CAs
			220,000	
	C		400,000	
		(£200,000 − £80,000) × 20%	24,000	
			424,000	

19 A
  A $^3/_{10}$ × £3,000
  B $^2/_{10}$ × £3,000
  C $^2/_6$ × £3,000
  D $^1/_4$ × £3,000

20 D
  A $^1/_4$ × £3,000
  B $^1/_6$ × £3,000
  C $^3/_{10}$ × £3,000
  D $^2/_6$ × £3,000

21 B   2 is the only one providing evidence that the risks and rewards of ownership are passed to the dealer.

22 D

23 B

24 D

25 B

26 A

27 C

28 The correct answer is C.

The possibility of case (i) being lost is remote, therefore it does not need to be disclosed. Case (ii) is possible though not probable (it is less than 50% probable), therefore disclose in the financial statements.

29 B
  A   20% × £4.8m
  B   20% × (£0.36m + £0.8m + £0.4m)
  C   £0.36 + (20% × [£0.8m + £0.4m])
  D   –

30 C

31 C

32 C
  A   £500,000 + £1,000
  B   £500,000 + £6,000
  C   £500,000 + £11,000

33 A

34   A

35   D   2   Private companies (but not public companies) can use a share premium account in purchasing or redeeming their own shares out of capital.

36   D   A   As D but with premium £50,000 charged against share premium account

        B   As D but with £8,000 of premium (premium on original issue) charged against share premium account.

        C   £160,000 less £30,000 (purchase price £90,000 less share premium account £60,000)

        D   £160,000 minus premium £50,000 minus CRR transfer (nominal value of share redeemed) £40,000

37   B   A   –

        B   £100,000 purchase price minus £80,000 profit and loss account

        C   £80,000 profit and loss account minus £50,000 premium on purchase

        D   Amount of premium on purchase

38   C

39   A   A   £500,000 – 360,000 = £140,000

        B   £500,000 – £300,000 = £200,000

        C   £500,000 – shares purchased in full

        D   –

40   C   2   A person exercising control over 20% of the company's voting rights is presumed to be a related party

        5&6   FRS 8 makes it clear that providers of finance and customers/suppliers are not related parties.

24   PREPARATION QUESTION: HENHAO

(a)   £

Land and buildings
At cost 31.12.X0 (Note 10)   100,000

Land and buildings
Accumulated depreciation at 1.1.X0   9,000
Depreciation charge for the year   1,000
Accumulated depreciation at 31.12.X0   10,000

Note 10: Land and buildings

The market value of the land and buildings is £1,500,000.

(b)   **Note to the directors**

It is usual to depreciate buildings, but not land. This is because land is regarded as having an unlimited life except in certain circumstances, for example where minerals are being extracted.

Buildings, however, have a limited life, the life of this building being estimated at 50 years. Accordingly it is appropriate to split the total cost of £100,000 between land and buildings and calculate depreciation on the cost of the building.

You may wonder why the buildings need to be depreciated when their market value far exceeds their book value. It must be emphasised that **the purpose of depreciation is to match the cost of the buildings against the benefits generated by them over their finite useful life**.

If the market value exceeds cost as in this case, it is permissible to record the market value of the property in the balance sheet and use this higher value to calculate depreciation. However, this is not required under the historical cost convention.

(c)   **Investment properties**

(i)   SSAP 19 distinguishes between investment properties and other fixed assets, including non-investment properties.

(ii)   Investment properties are held 'not for consumption in the business operations but as investments, the disposal of which would not materially affect any manufacturing or trading operations of the enterprise'.

(iii) **Matters of prime importance are therefore the current value of the investment properties and changes in their current value**, rather than a calculation of systematic annual depreciation.

25   T PLC II

> **Pass marks**. This question is based on FRS 15 but also requires some knowledge of SSAP 19. Part (b) is a standard external audit question.

(a)   **Impact of revaluation on depreciation charge**

(i)   Original depreciation charge (800 + 700 + 1,000) @ 2% =   £50,000

       Hotel A $\dfrac{1,300,000}{50}$ =   £26,000

       Hotel B $\dfrac{850,000}{30}$ =   £28,333

Hotel C $\dfrac{650,000}{40}$ £16,250

£70,583

There is therefore an increase in annual depreciation of £20,583 due to the revaluation.

NB. Hotel C has been revalued to an amount lower than NBV

	£'000
∴ NBV (1,000 – 140)	860,000
Revalued amount	650,000
Amount written off to P&L	210,000

(ii) **Revaluation reserve**

	£'000
Hotel A (1,300 – (800 – 180)) =	680
Hotel B (850 – (700 – 120)) =	270
Increase in the revaluation reserve	950

(iii) **Hotel depreciation policy**

The hotels are used on a **continuous basis** as **business assets**. This means that they are fixed assets as defined in FRS 15 and that they cannot be investment properties as defined by SSAP 19.

SSAP 19 defines a **business property** as an **interest in land or buildings** in respect of which all **construction work** has been **completed** and which is **held** for its **investment potential**. Any rental income received must be at arms length. The hotels are primarily being used by T plc to generate income. Sale of a hotel diminishes the trading income of the company.

FRS 15 states that **depreciation** must be charged on **fixed assets**. Depreciation represents the **use over time of an asset**, it is therefore matching the use of the asset with the revenue it generates.

In the case of the hotels, the directors have decided on a useful economic life of fifty years. The cost of the hotels is spread over this time. The fact that the **hotels may appreciate** in value is a **separate matter. The NBV of an asset does not need to equate to its market value.**

The directors **may adopt** a **policy of revaluing the properties** on a **regular basis** if they would like the balance sheet values to mirror market value. Where this policy is adopted, it must be **applied consistently** to **all assets** of the **same class**. However, they should **not avoid charging depreciation**.

FRS 11 states that a **review for impairment** of fixed assets should be done if changes in circumstances indicate that the carrying amount of a fixed asset may not be recoverable. **If T plc did not charge depreciation they would be required to conduct an impairment review instead.** This might produce the same overall impact as charging depreciation except there may be large expenses in the profit and loss in one year and none the next.

(iv) **Treatment of proposed repairs/refurbishment**

In terms of FRS 15, subsequent expenditure on tangible fixed assets should only be capitalised in three specific circumstances. The circumstance relevant to T plc is whether the expenditure enhances the economic benefits above previously assessed standards of performance.

The proposed programme of repairs and refurbishment is unlikely to be eligible for capitalisation as it does not appear that the work will enhance the existing assets or prolong their useful lives.

FRS 15 suggests that repairs are necessary to prevent the properties falling in value and to allow them to achieve their useful economic lives. This expenditure should be written off through the profit and loss account as its is incurred. This closely follows the rationale behind depreciation; the cost of the asset is matched to the revenue generated.

Replacement of existing furniture

The refurbishment involves the replacement of existing furniture. This may be capitalised under fixtures and fittings as long as the existing furniture is written off.

Decoration

The decoration may not be capitalised as it is again part of the upkeep of the building.

(b) (i) **External auditors' responsibilities**

The external auditors' responsibilities with respect to the financial statements are concerned with **reporting** to the **shareholders** on whether in their opinion:

(1) The balance sheet and profit and loss account give a **true and fair** view

(2) The financial statements have been **properly prepared** in accordance with relevant accounting standards and companies legislation.

However, it is the **directors** who are **responsible** for the **preparation** of the accounts and ensuring that these show a true and fair view. An **external audit** does **relieve** the directors of their responsibilities.

In addition to expressing an opinion, the auditor is required to **report**, inter alia, **by exception** on:

- The maintenance of proper accounting records by the company

- Adequacy of returns received from branches not visited

- Agreement of the accounts with accounting records

- Receipt of all necessary information and explanations

- Consistency of information shown in the Directors' Report with the accounts.

There is an '**expectation gap**' regarding the role of the external auditor regarding the **prevention** and **detection** of fraud. This is not a primary objective of an external audit. However, **true and fair accounts should not include material misstatement.** External auditors are therefore interested in any fraud or defalcations if they are material to the true and fair view given by the accounts.

(ii) **Unqualified audit report**

If the auditors' work leads them to conclude that the financial statements are free from material error or misstatement and that they give a true and fair view of the financial affairs of the company then they will issue an unqualified opinion.

This opinion covers the profit and loss account, the balance sheet, the statement of recognised gains and losses and the notes to the accounts. By convention the opinion usually covers the cashflow statement as well.

The directors report is also reviewed to ensure that this does not contain information which is materially misleading or which conflicts with elements of the financial statements.

The auditors' report is the statement of their opinion on these elements of the financial statements. They state explicitly that the balance sheet reflects the state of the company's affairs at the year end and that the profit and loss account gives the company's profit or loss for the year.

The report also covers a number of other elements, such as the fact that proper accounting records were kept, by exception.

Qualified audit report

A qualified report contains a qualified opinion because the auditors are concerned that the financial statements do not give a true and fair view. This may occur due to disagreement or uncertainty.

Disagreement occurs when the auditors form an opinion which conflicts with the view given by the financial statements.

Uncertainty arises when there is a limitation in scope and the auditors are unable to form an opinion.

The extent of the qualification is determined by whether the disagreement or uncertainty is **material** or **fundamental**.

When the auditors issue a qualified report it must contain a **full explanation** of the **reasons** for the qualification and, where possible, a **quantification** of the **effects** on the financial statements. This means that a qualified report will contain at least **one more paragraph** than an unqualified report.

The qualified report should leave the **reader** in **no doubt** as to its **meaning** and the **implications** it has on an **understanding** of the financial statements.

26   B PLC

> **Pass marks**. The calculations in this question are very straightforward but note that 19 marks are allocated to discussion.
>
> The examiner commented that each part of this question required a very specific response. 'It is very unusual for questions to test detailed knowledge of the requirements of an FRS and this is no exception. It is better to spend some time reading the question carefully and writing a few short paragraphs about each part than to reproduce from memory a page or more out of study materials.'
>
> The examiner also commented that 'it is often worth looking at the whole question before answering any of it. Thinking about one part will often provide clues and ideas that can help with other parts. For example, part (b) deals with accounting choice (between valuation at cost less depreciation or at market value) while part (d) deals with the impact of that choice on the interpretation of the resulting financial statements'.

(a)   **Relevant classes approach**

FRS 15 allows a **choice** as to whether fixed assets are **revalued or not**. If a company chooses to revalue its fixed assets then the **objective** is to **reflect current values** at the **balance sheet date**.

It should be remembered that one of the principles set out in the Statement of Principles and **FRS 18** is that information should be presented in the financial statements on a **consistent basis**.

If a company chooses to revalue some of its fixed assets then in the name of consistency **FRS 15** states that this **policy** must be **applied consistently** to all fixed assets in that class. This **prevents** company directors from 'cherry picking' the assets that they revalue in order to show the company in its best light. For example the directors might choose only to revalue assets that were to be revalued upwards and not those that were revalued downwards in order to boost the balance sheet.

Up-to-date requirement

Where a tangible fixed asset is revalued, its carrying amount should be its current value at the balance sheet date. For this reason **FRS 15 requires** the **valuations** to be **kept up to date**.

This does not mean an annual full valuation. The ASB has attempted to balance the benefits to users of up to date and reliable current values with the cost to preparers of obtaining annual full valuations. Therefore to show reliable current values FRS 15 requires:

- full valuation at least **every five years**

- an **interim valuation in year 3**

- an **interim valuation** in intervening years if it is likely that there has been a **material change** in value

(b) **Logic relating to option to revalue**

The logic behind the decision to allow companies a choice between revaluing its fixed assets or not is that the FRS is codifying current practice whereby valuation of fixed assets is optional. The ASB is leaving it to **individual preparers** of financial statements to **weigh up the costs and benefits** of revaluing or not.

Although there has been a move against allowing choices of accounting treatment in financial statements the ASB has decided to allow a choice for this major and fairly costly exercise of valuations.

FRS 15 addresses this freedom of choice to ensure **consistency** and **comparability** between companies which do revalue and those that do not by ensuring that there is **full disclosure** of the revaluations.

FRS 3 also requires a note of **historical cost profits and losses** which reconciles the reported profit to the profit that would have been earned if there were no revaluation. This again **improves** the **comparability** of companies who choose to revalue and those who do not.

(c) In the balance sheet the land and buildings would appear as

	£m
Factory A	160
Factory B	120
Factory C	40
	320

	£m
Factory A	
Cost	250
Depreciation	(70)
Net book value	180
Valuation	160
Loss on revaluation	20

As this loss is below the depreciated historical cost of the factory, this must be taken to the profit and loss account.

Factory B	£m
Cost	150
Depreciation	(60)
Net book value	90
Valuation	120
Gain on revaluation	30

This gain would be taken to the revaluation reserve and would appear in the statement of total recognised gains and losses.

Factory C	£m
Cost	134
Depreciation	(48)
Net book value	86
Valuation	40
Loss on revaluation	46

As this loss is due to a consumption of economic benefits, it should be shown in the profit and loss account.

(d) **Impact of revaluation of fixed assets**

The three main accounting ratios that will be affected by a revaluation of fixed assets are:

- Return on capital employed
- Gross profit on sales
- The gearing ratio

(i) **Return on capital employed**

Return on capital employed is calculated as the percentage of net profit to capital employed, or the total of the fixed assets and net current assets.

If fixed assets are revalued then the depreciation that is charged on these assets must be based upon the revalued amount. The figure for **fixed assets** will **increase** but so will the **future depreciation charge**. Therefore **profit** will be **lower** and **capital employed higher**, causing a **fall** in the **return** on **capital employed**. This may make the **business appear** to be **less efficient**.

However, in B plc's case, the net revaluation is a downwards revaluation meaning that depreciation will be lower in future and therefore profits higher. With capital employed also being lower due to the net downwards revaluation this will cause an increase in return on capital employed.

(ii) **Gross profit on sales**

Higher depreciation is likely to have the **knock-on impact** of reducing most of the profit-based ratios.

- gross profit on sales
- net profit on sales

However for B plc the lower depreciation charge will have the opposite effect.

(iii) **Gearing ratio**

The gearing ratio is the ratio of the long term loans to the shareholders funds plus long term loans, which is equivalent to fixed assets plus net current assets. If fixed assets are revalued upwards, then **shareholders funds plus loans** will **increase**, and in consequence the **gearing ratio will fall**. This will make the business appear **more stable** and **less volatile**.

On the other hand, with a downward revaluation, the value of the shareholders funds plus long term loans falls and the gearing ratio will thereby increase.

(iv) **Interpretation of changes**

If B plc does revalue its land and buildings, its return on capital employed should increase and its gearing ratio will also increase, and therefore the company may appear stronger due to the increased return on capital employed, although the increased gearing may worry some shareholders.

A further argument however, is that the **shareholders** will have **enough information** from the financial statements and the notes regarding the revaluation that they will be able to recognise that any increase or decrease in ratios is only due to the accounting policy of revaluation and therefore that the company is in fact neither stronger or weaker.

> **Pass marks**. The most common errors identified in answers were these:
> - Candidates failed to answer the question, which wasted time and generated few marks. For example, many answers to part (a) consisted of a summary of the requirements of FRS 15, rather than the explanation that was actually sought.
> - Answers to part (d) were often weak because they did not identify any ratios, merely talking about how revaluation might affect profit and balance sheet figures. Others dealt with ratios that would be barely affected, if at all, by the revaluation of fixed assets.

27 S LTD

> **Pass marks**. In part (c) you should have based your overhead valuations on normal production rather than actual production. In part (d) you should not simply apply the 'lower of cost and NRV' rule inflexibly; there is considerable evidence to suggest that the new product will be sold at a profit.

(a) SSAP 9 states that stocks should be valued at the lower of cost and net realisable value. This means that if a loss is foreseen, it is recognised immediately by writing down the stock value to net realisable value.

(b) (i) **Delivery and insurance**

SSAP 9 defines cost of purchase as comprising 'purchase price including import duties, transport and handling costs and any other directly attributable costs ...'.

Delivery costs and insurance may therefore be included **in the valuation of raw materials**. However, for consistency and comparability there should be a restatement of the opening stock.

(ii) **Prior period adjustment**

There should be a **prior period adjustment** to incorporate a **relevant proportion** of the 20X0/X1 costs in the raw material stock at 31 March 20X1.

Delivery and insurance costs incurred in the year to 31 March 20X2 should be included in the cost of purchases with the **relevant proportion** being **carried forward in year-end raw material stock**.

In the absence of such a prior period adjustment, the value of closing stock would be inflated relative to that of opening stock, thus artificially increasing the profit figure for the year.

(c) (i) **Overheads**

SSAP 9 states that 'in order to **match costs and revenues,** 'costs' of stocks should comprise that expenditure which has been incurred in the **normal course of business** in bringing the product or service to its **present location and condition**. Such costs will include all related production overheads ...'

Production overheads are defined as 'overheads incurred in respect of materials, labour or services for production, based on the **normal level of activity**, taking one year with another. For this purpose each overhead should be classified according to function so as to ensure the inclusion, in cost of conversion, of those overheads which relate to production ...'.

It follows that all **abnormal overheads** should be **excluded** from **stock valuation.**

(ii) **Value of overheads**

SSAP 9 states that the **allocation of overheads** should be **based on** the company's **normal level of activity**. All production overheads should be included whether fixed or variable, and should be allocated on the basis of normal production hours of 95,000.

	£
Rent, rates and insurance	150,000
Security	110,000
Light, heat and power	300,000
Depreciation of machinery	200,000
	760,000
Number of hours	95,000

Rate per hour $= \dfrac{760,000}{95,000} = £8$

Hours worked $= 500$

∴ Overhead absorption $£500 \times 8 = £4,000$

(d) (i) **Item by item: cost vs NRV**

SSAP 9 requires that the **valuation of closing stocks** at the **lower of cost and net realisable value should** be carried out on an **item by item basis**. **Comparison** of total realisable value of stocks with total cost could result in the **set-off** of **foreseeable losses** against **unrealised profits**.

(ii) **Obsolete stocks and new products**

The aggregate net realisable value of closing stock is irrelevant for the reasons stated in (c)(i) above.

Obsolete stocks should be written down to their scrap value of £500 as this is their net realisable value.

The **new product** is expected to realise more than cost and so should be included at cost of £90,000. If the product launch fails this will be an event of 20X2/X3 and the write down to scrap value would occur in that year. (Disclosure as an exceptional item may be appropriate.)

The need to disclose the possibility of a loss on this product in a contingency note in the 31 March 20X2 accounts should be considered. However, this is probably not necessary because of the positive findings from the market research carried out.

(e) **Effect of an unsuccessful launch**

This would be an adjusting post balance sheet event, according to SSAP 17, and the stocks of the new product should be written down to £1,000 as at 31 March 20X2. Reported profit for the year would be reduced by £89,000.

28   C PLC

(a)

	Maryhill bypass	Rottenrow centre
	£'000	£'000
Turnover	2,800	3,000
Profit/(Loss) (W)	622	(100)
Cost of sales	2,178	3,100
Current assets		
Amount recoverable on contract (2,800 – 2,600)	200	-
Current liabilities		
Payment on account (3,400 – 3,000)	-	(400)
Accrued cost of sales (2,178 – 1,400)	(778)	-
Accrued future losses (3,100 – 2,900)	-	(200)

Working

Maryhill: $[(9,000 - (1,400 + 5,600)] \times \dfrac{2,800}{9,000} = 622$

Rottenrow: $8,000 - (2,900 + 5,200) = (100)$

(b) **Accounting approach for long term contracts**

Long term contracts are recognised as such when the contract activity spans more than one accounting period. If they were not treated according to SSAP 9, then the costs incurred during the early years of the contract would be recognised but with no corresponding turnover. This would mean reporting several years of losses then one year of high profits regardless of how profitable the contract really was. The advantage of this approach however is that there would be no need to use estimates and forecasts.

The approach outlined in SSAP 9 is to take credit for ascertainable turnover and profit during the course of the project.

Turnover should be determined in a manner appropriate to the stage of completion. Where the outcome of the project can be assessed with **reasonable certainty**, the attributable profit should be calculated on a **prudent basis** and included in the accounts for the period under review.

Costs incurred with that **stage of completion** are matched with turnover, and hence the reported results can be attributed to the **percentage of work completed**.

This approach gives a fairer and more **relevant** representation of the underlying **financial substance** of the transaction and makes it easier for the user of the accounts to **assess** the **financial position** of the company.

(c) **Note to the commercial director**

The loss on the Rottenrow Centre has been determined based upon the current agreed contract price of £8 million. Although we are currently in negotiations with the customer to increase the price to £10 million as these negotiations have not yet been successfully completed then it would not be **prudent** to base the accounting for the Rottenrow Centre on this higher price of £10 million.

It could be argued that the additional £2 million is a **contingent asset.** FRS 12 defines a contingent asset as 'a possible asset that arises from past events and whose existence will be confirmed only by the occurrence of one or more uncertain future events' ie the negotiations. However, this does not affect the accounting treatment of the contract. Contingent assets should **never be recognised** in the financial statements but if they are **probable** they should be disclosed. In this case the lawyer's views should be taken into account and if they believe that the extra £2 million will probably be received from the customer then the details should be disclosed in a note to the financial statements.

29   QUAN PLC

> **Pass marks**. This question was designed to test understanding of an important SSAP, its relationship to accounting concepts and also to other standards. It was also intended to make you think about the approach which should be taken to the accounting treatment of stock and long term contracts in the answer to part (b).
>
> A good answer would demonstrate that you had thought about the logic behind the standards. That is important because, at least in theory, the spirit underlying the standard is more important than the letter of the rules. Furthermore, it is very difficult to apply the rules of an accounting standard to any kind of scenario or case without first understanding the logic behind the rules.
>
> In part (i), it is important to make the point that the element of subjectivity means that there will always be some level of inconsistency between companies' manner of recognising profits on partly completed contracts. In part (ii), the key is to focus on the issue of prudence.

(a)   (i)   **Inconsistency between companies**

Some businesses by their very nature frequently enter into long-term contracts, ie contracts that span more than one accounting period. The most obvious example is the building industry.

If the normal rules of not recognising profits until the completion of a contract were adhered to, the profit and loss account would not give a true and fair view of the organisation's financial activities during the accounting period. **Recording all of the profit in one accounting period would give a misleading impression of performance that year.**

SSAP 9 is based on the premise that it is fairer to recognise turnover and profit throughout the duration of the contract.

One of the reasons SSAP 9 was introduced was to promote consistency between companies accounting for long-term contracts. It does this by setting out guidelines for financial directors in apportioning profit and turnover between accounting periods. However, some might argue that it does not go far enough because an element of choice is given in the calculation of estimated turnover and attributable profit. **Different companies use different methods to determine the degree of completion of a contract, hence there is still some scope for manipulation of reported results.**

SSAP 9 attempts to address some of these problems by emphasising the need for disclosure of methods chosen.

However, regardless of the issue of choice, there is always going to be **an element of subjectivity involved** in estimating figures for inclusion in the accounts. Because of this, there will always be some level of inconsistency between companies in the manner in which they recognise profits on partly completed long-term contracts.

(ii)   **Additional costs**

Although the company has incurred additional costs of £800,000 and is hoping to recover them by raising the contract price accordingly, it is by no means certain that the lawyers will be successful in making the customer pay the higher price.

It would therefore be imprudent to assume that the contract price will be £4.8m rather than the original figure of £4m. For accounting purposes, FRS 18 and SSAP 9 dictate that a contract price of £4m only should be assumed. Per the provisions of FRS 12, the contingent gain of £0.8m should only be disclosed if it is a probable cash inflow.

(b)

> **Pass marks**. It is essential that you set your workings out clearly and legibly. All notes to the accounts should be referenced in to the face of the financial statements.
>
> This question is designed to provide a relatively simple trial balance and the rigour comes from the fact that the company had some reasonably complex adjustments in respect of its long-term contracts.

QUAN PLC
PROFIT AND LOSS ACCOUNT FOR THE YEAR ENDED 30 SEPTEMBER 20X8

	Notes	£'000
Turnover		19,000
Cost of sales		(12,080)
Gross profit		6,920
Distribution costs		(1,400)
Administrative expenses		(2,200)
Operating profit		3,320
Income from investments		480
Profit on ordinary activities before taxation		3,800
Taxation	1	(1,240)
Profit on ordinary activities after taxation		2,560
Dividends	2	(1,900)
Retained profit for the year		660
Retained profit brought forward		2,900
Retained profit carried forward		3,560

QUAN PLC
BALANCE SHEET AT 30 SEPTEMBER 20X8

	Notes	£'000	£'000
Fixed assets			
Tangible fixed assets	3		6,200
Investments			2,500
			8,700
Current assets			
Stock	4	680	
Debtors	5	1,660	
Bank		40	
		2,380	
Creditors: amounts falling due within one year	6	(2,020)	
Net current assets			360
			9,060
Share capital and reserves			
Called up share capital			5,500
Profit and loss account			3,560
			9,060

QUAN PLC
NOTES TO THE FINANCIAL STATEMENTS

	£'000
1 *Taxation*	
UK corporation tax for the year	740
Under-provision from prior year	500
	1,240
2 *Dividends*	
Interim paid	1,200
Final proposed	700
	1,900
3 *Tangible fixed assets*	
Cost	7,500
Depreciation	(1,300)
Net book value	6,200
4 *Stock*	
Long-term contract balances (W)	120
Finished goods	560
	680
5 *Debtors*	
Trade debtors	1,160
Amounts receivable on contracts (200 + 300)	500
	1,660
6 *Creditors due within one year*	
Trade creditors	380
Accrual for foreseeable loss	200
Taxation	740
Proposed dividend	700
	2,020

Workings

	£'000
Contract A	
Total contract value	5,000
Costs to date	(1,200)
Costs to complete	(1,500)
Total estimated profit	2,300
Turnover for the year	2,000
Profit for the year (2,300 × 2,000/5,000)	920
Cost of sales	1,080
Contract B	
Total contract value	4,000
Costs to date	(3,100)
Costs to complete	(1,200)
Total estimated loss	(300)
Turnover for the year	3,000
Total loss on contract	300
Cost of sales	3,300
Provision for foreseeable loss	
Cost of sales	3,300
Costs incurred to date	(3,100)
Accrual	200

	£'000
Turnover	
Per TB	14,000
Contract A	2,000
Contract B	3,000
	19,000
Cost of sales	
Per TB	7,700
Contract A	1,080
Contract B	3,300
	12,080
Stock	
Per TB	560
Long-term contract balance (1,200 – 1,080)	120
	680

30   S PLC 1

(a)   PROFIT AND LOSS ACCOUNT
      FOR THE YEAR ENDING 30 SEPTEMBER 20X3

	£'000
Turnover (W5)	3,000
Cost of sales (W5)	(3,076)
Gross loss (W5)	(76)

BALANCE SHEET AS AT 30 SEPTEMBER 20X3

	£'000
Work in progress (W2)	119
Amounts recoverable on contracts (W2)	150
Provision for foreseeable losses (W4)	650

Workings

1   *Deep-sea fishing-boat contract*

	Year to 30.9.X2	Cumulative two years to 30.9.X3	Year to 30.9.X3
	£'000	£'000	£'000
Total of contract turnover	3,000	3,000	
Cost incurred			
– year to 30.9.X2	(650)	(650)	
– year to 30.9.X3	-	(580)	
Estimated costs to complete	(1,300)	(790)	
Overall contract profit	1,050	980	
Percentage completed			
– year to 30.9.X2	30%	-	
– years 30.9.X2 to 30.9.X3 (30% + 25%)	–	55%	
∴Attributable profit	315	539	224
Turnover for year			
3,000 × 30%	900	-	-
3,000 × 55%	-	1,650	-
Balancing 25%	-	-	750
Cost of sales (balancing figure)	585		526
Profit for year, as above	315	539	224
			(W4)

2   *Deep-sea fishing boat ledger account*

CONTRACT COSTS ACCOUNT

		£'000			£'000
30.9.X2	Costs incurred	650	30.9.X2	Cost of sales	585
			30.9.X2	Balance c/d	65
		650			650
1.10.X2	Balance b/d	65	30.9.X3	Cost of sales	526
30.9.X3	Costs incurred	580	30.9.X3	Balance c/d	119
		645			645
1.10.X3	Balance b/d	119			

CONTRACT DEBTORS

		£'000			£'000
30.9.X2	Invoiced	900	30.9.X2	Cash received	800
			30.9.X2	Balance c/d	100
		900			900
1.10.X2	Balance b/d	100	30.9.X3	Cash received	700
230.9.X3	Invoiced	750	30.9.X3	Balance c/d	150
		850			850
1.10.X3	Balance b/d	150			

3   *Small passenger ferry contract*

	£000
Contract price	5,000
Costs to date	(1,900)
Estimated future costs	(3,400)
Foreseeable loss	(300)
Turnover (5,000 × 45%)	2,250
Cost of sales (bal fig)	2,550
Foreseeable loss	(300) (W5)

4

	£'000
Provision for future losses (2,550 – 1,900) (W3)	650

5   *Summary*

	Fishing boat	Passenger ferry	Total
Year ending 30.9.X3	£'000	£'000	£'000
Turnover	750 (W1)	2,250 (W3)	3,000 ★
Cost of sales	(526)(W1)	(2,550)(W3)	(3,076)
Profit ★	224	300	(76)

★   This figure is coincidently the same as the contract price for the deep sea fishing boat – do not let it confuse you.

(b) **SOP perspective on foreseeable losses**

(i)   *Technical position*

SSAP 9 requires a **foreseeable loss** on a **long-term contract** to be **recognised immediately** in the **profit and loss account**. According to the **Statement of Principles** a loss is effectively an **increase in a liability**. So we must apply this to foreseeable losses on long term contracts.

(ii)   *Obligation arising*

The **loss** that is to be incurred is **caused** by the **costs** of the contract **exceeding** the contract **price**. A **liability** must firstly be an **obligation** to **transfer economic benefits**. It would be highly unlikely that a business involved in a long-term contract could simply walk away from it at the point when the loss was recognised. The **contract must** be **completed** and **therefore** the company has an **obligation** to continue **incurring the costs involved in this contract**.

(iii) *Past actions or events*

A liability must also be as a result of **past actions or events**. It can be argued that although the foreseeable loss is caused by **future expected costs** that the costs already incurred are those that have caused the loss. As such the **costs** that are **to be incurred** which will **give rise to the loss** can be argued to be an **increase in a liability**.

(iv) *Accounts treatment*

This is either **recognised** as a **deduction** from **work in progress** in the **balance sheet** or as a **provision for losses**.

(c) **Prudence in relation to long-term contract accounting**

In terms of FRS 18, prudence relates to the uncertainty that may be associated with the **recognition** and **measurement** of **assets** and **liabilities**.

FRS 18 emphasises that prudence should not be invoked to justify setting up hidden reserves, excessive provisions or understating assets. **Prudence** should **not** be seen as a **tool for smoothing profits** in financial statements.

Some companies might **prefer** to **value work in progress on long-term contracts** at cost**,** and **defer taking** any **project** on the contract into the profit and loss account until the **contract** has been **completed**. This may, on the face of it, **seem prudent** but there may be an **underlying management motive** to **smooth profits**, especially where **uncertainty** is **not** a **key factor**.

FRS 18 emphasises that **if financial statements are not neutral they cannot be reliable**. Tension often exists between **neutrality** and prudence. This should be reconciled by finding a balance that ensures that the deliberate and systematic understatement of assets and gains, and overstatement of liabilities and losses, does not occur.

31 PREPARATION QUESTION: PATEL LIMITED

The questions to ask are whether the finance director's proposals involve a change to:

Recognition	No
Presentation	No
Measurement basis	Yes

FRS 19 allows entities to report deferred taxation on a discounted or undiscounted basis.

These are two different measurement bases and it is a matter of accounting policy which of these an entity chooses to adopt.

The conclusion is therefore that the proposed change would be a change of accounting policy.

32 TAXATION

> **Pass marks**. Remember to plan and structure your answer properly. Stay focused on the requirements of the question and avoid the temptation to waffle.

(a) **Deferred taxation**

(i) **Main disclosures and needs addressed**

The main disclosure required for deferred tax is the **balance sheet balance**. This must be **shown separately** on the face of the balance sheet under the heading of **provision for liabilities and charges** as it is a liability for additional tax that may have to be paid in the future.

In the **notes to the accounts** the balance sheet figure should be analysed to show:

- The amount attributable to each different type of timing difference
- The movement between the opening and closing balance sheet figures

These disclosures allow users of the financial statements to assess why there is a change in the deferred tax balance and an idea of the company's exposure to each type of deferred tax element.

The increase or decrease in the provision for deferred tax during the year is included in the **tax charge** in the profit and loss account. The tax charge note for the year should show separately:

- The amount relating **to current tax**
- The amount relating to **deferred tax**

This disclosure helps the user of the financial statements to **reconcile** the **accounting profit** reported for the year to the **tax charge**, as the charge for deferred tax is a method of matching the tax charge for the year to the accounting profit.

(ii) **Basis of calculation**

According to FRS 19 the **deferred tax balance** should be calculated **each year** on the basis of **full provision**. This means that **provision** should be made for **all timing differences** including:

- Accelerated capital allowances
- Pension costs
- Unrelieved tax losses
- Short term timing differences.

FRS 19 then **permits** companies, if they wish, to **discount** any deferred tax assets or liabilities but if this policy is chosen it must be used for all deferred tax balances.

(b) FRS 16 *Current tax* is a relatively recent accounting standard whose objective is to ensure that companies recognise current taxes in a consistent and transparent manner.

Current tax should normally be **recognised in the profit and loss account** for the period. However if the tax is attributable to a gain or loss that has been recognised in the statement of total recognised gains and losses then the associated tax should also be recognised in the STRGL.

Dividends, interest and other amounts payable and receivable should be recognised at an amount which **includes withholding taxes** but excludes other taxes such as attributable tax credits.

The measurement of the current tax charge should be based upon tax rates and laws that have been enacted at the balance sheet date.

As regards **disclosure**, the current tax charge in the profit and loss account should be disclosed showing UK tax and any foreign tax separately. Each element, UK tax and foreign tax, should show the current period tax charge and any adjustments in respect of prior periods.

(c) (i) **External auditors duties**

The **main duty** of the external auditor is to **express an opinion** on whether the financial statements as a whole show a **true and fair view** of the company's position. Therefore the auditor has to decide whether in his opinion each item in the financial statements has been accurately accounted for and shown on a fair basis.

With regard to the **deferred tax disclosures**, the auditor must satisfy himself that the calculation of the deferred tax balance is **technically** and **mechanically accurate**:

- Regarding the facts
- According to the requirements of the relevant accounting standard, FRS 19.

The external auditor must ensure that the company's accounting policy with regard to deferred tax is in line with the requirements of FRS 19 and that all of the disclosures required by FRS 19 have been made. Any **departures** from the **FRS** must be **disclosed** in the **notes** to the accounts.

With regard to the current taxes the auditor will be concerned with the calculation of the tax charge and its correct disclosure according to FRS 16.

(ii) **Impact of disagreement over disclosures**

If the external auditor **disagrees** with the disclosures or calculations made concerning any figure in the financial statements, including deferred tax and current tax, then he should **firstly inform** the **directors** of his concerns.

In most cases in practice the external auditor should be able to convince the directors of his arguments and in consequence the financial statements will be suitably amended, thereby securing **auditor and client satisfaction**.

If the directors are not prepared to change the financial statements then the auditor must consider whether to give a qualified audit report. A **qualification** of an audit report will **only** be made **if** the **matter is material.**

Therefore the auditor must consider whether the amounts involved are material. If not, then no further action needs to be taken.

If the auditor considers that the amounts involved are material and that users of the financial statements will be misled by the disclosures that the directors are making then his audit report must make this quite clear.

If the disagreement is regarding the deferred tax balance or current taxes then the audit response will be:

- Describe the nature of the problem
- Quantify its effects as far as possible
- State that the financial statements give a true and fair view except for the disagreement over the treatment of the deferred tax balance or current taxes.

33 H PLC

> **Pass marks.** The examiner makes the point that this question is deliberately structured to help candidates think through each stage. Each step in this question is progressively more difficult than the previous one, but should also be underpinned by the previous one. It was not attempted by many candidates, and was badly answered by those who did.

(a) NOTES TO THE FINANCIAL STATEMENTS

Tax on profit on ordinary activities - profit and loss account note

	£ million	£ million
Current tax		
Corporation tax on profits for the period		0.40
Deferred tax		
Reversal of timing differences (W)	(0.09)	
Effect of change in tax rate (W)	(0.04)	
Total deferred tax credit		(0.13)
Total tax charge		0.27

Deferred tax - balance sheet note

	£ million
Provision at 30 April 20X3	0.69
Deferred tax credit in profit and loss account	(0.13)
Provision at 30 April 20X4	0.56

Working

Deferred tax

	£ million
Timing difference at 30 April 20X3	2.30
Timing difference at 30 April 20X4	2.00
Deferred tax at 30 April 20X3 (2.30 × 30%)	0.69
Deferred tax at 30 April 20X4 (2.00 × 28%)	0.56
Reduction in deferred tax provision	0.13

The reduction in provision is made up of two elements:

	£ million
Reversal of timing differences ((2.30 – 2.00) × 30%)	0.09
Change in tax rate (2.00 × (30% – 28%))	0.04
	0.13

(b) **Helpfulness of reconciliation**

(i)   In many sets of company financial statements there may appear to be little **relationship** between the figure reported as the profit before tax and the actual tax charge that appears in the profit and loss account.

(ii)   Users of financial statements might well expect that the tax charge would be the reported profit multiplied by the tax rate.

(iii) Owing to the complexities of the tax system and the estimates and subjective decisions that the directors of a company must make in estimating the tax charge for the year, the actual tax charge may not be what users may expect at a glance.

(iv)   The purpose of the reconciliation between the actual tax charge and the reported profit multiplied by the standard rate of tax is to **highlight** to the users of the financial statements these **estimates and judgements**.

170

(v)   This reconciliation should clarify the effect of adjustments such as changes in tax rates, estimated tax charges differing from final agreed tax liabilities and other factors that have affected the amount that appears as the tax charge in the profit and loss account.

> **Pass marks.** The most common error in this question was the tendency to answer part (b) with a discussion of the creation of deferred tax liabilities due to accelerated capital allowances.

(c) **Role of FRRP**

(i)   The Financial Reporting Review Panel (FRRP) is part of the **enforcement structure** of the Financial Reporting Council's standard setting process. The Accounting Standards Board sets accounting standards and companies should comply with these accounting standards in their financial statements.

(ii)   The role of the FRRP is to **investigate** the financial statements of **public companies** and **large private companies** that have **departed** from current accounting standards.

(iii) The FRRP does **not itself monitor all sets** of company financial statements but instead **responds to matters** that are brought to its attention.

(iv)   Matters communicated to the FRRP may be due to a qualified audit report, investor complaint or press comment.

(v)   If the FRRP finds that the financial statements are in breach of accounting standards or the Companies Act then it will, as a **first resort**, request that the financial statements be **amended** and **re-published** or that the particular matter is dealt with differently in future financial statements and the comparatives amended with a prior period adjustment.

(vi)   The FRRP has the **power** to **apply** to the courts for an **order** requiring a set of financial statements to be **adjusted**.

(vii) In practice, companies tend to agree to the requests of the FRRP thereby avoiding the requirement for a court order.

(viii) The responsibilities of the FRRP relate only to the **annual published** and **audited financial statements** and not to the directors' report, summary financial statements or interim statements.

(d) **Role of external auditor**

(i)   The external auditor is appointed by, and reports to, the shareholders of a company on the **truth and fairness** of the financial statements

(ii)   The auditor has **no power to force a company's directors to comply** with accounting standards.

(iii) The greatest power the external auditor has is to issue a **qualified audit report** detailing the areas of disagreement with the directors' accounting treatment.

(iv)   The FRRP may well then investigate the financial statements themselves on the basis of this qualified audit report and the company may be forced to change its financial statements and accounting treatment. However the external auditor himself has no such powers.

(v)   The existence of the FRRP may also lead to situations where an auditor may not be prepared to accept a company's **creative accounting** by issuing an unqualified audit report as any subsequent investigation by the FRRP may lead to **criticism of the auditor** as well as the company concerned.

34 STATEMENT OF PRINCIPLES/SSAP 21

> **Pass marks**. In part (a) relate the definitions to the SSAP 21 determination of what is a finance lease. In part (b) remember the fixed asset disclosures as well as the creditor disclosures.

(a) **Accounting for finance leases**

SSAP 21 is an example of **substance** triumphing **over form**. In legal terms the lessor may be the owner of the asset, but the **lessee** usually **enjoys** all the **risks** and **rewards** which ownership of the asset would entail. This is the key element of SSAP 21. The lessee is deemed to have an asset because they must **maintain and run the asset** through its useful life.

The lessee enjoys the **future economic benefits** of the asset as a result of entering into the lease. What is capitalised in the lessee's accounts is not the asset itself, but his **rights** (to future economic benefits) enshrined in the contract. The definition of a finance lease is such that a lessee's rights are for practical purposes substantially similar to those of an outright purchaser. There is a **corresponding liability** which is the **obligation** to **pay** the **instalments** on the lease until it expires. Assets and liabilities cannot be netted off.

If finance leases were treated in a similar manner to the existing treatment of operating leases then no asset would be recognised and lease payments would be expensed through the profit and loss as they were incurred.

This is tantamount to **off balance sheet finance**. The company has assets in use and liabilities to lessors which are not recorded in the financial statements. This would be **misleading to the users** of the accounts and make it **appear** as though the **assets** which were recorded were **more efficient** in producing **returns** than was actually the case.

(b) The following need to be disclosed with regard to assets held under finance leases:

- the **gross amount** of assets held under finance leases and the related **accumulated depreciation**.

- the **depreciation charge** for the period for finance lease assets

- **obligations under finance leases** split between creditors falling due within one year and creditors falling due after more than one year

- the net obligation under finance leases should be **analysed** between amounts payable in the next year, in the second to fifth years and amounts payable thereafter

- the **finance charge** for the period

- the **accounting policy** for leases

(c) **Statement of Principles**

This provides a **framework** of principles for standard setters and those involved in the preparation of accounts. At one stage accounting standards were produced to address major flaws in the approach to preparing accounts. This was a fire fighting approach and led to some inconsistencies.

The Statement helps guide the **standard setters** as they produce standards. It also means that the process should be **more efficient** and **less controversial**. Those involved in accountancy are likely to be aware of the content of the Statement and therefore any objections to new standards should be based on how they compare with the guidelines in the Statement.

The **enforcement** of standards will be more straightforward as the underlying principles of financial reporting have been made more transparent by the Statement.

This **transparency** should enhance the standing of the accountancy profession and allow a platform for discussion and debate in the future.

35 Q HP

> **Pass marks**. You must make sure that your answers to both the written sections and the calculations are equally good.

(a) **Accounting treatment**

(i) Income arising on a hire purchase contract should be recognised when it is earned, therefore **Q Ltd's treatment of this sale is in breach of basic accounting concepts.**

(ii) The profit arising on the contract of £4,200 comprises two elements:

- the normal profit, as would arise on a cash sale (£2,560), and
- a financing element which is the balance.

This financing element is basically the interest earned on the outstanding balance over the period of the contract.

(iii) The **contract** is for a period of **two years** (and spanning **three accounting periods**) and under the **accruals concept** the interest should be **accounted for** in the **period** in which it is earned.

(iv) The 'normal' profit can be accounted for as if it were a cash sale, ie at the inception of the contract.

(b) Q LIMITED
PROFIT AND LOSS ACCOUNT (EXTRACTS) FOR THE YEAR ENDED 31 MARCH

	20X3 £	20X4 £
Sales	12,560	-
Cost of sales on HP	10,000	-
Gross profit on HP sales	2,560	-
HP interest receivable (W2)	641	840

BALANCE SHEET AS AT 31 MARCH (EXTRACT)

	20X3 £	20X4 £
Current assets		
HP debtors (W2)	7,101	2,541

Note. In the 20X3 accounts there should be a note to debtors that £2,700 is due in more than one year.

Workings

1   *Analysis of HP contract*

Total cost under HP agreement

	£
Deposit	3,400
Instalments (4 × £2,700)	10,800
	14,200
Cost of asset	10,000
Gross profit	2,560
Cash selling price	12,560
HP interest	1,640
HP selling price	14,200

2   *Allocation of finance charge*

Assume instalments paid on March 31 and September 30 for both 20X3 and 20X4.

		£
1 October 20X2	Sale	12,560
1 October 20X2	Deposit	(3,400)
		9,160
31 March 20X3	Interest (£9,160 × 7%)	641
31 March 20X3	Instalment	(2,700)
		7,101
30 September 20X3	Interest (£7,101 × 7%)	497
30 September 20X3	Instalment	(2,700)
		4,898
31 March 20X4	Interest (£4,898 × 7%)	343
31 March 20X4	Instalment	(2,700)
		2,541

(c) **Substance over form**

Purchasers should **include the assets purchased under hire purchase terms** because **their accounts** must **reflect the** *substance* **of the transaction rather than its** *legal form*.

The substance is that the purchaser has acquired the asset and has financed it by obtaining a loan from the seller. In this way the purchaser's accounts reflect the assets being used in the business and the seller's accounts show a debtor for the amount due under the hire purchase contract.

(d) PURCHASER
PROFIT AND LOSS ACCOUNT (EXTRACTS) FOR THE YEAR ENDED 31 MARCH

	20X3 £	20X4 £
Depreciation charge (12,560/5)	2,512	2,512
Finance charge payable	641	840

BALANCE SHEET (EXTRACTS) AS AT 31 MARCH

	20X3 £	20X4 £
Fixed assets:		
Cost	12,560	12,560
Accumulated depreciation	2,512	5,024
Net book value	10,048	7,536
Creditors: amounts falling due within one year		
Obligations under HP agreement	4,401	2,541
Creditors: amounts falling due after more than one year		
Obligations under HP agreement	2,700	–

36   HIRE PURCHASE

(a)   (i)
                                                          COMPUTERS

		£			£
30.6.X7	XF plc	8,000	31.12.X7	Balance c/d	8,000
1.1.X8	Balance b/d	8,000			
31.3.X8	XF plc	6,000	31.12.X8	Balance c/d	14,000
		14,000			14,000
1.1.X9	Balance b/d	14,000			
31.3.X9	XF plc	6,000	31.12.X9	Balance c/d	20,000
		20,000			20,000

(ii)
                              PROVISION FOR DEPRECIATION: COMPUTERS

		£			£
3.12.X7	Balance c/d	1,600	31.12.X7	Profit and loss (W1)	1,600
			1.1.X8	Balance b/d	1,600
31.12.X8	Balance c/d	4,080	31.12.X8	Profit and loss (W1)	2,480
		4,080			4,080
			1.1.X9	Balance b/d	4,080
31.12.X9	Balance c/d	7,264	31.12.X9	Profit and loss (W1)	3,184
		7,264			7,264

(iii)
                                          XF PLC

		£			£
30.6.X7	Bank	1,040	30.6.X7	Computer A	9,920
30.9.X7	Bank	740			
31.12.X7	Bank	740			
31.12.X7	Balance c/d	7,400			
		9,920			9,920
31.3.X8	Bank (740 + 720)	1,460	1.1.X8	Balance b/d	7,400
30.6.X9	Bank (740 + 550)	1,290	31.3.X8	Computer B	7,320
30.9.X9	Bank	1,290			
31.12.X9	Bank	1,290			
31.12.X9	Balance c/d	9,390			
		14,720			14,720
31.3.X9	Bank (740+550+720)	2,010	1.1.X9	Balance b/d	9,390
30.6.X9	Bank (740+550+760)	2,050	31.3.X9	Computer C	6,800
30.9.X9	Bank	2,050			
31.12.X9	Bank	2,050			
31.12.X9	Balance c/d	8,030			
		16,190			16,190

(Working 2 shows the calculation of the quarterly payments.)

(iv)
                              HIRE PURCHASE INTEREST SUSPENSE

		£			£
30.6.X7	XF plc	1,920	31.12.X7	Profit and loss (W3)	320
			31.12.X7	Balance c/d	1,600
		1,920			1,920
1.1.X8	Balance b/d	1,600	31.12.X8	Profit and loss (W3)	970
31.3.X8	XF plc	1,320	31.12.X8	Balance c/d	1,950
		2,920			2,920
1.1.X9	Balance b/d	1,950	31.12.X9	Profit and loss (W3)	1,380
31.3.X9	XF plc	800	31.12.X9	Balance c/d	1,370
		2,750			2,750

Workings

1   *Depreciation*

		Computer A £	Computer B £	Computer C £
20X7	£8,000 × 20%	1,600		
20X8	£(8,000 − 1,600) × 20%	1,280		
	£6,000 × 20%		1,200	
20X9	£(8,000 − 1,600 − 1,280) × 20%	1,024		
	£(6,000 − 1,200) × 20%		960	
	£6,000 × 20%			1,200

2   *Quarterly instalments*

Computer A (£9,920 − £1,040) ÷ 12	=	£740
Computer B (£7,320 − £720) ÷ 12	=	£550
Computer C (£6,800 − £720) ÷ 8	=	£760

3   *Interest*

		Computer A £	Computer B £	Computer C £
20X7	$^2/_{12}$ × £1,920	320		
20X8	$^4/_{12}$ × £1,920	640		
	$^3/_{12}$ × £1,320		330	
20X9	As 20X8	640		
	$^4/_{12}$ × £1,320		440	
	$^3/_8$ × £800			300

(b)   **Implicit interest rate**

The interest rate implicit in a lease is the discount rate that at the beginning of the lease, when applied to the amounts which the lessor expects to receive, produces an amount equal to the fair value of the leased asset.

(c)

		20X7 £	20X8 £	20X9 £
Computer A	$\frac{12+11}{78}$ × £1,920	566		
	$\frac{10+9+8+7}{78}$ × £1,920		837	
	$\frac{6+5+4+3}{78}$ × £1,920			443
Computer B	$\frac{12+11+10}{78}$ × £1,320	-	558	
	$\frac{9+8+7+6}{78}$ × £1,320			508
Computer C	$\frac{8+7+6}{36}$ × £800	-	-	467
		566	1,395	1,418

Workings

Sum of the digits:

Computers A and B	$\frac{12 \times 13}{2}$	=	78
Computer C	$\frac{8 \times 9}{2}$	=	36

37 T LTD

> **Pass marks**. The numbers in leasing questions are often daunting for students, so make sure you gain as many marks as possible from the written sections of this question. This means that you *must* allocate your time properly. As far as the value of the asset is concerned, the extract from SSAP 21 shows that it should be recorded at the present value of the minimum lease payments, *not* its fair value.
>
> *Other points*. Note that the question does not tell us whether lease payments are made in advance or in arrears. Make an assumption, state that assumption and be consistent. The answer assumes that lease payments are made in advance.

(a) (i) **90% Rule**

I do not agree with T Ltd's decision to classify its lease agreement with Lessor plc as an operating lease. Although the present value of the minimum lease payments amounts to less than 90% of the fair value of the leased asset, this does not necessarily justify treating the lease as an operating lease.

SSAP 21 states that a finance lease is one which transfers substantially all of the risks and rewards of ownership with the 90% rule giving a presumption that this has occurred.

Conversely, the presumption that a lease which fails the 90% test is not a finance lease may be rebutted.

However, further evidence of the transfer of risks and rewards (the criteria for recognition of assets under FRS 5 *Reporting the substance of transactions*) is that T Ltd is responsible for maintenance of the machinery and for insurance. Furthermore, the asset was built and purchased specifically for T Ltd, so Lessor plc might not be able to find another user for the asset. The lease will continue for most of the useful life of the asset, which will effectively be obsolete at the end of the lease term.

Added to the fact that the minimum lease payments amount to 88% (ie nearly 90%) of the fair value of the asset, I believe that the lease should be treated as a finance rather than an operating lease.

(ii) **Lease calculations**

	£'000
Profit and loss account	
Depreciation	820
Finance charges	582

	£'000
Balance sheet - fixed assets	
Present value of lease	4,100
Less depreciation	(820)
Net increase	3,280

	£'000
Current liabilities	
Obligations under finance lease	706

	£'000
Long-term liabilities	
Obligations under finance lease	2,776

Workings

20X6	£'000
Capital sum at start of period	4,100
Finance charge (14.2%)	582
Lease payment	(1,200)
Capital sum at end of period	3,482

	20X7	£'000
	Capital sum at start of period	3,482
	Finance charge (14.2%)	494
	Lease payment	(1,200)
	Capital sum at end of period	2,776

	Liabilities (split <1 year, > 1 year)	£'000
	Due within one year	1,200
	Less interest	(494)
		706
	Due after one year (balance)	2,776
	Total liability	3,482

Depreciation

$$\text{Depreciation} = \frac{\text{PV of lease}}{\text{Lease term}} = \frac{£4.1m}{5} = £820,000$$

(iii) **In Lessor Ltd's a/cs**

PROFIT AND LOSS ACCOUNT (EXTRACTS)

	£'000
Turnover	4,100
Cost of sales	3,900
Lease costs receivable	582

BALANCE SHEET (EXTRACTS)
Current assets

Lease debtor	3,482

£2,776,000 included in debtors is receivable after more than one year.

(b)

Pass marks. This part of the question concentrates on two very important ratios. Note how few marks are given to their calculation: it is interpretation of the ratios which gains marks.

Remember, an accountant who relies on memorised formulae will not be able to explain whether the resulting figure is good or bad.

If you did badly here work on your written answers. There is a strong written element in each exam, even more so in the interpretation questions.

(i) **Definition**

The gearing ratio measures the proportion of the total long-term capital of the company which is financed by long-term debt capital as opposed to share capital and reserves.

$$\text{Gearing} = \frac{\text{Long-term debt capital}}{\text{Total capital}}$$

Gearing and profit

Gearing is an important measure of stability (ie financial risk) because of the nature of long-term debt capital. This type of capital requires annual interest to be paid, usually at a fixed rate, if the terms of the loan are not to be breached. In addition, the loan will have fixed repayment terms, either in instalments over the period of the loan or in total at the end of the loan period.

Share capital, on the other hand, only requires the payment of dividends, which unlike interest only need be paid when profits allow, ie they are discretionary. (Preference share dividends, whilst fixed, can be deferred but arrears must be paid before any ordinary share dividends can be declared.)

Repayment

Ordinary share capital is only repayable on the winding up of the company. It is the most stable form of capital because it does not demand a return and does not have to be repaid.

Long-term debt is less stable as interest must be paid when due and the loan requires repayment on a fixed date.

Effect of high gearing

The higher the gearing ratio then, the less stable is a company's capital base. Therefore, companies that are already highly geared may be unable to obtain further borrowings and thus may be forced into liquidation in difficult times.

(ii) **Return on capital employed** $= \dfrac{\text{Profit before interest and taxation}}{\text{Capital employed}}$

$$= \dfrac{4,600,000}{4,000,000 + 10,500,000} \times 100\% = 31.7\%$$

Gearing $= \dfrac{4,000,000}{14,500,000} \times 100\% = 27.6\%$

(iii) (1) **Return on capital employed**

If the lease was reclassified, profit would not change greatly as the reduction in lease charges would be offset by the increase in depreciation charge (see 2(a) above). Capital employed would also only change very little (the fixed asset increase is offset by recording the liability under the lease) and therefore return on capital employed would remain roughly the same.

Gearing

Long-term debt would increase substantially and so would total capital with little effect on equity interests. The gearing ratio would therefore increase significantly.

(2) **Impact on planning and management decisions**

The ratios discussed above (ie with the transaction treated as a finance lease) would be more relevant as they give a truer picture of the actual way that the company is financed and the costs of that finance.

It will allow management to appreciate the true debt and gearing of the company before any further long-term debt is incurred. It also gives a more realistic picture of what return the company is earning on all the assets employed (whether owned or not).

The directors are unlikely to mislead future potential lenders if the transaction is treated as an operating lease, because such lenders will be able to recognise the nature of the transaction from the information in the accounts.

38   S PLC 2

> **Pass marks**. This question is broadly about accounting choices and the impacts that these can have on the interpretation and analysis of financial statements.

(a) **Impact of operating lease treatment**

Balance sheet impact

If the lease is treated as an operating lease rather than a finance lease the main differences will be seen on the balance sheet. As a finance lease the asset is shown as a fixed asset on the balance sheet together with a related creditor. If the lease is an operating lease then there is no capitalisation of the asset or the recognition of a creditor.

Profit and loss impact

In the profit and loss account the effective quantitative difference between the two alternative treatments is not so significant. If the lease is treated as an operating lease then the full lease rental will appear as an expense in the profit and loss account. However if the lease is treated as a finance lease the lease payment is split between the interest element and the capital repayment. Only the interest element is shown as the finance cost in the profit and loss account. However as the asset has been treated as a fixed asset under the finance lease then the profit and loss account will also have a charge for depreciation each year.

Accounting ratios impact

The two main ratios that may be affected by the treatment of the lease are return on capital employed and gearing. Return on capital employed is calculated as net profit before interest divided by capital employed. The net profit is likely to be similar quantitatively whether the lease is treated as an operating lease or a finance lease.

If the net profit before interest is used then the capital employed figure is the equity capital plus any long term creditors. Part of the finance lease creditor will appear in long term creditors and therefore will be part of capital employed therefore reducing the return on capital employed.

In the same way if the gearing is measured by comparing all long term loans and long term creditors to the equity then the measure of gearing will increase if the lease is treated as a finance lease.

(b) **Effect on the financial statements**

If C Bank were to treat the lease to S plc as an operating lease the asset would remain on the balance sheet of C Bank as a **fixed asset** and would be depreciated as such. The **rental income** from the lease would be recognised in the profit and loss account on a **straight line basis**.

However if C Bank were to treat the lease as a finance lease then the asset itself would not appear on the balance sheet. Instead there would be a **debtor** for amounts due from finance leases being the capital value of the lease yet to be paid by S plc. In the profit and loss account the **finance element** of the lease rentals would be recognised as income whereas the capital element of the lease rentals would be set off against the debtor. The element of the debt that was due after more than one year would need to be disclosed in the notes to the accounts if material.

(c) **Selection of accounting treatment**

SSAP 21 *Accounting for leases and hire purchase contracts* requires a lease to be treated as a finance lease if substantially all of the **risks** and **rewards** of ownership are transferred to the lessee.

An important element of evidence of the transfer of risks and rewards is whether the lessee has the use of the asset for substantially all of its **useful life**. The terms of S plc's lease with C Bank is such that it is almost definite that S plc will have the use of the asset for all of its useful life.

The asset is vital to the production process and the cost of refurbishing it is prohibitively expensive therefore it is almost certain that S plc will continue for the entire six years of the lease.

The lease should be treated as a **finance lease**.

(d) **Motivations for minimising gearing ratio**

If a company is partly financed by debt capital this increases the **risk** to the equity shareholders and sometimes also to the debt holders themselves. The interest payment on any debt capital must be paid before any dividend can be paid out to the ordinary shareholders, therefore if profits are low then there is less chance of an ordinary dividend being paid. As the amount of debt capital in issue increases the amount of **interest** that must be paid out of profits increases.

The payment of interest out of profits also increases the **variability** of the profits available for shareholders as the amount of debt interest is fixed. If large profits are made then there is a high proportion available for the shareholders. If there is a large amount of debt capital however and profits are low there will be very little, if any, available for the ordinary shareholders.

High levels of debt capital can also increase the risk to the providers of the debt themselves as if the company fails there may be a large amount of debt which is due to be paid off before that particular lender.

The **gearing ratio** measures the amount of debt in the company's financing structure. Therefore the gearing ratio is a measure of the riskiness of the company. If the gearing ratio can be minimised then the company can appear to be less risky and therefore more attractive to equity shareholders and future lenders alike.

(e) **Potential scope to influence accounts balances**

The rules governing the preparation of financial statements are covered by the Companies Act, SSAPs and FRSs. The Companies Act covers the basic format of the financial statements but the detailed accounting treatments are dealt with in SSAPs and FRSs. Some SSAPs and FRSs deal with very specific areas such as **SSAP 21** and leasing and **FRS 15** and fixed assets. However others are of a more general nature such as **FRS 5** and the substance of transactions.

If consideration is taken of both the specific and general accounting standards there are very few areas of accounting that will not fall under the remit of an accounting standard. However, although now difficult, it is still possible to influence the profit figure or the balance sheet position in a number of ways.

One example is the possible treatment of the lease in S plc. By choosing to treat the lease as an operating lease the directors of S plc were taking a very literal approach to SSAP 21 by treating each two year period as effectively a separate lease. It is unlikely that S plc's auditors would agree to this treatment.

A possibly easier approach is to bias the figures whilst remaining within the spirit of an accounting standard. For example **FRS 15** allows a company to choose the most appropriate method of depreciation for its fixed assets and the best estimate of useful economic life. By choosing a long useful economic life the annual depreciation charge can be reduced or by choosing a high percentage reducing balance method of depreciation there can be large depreciation charges in the early years of the asset's life and much lower charges in later years.

39   PREPARATION QUESTION: RESEARCH AND DEVELOPMENT

(a) **Applied research vs development expenditure**

(i)   SSAP 13 states that '**pure and applied research** can be regarded as part of a continuing operation required to maintain a company's business and its competitive position. In general, no one particular period rather than any other will be expected to benefit and therefore it is appropriate that these costs should be **written off** as they are incurred'.

This is in keeping with the **accruals** concept envisaged by FRS 18 which specifies that the non-cash impacts of transactions should be reflected in the financial statements for the accounting period to which they relate, rather than in the period any cash involved is received or paid.

(ii)   **FRS 5** defines **assets** as 'rights or other access to future economic benefits controlled by an entity, as a result of past transactions or events'.

(iii) The key difference between research and development is that research is speculative whereas development builds on successful research: 'development is normally undertaken with a reasonable expectation of specific commercial success and of future benefits arising from the work ...' (SSAP 13, Paragraph 9). Development expenditure is therefore capable of linkage with revenue but applied research is not. Development expenditure falls within the definition of an asset as it gives access to future economic benefits.

Accounting treatment

This has the effect that applied research costs must be written off as incurred but development expenditure can be deferred (that is, capitalised as an intangible asset) and amortised over the life of the product, service, process or system developed. This treatment is only permissible if the project meets certain criteria designed to ensure that deferral is prudent.

(b) **Definitions of research and development**

(i)   **Market research** is not normally considered to be research and development activity. It is specifically excluded by SSAP 13. This is presumably because it does not depart from routine activity and it does not contain an appreciable element of innovation.

(ii)   **Testing of prototypes** is included in SSAP 13's list of activities normally to be considered as research and development. A prototype must be constructed and tested before full-scale production can be risked and so it is an essential stage in the development process.

(iii) '**Operational research** not tied to a specific research and development activity' is an activity which SSAP 13 considers should not normally be included in research and development. 'Operational research' is presumably used here to denote the branch of applied mathematics which includes techniques such as linear programming and network analysis. The implication is that routine use of such techniques (to improve production efficiency, for example) does not fall within SSAP 13's jurisdiction, in spite of the use of the word 'research'.

(iv)   '**Testing** in search for, or evaluation of, product, service or process alternatives' is considered to be research and development work. It would fall within the definition of applied research.

40 **PREPARATION QUESTION: GOVERNMENT GRANTS**

(a) **SSAP 4 vis-à-vis FRS 18**

Going concern

(i) Under the going concern concept, the enterprise is viewed as **continuing in operation** for the **foreseeable future** and the accounts should be prepared on the assumption that the organisation has neither the intention nor the necessity of liquidating or of curtailing significantly the scale of its operations.

(ii) It is in accordance with this concept that **SSAP 4** does **not require** the **postponement of recognition** of a grant until all possibility of **repayment** is removed or the disclosure of a contingent liability by way of a note that the grant may have to be repaid. This is because in a **going concern** a grant will not have to be repaid.

Accruals

(i) The accruals concept requires that revenues and costs should be dealt with in the profit and loss account of the period to which they relate, rather than in the period any cash involved is received or paid.

(ii) **The treatment of government grants as laid down by SSAP 4 is consistent with this**; grants are to be recognised in the profit and loss account so as to match them with the expenditure towards which they are intended to contribute.

(b) (i) **Grant relating to fixed asset**

The correct treatment is to **show the asset at cost in the balance sheet and to set up a deferred income account**. Over the ten year period of the asset's useful economic life, the grant will be credited to the profit and loss account in ten annual instalments, the corresponding debit being to the deferred income account.

The fact that the asset was purchased by means of a five year loan is irrelevant to the accounting treatment of the grant.

(ii) **Grant towards revenue expenditure**

SSAP 4 requires that government grants should be matched with the expenditure to which they relate. In the case of revenue expenditure, therefore, **the grant should be credited to the profit and loss account in the year in which the revenue expenditure takes place**.

Each year, however, the company should consider whether it is likely that the grant will have to be repaid. If this is probable, provision should be made. If repayment is possible, the fact should, in accordance with FRS 12 *Provisions, contingent liabilities and contingent assets*, be disclosed in a note to the accounts.

(iii) **Grant towards consultancy costs**

The consultancy costs are revenue expenditure. They cannot be capitalised but must be written off to the profit and loss account in the year in which they are incurred. Accordingly the grant should be credited to the profit and loss account in that year.

41 **PREPARATION QUESTION: ACE (FRS 8)**

> **Pass marks**. This question deals with related party disclosures. It calls for a discussion of the principles of FRS 8.

Prior to the issue of **FRS 8** in 1995, disclosures in respect of related parties were focused on transactions with directors and their relationship with the group. The ASB extended this definition and also the required disclosures. This reflects the objective of the ASB to provide **useful data** for investors in addition to the need for companies to report on stewardship activities.

The **objective** of FRS 8 is to ensure that financial statements disclose to shareholders the possibility that the reported financial position and results have been affected by the existence of related parties and transactions with them.

It is usually assumed that a reporting entity conducts its transactions on an 'arm's length' basis. However, these assumptions may not be justified when related party relationships exist, because the necessary conditions for competitive, free market dealings may not be present. The parties involved may well endeavour to deal at arm's length, but the very nature of the relationship may preclude this.

Some **examples** of typical related party transactions encountered in practice include the following.

- Purchases or sales of goods (finished or unfinished)
- Purchases or sales of property
- Rendering or receiving of services
- Provision of finance (including loans and equity contributions)
- Management contracts

The above are relevant, whether or not a price is charged. Disclosure is required if the transaction is material.

FRS 8 brings the UK more into line with international practice and requires all **material related party transactions** to be disclosed.

It should be noted that related party transactions are not necessarily fraudulent or intended to deceive. Without proper disclosure, investors may be disadvantaged – FRS 8 seeks to remedy this.

42   VARIOUS: D PLC

> **Pass marks**. This question asked you to discuss five situations in the light of the applicable accounting standard. It is important not merely to discuss the standard but to relate it to each of the situations.
>
> Remember that you should not be afraid of committing yourself to a preferred course of action when answering this type of question.

(a)   **Post balance sheet event (SSAP 17)**

The **fire** at the company's factory on the 4 April 20X3 arose after the balance sheet date and this type of event is specifically identified as **a non-adjusting** event in the list provided in the appendix to SSAP 17.

In this case SSAP 17 requires disclosure of the nature of the event and its financial impact which here will comprise the uninsured costs.

The **liquidation of a major customer** is **an adjusting post balance sheet event** per the examples given in the appendix to SSAP 17.

Hence **full provision** for the **debt** should be made at 31 March 20X3 and the adjustment disclosed in the notes.

(b) **Possible investment property (SSAP 19)**

SSAP 19 defines an **investment property** as an **interest in land** and/or **buildings** which is held for its **investment potential**. The investment property is included in the accounts at its **open market value** and is **not depreciated**.

However, **SSAP 19 specifically excludes properties owned** and **occupied** by a **company** from being categorised as investment properties.

Hence at 31 March 20X3 the office building should be treated as a tangible fixed asset and depreciated in the normal way. Once it is no longer occupied by the company it can then be reclassified as an investment property.

(c) **Possible development expenditure (SSAP 13)**

SSAP 13 states that **development expenditure** should be **written off** in the **year of expenditure except** in the **following circumstances** when it may be **deferred to future periods**:

(i)   There is a **clearly defined project**

(ii) The related **expenditure is separately identifiable**

(iii) The outcome of such a project has been assessed with reasonable certainty as to:

    (1) Its **technical feasibility**

    (2) Its ultimate **commercial viability** considered in the light of factors such as likely market conditions, public opinion, consumer and environmental legislation.

(iv) The aggregate of the deferred development costs, any further development costs, and related production, selling and administration **costs** is reasonably **expected to be exceeded by related future sales or other revenues**.

(v)   **Adequate resources exist,** or are reasonably expected to be available, **to enable the project to be completed** and to provide any **consequential increases** in **working capital**.

From this definition the company will be able to carry forward the money advanced to develop the new pulping process to the extent that the amount will be covered by future savings on raw materials.

The project to develop a new species of tree has not been successful and will not result in any future income stream. Hence the costs should be written off fully in the year to 31 March 20X3.

(d) **Possible contingent liabilities (FRS 12)**

FRS 12 states that an entity should **never recognise** a **contingent liability** in the financial statements. The FRS requires a contingent liability to be **disclosed unless** the possibility of any **outflow of economic benefits to settle it is remote**.

In **this case** the contingent liability would merely be **disclosed** in the **notes** to the accounts as follows.

(i)   The **nature** of the contingency
(ii) The **uncertainties** which are expected to **affect** the **ultimate outcome**
(iii) A **statement** that it is **not practicable** to make an **estimate** of the **financial effect**

The employee's claim should be disclosed as a contingent liability, since it is likely that a payment will have to be made.

The customer's claim would not be disclosed in the accounts, as the company's lawyers consider the possibility of a liability arising to be remote.

(e) **Convertible debentures (FRS 4)**

According to **FRS 4** *Capital instruments* the issue costs should be written off over the life of the capital instrument. Therefore instead of charging them to the current year profit and loss account they should be deducted from the issue proceeds of the debentures. The convertible debentures will then be initially recorded at **issue proceeds less issue costs**.

FRS 4 also states that convertible debentures must always be treated as **liabilities** rather than as part of shareholders funds no matter how certain it is that they will be converted. Therefore the convertible debentures must be shown as a creditor falling due after more than one year.

43 V PLC

> **Pass marks**. This question tests understanding of financial regulations in the preparation of accounts in the context of applying specific standards to a scenario. Part (b) requires knowledge of the accounting entries for share issues.

(a) (i) (1) **Useful economic life**

The installation of a more advanced computer system by V plc's main competitor suggests that the directors of V plc need to assess the estimated useful life of its own computer system.

Although it is probable that the system will operate reliably for ten years, nowadays this is not the primary criterion for measuring useful life. It is likely that most systems will be technologically obsolete within a much shorter period.

V plc might decide not to replace the system immediately as it may wish to assess the effect (if any) of its competitor's new system. In addition it may wish to ensure that all technical problems have been resolved by the software suppliers before it invests in something similar.

Hence the directors' assessment must take into account all these aspects of the situation before they decide on a revised useful life for this system. As this review will almost certainly result in a reduction in the useful life, the accounts to 30 September 20X7 should reflect this change and the additional depreciation incurred.

(2) **Window dressing**

This transaction would be classified as a non-adjusting event by SSAP 17 *Accounting for post balance sheet events* as **it is basically window dressing,** ie an arranging transaction designed to alter the appearance of the balance sheet. The standard requires disclosure of the alteration in a note to the accounts.

Further information may need to be disclosed if it was always the directors' intention to treat the loan as short term. In that case the nature of the transaction and its financial effect will also need to be disclosed.

(3) **Net realisable value**

This will involve the directors assessing the **future sales** of this production. It will be of its nature a **subjective judgement**.

A review of post year end sales, orders being processed etc may give an indication. The directors may consider that a small modification is all that the product requires, basing this on the product reviews and technical feedback. Ultimately stock needs to be valued at the lower of cost and net realisable value. Hence the accounts to 30 September 20X7 will need to reflect any write-down of this stock that the directors may consider necessary or the cost of making any modifications to make it saleable.

(4) **Warranty income**

The **accruals** basis of accounting as stated in FRS 18 requires that the non-cash impacts of transactions be reflected in the financial statements for the accounting period in which they occur rather than in the period when the cash is received or paid.

If the company is going to include the fees in the accounts to 30 September 20X7 it needs to make **provision** for the costs that are likely to arise during the three year warranty period.

Alternatively the fees should be credited to the profit and loss account over the period of the warranty. However, a straight write-off would not be appropriate as the majority of costs are expected to occur in the third year. Hence the bulk of the fees should be recognised then.

This would probably need to be a stepped write-off of fees eg 15% in first year, 25% in second year 60% in third year or something similar.

(b) (i)

APPLICATION AND ALLOTMENT

	£		£
Share capital (200,000 × 50p)	100,000	Bal b/fwd	110,000
Bank	10,000		
	110,000		110,000

CALL ACCOUNT

	£		£
Share capital (200,000 × 20p)	40,000	Bank	118,800
Share premium (200,000 × 40p)	80,000	Forfeited shares	1,200
	120,000		120,000

FORFEITED SHARES

	£		£
Call a/c	1,200	Bank	900
		Share premium	300
	1,200		1,200

SHARE CAPITAL

	£		£
		Bal b/fwd	1,000,000
Bal c/fwd	1,140,000	App and all	100,000
	1,140,000	Call	40,000
			1,140,000

SHARE PREMIUM

	£		£
Forfeited shares	300	Call	80,000
Bal c/fwd	79,700		
	80,000		80,000

(ii)   *Share capital*

		£
1,000,000 £1 shares fully paid		1,000,000
200,000 £1 shares 70p paid		140,000
		1,140,000
Share premium		79,700

44   H PLC I

> **Pass marks**. SSAP 13 is a straightforward and well known accounting standard but this question requires you to think carefully about the issues involved. The examiner commented that as is so often the case, the key is to read the question carefully and to make use of as many cues as possible to assist in the structuring of these opinions.

(a)   **Justification for capitalising research costs**

Capitalisation of research costs may be justifiable if the costs could be shown to be a true asset, in that they give rights or other access to future economic benefits and that they can be measured at a monetary amount with sufficient reliability. The research costs can be measured at a monetary amount as payment is made for this academic research.

The question is whether the research gives rise to future economic benefits. Certainly to date it would appear that the research in total would fulfil this criteria as the one successful project each year has created enough profit to cover all of the research costs.

However on the grounds of prudence, as the nature of the research is that only one in twenty projects reaps such rewards, it would probably not be advisable to capitalise the research costs.

FRS 18 specifies that in **conditions of uncertainty, more confirmatory evidence** should be **obtained** for the **occurrence of an asset than a liability**. Therefore these costs should probably not be recognised as an asset on the grounds of prudence.

(b)   **Reasons for SSAP 13 approach regarding capitalisation**

The capitalisation of development costs concerns a conflict between two of the important accounting concepts, accruals and prudence.

The **accruals concept** argues for **writing off of expenditure** to profit and loss in the **period to which it relates, rather than in the period of payment.**

The argument for capitalising development costs is, however, that these costs will be earning revenues in the future and therefore the development costs should appear as an intangible fixed asset until the revenues are earned and will then be written off to the profit and loss account and related to those revenues. The prudence concept however specifies where there is **uncertainty more confirmatory evidence is required in order to recognise an asset than a liability**.

The purpose of the rules in SSAP 13 regarding the writing off of all research costs and the capitalisation of development expenditure is to ensure the **correct balance between the accruals and prudence concepts.**

The **SSAP 13 criteria** state that there must be a **clearly defined project** and **separately identifiable expenditure**. This is in order to assess whether there is actually an asset and whether the asset can be measured with sufficient certainty. Development costs are capitalised in order to be matched with the future revenues from the project. Therefore SSAP 13 requires that the future of the project is assessed in detail to ensure that there will be such revenues and that these **revenues** will be **large enough** to **cover the costs.**

(c) **Impact of SSAP 13 on research investment**

It could be argued that the fact that research costs have to be written off immediately in the income statement on the grounds of prudence might discourage companies from investing in such activities as this will have an immediate effect on the profit and loss account figures. However, this is also the case for many other types of discretionary expenditure such as training or advertising.

A **company's decision** as whether to invest in training its employees or whether to enter into a large advertising campaign will be **based upon a cost/benefit analysis** of the **activity in question**. If it is felt that the activity will earn long term profits for the business then the company will normally go ahead with the project even though the cost would be written off to the profit and loss account and would reduce immediate profits.

The decision regarding **investment in research** is exactly the **same** in that the research should be assessed to determine whether it is a **worthwhile long term investment** and should be entered into if it is, **no matter what the accounting treatment of the costs**.

It can further be argued that even if research costs were capitalised they do not stay permanently on the balance sheet and will be written off to the profit and loss account in future years to match with the income from the project. **Therefore the writing off** of **the research cost is a matter of timing, now or in the future, and should therefore not affect the decision as to whether to invest in the research.**

A final argument that could be put forward is that the **shareholders** of the company will **not** be **concerned** about the **accounting treatment** of the research costs in their valuation of the company. The shareholders and the market in general will value the company on the basis of the **present value** of the **net cash flows** from its operations and investments and therefore the accounting treatment of items of expenditure will be irrelevant to their thinking. On the basis of this the accounting treatment of the research costs should not play a key part in the company's decision as to whether to invest in the research.

(d) **Advantages and disadvantages of true and fair override**

Accounting Standards are designed to be applicable to **companies in general** and are **not tailored** to the **specific circumstances** of **individual companies**. Therefore one advantage of the true and fair override is that if the treatment required by an accounting standard does not suit the circumstances of a particular company then the override can be invoked.

In the setting of accounting standards, the standard setters may feel that the most appropriate accounting treatment is one which would not normally be allowed by the Companies Act. However, the appropriate accounting treatment can still be used by invoking the true and fair override. For example, the Companies Act states that all fixed assets with a limited useful economic life must be depreciated. SSAP 19 allows investment properties to be included in the balance sheet at open market value and not depreciated.

The **disadvantage** of offering companies the option of the true and fair override is that it could be used to **manipulate financial statements** or to **show** the financial statements in the **best light by the directors of the company** even though the accounting treatment chosen is not allowed by either the Companies Act or accounting standards.

(e) FRS 18 *Accounting policies* sets out the principles to be followed in selecting accounting policies and the disclosures required to help users to understand the accounting policies adopted and how they have been applied.

Accounting policies should be consistent with accounting standards, UITF Abstracts and companies legislation and where these requirements allow a choice then the accounting policy that a company chooses must be the **most appropriate** to its particular circumstances for the purpose of giving a true and fair view. The appropriateness should be judged against the objectives of **relevance, reliability, comparability** and **understandability**.

The accounting policies used should be **reviewed** regularly to ensure that they remain the most appropriate and should be changed if a new accounting policy is judged to be more appropriate.

> **Pass marks**. The examiner commented that this question was answered badly by most candidates. Many candidates did little more than recite the SSAP 13 conditions for the capitalisation of development expenditure, which was largely irrelevant.

45 L PLC

> **Pass Marks**. The examiner commented that questions involving the practical application of accounting standards usually focus on the main requirements. The fact that there were four circumstances to deal with suggests that a range of responses was required and so answers that treated all four as, say, contingent liabilities appeared rather naïve. A careful reading of the question would have helped decide which response was most likely to be appropriate in each case.

(a) **Accounting treatment**

(i)   Normally this situation would require a provision in the financial statements as L plc has an **obligation to pay** the amounts due on the outstanding cards. However in this case it is **not possible** to **determine** the **amount** that is due with any **reasonable accuracy** therefore **no provision** can be recognised in the balance sheet. Instead a **contingent liability** should be disclosed in the notes to the financial statements.

(ii) This is a liability of L plc. The company is **obliged to pay the claim** unless it proves to be fraudulent which would appear to be unlikely. Therefore the full amount of £200,000 should be **accrued** for in the financial statements and shown as a **current liability** in the balance sheet.

(iii) **Potentially** this could be a **contingent liability**. However the **likelihood** of L plc having to pay out on this claim appears to be **remote** as it is most probably a forgery. **Therefore** there should be **no disclosure** as this would be **misleading** in the financial statements.

(iv) Any amounts payable will only be provided for or disclosed as a **contingent liability** if there is a **legal or constructive obligation** to make the payment. In this case there is no legal obligation and a constructive obligation would only be created if the prize-winners had been informed of the directors' decision to pay out half of each claim. However by the balance sheet date this has not happened and therefore for there should be neither a provision in the financial statements nor disclosure of any contingent liability.

(b) (i) **Reasons for insufficient attention**

- The main reason why insufficient attention might be paid to contingent liabilities is that the information regarding them is in a **note to the financial statements** rather than in the financial statements themselves.

- **Many users** of financial statements, rather than studying them in depth, will tend to concentrate on the profit and loss account and balance sheet and may **not read the notes** that accompany these at all.

- Many users now **access** financial statements from **on-line sources** and many of these are a **summarised version** of the financial statements which does not include notes such as contingent liabilities.

- Even if users do read the contingent liability note there may be a **temptation to ignore the importance of these matters** as it will not always be clear whether in fact any liability will eventually be incurred, when it might be incurred and indeed how much the liability actually is.

(ii) **FRS 12 approach**

- There is a fine dividing line between a provision and a contingent liability.

- FRS 12 defines a provision as a liability that is of uncertain timing or amount. This follows the Statement of Principles definition of a liability that is an obligation to transfer economic benefits due to a past transaction or event. This obligation can be a legal obligation or a constructive obligation. If there is such an obligation therefore a provision must be made in the financial statements even if either the amount or the timing of the obligation is uncertain.

- In contrast a contingent liability is either a possible obligation or a present obligation which is not treated as a provision because it is not probable that the transfer of economic benefits will take place or because the amount of the obligation cannot be measured with sufficient reliability.

Pass marks. The examiner said that most errors arose from a failure to think about the information in the question. He gave the example that it would be impossible to provide for a liability without having a rough idea of its value. Despite this, many candidates suggested a provision for the Chance Cards, despite the fact that the question did not provide an estimate and claimed that it would be impossible to do so.

(c) **Wealth creation and financial statements**

(i) Wealth for shareholders is created in two main ways - by making a **profit** and by **increases** in the **value** of the business's **assets**. Both of these aspects of wealth creation are expanded upon in a set of financial statements.

(ii) The profit and loss account indicates not only the profit that has been made but also the **manner** in which this **profit** has been **made**. The figures that make up the operating profit, turnover and costs must be analysed between continuing operations, showing any acquisitions separately, and discontinued operations. This gives users of the financial statements an **indication** of how profits might be generated in **future years**.

(iii) Any **exceptional items** must be shown either on the face of the profit and loss account or in a note to the accounts indicating figures that are **not likely to occur on an on-going basis**.

(iv) SSAP 25 also requires **segmental analysis** of the profit for the period showing the profit made by each **geographical region** and **line of business**. Again this will provide shareholders with more information about the **quality** of the **profits** of **each area** of the business.

(v) The second way in which wealth is created for shareholders is by increases in the value of the assets of the business. Both the Companies Act and FRS 15 allow revaluation of tangible fixed assets and if this policy is chosen any **revaluations** during the year must be shown in the **Statement of Total Recognised Gains and Losses**. The information about revaluations is therefore available in a **primary financial statement** and gives shareholders an indication of any future changes in profit due to the revaluation such as increases in depreciation. The **note reconciling the actual profit to historical cost profit** also gives users an indication of the effect on profits of a policy of revaluation of tangible fixed assets.

46   FRS 12

(a) **Classification of contingencies**

> **Pass marks**. We have provided you with a relatively full suggested solution.

(i) FRS 12 requires that there are **different treatments** for contingencies depending upon the nature of any obligations involved and their **probabilities**. This provides users of financial statements with a clear and logical framework for understanding the various items they read regarding contingencies as well as what might not be disclosed.

(ii) When assessing the accounting treatment it is important to determine whether:

- The obligation arises from **past events** or depends on **uncertain future events**

- The **probability/possibility** of an **outflow of economic benefits**

(iii) The position with respect to liabilities can be summarised in terms of the following four scenarios.

Scenario	Accounting treatment
• There is a **present obligation** arising from a **past event** for which there is: – a **reliable estimate** – a **probable outflow of economic benefits**	Recognise as a provision in accounts
• There is a **present obligation** arising from a **past event** for which there is: – a **reliable estimate** – a **remote possibility** of an **outflow** of economic benefits	Disclose by way of note as a contingent liability
• There is an **obligation**: – **dependent** on **uncertain future benefits** – there is a **probable outflow of economic benefits**	Disclose by way of note as a contingent liability
• There is an **obligation**: – **dependent** on **uncertain future benefits** – there is a **remote possibility** of an **outflow** of economic benefits	None; no recognition nor any disclosure

(iv)   The position with respect to assets can be summarised in the following scenarios

Scenario	*Accounting treatment*

• **Past event:**
  – Confirmed by the **occurrence** of **future events**
  – **Inflow** of **economic benefits** is **probable**
	Recognised as a contingent asset in accounts

• **Past event:**
  – Confirmed by the occurrence of **future events**
  – **Inflow** of **economic benefits** is **not probable**
	None: do not recognise nor disclose

• **Past event:**
  – Confirmed by the occurrence of **future events**
  – The inflow of **economic benefits** is **certain**
	Recognise asset

(b)   (i)   *Leaking roof*

There is a **probability** that there will be an **outflow** of £100,000 in respect of the necessary remedial work on the roof. Therefore it should not be treated as a contingency but instead should be recognised in the financial statements as a provision for repairs of £100,000, the **best estimate** of the repairs.

(ii)   *Claim against sub-contractor*

This is potentially a contingent asset. However as the **subcontractor appears** to be almost **insolvent** then the **likelihood** of receiving any **compensation** has to be remote and therefore there is **no requirement to disclose** any information about it.

(iii)   *Provision for defects*

The provision must be **updated** by a charge of £40,000 to the profit and loss account in order to bring the amount of the provision up to £120,000. This is a liability that will probably arise.

(iv)   *Claim for delayed completion*

If the Chief Accountant is **virtually certain** that this **amount** will be **received** the it should be **treated as income** and **recognised as a debtor**. However if there is any shadow of uncertainty which means that the **receipt is only probable** then **disclosure only** should be made **not recognition**.

There is a fine dividing line to be drawn here between virtually certain and probable.

(v)   *Stolen computer*

There are two potential elements to this problem:

- Firstly it appears to be clear that the **claim** for £90,000 is **remote** and therefore would **not** be **disclosed** as a **contingent liability**.

- However there is also the possibility that a **trivial sum** might have to be paid in compensation for the hardware.

- Normally a **possible contingent liability** would be disclosed if the **sum is trivial** then it most **probably** is **not material** and therefore would **not require disclosure**.

(c)   (i)   *Advanced billing based on forecast requirements*

On the face of it, this appears to be an arrangement designed to **accelerate** the **recognition of revenue**. In terms of the SOP, profit should only be recognised on a transaction where there has been an increase in net assets; VJ Ltd needs to confirm that it controls the **right** to **future economic benefits** resulting from **past transactions** or events, ie VJ Ltd has delivered value to Acme plc and payment will be made.

The SOP (and FRS 18) cautions that where **uncertainty** exists in the recognition of assets, **prudence** must be exercised and an appropriate degree of **evidence** obtained on the **existence** of an asset.

No performance has taken place and anything could happen, eg Acme plc might cease to trade. Hence the potential sale of £800 million and costs of £300 million should not be recognised by VJ Ltd.

(ii) *Cancellable contract*

This scenario appears to involve even more **uncertainty** than scenario (i) above. **Prudence** would suggest that the transaction should **not be recognised** as a **sale.**

47   AIMS OF ASB

Pass marks. Note that part (i) asked about the *usefulness* of these standards, not their *requirements* - you must read the question and answer it accordingly. It is important to appreciate why standards were introduced in order to apply their spirit.

(a) **Providing financial information on performance and position**

(i) **FRS 3**

FRS 3 *Reporting financial performance* **aims to give users information about the core activities of the business which are expected to continue for the foreseeable future**.

It attempts to do this by requiring a structure for the profit and loss account which shows an analysis to the level of operating profit of **continuing** operations, **discontinued** operations and **acquisitions**.

In addition, separate disclosure is required of:

- profit and losses arising on the sale or termination of an operation
- costs of fundamental reorganisation or restructuring
- profits and losses on the disposal of fixed assets.

The profit and loss account format gives an analysis of any business which was discontinued during the year, showing the profit or loss for the period, so that the future impact of its closure can be appreciated. Prior to FRS 3 it would have been difficult to predict the impact of discontinued operations.

Exceptional items/additional statements

FRS 3 **requires all exceptional items to be highlighted, either on the face of the profit and loss account or in the notes to the accounts.**

Additional statements required, with the aim of providing users with more **information for decision making** are:

- **a statement of total recognised gains and losses**
- **a reconciliation of opening and closing shareholders' funds**

(ii) **SSAP 25**

SSAP 25 requires larger companies (ie plcs, banking and insurance companies or those meeting ten times the medium sized company criteria) to provide, where applicable, an analysis of turnover and operating profit attributable to different classes of business and an analysis of turnover attributable to each geographical market.

Segmental net assets are also required to be disclosed.

The purpose of **SSAP 25 disclosures** is **to provide users with information as to which classes of business**:

(1) **Earn the best rate of return**
(2) **Have a lower degree of risk**
(3) **Show the best growth rates**
(4) **Demonstrate the best potential for future development.**

The segmental information provided shows the different results achieved for each class of business (both continuing and discontinued) and information about segmental net assets. The user of the financial statements can see any differing operating profit margins in different areas of the business.

(iii) **FRS 12**

FRS 12 deals with the treatment of provisions, contingent gains or contingent losses in financial statements. The standard states that **an entity should never recognise a contingent liability. It should, however, disclose contingent liabilities unless the possibility of any outflow of economic benefits to settle it is remote.**

The standard also lays down strict rules about provisioning to ensure that **appropriate** provisions are accounted for but that profits are not **manipulated** by excessive provisioning.

It should be remembered that FRS 18 states that it is not necessary to exercise prudence where there is no uncertainty. Nor is it appropriate to use prudence as a reason for creating hidden reserves or excessive provisions because that would mean that the financial statements are not neutral and therefore not reliable. In this vein FRS 12 ensures that unnecessary provisions are not made but that there is **adequate disclosure** of possible liabilities.

(b) **SSAP 17**

Adjusting events. SSAP 17 cites a number of post balance sheet events which normally should be classified as adjusting events.

(1) **Fixed assets**: the subsequent determination of the purchase price or of the sale proceeds of assets purchased or sold before the year end.

(2) **Property**: the valuation of a property which provides evidence of impairment in value.

(3) **Investments**: the receipt of a copy of the financial statements or other information in respect of an unlisted company which provides evidence of an impairment in the value of a long-term investment.

(4) **Stocks**: the receipt of proceeds of sale or other evidence after the balance sheet date concerning the net realisable value of stock.

(5) **Work in progress**: the receipt of evidence that the previous estimate of accrued profit taken on a long-term contract was materially inaccurate.

(6) **Debtors**: the re-negotiation of amounts owing by debtors, or the insolvency of a debtor.

(7) **Claims**: amounts received or receivable in respect of insurance claims which were in the course of negotiation at the balance sheet date.

(8) **Discoveries**: the discovery of errors or frauds which show that the financial statements were incorrect.

Some events occurring after the balance sheet date, such as a deterioration in the company's operating results and in its financial position, may indicate a need to consider whether it is appropriate to use the *going concern* concept in the preparation of financial statements. Consequently such events may fall to be treated as adjusting events.

In addition, there are certain events which because of statutory or conventional requirements, are reflected in financial statements:

• Resolutions relating to proposed dividends and amounts appropriated to reserves

• The impact of changes in taxation rates

Non-adjusting events

The key examples given in SSAP 17 are as follows:

(1) **Issues of shares** and debentures

(2) Purchases and sales of **fixed assets** and **investments**

(3) **Losses of fixed assets** or stocks as a result of a catastrophe such as fire or flood

(4) Opening **new trading activities** or extending existing trading activities

(5) **Closing** a significant **part of trading activities** if this was not anticipated at the year end

(6) **Decline in value of property and investments** held as fixed assets, if it can be demonstrated that the decline occurred after the year end

(7) **Government action,** such as nationalisation

(8) **Strikes** and other labour disputes

> **Tutor's hint**. The question only requires five adjusting events and five non-adjusting events. The suggested answer is given in more detail to help you revise for potential scenarios which might come up in your exams.

48 NEWCARS PLC

> **Pass marks**. Take care to explain the relevance of the facts given in the question and also identify the additional information required.

(a) **Assessment of related party situation**

One of the key elements of FRS 8 in determining whether parties are related is the concept of control or influence and whether parties are under **common control** or **influence**.

There would appear to be little doubt that Arthur is a related party of both Newcars plc and Oldcars plc. He has **more than a 20% shareholding** in each company and as such a **significant influence** over the companies would **normally** be **presumed** and to reinforce this he is also a member of the board of directors of both companies.

The above scenario indicates that under FRS 8, Arthur would be presumed to be a related party of both companies unless it can be demonstrated otherwise.

The question however is whether Newcars and Oldcars are related parties of each other. FRS 8 sets out a number of situations where parties are deemed to be related parties but the relationship between Newcars and Oldcars does not fit into these categories.

FRS 8 states that **two parties** subject to **common influence**, ie Arthur, are only deemed to be related parties to such an **extent** that **one** of the **parties subordinates** its **own separate interests in a transaction**.

Therefore in order to determine whether these two companies are related we would need more information about the nature of the sales and purchases between the two companies. If it can be shown that one of the companies has subordinated its own interests, for **example** by making **sales** of cars at **less than market value**, then the two companies would be related in terms of FRS 8.

More information will therefore be required concerning the terms of trade between Newcars plc and Oldcars plc and the prices at which the cars are transferred between the companies. If it can be shown that the prices of the cars are not those of a **normal arm's length transaction** then the parties will be deemed to be related as Arthur will be presumed to have influenced the relationship between the two companies.

Given the nature of the trade between the two companies, second hand cars, it may be difficult to judge whether the prices of the sales are at market value as a market value for a second hand car is subjective and will depend upon factors such as the condition of the car. However second hand car valuation guides do exist and these should be consulted to try to discern whether the sales are being made on an arm's length basis.

Until the precise nature of the sales between the two companies has been examined it is not possible to state whether Newcars and Oldcars are indeed related parties.

(b) **Related party disclosures**

Assuming that Newcars plc and Oldcars plc are related parties then FRS 8 requires a variety of disclosures of names and transaction details. The following disclosures will be required:

- each company must state the other's name as a transacting related party;
- there must be a description of the relationship between them which would need to include mention of Arthur and that both companies are subject to influence from him;
- a description of the transactions;
- the amount of the transactions – this can be given in total;
- any other elements of the transactions that are necessary for an understanding of the financial statements such as any unusual trade terms or the fact that the sales were not made at an arm's length price if this was the case;
- any amounts due to or from the other company at the balance sheet date.

(c) **Reason for disclosures**

When a **user of financial statements** reads the financial statements they will **assume** that the **transactions** are all at **arm's length** and that the **organisation** has always **acted in its own best interests**. If there are **transactions with related parties** then these **assumptions may not be valid** and therefore it is necessary to **provide users** with **enough information** about the **related parties**, the relationship and the transactions in order that **users can make informed decisions** from the financial statements.

197

For example if transactions had taken place between two related parties and these sales were not at a fair market value then the sales or cost of sales figures may be distorted. The detail of disclosures that are required by FRS 8 mean that a user can assess the effect of these transactions and adjust the figures accordingly in order to gain a view as to the true profitability of the business.

Even if the transactions have been at arm's length it is still useful information for users to know of the existence of any related parties and particularly if the relationship is such that the business can be compelled to enter into transactions that are not necessarily in its own best interests.

(d) **Identifying the related parties**

FRS 8 provides a list of parties that are related parties of a company and a further list that are presumed to be related unless it can be demonstrated otherwise.

Many of these potential related parties are fairly easily determined, for example: the parent company; any subsidiary or associate companies; the directors of the company itself; directors of any parent companies; key management. Other related parties can be determined from other evidence, for example, any 20% shareholders will be apparent from the share register.

However FRS 8 also states that certain other parties, who might be far harder for the auditor to identify, are also presumed to be related parties. These are members of the close family of any directors, major investors or key management and any partnerships, companies or trusts in which any director, major investor or key management or their close family has a controlling interest. Clearly this wide net of individuals and organisations makes it harder for the auditor to be satisfied that all related parties with whom transactions have been undertaken have been identified.

Material transactions

The financial statements must disclose all material related party transactions. The issue of materiality in this context can also be a practical problem. Obviously related party transactions are material if they are **material** to the company. However FRS 8 also states that related party transactions are material if they are **material in relation to the related party** if the related party is a director, key manager, member of the close family of directors or managers or an entity controlled by a director, key manager or close family. This means that a transaction which is not material to the company itself may need to be disclosed if it is material to the other individual who is party to the transaction - not an easy task for the directors to determine nor the auditors to verify.

49   PREPARATION QUESTION: ISSUE OF SHARES

Journal entries

			Dr £	Cr £
23 Mar	DEBIT	Bank	30,000	
	CREDIT	Application account		30,000
		Being amounts received on application		
5 Apr	DEBIT	Bank	60,000	
	CREDIT	Allotment account		60,000
		Being amounts received on allotment		

				Dr £	Cr £
5 Apr	DEBIT		Application account	30,000	
			Allotment account	60,000	
	CREDIT		Share capital account		45,000
			Share premium account		45,000
			Being allotment of shares		
30 Apr	DEBIT		First call account	52,500	
	CREDIT		Share capital account		52,500
			Being first call of 35p per share		
4 May	DEBIT		Bank	49,000	
	CREDIT		First call account		49,000
			Being first call received on 140,000 shares		
25 Jun	DEBIT		Second call account	52,500	
	CREDIT		Share capital account		52,500
			Being second call of 35p per share		
29 Jun	DEBIT		Bank	49,000	
	CREDIT		Second call account		49,000
			Being second call received on 140,000 shares		
31 Jul	DEBIT		Forfeited shares account	7,000	
	CREDIT		First call account		3,500
			Second call account		3,500
			Being the forfeiture of 10,000 shares		

50   PREPARATION QUESTION: PURCHASE OF OWN SHARES

> **Pass marks**. If you have studied and understood this topic you will do well as it only asks for the basic rules to be followed when carrying out such a transaction. The second part of the question should present no problems, as long as you apply common sense when considering the effects of such a purchase of shares and what it may achieve.

(a)   **Accounting requirements – plc buying own shares**

The accounting requirements for a public listed company when it purchases its own shares are as follows.

(i)   The basic accounting entry to effect the purchase (or redemption) is to **debit the share capital account** and **credit cash** with the **nominal value of the shares** (if they are being purchased at nominal value).

(ii)   Alternatively, the entry can be made to a share purchase or redemption account, which will be cleared by a cash payment when all the necessary journal entries have been made.

This transaction has caused the **'creditors' buffer'** (capital and reserves excluding debenture capital) to shrink by the nominal value of the shares purchased.

This is not permitted, and to rectify the situation a transfer is made from distributable profits to a capital redemption reserve (CRR) equal to the nominal value of the shares.

The purchase must therefore be made out of **distributable profits,** or alternatively out of the **proceeds of a fresh issue** of shares. Where such shares are issued, the transfer to the CRR need only be the excess (if any) of the nominal value of the shares purchased over the proceeds of the new issue.

Any premium on purchase must be charged to distributable profits, unless the shares were originally issued at a premium and there is a fresh issue of shares. In this case any premium may be charged to the share premium account.

In this last case, there is an additional restriction because it is not possible to have a debit balance on the share premium account. This means that the amount that may be charged to the share premium account is limited to the lower of:

(i) The **premium received** on the original issue of the shares now being purchased.

(ii) The **proceeds of the fresh issue of shares.**

(iii) The current balance on the share premium account, after accounting for any premium on the fresh issue of shares.

Other rules regarding the transaction are as follows.

(i) The **articles** of association of the company must allow the purchase.

(ii) The shares must all be **fully paid** on redemption.

(iii) The shares purchased by the company must be **cancelled**.

(iv) There must be **shares remaining** in issue after the purchase which are not redeemable.

(v) The company must make a **return to the registrar** within 28 days of the purchase stating all the details (nominal value of the shares, date of transaction, amount paid and so on).

In summary, the journal entries are as follows.

		£	£
DEBIT	Ordinary share capital	X	
CREDIT	Bank		X

Being the payment for the nominal value of the shares purchased

DEBIT	Profit and loss account	X	
CREDIT	Capital redemption reserve		X

Being the transfer of the nominal value of the purchased shares to the CRR to maintain the creditor's buffer

DEBIT	Profit and loss account	X	
CREDIT	Bank		X

Being any premium on redemption or purchase

(b) **Advantages of purchase of own shares**

The following are advantages which a company gains when purchasing its own shares.

(i) The purchase allows the **distribution of surplus cash**, enabling the shareholders of the company to find other (perhaps better) uses for their money.

(ii) Companies with **employee share schemes** may wish to buy the employees' shares when they leave employment with the company.

(iii) It is possible to **buy out dissident shareholders**, which will allow the company to develop in the way the majority of the shareholders wish. Fewer shareholders also means that the company is less vulnerable to takeover.

(iv) By reducing the number of shares on the market, the **value of the remaining shares may rise** as part of the supply and demand mechanism, thus improving the marketability of the shares. (Note the effect on EPS and therefore the P/E ratio.)

(v) Companies which have messy and complicated capital structures may be able to simplify matters by buying whole classes of shares and issuing only one class in return.

(vi)   It may be possible to reduce the level of overall dividend paid out. Retaining earnings in the business would encourage growth.

51   PREPARATION QUESTION: PURCHASE OF OWN SHARES (CALCULATION)

Balance sheet of Gregory Ltd after redemption of shares.

	£	£
Ordinary shares £1 each £(82,500 + 15,000)		97,500
Share premium account (W2)		32,500
Capital redemption reserve (W3)		11,400
		141,400
Sundry fixed assets		65,000
Sundry net current assets	81,250	
Bank overdraft (W4)	(4,850)	
		76,400
		141,400

Workings

1	*Permissible capital payment*		£
	Cost of redemption (£40,000 × 1.09)		43,600
	Proceeds of new issue (15,000 × £1.50)	(22,500)	
	Profit and loss account	(15,000)	
			(37,500)
	Permissible capital payment		6,100

2	*Share premium account*		£
	Balance per balance sheet		25,000
	Plus premium on new issue of shares		7,500
			32,500

3	*Profit and loss account*		£
	Balance per balance sheet		15,000
	Premium on redemption	(3,600)	
	Transfer to CRR	(11,400)	
			(15,000)
			-

4	*Bank overdraft*	£
	Cash b/f	16,250
	Proceeds from share issue (15,000 × £1.50)	22,500
	Redemption of shares (£40,000 × 109%)	(43,600)
		(4,850)

52   H PLC II

> **Pass marks**. Part (b) reminds you that a transfer to capital redemption reserve is required.

(a)   BALANCE SHEET AT 30 APRIL 20X1 (AFTER SHARE REPURCHASE)

	£m
Net assets (18 – 4.5)	13.5
Share capital (7 – 2)	5.0
Capital redemption reserve	2.0
Profit and loss (11 – 4.5)	6.5
	13.5

BPP))) PROFESSIONAL EDUCATION

(b) **Interests of lenders on repurchase of shares**

The concept of capital maintenance concerns the safety margin of the liabilities of the company. The balance sheet equation can be expressed as follows.

$$\text{Assets} = \text{capital} + \text{liabilities}$$

If the company should go into liquidation its liabilities will be paid out of the proceeds of the disposal of the assets of the business. Even if the assets do not realise their full value, the liabilities are still covered as they must be paid before the shareholders receive any funds. Therefore, provided that the shortfall does not exceed the amount of the capital, then the liabilities will be repaid.

Some of the capital of a company is distributable to the shareholders as a dividend, normally the accumulated retained profits of the business. However other elements of capital such as the **nominal value of the share capital** and any **share premium** balance **cannot be distributed** to the shareholders **as dividend**. These elements therefore form a permanent balance of capital that is available, if necessary, to pay off the liabilities if the company fails.

If a company **repurchases some of its shares** then the **share capital will be reduced** thereby **reducing the buffer of capital for repayment of the liabilities**. For this reason a **transfer is required out of the distributable profits** of the business in order to maintain the buffer of undistributable capital. This transfer is to the **Capital Redemption Reserve**.

In the case of H plc prior to the repurchase the undistributable capital totalled £7 million, the balance on the share capital account. After the repurchase the share capital is reduced to £5 million but the transfer to the Capital Redemption Reserve of £2 million means that the undistributable capital remains at £7 million.

(c) **Reasons for permission to repurchase shares**

The two main reasons why companies are permitted to buy back their own shares are:

- To use up surplus cash
- In order for shares of a private company to be sold by a shareholder

If a company has surplus cash but no profitable investment opportunities then it may be useful for it to buy back some shares from shareholders who are willing to sell. This will then mean that in future there are less shares on which to pay a dividend and it may also see a rise in the share price as there are less shares with an interest in the future profits of the business.

In a private company there is no ready market for the sale of shares. Suppose that one of the shareholders in a **family owned private company** wishes to sell his shares. The family may wish to keep the shares within the family but cannot find the funds to repurchase the shares. If the shares are repurchased by the company then the **control of the company remains with the family**.

Similarly if a **shareholder in a private company wishes to exit** for some reason there is **no ready market** in which he can sell the shares. Therefore **repurchase** by the company is **often the only option**.

(d) There are a number of reasons why a company might wish to purchase its own shares.

Some companies may find that they have a **surplus of cash** and not enough investment opportunities to use this cash. Cash is a wasted asset in many ways and if there are shareholders that are willing to have their shares repurchased then this is often a useful way for companies to use this surplus cash in order to reduce the number of shares on which a dividend will be paid. The reduction in the number of shares may also increase the value of the remaining shares due to market forces.

In private companies there is often no open market for the sale of shares therefore if a **shareholder** wishes to sell his shares then the only opportunity may be to sell them back to the company.

If there are a small number of **dissident shareholders** in a company then the repurchase of their shares may allow the company to follow the path that the majority of shareholders wish for.

If a company has an **employee share scheme** then it may wish to repurchase the shares of employees, particularly those with significant interests, if they leave the company.

If a company has a **complicated capital structure** after years of equity and non-equity issues it may decide to simplify this structure by repurchasing some classes of shares.

53   CAPITAL TRANSACTIONS

(a)

SHARE CAPITAL ACCOUNT

	£		£
		Balance b/d	4,000,000
		Application and allotment	700,000
Balance c/d	5,000,000	Call account	300,000
	5,000,000		5,000,000
		Balance b/d	5,000,000

SHARE PREMIUM ACCOUNT

	£		£
		Balance b/d	1,250,000
		Application and allotment	200,000
Balance c/d	1,450,400	Investment in own shares	400
	1,450,400		1,450,400
		Balance b/d	1,450,400

APPLICATION AND ALLOTMENT ACCOUNT

	£		£
Cash returned (100,000 × 25p)	25,000	Cash (2,100,000 × 25p)	525,000
Share premium (1,000,000 × 20p)	200,000	Cash (998,000 × 40p)	399,200
Share capital	700,000	Investment - own shares	800
	925,000		925,000

INVESTMENT IN OWN SHARES ACCOUNT

	£		£
Call	800	Cash - reissue (2,000 × 60p)	1,200
Share premium	400		
	1,200		1,200

Note: There are other methods that use a *'forfeited shares'* account and a *'Reissue of forfeited share accounts.'* So do not be put off if you see such terminology in an exam. Remember the transactions and entries are the same; only the names of the accounts are different.

CALL ACCOUNT

	£		£
Share capital - final call			
(1,000,000 × 0.30)	300,000	Cash	300,000
	300,000		300,000

(b) **Bonus issues from distributable reserves**

    (i) *Impact on company's capital structure*

        If X Ltd makes a **bonus issue** of new shares out of **distributable profits** the effect on the capital structure of the company will be that:

- The **share capital increases** by the number of new shares issued and the **profit and loss reserve** will be **reduced** by the same amount.

- The total of share capital and reserves will **remain** the **same**.

    (ii) *Impact on shareholders' interests*

- They now hold more shares each but they still hold the **same proportion** of the **total share capital** as they did before as the bonus shares are issued in proportion to the current holding of shares.

- The shareholders now own more shares and therefore will receive dividends in future on those shares. However, the **profits** that are **available** for **payment** of the **dividend** have been **reduced**. One scenario is that it is possible that the **dividend** per share might be **reduced** in the future **depending** upon the **future profitability** of the company.

- Another scenario is that market sentiment might improve if it perceives the bonus issue presaging a future dividend increase. Hence the overall value of the shares could increase.

- The bonus issue will also impact on the EPS calculation.

- The shareholders have not paid for the bonus shares and therefore the **net assets** of the company have **not increased**. It is therefore possible that the **market value** of each share **may decrease slightly** as the market value of the company remains the same in total but is **now spread across more shares**.

    (iii) *Impact on creditors' position*

- They are likely to be **comparatively safer** after the bonus issue.

- The effect of the bonus issue has been to **transfer profits** that were previously distributable to the **share capital account** which is **not distributable**.

- **More assets** must now be **retained** within the company for the **eventual settlement** of **liabilities** if the company did go into liquidation.

- The total of share capital and reserves is still the same and in consequence there will be **no effect** on the **gearing ratio** of the company.

(c) **Classification of share capital types**

    (i) *Types of share capital*

        Companies can issue **many different types of share capital**. It is possible to issue:

- Shares that may be **redeemable** at some point in the future

- Shares that may be **converted** to ordinary shares in the **future**

- Shares which **carry** the **right** to a **fixed** amount of **dividend** in each period

- Shares with **combinations** of the above **attributes**

- FRS 4 *Capital instruments* requires that the **shareholders' funds** should be **disclosed** showing the split between **equity interests** and **non-equity interests**.

(ii) *Non-equity interests*

These are any shares that have any of the **attributes** of **loan capital**. Hence, the following:

- Any redeemable shares should be shown as non-equity.

- Any shares such as preference shares which have a fixed percentage dividend each period

- The remaining shares are equity shares.

(iii) *Equity shares*

- The distinction is important as the **equity shares** are the ones which have **no rights** to a **dividend** unless the **directors** of the company **recommend** that a dividend is paid.

- In the eventuality of the **liquidation** of the company the **equity shareholders** also have **no rights** to any of the **assets** of the company **until all** of the **creditors** of the company and the **non-equity shares** have been **paid**.

(iv) *Overall*

- Shareholders need to appreciate the risks and returns associated with each category of share capital.

(d) **Redemption of shares in private companies**

For **private companies** there is a significant departure from the principle that shares must not be purchased or redeemed in a way which reduces non-distributable equity reserves. This rule applies to private companies only (provided that their articles of association authorise them to do so).

A private company may redeem or purchase its own shares out of *capital* (ie non-redeemable share capital, capital redemption reserve, share premium account or revaluation reserve) but only on **condition** that the **nominal value of shares redeemed (or purchased) both**:

(i) **Exceeds** the **proceeds** of any **new share issue** to finance the redemption (or purchases).

(ii) **First exhausts** the **distributable profits** of the **company entirely.**

In such a situation, a **transfer** must be made to the **capital redemption reserve** of the amount by which **distributable profits exceed** the **premium on redemption or purchase.** (If the premium on redemption or purchase exceeds the total of distributable profits, the difference must be deducted from non-redeemable share capital, and there will be no capital redemption reserve.)

PERFORMANCE

OBJECTIVE TEST ANSWERS: PERFORMANCE

1	B			
2	B	1		A high current ratio is not necessarily an indication of efficiency
		2		Highly geared companies are usually more risky than companies with a low gearing ratio
		4		Treating leases as finance leases, not as operating leases, will increase the gearing ratio
3	D			
4	D			
5	A			
6	C	A	$^{180}/_{12}$	
		B	$^{30}/_{12}$	
		C	$^{24}/_{12}$	
		D	$^{36}/_{12}$	
7	A	A	32/400	
		B	32/200	
		C	35/400	
		D	17/400	
8	D	A	300/50	
		B	300/32	
		C	300/35	
		D	300/8 (or 400 × £3 /32)	

54 PREPARATION QUESTION: OVERTRADING

Overtrading generally refers to a depletion in net current assets over time, resulting in serious problems for management in finding cash to meet its commitments as they fall due. This **can result from two types of factor**.

(a) **Internal factors**

    (i) **Increasing stock levels.** There may be sound competitive reasons for a company to have higher stock levels (for example, if a large amount of stock was acquired in a bargain purchase, or in anticipation of a large order to be satisfied after the balance sheet date), but if the higher stock levels have been financed only out of existing funds, overtrading is a real risk.

    (ii) **Increasing debtors' levels.** Again there may be genuine reasons to allow debtors to rise (for example, favourable credit terms will attract more business to the company) but the liquidity position of the company will worsen unless new funds are introduced.

    (iii) **Using cash or short-term borrowings to acquire new fixed assets.** The fixed assets will generate cash receivable in the longer term, but in the shorter term working capital will have been depleted.

    (iv) **Using cash or short-term borrowings to acquire investments or to make loans.**

(v) **Redeeming shares, debentures or loan stock without issuing new equity or borrowings**. This must reduce the liquid resources at the company's disposal leaving fewer resources to pay other creditors.

(vi) **Over-reliance on short-term borrowings**. Long-term assets (fixed assets and longer-term stocks) must be financed by long-term liabilities (equity and loans). Short-term creditors and bank overdrafts should be reduced to appropriate levels by raising new funds through issuing more equity and long-term loans.

(b) **External factors**

(i) **Overheating of the economy itself** may lead to inflationary pressures. When general prices rise, increased cash resources will be needed to maintain the operating capability of a company in replacing fixed assets, stocks and net monetary working capital. Fresh capital will continually be needed if the liquidity position is not to worsen.

(ii) **Government fiscal policies can increase the pressure on cash resources**. For example, the introduction of the payment of corporation tax by instalments will impact a company's cash flow.

(iii) **Rising interest rates** may drive up the cost of overdrafts and similar short term finance.

(iv) **Economic recession** might leave a business stranded with high stock levels and excess production capacity.

55 PREPARATION QUESTION: ANN NAIDU

(a)

REPORT

To: Ann Naidu
Form: A. Student
Subject: Relative Profitability of Blue Ltd and Red Ltd   Date: 28 January 20X5

The purpose of this report is to help you to assess the relative profitability of Blue Ltd and Red Ltd. This will be done using certain key ratios, the meaning of which will be explained. Other information provided in the management accounts of the two companies will also be taken into consideration.

(a) **Return on capital employed**

- This ratio shows in percentage terms how much profit is being generated by the capital employed in the company.

- Red Ltd shows a higher return on capital employed, and is therefore more profitable per £ of capital employed in the business.

- However, it should be noted that in absolute terms, Blue Ltd is making more profit; it is just not using its capital as effectively.

(b) **Gross profit margin**

- This ratio shows the percentage of gross profit generated by the company's sales, and is thus an indication of the gross profit margin on sales.

- The gross profit margin of Red Ltd is higher than that of Blue Ltd, indicating that it is selling at higher margins.

- Blue Ltd's higher turnover may be at the expense of lower margins.

- Gross profit margin is also impacted by **non-financial factors** that must be taken into consideration:

  - Pricing policy, discounts allowed etc

  - Sales mix

  - Production efficiency and waste

  - Effectiveness of physical controls over stocks/materials

  - Impact of inflation/market factors

  - Shrinkages and pilferage

  - Sourcing of supplies, discounts received etc

  - Stock valuation issues (obsolescence, overhead absorption, NRV etc)

(c) **Net profit margin**

- The net profit margin shows the operating profit as a percentage of sales thus indicating the overall profitability of the company after all the operating expenses have been charged

- The net profit margin of Red Ltd is significantly higher than that of Blue Ltd which in turn has led to the higher return on capital employed of Red Ltd

- The net profit margin is affected by the gross profit margin and also by the operating expenses of the business. In this case the higher net profit margin in Red Ltd is not only due to Red Ltd's higher gross profit margin but also the fact that Red Ltd's operating costs as a percentage of sales are lower than those of Blue Ltd.

(d) **Earnings per share**

- This is a measure of the return to shareholders in the year and shows, in pence, the profit after tax earned for each ordinary share.

- Red Ltd's earnings per share is considerably higher than that of Blue Ltd, showing that shareholders are **getting more out of their investment.**

Conclusion

Red Ltd is the more profitable, in terms of all four key ratios. Although Blue Ltd is the larger company in terms of turnover, profit and asset base, it is clear that Red Ltd is making better use of those assets and giving a better return to shareholders.

Signed

A. Student.

(b) **Practical limitations of ratio analysis**

These can be summarised as follows.

- Different accounting policies give different ratios
- Availability of comparable information
- Use of historical/out of date information
- Ratios are not definitive - they are only a guide
- Interpretation needs careful analysis and should not be considered in isolation
- It is a subjective exercise
- It can be subject to manipulation
- Ratios are not defined in standard form

56   RATIOS: T plc

> **Pass marks**. In part (a) you should read the requirement carefully. The calculation of ratios must take account of the required adjustments. In part (b), do not just talk about the usefulness of ROCE in general terms; you are asked about *monthly* calculation of the ratio.

(a) (i)   **Gross profit percentage**

October

$$\frac{532}{900 - 200} = 76\%$$

September

$$\frac{525}{700} = 75\%$$

Sales have been adjusted for sales made at cost to the charity. Inclusion of these figures would distort the gross profit percentage as no margin was earned on these sales, so making it artificially low.

(ii)   **Current ratio**

October

$$\frac{1,042 - 371 + 400}{185} = 5.8{:}1$$

September

$$\frac{952}{360} = 2.6{:}1$$

The bank overdraft shown in the October accounts has arisen because of a short-term need to raise funds to purchase plant. As this will be replaced by a long-term loan in December, to include it as a current liability would distort the current ratio.

(iii) **Debtor days**

October

$$\frac{1,010}{900} \times 31 = 35 \text{ days}$$

September

$$\frac{720}{700} \times 30 = 31 \text{ days}$$

(iv)   **Creditor days**

October

$$\frac{185}{368 - 220 + 32} \times 31 = 32 \text{ days}$$

September

$$\frac{360}{175 - 37 + 220} \times 30 = 30 \text{ days}$$

(v)   **Stock turnover days**

October

$$\frac{(220 + 32)/2}{368} \times 31 = 11 \text{ days}$$

September

$$\frac{(37 + 220)/2}{175} \times 30 = 22 \text{ days}$$

Average stock has been used to smooth out the distortions in the stock-holding pattern.

(vi)   **Return on capital employed**

October

$$\frac{292}{2,384} \times 100 = 12.2\%$$

September

$$\frac{275}{2,092} \times 100 = 13.1\%$$

(b) A return on capital employed ratio based on monthly financial statements may be of limited use because it could easily be distorted by monthly fluctuations.

Any adjustment or unusual transaction made in a particular month would have the capacity to distort the ratio whilst such adjustments, unless they are exceptional, would be smoothed out over a year. In addition a monthly ROCE would take no account of seasonal fluctuation in results.

(c)   **Cash flow – October 20X7**

	£'000
Cash received from customers	610
Payments for materials consumed	(353)
Other operating costs	(240)
Purchase of fixed assets	(400)
Net outflow for the month from operating activities	(383)

Workings

(i)

	b/f	Additions	Depreciation	c/f
	£'000	£'000	£'000	£'000
Fixed assets	1,500	400	(2)	1,898

(ii)

	b/f	Change	Cash/ consumed	c/f
	£'000	£'000	£'000	£'000
Debtors/sales	720	900	(610)	1,010
Stocks/materials consumed	220	178*	(366)**	32
Creditors/purchases	(360)	(178)*	353	(185)

* Purchases

**	£'000
Cost of sales	368
Depreciation – fixed assets	(2)
	366

(Note: You may prefer to use T accounts rather than a column format.)

---

57   PERFORMANCE INDICATORS

> **Pass marks**. The question gave all the clues to the approach required here. Don't automatically assume that you are simply required to compare a ratio with that of the previous year and say whether it is higher or lower. The issues here are more complicated.
>
> A good answer would state why the trend information might indicate why one company was more *risky* than the other.

(a)   **Benchmarking and trends**

Ratios on their own may reveal very little if they are merely isolated indicators of a company's performance. It is therefore important that **the trend of a particular ratio is benchmarked over time for a particular company or against an industry norm**. This enables the company's performance to be viewed in relative terms against its past performance or against that of its competitors.

Volatility and risk

In particular, the volatility of a company's performance can be measured over time, giving an indication of the *risk* associated with the business. Are results slowly improving or are they lurching from good to bad to very good with no real pattern?

Investors (usually) prefer slow steady growth with low risk so that they can predict the company's performance and hence the likely return on their investment.

Constant ratios

A ratio may appear unfavourable unless it is compared to that of other periods. If the ratio has stayed roughly the same for some time, then the company is obviously able to operate with the ratio at that level in the long term, even though the ratio may *appear* to be adverse.

Sudden changes

Conversely, **sudden changes in ratios over time may indicate substantial problems to come**. Changes can indicate to investors that the managers of the company may not be able to cope with a suddenly different situation.

(b) **Sales and gross margins**

The sales of X and Y for 20X5 are at a similar level, with X showing a significant increase in sales of 56% over the three year period. Y's increase in sales has been more modest, amounting to less than 11% over the same period. However, the increase in X's sales have been achieved by a deterioration of gross profit which has fallen every year from 20X3 to 20X5. Y on the other hand has maintained a steady level of gross margin which has exceeded that of X in each year.

In contrasting the businesses, it appears that Y has retained margins, perhaps offering an up market, quality service, while X's rapid increase in sales indicates a low price, down-market operation. H plc may prefer to be associated with a 'quality' company.

Current and quick ratios

X's current ratio is better than Y's and improving. However, its quick ratio has fallen substantially over the three year period although only to the level of Y. Y's current and quick ratios have remained at the same level throughout the period under review. This indicates that X has increased its stock holding substantially over the period. In contrast, Y's stock levels and general liquidity position have remained relatively constant.

ROCE

X's return on capital employed has improved significantly and now equals that of Y. This indicates that the increase in sales has been achieved without a corresponding increase in capital. However, the level of gearing, which has increased significantly over the three years, shows that any increases in capital that have been made have been achieved through non-equity finance such as debentures and even an increased overdraft (depending on how the ROCE has been calculated). The management of X may be struggling to deal with the growth in sales. They may not have the ability to recognise the need for further capital to underpin the rise in sales and steady the company's position.

Y again has maintained return on capital employed at a steady level with only a small increase during the period. Gearing peaked in 20X4 and has begun to decline.

Summary and decision

Given that H plc prefers a distributor which is unlikely to collapse, Y seems the safer choice.

(i) Its growth rate has not equalled that of X but it has shown a steady increase in both gross margin and return on capital employed.

(ii) Y's level of gearing is falling, indicating a reduction in dependency on prior charge capital.

(iii) Y's stock levels and liquidity are constant, indicating that the company has avoided 'overtrading' (compared to X).

(iv) Y is also able to manage its working capital very well, surviving on what some would consider the low current ratio of 1.7: 1.

Altogether the ratio analysis of Y indicates a steady company with a trend of continually improving results and low risk of bankruptcy, and therefore it should be H plc's choice.

(c) **Other information to review when interpreting accounts**

  - Comments in the chairman's report and directors' report

  - The age and nature of the company's assets

  - Current and future developments in the company's markets, at home and overseas, recent acquisitions or disposals of a subsidiary by the company

  - Exceptional items in the profit and loss account

  - Any other noticeable features of the report and accounts, such as post balance sheet events, contingent liabilities, a qualified auditors' report, the company's taxation position, and so on

(d) **Revaluation versus historical cost**

If one company revalues its fixed assets whereas the other does not this will affect the return on capital employed, gross margin and gearing ratios. The capital employed will be higher in the company that revalues and its profit will be lower due to higher depreciation charges so the return on capital employed will be lower.

Again as shareholders' funds increases by the amount of the revaluation gain the gearing level of the company which revalues will appear to be lower.

Capitalisation of development costs

If one company capitalises development costs while the other company writes off all such costs to the profit and loss account this will again affect return on capital employed and gearing ratios.

The company which capitalises development costs will have a higher level of capital employed. In the short term it is likely to have a higher level of profit as the development costs are not being written off in the profit and loss account. These two factors may almost cancel each other out but they will have some effect on return on capital employed.

However, it is important to remember that, because development costs are amortised, the effect of the policy is simply to change the periods in which the costs pass through the profit and loss account.

The company which capitalises development costs will have a higher capital employed and therefore the gearing ratio may appear lower than in the company which writes off its development costs.

Where trends are considered, capitalising development costs may have little overall effect on profits and return on capital employed.

58   BENCHMARKING: CUTLERS

> **Pass marks**. Remember that it is the analysis of the figures which is important: it should be well argued and well written.

(a)   *CE Ltd*   *Industry average*

$Return\ on\ shareholders'\ equity = \dfrac{110}{424} \times 100 = 26\%$ 33%

$Return\ on\ total\ capital\ employed = \dfrac{(110 + 15)}{(424 + 150)} \times 100 = 22\%$ 29%

$Gross\ profit\ percentage = \dfrac{180}{900} \times 100 = 20\%$ 30%

CE Ltd		*Industry average*
Current ratio =	$\frac{221}{147} = 1.5{:}1$	1.9:1
Stock turnover =	$\frac{96}{720} \times 365 = 49$ days	37 days
Debtors turnover =	$\frac{120}{900} \times 365 = 49$ days	41 days
Gearing =	$\frac{150}{574} \times 100 = 26\%$	40%

Comment

CE Ltd is generally underperforming compared to the industry benchmarks. Shareholders are receiving a return below that which they should expect for each £1 invested. The company is obviously not using the funds available to it in the most efficient way.

The gross profit percentage is much lower than the industry average. This could mean that CE Ltd is not controlling costs very well, or that sales prices are lower than the average, perhaps due to local competition problems.

CE Ltd's current ratio, while lower than the industry benchmark, is not unhealthy and has certainly not reached the stage where liquidity might be a problem.

The company has a longer stock turnover period than average, which means that cash is tied up in stock for longer, thus affecting cash flow. The case is similar for debtors, with CE Ltd taking eight days longer to extract cash from debtors.

CE Ltd has much lower gearing than the industry average and with debenture interest at 10% and return to equity 22% CE Ltd should perhaps consider the use of more debt finance.

(b) Four reasons why **the above analysis could be misleading** are as follows.

(i) **Accounting policies etc**

Inter-firm comparisons (including comparison with industry benchmarks) do not take into account the different accounting policies and treatments adopted by different companies.

Accounting standards may give scope to select from two or more treatments and such a choice can have a significant impact on the results of different businesses. For example, under SSAP 13 development costs can be capitalised and amortised or written off immediately.

(ii) **Industry segment**

CE Ltd may operate in that part of the industry which operates with a higher turnover but lower margins, for example the part of the industry which produces cheap cutlery rather than high quality cutlery. Alternatively, CE Ltd may be producing very high quality, low volume products which might have the same effect.

(iii) **Size of business**

CE Ltd may be a much smaller company than is usual in the industry. It will thus have less opportunity to achieve the **economies of scale,** terms with debtors and creditors and so on which larger companies can obtain.

(iv) **Age of fixed assets**

The age of CE Ltd's fixed assets may be very different to that of the industry in general. If CE Ltd is a new company then its fixed asset values are likely to be high thus reducing ROCE. Similarly after a period of fixed asset replacement, ROCE and gearing would both be reduced.

59   INHERITANCE: BUSINESS STRATEGY

(a)   Four major changes to the running of the company are

- Increased turnover
- Investment in new machinery
- Significant increase in borrowings
- Working capital policy

Turnover

Turnover has increased threefold. The company has increased sales significantly. The gross margin has fallen from 60% to 40%. This decrease in pricing may have helped increase sales.

It is not clear how this price strategy affects the company's market share or how the company's competitors are responding to this. The company may be filling a new niche or staging a price war to consolidate the market.

Bad debts have risen and may be a cause for concern. This may be due to various factors such as

- Poor credit control
- Falling product quality

Net margin has fallen from 34% to 11%. This is due to the increases in bad debts, depreciation and interest.

Selling expenses have not increased in proportion to the increase in turnover pointing to increased efficiency in this area. Perhaps the company is selling more to existing customers.

Machinery

Investment in machinery has seen the balance sheet figure increase by 3.6 times. There has been no revaluation as there is no corresponding revaluation reserve.

The increase in machinery may go some way to explaining the increase in turnover. Capacity has been increased. The sales generated by the machinery are now 1.6 times (19X9: 1.8 times) the machinery's value.

It is likely that the machinery has only been in use for part of the year and there would be a period where production would be hindered whilst the machinery was delivered, installed and 'bedded in', so this rate of asset turnover would seem quite healthy in comparison with the previous year.

Borrowings

The loan is £4.5m higher than the previous year. Borrowings are therefore 16 times greater. The majority of the loan appears to have been used to buy the machinery (£4.4m).

The gearing of the company has increased significantly (to 56%) which in turn increases the financial risk of the company.

The cash position of the company has worsened with an overdraft of £33,000 replacing a cash balance of £36,000. The cash position may be a short term problem. There may be a delay between earning financial profits and seeing the beneficial cashflows and an improvement in managing working capital may help this situation.

Working capital management

There has been a fairly drastic change in working capital management policy. Stock turnover has increased by 22 days, debtors turnover has almost doubled to 76 days whereas creditors turnover is almost the same as in the previous year. This means that the overall working capital cycle is now 90 days rather than 28 days. This has obviously had a significant effect on cash flow with the bank balance of £36,000 in 19X9 reduced to an overdraft of £33,000.

It is entirely possible that the debtors turnover increase is part of the policy of increasing sales by offering longer periods of credit to customers. The increased stock turnover could be due to holding a wider range of stocks or stockpiling to meet the increased demand. If the situation continues it could be indicative of overtrading and may have serious liquidity consequences.

(b) **Impact of one year**

The changes discussed in part (a) are quite dramatic. We have assessed the impact they have had so far but not the impact they may have in the future. We do not know when the changes were made.

There is inevitably a lag between the decision making stage and the implementation of the decision. If the machinery was installed in June 20X0 and the sales relied upon increased production then we could expect sales to be as high as £14m in 20X1.

The cash and debtors positions should improve as the increased profits are translated into cashflows. The new director may be looking at a longer term strategy which involves undercutting competitors and gaining a dominant market position. It would be useful to gain more information as to the director's plans in order to make more sense of the position of the company to date.

Workings

1 *Sales* $\frac{8,400}{2,700} = 3.1$ increase

   Gross margin   19X9: $\frac{1,620}{2,700} = 60\%$ 20X0: $\frac{3,360}{8,400} = 40\%$

   Net margin   19X9: $\frac{906}{2,700} = 33.6\%$ 20X0: $\frac{930}{8,400} = 11.1\%$

2 *Machinery* $\frac{5,289}{1,470} = 3.6$ increase

   Sales generated   19X9: $\frac{2,700}{1,470} = 1.8$ times   20X0: $\frac{8,400}{5,289} = 1.6$ times

3 *Loan* $\frac{4,800}{300} = 16$ increase

   Gearing   19X9: $\frac{300}{300+900+1,887}$ 20X0: $\frac{4,800}{4,800+900+2,817}$

   $= 9.7\%$ $= 56.4\%$

   Debt equity   19X9: $\frac{300}{900+1887} = 10.8\%$ 20X0: $\frac{4,800}{900+2,817} = 129.1\%$

   Loan application: machinery $5,289 - 1,470 + 624 - (1,350 - 1,323) = £4,416$

4 *Working capital*

   Stock turnover   19X9: $\frac{90}{1,080} \times 365$ 20X0: $\frac{714}{5,040} \times 365$

   $= 30$ days $= 52$ days

$$Debtors\ turnover \quad 19X9: \quad \frac{249}{2,700} \times 365 \qquad 20X0: \quad \frac{1,749}{8,400} \times 365$$

$$= 34\ days \qquad\qquad = 76\ days$$

$$Creditors\ turnover \quad 19X9: \quad \frac{108}{1,080} \times 365 \qquad 20X0: \quad \frac{525}{5,040} \times 365$$

$$= 36\ days \qquad\qquad = 38\ days$$

60 REDUCING OVERDRAFT: LINDA PLC

> **Pass marks**. Do not include cash sales in the debtors turnover calculation.

(a) **Debtors turnover**

$$\frac{2.2}{14} \times 365 = 57\ days$$

(b) **Debtors turnover**

$$\frac{2.2 - 0.6}{14} \times 365 = 42\ days$$

(c) (i) **Debtors balance**

March sales : £14m × 31/365 × 60% = £713,425

February sales: £14m × $\dfrac{57-31}{365}$ = £997,260

Total = £1,710,685

(ii) **Estimated overdraft**

	£
Existing overdraft	800,000
Less decrease in debtors: 2.2m – 1,710,685	(489,315)
Add discount (£14m × 31/365 × 40% × 2%)	9,512
	320,197

(d) (i) **Impact of manager's proposal**

The manager's proposal would have rendered the financial statements misleading because it is a **one-off transaction** designed to improve the year end balance sheet.

The balance sheet, which is effectively a **snapshot** of the company's financial position at the year end date, would show both trade debtors and the overdraft at a lower figure than normal. Hence these figures would **not** be **comparable** with either past or future periods and analytical review would be meaningless.

(ii) **Accounting for settlement discounts**

The discount of £9,512 would be included in **administrative expenses** as it is a settlement discount.

(e) **How to avoid a qualification**

If the policy of offering discounts was only for the month of March and the company then returned to its previous policy then it is likely that the auditor would consider this to be a '**window dressing**' type of transaction. According to SSAP 17, Post balance sheet events, disclosure would be required of the reversal or maturity after the year end of this situation as the substance is to alter the appearance of the balance sheet at the balance sheet date . In order to satisfy the auditor and ensure that there is no audit qualification the directors would require a **note** to the financial statements disclosing the **debtors** position and **overdraft** amount once the March discount policy was no longer in force.

(f)   **Information provided by cash flow statements**

Cash flow statements provide information that assists in the assessment of a business's **liquidity**, **solvency** and **financial adaptability**.

61   K PLC

Pass marks. You should notice that rather than simply commenting on the superiority or inferiority of each company, the question asks for a discussion of the business practices adopted by each.

The examiner said that calculating ratios is not enough in itself in this question. 'The question requires careful selection of ratios and also some thought about how each is to be interpreted. There were some quite deliberate clues given in the question (for example the names of the companies were intended to suggest something about their pricing and investment strategies).'

(a)   **Ratios**

	K plc	Pricecut Ltd	Bigstore plc
Gross profit margin	$\dfrac{3,500}{5,000} = 70\%$	$\dfrac{2,000}{4,000} = 50\%$	$\dfrac{8,250}{11,000} = 75\%$
Net profit margin	$\dfrac{2,150}{5,000} = 43\%$	$\dfrac{960}{4,000} = 24\%$	$\dfrac{5,060}{11,000} = 46\%$
Return on capital employed	$\dfrac{2,150}{5,018} = 43\%$	$\dfrac{960}{1,320} = 73\%$	$\dfrac{5,060}{8,017} = 63\%$
Advertising/sales	$\dfrac{400}{5,000} = 8\%$	$\dfrac{480}{4,000} = 12\%$	$\dfrac{880}{11,000} = 8\%$
Sales staff wages/ sales	$\dfrac{350}{5,000} = 7\%$	$\dfrac{400}{4,000} = 10\%$	$\dfrac{880}{11,000} = 8\%$
Asset turnover	$\dfrac{5,000}{5,018} = 1.0$	$\dfrac{4,000}{1,320} = 3.0$	$\dfrac{11,000}{8,017} = 1.4$
Stock turnover days	$\dfrac{123}{1,500} \times 365 = 30$	$\dfrac{99}{2,000} \times 365 = 18$	$\dfrac{286}{2,750} \times 365 = 38$
Creditors days	$\dfrac{115}{1,500} \times 365 = 28$	$\dfrac{82}{2,000} \times 365 = 15$	$\dfrac{286}{2,750} \times 365 = 38$

Pricecut Ltd

(i)   Pricecut Ltd operates at a much **lower gross profit margin** than K plc which, if Pricecut is selling the same product range, indicates that it is selling the goods at a lower price.

(ii)   Pricecut Ltd's **net profit margin** is almost half that of K plc which is not only due to the low gross profit margin but also due to Pricecut Ltd's expenses policy.

(iii)   Pricecut spends relatively more on advertising and sales staff remuneration than K plc indicating that it has an **aggressive selling policy** although admittedly lower turnover than K plc.

(iv)   Pricecut Ltd holds its stock for almost half the time that K plc does again indicating a **fast turnover of stock,** supporting the aggressive selling policy, and also therefore lower **stock holding costs**.

(v)   Pricecut Ltd appears to have a low price policy but this has not affected return on capital employed which is significantly higher than that of K plc.

(vi) The reason for the above is that, despite the lower gross profit margin and net profit margin, Pricecut Ltd has a considerably higher **asset turnover** than K plc.

(vii) The available evidence suggests that Pricecut Ltd has a positive policy of minimising its **investment in fixed assets**.

(viii) Finally Pricecut Ltd has a short creditors' payment period indicating that either suppliers are paid quickly. This may be important so as to maintain goodwill and the guaranteed supply that is essential when stock turnover is so quick.

(ix) The short creditor days figure may also indicate that a or that a substantial amount of suppliers are paid in cash.

(x) Quick **turnover** of stock is probably produced by advertising and well-paid sales staff and seems to be supported by suppliers.

(xi) Pricecut may also be operating a more relaxed **trading environment**, that accepts a certain amount of loss owing to **shrinkage** which has an adverse impact on the gross margin.

(xii) In conclusion it would appear that Pricecut Ltd is operating in the lower end of the market with a **policy** of low prices and minimum fixed asset investment.

Bigstore plc

(i) Bigstore plc operates with a higher **gross profit** margin than K plc indicating higher prices if the range of products is the same.

(ii) There may also be less losses from shrinkage.

(iii) Bigstore plc's **net profit margin** is also higher than K plc although in line with the gross profit margin difference as the advertising, sales staff and other expenses as a percentage of sales are in line with those of K plc.

(iv) Bigstore plc is also clearly a **much bigger operation** than K plc with more than twice K plc's turnover.

(v) The main difference in profitability therefore appears to be Bigstore plc's ability to charge more for its products than K plc can.

(v) Consideration must be given to **non-financial business orientated factors** such as better quality, superior sales staff personal skills, returns policy, customer care and corporate image.

(vi) Bigstore plc's **return on capital employed** is significantly higher than that of K plc due not only to the better profit margins of the bigger company but also to Bigstore plc's better **use of assets** as indicated by its higher **asset turnover**. Bigstore plc has a longer period of **stock turnover** than K plc which may indicate that it sells a wider range of products which may be part of its success.

(vii) Bigstore plc's **creditors' payment period** is also significantly longer than that of K plc perhaps indicating that Bigstore is a well-established player in this market with good supplier relations and possibly significant **trade discounts** which could also account for the higher gross profit margin.

(viii) Bigstore plc has **far higher turnover** than K plc and appears to be able to sell its products at a higher price, or buy them at a lower cost, than K plc.

(ix) Bigstore plc would appear to be an established company in this market with good profit margins and good use of its asset backing. Bigstore seems to be a successful 'brand' in itself which gives it a sharp **competitive edge**.

(b) **Limitations of the annual report**

> **Pass marks.** The examiner commented that part (b) was quite closely related to part (a). Thinking about the first part should have raised some concerns that the underlying analysis was flawed by the suitability of the information provided for the purpose. To that extent, candidates should have found the second part quite straightforward.

The directors of K plc are suggesting that they should compare their company's business practices and performance with that of these two other companies based upon the companies' annual reports. There are a number of problems with this approach.

(i) The annual report contains aggregated and simplified information. For example there is no analysis between credit sales and purchases and cash sales and purchases which may affect ratios such as profit margins and creditors payment period.

(ii) The figures that appear in the annual report are also affected by the **accounting policies** that each company has. A particular example might be in respect of revaluation of tangible fixed assets. K plc appears to have much higher tangible fixed assets than Pricecut Ltd but if K plc regularly revalues its fixed assets whereas Pricecut Ltd's are valued at cost then this would distort the position shown by the ratios.

(iii) There may also be different approaches to developing **estimates** eg determining the useful life of assets etc.

(iv) Accounts cannot reflect the quality of a company's assets. One company may spend £250,000 on building a top class business premises, whereas for the same cost, another company might get a sub-standard premises.

(v) Stock valuation policies may be different affecting both profit margins and stock turnover periods.

(vi) Published accounts do not directly reflect the strengths or weaknesses of a company's internal control systems.

(vii) Financial statements do not reflect the quality of the company's human resources. Are they well trained and highly motivated or is skills deficiency and poor morale causing customer dissatisfaction?

(viii) Many companies will disclose only the **bare minimum** of information required by the Companies Act and accounting standards in order to **avoid giving** any **useful information to competitors**. Therefore the annual report of such companies may be of little use for comparison of business practices.

(ix) Many ratios, particularly working capital ratios, are based upon **year end figures** and these may not necessarily be indicative of the general position.

(c) **Ratios affected by revaluation**

(i) The main profitability ratio that is likely to be adversely affected by a major investment in tangible fixed assets during the year is the return on capital employed.

(ii) ROCE is based upon the profit for the year and the capital employed at the end of the year. An investment in tangible fixed assets increases capital employed. It also tends to decrease profits due to higher depreciation charges.

(iii) In addition, the profit figure for the year does not normally reflect a full year's use of the asset as they are not operational (and therefore generating profits) for the entire year.

(iv) Therefore the profit figure will be lower than if the additional tangible fixed assets had been in operation for the entire year but the capital employed figure will be higher reflecting the assets purchased thereby causing ROCE to appear lower than it might otherwise have done.

(v) Further ratios that may be adversely affected are asset turnover and fixed asset turnover. The turnover figures, as with profit, will not reflect a full year's use of the assets. However the capital employed or fixed asset total shows all of the assets at the end of the year. With low turnover, high capital employed and high fixed assets both of these ratios may appear lower than would be anticipated.

62 J PLC

> **Pass marks**. You must know the full definition of discontinued operations and be able to apply it to specific situations.

(a) (i) Classification criteria - discontinued operations

The criteria for classification of discontinued operations as laid out by FRS 3 are:

(1) The operation must have discontinued within the reporting period or within three months after the year end (or when the financial statements were approved, if earlier)

(2) The activity must have ceased permanently

(3) The discontinuance must be material. It must represent a material reduction in the entity's operating facilities either because the entity has withdrawn from a market or experienced significantly reduced turnover in continuing markets

(4) The results can be clearly identified both on a physical and operational basis.

All these criteria must be fulfilled.

The operation must be discontinued on or around the period end. This means that only the costs in the final period of the discontinued segment's existence can be disclosed separately. **Costs incurred earlier** than this will be classed as part of the **continuing operations**.

The first and second criteria both establish that events are such that a reversal of the decision to discontinue the operation is remote. This prevents business segments being classed as discontinued based purely on management decisions, which can more easily be reversed.

The third and fourth points prevent time being wasted on unnecessary and confusing disclosure.

They help **prevent** any **creative accounting**. The discontinued operation must be a **discreet** and **identifiable entity**. This means that a general slump in overall turnover cannot be attributed to a business segment to which it does not actually relate. Whereas, the **rationalisation** of a business segment or the **closure** of a **branch** can be **disclosed** under **discontinuing operations** if the **nature** and **focus** of the business have been **affected**.

(ii) Usefulness of information

The information stipulated by FRS 3 is designed to help users of the accounts assess the **profitability** and **financial performance** of an entity.

The information relating to discontinued operations allows the user to **analyse** the **continuing** and **newly acquired operations** of the business in order to assess the **future prospects** of the entity.

However, FRS 3 has helped **bring the emphasis away from the bottom line profit** figure and the earnings per share. The ASB has been concerned with investors and other interested parties being too focused on these figures and has stressed that other elements of the financial statements are equally important.

FRS 3 disclosure requirements reflect an **'information set' approach** that highlights a range of important aspects of performance. This is intended to provide a **framework** that will facilitate the **analysis and interpretation** of the various aspects of **performance.**

(b)

> **Pass marks.** A typical ratio analysis question. You should be prepared to calculate the ratios and to discuss the results obtained.

(i) **Calculation of ratios**

		A Ltd	B Ltd
(1) ROCE			
$\dfrac{\text{Profit before interest and taxation}}{\text{Equity}+\text{Loans}} = \dfrac{170}{290+200}$		34.7%	
$= \dfrac{140}{767+223}$			14.1%
(2) ROE			
$= \dfrac{\text{Profit}}{\text{Equity}} = \dfrac{138}{290}$		47.6%	
$= \dfrac{111}{767}$			14.5%
(3) Gearing			
$= \dfrac{\text{Long term loans}}{\text{Equity}+\text{Loans}} = \dfrac{200}{490}$		40.8%	
$= \dfrac{223}{990}$			22.5%

(ii) *B Ltd - restated figures*

	£'000
Operating profit (140 + 14)	154
Interest	(29)
	125
Fixed assets (940 - 450 + (14 × 5))	560
Net current assets	50
	610
Loans	(223)
	387
Share capital	65
Revaluation reserve (450 - 450)	-
Profit and loss account (252 + (14 × 5))	322
	387

$$\text{ROCE} = \frac{154}{387+223} = 25.2\%$$

$$ROE \quad = \quad \frac{125}{387} \qquad = 32.3\%$$

$$Gearing \quad = \quad \frac{223}{387+223} \qquad = 36.6\%$$

(iii) **Comparison of companies**

Company A Ltd has a ROCE of 34.7% compared to 25.2% for company B Ltd, on the restated basis. A Ltd, therefore, appears to be making better use of the company's assets in earning profits. This may be due to a higher selling price or better control of costs.

A Ltd's ROE of 47.6% is again better than B Ltd's restated ROE of 32.3%. Although A Ltd is paying more interest than B Ltd (although on lower value loans) its operating profit is higher and so it is showing a much better return on equity.

B Ltd's loans at the year end are higher than A Ltd's but the interest charge is lower, it therefore seems likely that B Ltd has increased its loans towards the year end. If this is the case, then B Ltd's interest charge is likely to increase during the current year reducing ROE further.

A Ltd's gearing of 40.8% is higher than B Ltd's gearing of 36.6%. Although A Ltd has borrowed less than B Ltd at the year end, A Ltd's lower reserves brought forward mean that its gearing is higher than B Ltd.

Without industry norms to benchmark against, it is difficult to say whether A Ltd's gearing is too high; but (given the ROCE and ROE figures) it seems likely that the gearing is under control by management.

Therefore, it would appear that A Ltd is the better managed company of the two.

(iv) **Impact of revaluation**

The revaluation of B Ltd's fixed assets drastically lowered its ratios based on equity, as the revaluation reserve forms part of the equity figure. This shows the importance of identifying different companies' revaluation policies when comparing ratios. A revaluation can lead to an artificially low ratio compared to a company that does not revalue.

Reasons for revaluing

A company might still wish to revalue its fixed assets. This would be in order to reflect the current market value of its assets, as opposed to historic cost.

The revaluation would give the accounts users a better idea of the current value of the assets used in the business. Shareholders would have a better idea of the true value of their funds and the equity being used to generate profits.

Although the ratio analysis carried out above shows a reduction in ratios as a result of the revaluation, these reflect the true returns that the business is making better than historic cost.

63 **Q LTD I**

> **Pass marks**. You must ensure that your answers show good commercial awareness in a real world sense.

(a) (i) **Current working capital cycle**

		Days
Stock turnover	$\frac{480,000}{2,400,000} \times 365 =$	73
Debtors days	$\frac{630,000}{3,600,000} \times 365 =$	64

Less: creditors days	$\dfrac{200,000}{2,400,000} \times 365 =$	(30)
		107

(ii) Directors' hypothetical working capital cycle

		Days
Stock turnover	$\dfrac{336,000}{2,400,000} \times 365 =$	51
Debtors days	=	40
Less: creditors days	=	(50)
		41

(b) Importance of monitoring working capital cycle

High levels of stocks and debtors **tie up** cash that might be **profitably utilised elsewhere** in the business. Moreover, the amount of cash tied up in the stock and debtors might mean that the company has a **large overdraft** and has to bear the cost of the **interest** on that.

Equally if creditors are being paid relatively quickly, this means that cash is going out of the business which could have been profitably utilised within the business or could have been applied to reduce the overdraft.

This is why it is important that companies **monitor** their **working capital cycles**. If the working capital cycle is too long, cash is unnecessarily tied up in the working capital. If the working capital cycle can be reduced, **more cash** will become **available** for the company.

For example in Q Ltd, if the stock turnover is reduced from 73 days to 51 days, this reduces the working capital cycle by 22 days and would release £144,000 of cash (£480,000 – £336,000).

Management must also ensure that there is sufficient working capital within the business and that the working capital cycle is not reduced to too low a level. If stock turnover is reduced this will reduce the working capital cycle but it may also mean that there is a **risk** of not being able to **supply customers** or the **production departments** with the goods that they require.

If debtors levels are reduced again this reduces the working capital cycle but there is a risk of **losing customer goodwill** and orders.

The working capital cycle can also be reduced by increasing the period of credit taken from suppliers but again this may mean a loss of goodwill and associated service and/or **discounts** from suppliers.

(c) Potential cash release from proposed policies

		Stocks £	*Debtors* £	*Creditors* £	*Total* £
Stock	Old level	480,000	630,000	200,000	
	New level	336,000	394,521*	328,767**	
Cash released		144,000	235,479	128,767	508,246

* £3,600,000/365 × 40 = £394,521

** £2,400,000/365 × 50 = £328,767

(d) Potential problems implementing proposed policy

The directors wish to reduce levels of stock and debtors and to increase the time taken to pay suppliers. Each of these will have its own difficulties.

Reducing stock levels is probably the easiest to implement. This can be done by allowing stock levels to fall to a lower level before placing an order or by placing smaller but more frequent orders in the future. For each major stock line a **decision** must be made as to which **method** is the **least costly**. This will involve taking into account **ordering costs, lead times** and the costs involved in not being able to **satisfy customer demand** if the company runs out of stock.

Reducing the period of credit allowed to customers from 64 days to 40 days is likely to be more problematic. To collect cash from debtors more quickly, the credit control department of Q Ltd will have to start chasing debtors for payment earlier. Because these debtors are accustomed to being allowed a **fairly long credit period** they may be unhappy with the new situation.

This may mean that some customers look to take their business elsewhere. The push to **accelerate payment** may also be interpreted as a signal by customers that Q Ltd is in financial difficulties and this may also prompt them to consider turning to other suppliers or negotiating with Q Ltd for **special prices or terms** before placing an order.

In trying to extend the creditors payment period from 30 days to 50 days Q Ltd runs the risk of losing the goodwill of its suppliers. This might mean a **loss of trade discounts from suppliers,** a **deteriorating credit rating,** an **increase in prices** or at worst the **refusal of a supplier to sell the goods required**. Some suppliers may be willing to allow a longer period of credit particularly if there is reasonable competition in the market for these goods. However care should be taken with a blanket increase in creditors payment period.

(e) There are a number of other ways in which the directors could try to alleviate the company's cash flow problems.

Settlement discounts or special prices

The directors could encourage debtors to pay more quickly either by offering all customers a cash or settlement discount for payment within say 10 or 14 days of the invoice date or alternatively offer specific individual customers special prices for immediate or swift payment.

Rationalisation of stock lines

The company's stock holding may be high because it carries a large variety of different stock lines which must all be held in stock. If the number of stock lines were rationalised it may be possible to reduce the overall stock holding period and thereby reduce the working capital cycle.

Sale of surplus assets

A review of the fixed assets of the company may result in surplus or unused assets being identified that can be sold.

Negotiation of an overdraft

The shortage of cash could be dealt with by the negotiation of an overdraft with the company's bank. The directors may not wish this to become a permanent feature of the company finances but it might alleviate any short term problems.

Additional long term finance

The directors could consider the possibility of raising additional long term finance by taking out a medium or long term loan. The company might also issue additional shares although being a private company this may not always be possible unless interested investors can be found. However the directors may also feel that it is not appropriate to fund short term cash flow problems with long term finance.

64   Q LTD II

> **Pass marks**. In your analysis you are required to concentrate on profitability and efficiency. Think about the overall context of the financial statements remembering that these companies are in the hotel industry.
>
> The examiner offered this suggested approach in his comments.
>
> 'Firstly, think about the key ratios and calculate these. There is no point in calculating every ratio that exists because some will be less relevant than others. It is usually better to calculate all relevant ratios and present them together just in case there are any patterns or relationships between ratios. The interpretation of the ratios is more important than their calculation. Finally, always think about the limitations of ratio analysis – it is a very powerful tool, but it is not infallible.'

(a)   RATIOS

	Hotel A	*Hotel B*
Room hire gross profit margin		
$478/900 \times 100$	53%	
$365/800 \times 100$		46%
Bar and restaurant gross profit		
$181/400 \times 100$	45%	
$157/450 \times 100$		35%
Overall gross profit margin		
$478 + 181/900 + 400 \times 100$	51%	
$365 + 157/800 + 450 \times 100$		42%
Housekeeping staff/room receipts		
$180/900 \times 100$	20%	
$136/800 \times 100$		17%
Net profit margin (operating profit)		
$489/1,300 \times 100$	38%	
$421/1,250 \times 100$		34%
Return on capital employed		
$489/2,702 + 200 \times 100$	17%	
$421/1,838 + 1,000 \times 100$		15%
Asset turnover		
$1,300/2,902$	0.45	
$1,250/2,838$		0.44
Current ratio (including tax)		
$55/153$	0.36 : 1	
$51/113$		0.45 : 1
Stock turnover		
$3/80 \times 365$	14 days	
$6/104 \times 365$		21 days
Debtors turnover		
$45/1,300 \times 365$	13 days	
$40/1,250 \times 365$		12 days
Creditors turnover (excluding tax)		

| 153- 144/80 × 365 | 41 days | |
| 113 -107/104 × 365 | | 21 days |

Gearing

| 200/2,902 × 100 | 7% | |
| 1,000/2,838 × 100 | | 35% |

> **Pass marks**. In the examiner's marking scheme, up to 5 marks were available for the calculation of the ratios, and up to 8 marks were available for their interpretation, to an overall maximum of 12.

Profitability

The ratios calculated indicate the profitability of hotel A to be greater than hotel B in all areas. The gross profit margins for both room hire and the bar and restaurant are significantly higher in A. This suggests that hotel A is able to sustain a **higher pricing policy**. A potential reason is that hotel A can give its customers greater 'added value'.

Hotel A's **occupancy levels** may also be higher than for hotel B.

However the room hire figures might be a little misleading. The main difference in room costs is in the much higher depreciation charge for B, 30% of receipts compared to only 22% of receipts for A.

The other main cost for room hire are the housekeeping staff costs which are only 17% in B compared to 20% in A. Hotel A's greater level of expenditure on housekeeping staff may be a contributory factor in improving the **quality perceived** by guests and thereby **enhancing customer satisfaction, value added** and hence the room rates chargeable. If the depreciation is ignored the gross profit for room hire for B is 76% compared to 75% for A.

Overall the total gross profit margin of A at 51% is significantly higher than that of B at 42%. However the difference in margins becomes less significant as we move further down the profit and loss account.

The net profit margin using the operating profit of A is 38% compared to 34% in B. The main reason for B closing the gap on A here is that A's management are paid significantly more than those of B with A's management receiving 12.5% of receipts whereas B's only receive 7%. A's **management team** are either **better remunerated** or there is a **bigger team**.

Efficiency

Both hotels have very **similar asset turnover** indicating that they are both using their capital employed to earn similar amounts of revenue.

As far as working capital control is concerned, if the current ratio is calculated with the tax creditor included, then A has a current ratio of just 0.36 to 1 and B 0.45 to 1. This might indicate that both hotels will have difficulty finding the cash to pay the tax liability that will fall due during the forthcoming year.

Creditors turnover is 41 days in A and 21 days in B. These are presumably creditors for food and drink and it might be thought that B is paying its creditors very early.

Assessment

On balance it is quite clear that hotel A is the **more profitable** of the two hotels and on the whole that costs are **better controlled**. However in terms of **working capital efficiency** both hotels appear to be **managed on a fairly similar basis** although A does take a more reasonable period of credit from its suppliers than B.

(b) **Problems using accountancy ratios re management teams**

The **ratios** that can be calculated from the financial statements can give some **insight into the management** of each of the hotels. However, there are a number of problems and limitations - there are some **general problems** of ratio analysis and also some **specific problems** in this scenario.

In general terms when comparing the financial statements of two companies they will only be **truly comparable** if the **assets** are of **similar age**. Older assets will have been depreciated for longer and will have a lower net book value. This will mean that the company with the older assets will have a relatively higher asset turnover and potentially higher return on capital employed.

In practice, an approach which relies on old fixed assets may be an **indicator of other business issues and management attitudes**. This is a scenario that demonstrates the importance of looking at the **big picture** and **developing a proper understanding of the industry and the business itself**.

There is a further general problem with ratio analysis particularly when calculating efficiency ratios such as stock turnover, debtors and creditors turnover and current and quick ratios. These ratios are calculated using the balance sheet figures for stock, debtors and creditors and the question has to be asked as to whether these year end balances are representative of the balances throughout the year. Again, it is **important to examine the business issues behind the figures**.

The ratios that can be calculated from a set of financial statements are certainly a **starting point** for investigating a business and identifying management strengths and weaknesses. The process of analysing the **quantitative ratios** will identify more questions that will need to be answered. The ratios will not be enough - more **qualitative details** will be needed.

Accounting ratios are an important part of an **accountant's tool kit** in analysing a business. In practice, where possible, it is also important to **understand** the **business** itself, the **industry** in which it operates, its **strategies** and the **attitude** and **quality** of its **management**.

(c) **Unusual figures and ratios**

There are also some specific issues in the financial statements given and the ratios calculated which appear unusual.

Has hotel A's loan been outstanding all year? If it has, then the rate of interest charged is only 5% compared to 9% on B's loan. If A's loan has been outstanding all year then A have managed to negotiate a far **better rate of interest** than B which may be due to the market's view of B's efficiency and management.

Why are there debtors of 12 to 13 days in each hotel? Who are these debtors? In a hotel business the rooms should usually be paid for on leaving the hotel and bar and restaurant customers would not normally be allowed credit. The answer could be credit card companies but it is unlikely that they would take so long to pay the hotels. Another possibility is large corporate customers eg running conferences. An **understanding of the target market and customer mix of the hotels**, and any changes therein, might be good pieces of management information required to help interpret the figures.

Having taken out the tax liability, who are the other creditors? In the calculations of creditors turnover they have been assumed to be creditors for food and drink. However they could also include creditors for VAT, PAYE and National Insurance contributions.

Hotel A has a **different year end** to hotel B and consideration should be given to where this relates to each hotels **annual business cycle** and the impact on the level of the various account balances.

The book value of hotel A is higher than for hotel B. This might suggest that hotel A is **newer** or has been **more recently renovated** than hotel B. However, this does not provide much guidance in terms of **customer preference** and **added value. Success factors** as **service style**, decorative style, traditional or modern, nature and duration of facilities, ambience, **quality** and **choice** of **food** and **beverages** etc are not reflected in accounting ratios. Hotels are very much a **service industry** and **customer satisfaction** is likely to be a **key variable in determining business success**.

Pass marks. The examiner said of this type of question that it is very predictable, but can rarely be approached mechanically. It is necessary to think about which ratios might be relevant and to decide how a particular result ought to be interpreted. The most common errors were these:

- Many solutions had technical errors in the construction of the ratios themselves. Ratios can only be interpreted when the numerator and denominator are consistent.

- Many answers dealt with areas that were peripheral to the overall requirements of the question.

- Many candidates insisted on combining the results of the two main business segments, even though it might have provided a more interesting comparison if each had been looked at separately.

---

65   P PLC

(a)   **Profitability and performance**

   (i)   *The comparative big picture*

     The shareholders view is likely to have been influenced by the following comparisons

	P plc £ million	Q plc £ million	Q plc greater by
Shareholders equity	1,732	2,098	21.1%
Turnover	1,845	2,978	61.4%
After tax profit	717	1,165	62.5%

- Hence at a glance, Q plc's in only a little bigger than P plc sizewise but its trading operation is significantly larger.

- These perceptions are supported by P plc's ROCE of 24% as compared to Q plc's ROCE of 31%.

   (ii)   *Trading strategy*

- P plc's gross profit margin is slightly better than that of Q plc. Superficially this looks good for P plc but the impact of the **relative pricing policies** probably need further investigation;

     – What is the **price sensitivity** of the market?

     – Are P plc **prices high** in comparison with Q plc?

     – Is P plc **skimping on quality** to get a better margin?

(iii) *Distribution policy*

- Q plc's distribution costs seem to be relatively higher than those of P plc.

- This might indicate a **different marketing strategy** between the two companies which may need more in-depth investigation to **understand their commercial approaches**.

  - Is Q plc providing a **better customer service** with more **delivery staff,** use of first class post for mailed items, **better paid,** better **trained** and more **motivated** staff?

  - Does Q plc have more **distribution outlets,** situated in better **strategic locations**?

  - Does Q plc spend more money on **distribution management systems,** the latest IT software, efficient shelving and picking systems?

  - Are Q plc's **marketing skills simply better** than those of P plc?

(iv) *Administrative cost structure*

- P plc's administrative costs are comparatively almost twice as high as that of Q plc.

- P plc may need to review both its **detailed P&L** account administration cost accounts as well as its **working practices** to see if:
  - They are **cost efficient**
  - **Add value** to the business

(v) *Asset utilisation strategy*

The asset turnover of P plc is only 0.49 whereas that of Q plc is 0.69. This means that P plc is only earning 49 pence for every £1 of net assets employed whilst Q plc is earning 69 pence from its net assets. There is a similar picture with fixed asset turnover of just 46 pence in P plc but 68 pence in Q plc. More information is needed on

- The relative age and quality of fixed assets
- The accounting policies of each company regarding fixed assets

(vi) *Stock and debtors management*

This difference in efficiency of asset usage would appear to be confined to the fixed assets of the two businesses as the stock turnover periods and debtors turnover periods are substantially the same.

(vii) *Creditors turnover*

There is a marked difference in creditors turnover period but as there is no breakdown of the creditors figure this is difficult to analyse.

Workings

Ratios

		P plc	Q plc
Gross profit margin	1,087/1,845 × 100	59%	
	1,668/2,978 × 100		56%
Distribution costs to turnover	136/1,845 × 100	7.4%	
	273/2,978 × 100		9.1%
Administration costs to turnover	61/1,845 × 100	3.3%	
	51/2,978 × 100		1.7%
Return on capital employed	890/(4,045 – 291) × 100	24%	
	1,344/(4,548 – 250) × 100		31%
Fixed asset turnover	1,845/4,002	0.46	
	2,978/4,380		0.68
Asset turnover	1,845/(4,045 – 291)	0.49	
	2,978/(4,548 – 250)		0.69
Stock turnover period	42/758 × 365	20 days	
	74/1,310 × 365		21 days
Debtors turnover period	180/1,845 × 365	36 days	
	293/2,978 × 365		36 days
Creditors turnover period	292/758 × 365	141 days	
	317/1,310 × 365		88 days

(b) **Earning per share**

   (i) *Calculation*

   - The earnings per share calculation is performed by taking the **profits available** to the ordinary shareholders for the year and **dividing** this by the **number of shares** in **issue** and **qualifying** for **dividend**. The calculations for the two companies are therefore:

   P plc   £717m/600m   =   119 pence
   Q plc   £1,165m/2,800m =   42 pence

   - Although Q plc has a much higher absolute level of profit than P plc it is shared between almost 5 times as many shares as in P plc, as the shares in Q plc are 25 pence nominal value shares.

   (ii) *Purpose of EPS*

   - The purpose of earnings per share for shareholders is to give them an **indication** of the **earnings** that have been made by the company for **each share** that they hold and they can then **compare** that figure to **others such as** the **dividend per share**.

   - Earnings per share is also **widely used** in the **market place** as part of the **calculation** of the price **earnings ratio** of the company which is the **current share price divided by the most recent EPS figure**.

   - The higher the PE ratio, the higher the indication that shareholders are willing to pay a price for the company's shares relative to its earnings.

   - The key benefit of EPS is that it provides a useful **performance indicator** of earnings from **one year to the next**.

(iii)   *Limitations of EPS*

- One of the limitations of EPS can be illustrated with P plc and Q plc. On the face of it P plc appears to be performing far better than Q plc with a much higher EPS but this is simply due to the fact that **Q plc has many more shares in issue than P plc**. It is still the case that a 1% shareholder in P plc would only have earnings of £7.17m attributed to him whilst a 1% shareholder in Q plc could be said to own earnings of £11.65m.

- A further limitation of EPS is that it tends to **focus on this single 'bottom line' profit figure**. This **earnings figure is after all income and expenses including** any **exceptional items**. The EPS that is calculated **may therefore not be a measure of the sustainable earnings of the company** if this includes **one off exceptional items** that will **not recur in future years**.

(c)   **Usefulness of financial statements**

(i)   The use of financial statements and financial ratios to **compare** the **performance** of two companies can provide some **useful information** about their comparative performances.

(ii)   However there are a **number of factors** which may make such **comparison less than meaningful**.

Choice of accounting policies

- In many areas of accounting there are **choices of accounting** policies that can be made.

  – For example **some companies** may carry their **fixed assets** at **depreciated historical cost** whereas **other companies** may regularly **revalue their fixed assets**. Similarly **some companies** may **capitalise development costs** wherever possible whereas **others write them off** to the profit and loss account.

  This will **affect** the figures calculated as ratios such as **return on capital employed, profit margins, fixed asset turnover** and **gearing levels**.

Choice of estimation techniques

- There are also many **choices in estimation techniques** that companies can choose such as **methods of depreciation** or methods of **stock valuation** which will mean that profit and loss accounts and balance sheets are **not strictly comparable**.

Choice of financing methods

- Companies may choose different methods of funding fixed assets. Some companies **purchase their fixed assets outright** whereas others will enter into **finance leases** to provide the fixed assets required.

- Others may prefer to use genuine operating leases.

- Again these policies will have an effect on ratios that are calculated such as the gearing ratio.

Age of fixed assets

- It will often be **difficult** from a set of financial statements to **determine** the **age** of the **fixed** assets of a company.

- If one company has relatively new plant and machinery compared to another company then that may perform more efficiently thereby improving company performance.

Non-financial factors

- Finally comparison of two companies using their financial statements ignores the many other factors that are not shown in a set of financial statements such as market reputation, goodwill, quality of customer bases, quality of the management team, employee skills, effectiveness of business process and working practices, sophistication of IT infrastructure, systems and software etc.

Generally, two businesses may superficially appear similar on paper in financial statement terms but may in reality be very different strategically, culturally, managerially and operationally.

(d) Accounting ratios are only one part of the accountants diagnostic kit for analysing and interpreting financial statements. Other useful tools or sources of information, if available may comprise:

(i) The company's business plan
(ii) Annual budgets
(iii) Cash flow projections
(iv) Management accounts
(v) Historic accounts figures (past trends)
(vi) SWOT analysis
(vii) Industry benchmark surveys
(viii) Any other strategy or planning documents
(ix) On line company and text search services
(x) Press releases and comments

EXTERNAL AUDIT

OBJECTIVE TEST QUESTIONS: EXTERNAL AUDIT

1   A

2   C

3   A

4   B

5   C

6   A

7   C

8   D

66   PREPARATION QUESTION: REPORTING

(a)   **Qualifications owing to inherent uncertainty**

Two sets of circumstances in which auditors may qualify their report owing to **inherent uncertainty**:

(i)   Where the auditors have not been able to verify the value of provisions for legal costs, because of uncertainty over the outcome of impending litigation.

(ii)   Where there is doubt about whether the company is a going concern in that the company has to repay a substantial loan and there is as yet no financing available for this.

(b)   **Emphasis of matter because of inherent uncertainty**

Four circumstances in which the auditors may include an emphasis of matter as a result of disagreement with the directors:

(i)   Where there has been a departure from a SSAP or FRS relevant to the company and where non-compliance, in the auditors' opinion, distorts the true and fair view shown by the accounts.

(ii)   Where the company has failed to make adequate provision for a bad debt in respect of a major customer who is in liquidation, the liquidator having indicated that the company is unlikely to receive any dividend.

(iii) Where the accounts do not provide adequate disclosure of information required by the provisions of the Companies Act 1985.

(iv)   Where the auditors do not agree that a particular accounting policy adopted by the management is conducive to the accounts showing a true and fair view.

67   MOWBRAY COMPUTERS

> **Pass marks**. You would not have needed to mention all the points we have to gain full marks in (a).

(a)   **Going concern indicators**

The directors are responsible for assessing whether there are **significant doubts** about an entity's ability to continue as a going concern. In making this assessment, **material uncertainty** must be considered as well as **all available information** about the

foreseeable future. The assessment must be based on the **facts in each case,** but in general terms these include **past, current and expected profitability, debt repayment schedules** and **access to financial resources**.

Companies usually fail because of **liquidity** or **financial adaptability** problems: either the bank calls in the loan or overdraft, or other lenders (eg debenture holders) call in a receiver or liquidator. The liquidity problems are usually related to profitability and other problems.

Profitability problems

(i)   **Recurring losses/low profits**. This means that fixed assets cannot be purchased and working capital is not funded for inflation or expansion, ie losses produce liquidity problems.

(ii)   **Recession** in the economy/industry, reducing profits as sales prices fall.

(iii)   **Loss of customer(s),** particularly where the company has one major customer or only a few large customers. It may take time to gain new ones.

(iv)   **Loss of supplier**. The product(s) may not be available from another source or only at a much higher price.

(v)   **Rapid technological change** makes the company's products (or even production processes) redundant and out of date (fashion may have an impact here).

(vi)   **Funding** for research and development is not available, so new products cannot be developed.

(vii)   **Foreign competition** with lower labour costs and more advanced technology may make cheaper products and take market share.

(viii)   **Foreign sourcing by competitors** may make their products cheaper.

(ix)   **Changes in fashion or purchasing behaviour** may result in loss of custom, if the business does not keep up with market trends.

(x)   **Political and external factors** such as foot and mouth disease and terrorism may have an impact on affected industries.

(xi)   **Currency movements** (£ vs other currencies) may adversely affect both importers and exporters. Prices may be forced up or margins reduced.

(xii)   **Low interest cover** indicates that the company is only just covering interest costs, leaving little for distribution or reinvestment. Any increase in gearing (ie more loans) would exacerbate the problem.

(xiii)   **Development of substitute products** or markets, eg second hand computer shops.

(xiv)   **Market saturations** where most consumer needs for the relevant product are reasonably satisfied.

Liquidity problems

(i)   A (large) **bank overdraft**, always fully utilised, or even exceeded on a regular basis.

(ii)   **High gearing**. In general terms borrowers (particularly banks) will be concerned if gearing is greater than 50% of total capital, particularly if it is increasing, although the industry norms should be taken into account.

(iii)   **High levels** of stock (hard to sell? obsolete? overvalued?); high levels of debtors (increased risk of bad debts); and high levels of creditors (paying creditors slowly, exceeding credit limits).

234

(iv)   **Overtrading** problems, where working capital is not sufficient to deal with rapid increases in sales (because profits have yet to be taken) and so the increases in working capital and fixed assets must be funded by borrowings.

(v)   **New fixed assets** are purchased before sufficient sales and profits have been generated to pay for them. In particular, the acquisition of fixed assets under leases may indicate a lack of resources.

(vi)   **Factoring of debts** often indicates liquidity problems, although it may decrease borrowings.

(vii) **Knock-on impacts of recession** where debtors themselves experience liquidity problems.

Financial:

(i)   An excess of liabilities over assets

(ii)   Net current liabilities

(iii) Necessary borrowing facilities have not been agreed

(iv)   Default on terms of loan agreements, and potential breaches of covenant

(v)   Significant liquidity or cash flow problems

(vi)   Major losses or cash flow problems which have arisen since the balance sheet date and which threaten the entity's continued existence

(vii) Substantial sales of fixed assets not intended to be replaced

(viii) Major restructuring of debts

(ix)   Denial of (or reduction in) normal terms of trade credit by suppliers

(x)   Major debt repayment falling due where refinancing is necessary to the entity's continued existence

(xi)   Inability to pay debts as they fall due

Operational:

(i)   Fundamental changes to the market or technology to which the entity is unable to adapt adequately

(ii)   Externally forced reductions in operations (for example, as a result of legislation or regulatory action)

(iii) Loss of key management or staff, labour difficulties or excessive dependence on a few product lines where the market is depressed

(iv)   Loss of key suppliers or customers or technical developments which render a key product obsolete

Other:

(i)   Major litigation in which an adverse judgement would imperil the entity's continued existence

(ii)   Issues which involve a range of possible outcomes so wide that an unfavourable result could affect the appropriateness of the going concern basis.

(b) **Form of audit report**

Inherent uncertainty about the validity of the **going concern** basis will be **fundamental** here.

(i) **Financial statements – sufficient disclosure of going concern problems**

If the uncertainty is adequately accounted for and disclosed in the financial statements, SAS 600 requires that an **explanatory paragraph** be included in the audit report.

This paragraph appears **before the opinion paragraph** and will start as follows.

> 'In forming our opinion, we have considered the adequacy of disclosures made in the financial statements concerning ..... '

It will then go on to **explain** the **circumstances,** ie the recession and strong competition and the resulting fall in sales and gross profit margin, and state that the accounts have been prepared on a **going concern basis,** and **refer** to the **note** which deals with this issue. The paragraph is likely to **add** that the business's continuation **depends** on **increased profitability** etc, and the **support** of the company's **bank** and **creditors.** The paragraph will **end** with the **statement; 'our opinion is not qualified in this respect'.**

(ii) **Financial statements – no disclosure of going concern problems**

SAS 600 requires that where **adequate disclosure** is **not given** in the financial statements it is necessary to **decide** whether the **effect** is **so material** or **pervasive** that the financial statements as a whole are **misleading.** Where this is so, as in the case of Mowbray Computers Ltd, an **adverse opinion** should be given.

The **opinion paragraph** will be **titled 'Adverse opinion'.** It will **explain** the **circumstances,** ie the recession and strong competition and the resulting fall in sales and gross profit leading to **questions** about the **validity** of the **going concern basis.** It will go on to **state** that because of the **failure** to **disclose** the **going concern problems** the **financial statements do not give a true and fair view.**

68 AUDIT REPORTS

> **Pass marks.** You should be familiar with SAS 600, the audit report SAS. Although you will not be asked to reproduce a full audit report, you should know its main contents hence question (b) is quite legitimate. Part (c) requires a full understanding of the different types of qualification available under SAS 600. Answers in (c) had to be justified.

(a) The duties of an auditor can be summarised as follows:

- to **report** to the **shareholders on** whether the financial statements show a true and fair view

- to consider whether the other information in the directors' report, chairman's statement etc is **consistent** with the financial statements

- to provide details of **statutory information** such as transactions with directors if they are not provided in the financial statements

- to form an opinion as to whether **proper accounting records** have been kept, the accounts are in agreement with the accounting records, the profit and loss account and balance sheet totals are **fairly stated** and that the appropriate information and explanations have been provided

(b) **Contents of an unqualified audit report**

    (i)   A **title** identifying the person or persons to whom the report is addressed, ie the shareholders of the company being audited.

    (ii)   An **introductory paragraph identifying the financial statements** audited (ie statements and notes but not directors' report or other such information). The basis of preparation is then stated (eg, modified historical cost).

    (iii)   A section which deals with **respective responsibilities of directors and auditors**. This should include:

        (1)   A statement that the financial statements are the responsibility of the reporting entity's directors

        (2)   a reference to a description of those responsibilities when set out elsewhere in the financial statements or accompanying information

        (3)   A statement that the auditors' responsibility is to express an opinion on the financial statements.

    (iv)   A section dealing with the **basis of the auditors' opinion** will include:

        (1)   A statement that the audit was performed in compliance with auditing standards

        (2)   A statement that the audit process includes

- examining, on a test basis, evidence relevant to the amounts and disclosures in the financial statements

- assessing the significant estimates and judgements made by the reporting entity's directors in preparing the financial statements

- considering whether the accounting policies are appropriate to the reporting entity's circumstances, consistently applied and adequately disclosed

        (3)   A statement that they planned and performed the audit so as to obtain reasonable assurance that the financial statements are free from material misstatement, whether caused by fraud or other irregularity or error, and that they have evaluated the overall presentation of the financial statements.

    (v)   The **auditors' opinion** on the financial statements will come next.

    (vi)   The manuscript or printed **signature** of the auditors and the date of the auditors' report should end the report.

(c)   (i)   **Inherent uncertainty – value of tangible fixed assets**

The inherent uncertainty regarding the value of tangible fixed assets in the loss-making branch can be considered to be **material** to the financial statements.

However, the disclosure made in the financial statements by the directors, and the audit evidence I have obtained on this matter are such that I am satisfied that the financial statements give a true and fair view.

Therefore the audit opinion will be unqualified.

    (ii)   **Disagreement – failure to write down fixed assets material but not fundamental**

In this case I disagree with the treatment of the branch's tangible fixed assets and I consider that they should be written down to a nil valuation. However, except for this disagreement I am satisfied that the financial statements show a true and fair view.

This is because the failure to write down the value of the branch's tangible fixed assets has not had such a fundamental effect on the financial statements that they are seriously misleading.

Hence my audit opinion would be **qualified on grounds of disagreement**. I would explain the matter on which I disagree, that tangible fixed assets are overstated by £710,000 and why I consider that this is the case. My audit opinion would then conclude with the statement '**except for** the absence of the provision against tangible fixed assets, in our opinion the financial statements give a true and fair view'.

(iii) **Limitation in scope - fundamental**

I have not received all the evidence I would normally expect to be available in relation to custody of stock and cash takings. Also, if the uncertainty about the misappropriation of stock and cash takings relates to all the company sales, it must be considered to be pervasive, so making the financial statements misleading.

Hence I would issue a **disclaimer of opinion** drawing attention to the limitation in the scope of the audit. My opinion will take the following form.

> '... However, the evidence available to us was limited because £X of the company's recorded turnover comprises cash sales, over which there was no system of control on which we could rely for the purposes of our audit. In addition there was no system of control over custody of stock, appearing in the balance sheet at £X. There were no other satisfactory audit procedures that we could adopt to confirm that cash sales and stock were properly recorded. In forming our opinion we also evaluated the overall adequacy of the presentation of information in the financial statements.
>
> *Opinion: disclaimer on view given by the financial statement.*
>
> Because of the possible effect of the limitation in evidence available to us, we are unable to form any opinion as to whether the financial statements give a true and fair view of the state of the company's affairs at .... or of its profit (loss) for the year then ended. In all other respects in our opinion the financial statements have been properly prepared in accordance with the Companies Act 1985. In respect of the limitation on our work relating to cash sales and stock:
>
> (1)   we have not obtained all the information and explanations that we considered necessary for the purpose of our audit; and
>
> (2)   we were unable to determine whether proper accounting records had been maintained.'

(iv) **Limitation in scope – material but not fundamental**

As in (iii) above I have not received all necessary evidence, and in this case it is necessary to decide on the extent of the uncertainty. Here, the uncertainty only affects 10% of the company's sales. Hence the uncertainty is material but not so pervasive that it makes the financial statements misleading.

Therefore I would issue an **'except for' audit opinion** which would be very similar to that in (iii) above. The basis of the opinion paragraph would be the same except that the value of recorded turnover to which uncertainty related would only amount to 10% of the total turnover.

The opinion paragraph would start as follows.

> '*Opinion: qualified opinion arising from limitation in audit scope*
>
> Except for any adjustments that might have been found to be necessary had we been able to obtain sufficient evidence concerning cash sales and the custody of stock, in our opinion the financial statements give true and fair view .... '

The paragraph would end with a similar statement as to the limitation on our work as given in (iii) above.

69 AUDIT REPORTING

(a) **'Except for' situations**

The auditor would report by exception if any of the following conditions were not fulfilled:

(i) **Proper accounting records** have been kept and proper returns adequate for the audit received from branches not visited.

(ii) The **accounts** agree with the **accounting records** and **returns**.

(iii) **All information and explanations** have been **received** as the auditors think necessary and they have had access at all times to the company's books, accounts and vouchers.

(iv) **Details** of **directors' emoluments** and **other benefits** have been correctly **disclosed** in the financial statements.

(v) Particulars of **loans** and **other transactions** in favour of **directors** and others have been correctly disclosed in the financial statements.

(vi) The **information** given in the **directors' report** is **consistent** with the **accounts**.

(b) (i) **Basis of opinion**

The situation described would give rise to a **limitation in the scope** of the auditor's work. Therefore the standard **basis of opinion** paragraph would be amended as follows.

(1) We would state in the first line of this paragraph that whilst our audit was carried out in accordance with auditing standards the **scope** of our work was **limited**.

(2) We would state that we planned our audit so as to obtain all **information necessary**. The reference to performance would be dropped.

(3) We would include an explanatory paragraph stating that, as a majority of the company's books and records were destroyed by fire, the **evidence** available to us was **limited**. In this case it would be **difficult to quantify** the financial impact.

Opinion paragraph

Our audit **opinion** would be a **disclaimer** on the grounds of **fundamental uncertainty**. We would have to state that due to the **limitation in scope** of our work we were **unable to form an opinion** regarding the truth and fairness of the information.

We would also have to report by exception that we had **not obtained all the information and explanations** which we considered necessary, and that we were **unable to determine** whether **proper accounting records** had been **maintained**.

These points would be included in an additional paragraph after the opinion paragraph.

(ii) **Audit opinion – the reasons**

A lack of accounting records results in **uncertainty** due to a **limitation in scope**; the auditors cannot obtain all the evidence which they would normally expect to collect, and will therefore have difficulty in forming an opinion.

This **uncertainty** may be **material or fundamental**. In this situation it would seem more likely that a fundamental uncertainty qualification would be appropriate as the destruction of the records will have had a significant impact on most of the balances rather than one particular item.

I am also assuming that destruction of the information is such that it is not possible to obtain any other satisfactory information to support the estimates made by the accountant.

The work that we have been able to do has been inconclusive.

(iii) (1) **Disagreement**

The auditor may qualify the audit report due to **disagreement** with any of the following:

- **Non-compliance** with **Companies Act**
- **Non-compliance** with **SSAPs/FRSs**
- **Disagreement** due to known facts
- **Inadequate disclosure** by the directors of inherent uncertainties and/or the assumptions made

If the disagreement is material but does not render the accounts as a whole meaningless an **'except for'** qualification would be used. The opinion would state that the accounts give a true and fair view overall apart from this one specific item.

The **opinion paragraph** would be headed up as **qualified** on these grounds and would include an **explanation** of the **disagreement**.

(2) **Disclaimer**

A **disclaimer** by contrast is a qualification due to a **fundamental uncertainty**. This would arise due to a limitation in the scope of the auditors' work which has such a severe impact that the auditors are **not able** to **form an opinion** on the truth and fairness of the accounts at all.

The **audit opinion** would be headed up as a **disclaimer**.

Normally the audit report would **not be qualified** in respect of **proper preparation of the accounts**.

(3) **Adverse opinion**

An **adverse opinion** would be given where a **disagreement** is not just material as in (1) but has such an impact on the **accounts** that they are rendered **meaningless** as a whole. The basis for such disagreements are listed in part (1). Here the audit opinion would be headed up as an adverse opinion and would state that the accounts do **not give a true and fair view**. Depending on the nature of the disagreement the proper preparation opinion may also require qualification.

(c) **The legal rights of an external auditor are:**

- the right of **access** to the books, records, documents and accounts of the company

- the right to require from officers of the company such **information** and explanations as he thinks necessary for the performance of his duties

- the right to receive all **notices** relating to any general meeting of the company, the right to attend any general meeting and to be heard at any general meeting on any part of the business which concerns him as auditor

- the right to receive a copy of any **written resolutions** proposed

- the right to be sent by the company a copy of a notice of intention to propose his **removal** or replacement as auditor and the right to make written or oral representations

- the right to require the directors to requisition a general meeting on his **resignation** and to attend and be heard at that and any other meeting which concerns him as auditor.

Practice objective test questions

These two practice objective tests contain 10 items from topics across the syllabus. You should practise them under timed conditions (36 minutes each) before you tackle the mock exams.

PRACTICE OBJECTIVE TEST: TEST 1

1   What is the main function of the Urgent Issues Task Force (UITF) ?

A   To maintain a continuous review of accounting standards and recommend changes when necessary.

B   To enquire into annual accounts that appear not to comply with the Companies Act or accounting standards.

C   Producing Abstracts for publication by the Accounting Standards Board when unsatisfactory or conflicting interpretations of existing accounting standards arise.

D   Undertaking preparatory work under the guidance of the Accounting Standards Board when a new accounting standard is under development.

2   FRS 3 Reporting Financial Performance requires an analysis in the profit and loss account showing discontinued and continuing activities separately.

Which of the following statements about this analysis are correct?

1   Acquisitions during the year must be shown separately as a component of continuing activities.

2   An activity is treated as discontinued if it ceased during the period or within three months after the end of the period (or the date the financial statements are approved if earlier).

3   If an activity is treated as discontinued because it ceased in the three months after the balance sheet date, the financial statements to that date must include the results of operations up to the actual date of discontinuance.

4   The analysis should normally be shown up to the calculation of profit on ordinary activities before interest.

A   1, 2 and 3
B   1, 2 and 4
C   1, 3 and 4
D   2, 3 and 4

3   SSAP 25 Segmental Reporting requires certain companies to disclose segmental information.

Which of the following lists correctly identifies the analysis headings required by SSAP 25?

A   Turnover, profit and net assets for each class of business and geographical area.

B   Turnover and profit for each class of business and geographical area.

C   Turnover and profit for each geographical area.

D   Turnover and profit and for each class of business, plus turnover only for each geographical area.

4   A company had 1,000,000 ordinary shares of 50p each in issue on 1 January 20X2. On1 July 20X2 the company made a bonus issue of one share for every two held. Its profit for the year ended 31 December 20X2 was £120,000. What will the company's earnings per share (EPS) be for the year ended 31 December 20X2?

A 12p per share.
B 10p per share.
C 8p per share.
D 16p per share.

5 A company's fixed assets include the following properties:

1 A freehold office block that had cost £800,000, with a current open market value of £1,100,000. This property is let to tenants. No depreciation has been provided on the property.

2 A leasehold property purchased ten years ago for £1,000,000 with a current open market value of £500,000.

At the time of purchase the lease had 25 years to run and it is being depreciated at 4% per annum on the straight line basis. This property is also let to tenants.

What figure should appear for these properties in the company's balance sheet under the headings of Investment Properties?

A £800,000
B £1,100,000   *mv of POP*
C £1,600,000
D £1,400,000

6 Which one or more of the following statements about SSAP13 Accounting for Research and Development are correct?

1 Research expenditure, other than capital expenditure on buildings and equipment for research purposes, must be written off as incurred.

2 All companies must disclose in their financial statements the total amount spent on research and development and the movements on deferred development expenditure during the period.

3 If development expenditure is capitalised, it must be amortised over a period not exceeding five years.

A 1 only
B 1 and 2
C 2 and 3
D 1 and 3

7 In compiling its financial statements, the directors of a company have to decide on the correct treatment of the following items.

1 An employee has commenced an action against the company for wrongful dismissal. The company's solicitors estimate that the ex-employee has a 40 per cent chance of success in the action.

2 The company has guaranteed the overdraft of another company, not at present in any financial difficulties. The possibility of a liability arising is thought to be remote.

3 Shortly after the balance sheet date, a major installation owned by the company was destroyed in a flood. The company's going concern status is not affected.

What are the correct treatments for these items, assuming all are of material amount?

A   All three should be disclosed by note

B   A provision should be made for item 1 and items 2 and 3 disclosed by note

C   Items 1 and 3 should be disclosed by note, with no disclosure for item 2.

D   Item 2 should be disclosed by note. No disclosure is required for items 1 and 3.

8   According to SSAP 4 Accounting for Government Grants and the Companies Act 1985, what is the correct treatment of grants received to contribute to capital expenditure?

1   Credit grant to profit and loss account when received

2   Credit grant to a non-distributable reserve to be maintained permanently in the balance sheet.

3   Credit grant to the related fixed asset account and base depreciation on the reduced amount

4   Credit grant to a deferred credit account to be released to profit and loss account in step with depreciation of the related asset

A   All four treatments are acceptable

B   3 and 4 only

C   4 only

D   1 or 2 only

9   At 1 January 20X4, a company's share capital consisted of 1,000,000 ordinary shares of 50p each, and there was a balance of £800,000 on its share premium account.

During 20X4, the following events took place:

1 March   The company made a bonus issue of 1 share for every 2 held, using the share premium account. *500,000 shares*

1 July   The company issued 600,000 shares at £2 per share *£1200,000 → 300k share cap 900k premium*

1 October   The company made a rights issue of 1 share for every 3 held at £1.80 per share. *700,000 shares*

What are the balances on the company's share capital and share premium accounts at 31 December 20X4? *1260*

	Share capital £	Share premium £
A	1,400,000	2,960,000
B	2,800,000	1,460,000
C	1,800,000	2,320,000
D	1,400,000	2,360,000

1450
910

10   There is a major uncertainty facing Z plc – actions are pending against the company for allegedly supplying faulty goods, causing widespread damage

The directors have fully described the circumstances of the case in a note to the financial statements.

What form of audit report is appropriate in this case?

A   Qualified opinion – limitation on auditors' work.

B   Disclaimer of opinion

C   Unqualified report with an additional explanatory paragraph.

D   Qualified opinion – disagreement

PRACTICE OBJECTIVE TEST: TEST 2

1   Which of the following items are required by the Companies Act 1985 to be disclosed in the financial statements of a public limited company (plc)?

    1   Auditors' remuneration. ✓
    2   Directors' remuneration ✓
    3   Staff costs ✓
    4   Depreciation

    A   1 and 4 only.
    B   1 , 2 and 3 only.
    C   2, 3 and 4 only.
    (D) All four items

2   Which of the following statements about FRS 18 Accounting Policies are correct?

    1   The decision to carry forward unexpired revenue expenditure at the balance sheet date depends on whether the item being considered meets the definition of an asset in FRS 5 Reporting the Substance of Transactions.

    2   The decision to carry forward unexpired revenue expenditure at the balance sheet date depends on whether there is a reasonable expectation of related future revenue.

    3   If a company is to be liquidated shortly after the balance sheet date, the directors may decide to prepare the company's financial statements on a basis other than that of a going concern.

    4   If a company is to be liquidated shortly after the balance sheet date, the financial statements must be prepared on a break-up basis.

    A   1 and 3
    B   1 and 4
    C   2 and 3
    D   2 and 4

3   Which of the following events would require a company to make a prior period adjustment, if material, according to FRS 3 Reporting Financial Performance and FRS 18 Accounting Policies?

    1   A change of depreciation method. ✗
    2   The correction of a fundamental error.
  ✓ 3   A change in the allocation of overheads between distribution cost and cost of sales.
    4   A decision to write off all development costs as incurred, instead of capitalising such costs when allowed by SSAP 13 Accounting for Research and Development.

    A   1, 2 and 3.
    B   1, 2 and 4
    C   1, 3 and 4
    (D) 2, 3 and 4

4   In calculating diluted earnings per share, in what order are potential ordinary shares included in the calculation?

    (A) Most dilutive first and least dilutive last, ignoring antidilutive items.
    B   Most dilutive first, followed by less dilutive, with antidilutive shares dealt with last.
    C   It makes no difference, as the arithmetic produces the same answer regardless of order.
    D   Least dilutive first and most dilutive last, ignoring antidilutive items.

5   The position of a long-term contract at 30 June 20X6 is as follows:

	£
Contract price	900,000
At 30 June 20X6	
Costs to date	720,000
Estimated costs to completion	480,000
Progress payments received	400,000
Percentage complete	60%

[handwritten annotations: (300) loss ; Turnover 540 ; Cost TO 720 ; Provision (180) ; 120]

What figures should appear for this contract in the accounts at 30 June 20X6, according to SSAP9 Stocks and Long-term Contracts?

		Profit and loss account		Balance sheet
A	Turnover	£540,000	Debtors	£140,000
	Costs	£720,000		
	Provision for loss	£120,000	Provision for loss	£120,000
B	Turnover	£540,000		
	Costs	£720,000		
C	Turnover	£540,000		
	Costs	£720,000	Stocks-long-term contents	£20,000
	Provision for loss	£120,000		
D	Turnover	£540,000	Debtors	£140,000
	Costs	£720,000		

[handwritten check mark by option A]

6   Which of the following statements about SSAP 21 Accounting for Leases are correct?

1   A finance lease is one which transfers substantially all the risks and rewards of the ownership of an asset to a lessee. *[✓]*

2   A leased asset should be depreciated over the shorter of the lease term and the useful life of the asset. *[✓]*

3   All obligations under finance leases will appear in the balance sheet under the heading of 'Creditors: amounts falling due after more than one year '.

4   An asset held on an operating lease should appear in the balance sheet as a fixed asset and be depreciated over the term of the lease. *[handwritten: not capitalised]*

A   1 and 3 only
B   1 and 2 only *[handwritten ✓]*
C   2 and 4 only
D   All four statements are correct

7   Which of the following statements about SSAP 17 Accounting for Post Balance Sheet Events are correct?

1   Notes to the financial statements must give details of all material adjusting events reflected in those financial statements.

2   Notes to the financial statements must give details of non-adjusting events affecting users' ability to understand the company's' financial position.

3   A non-adjusting event may still have to be adjusted for in the financial statements if it jeopardises the going concern status of the company.

A   All three statements are correct

B   1 and 2 only

C   1 and 3 only

D   2 and 3 only

8   A company's debtor collection period is 90 days, when 60 days is a reasonable figure.

Which one of the following could NOT account for the high level of 90 days?

A   The company's trade is seasonal

B   The company's credit control procedures are weak ✓ *so collection long*

C   The company made a large credit sale in the last month of its accounting year

(D) A downturn in the company's credit sales in the last three months of its accounting year ✗

Debtor days = Debt / Turnover ✓

9   Which of the following statements about the auditors of a limited company are correct?

1   The auditors must carry out their work so as to have a reasonable expectation of detecting material misstatements in the financial statements arising from error or fraud.

2   The auditors carry out walk-through tests to confirm their understanding of the client's accounting system.

3   At the end of their audit the auditors are required by the Companies Act 1985 to report to the directors expressing their opinion of the financial statements.

4   Substantive tests are designed to confirm that internal controls operated effectively throughout the relevant period.

A   3 and 4 only

B   2 and 3 only

(C) 1 and 2 only

D   All four statements are correct

10   A Limited's balance sheet is as follows:

	£
Called up share capital	
Ordinary shares of £1 each, fully paid	280,000
Profit and loss account	80,000
	360,000
Sundry net assets	360,000

The company is to buy 50,000 of its own shares at £2 each.

What transfer, if any, must be made to capital redemption reserve?

A   No transfer is required because A Limited is a private company

B   £20,000

(C) £30,000   *50,000 @ £2*

D   £50,000

Practice objective test answers

PRACTICE OBJECTIVE TEST: TEST 1

1   C

2   B

3   A

4   C   A   £120,000/1,000,000

      B $^6/_{12}$(£120,000/1,000,000) + $^6/_{12}$(£120,000/1,500,000)

      C   £120,000/1,500,000

      D   £120,000/750,000

5   B   A   Cost - property 1 only

      B   Market value - property 1 only

      C   Market value - properties 1 and 2

      D   Cost - property 1 plus depreciated cost property 2

6   A   Private companies that satisfy the criteria for a medium sized company multiplied by 10 do not have to disclose the amount of research and development charged in the year to the profit and loss account.

7   C

8   C   Although SSAP 4 allows treatment 3 this is not allowed by the Companies Act.

9   D   A   Share capital   £500,000 + £250,000 + £300,000 + £350,000
         Share premium   £800,000 + £250,000 + £900,000 + £910,000

      B   Share capital   £1,000,000 + £500,000 + £600,000 + £700,000
         Share premium   £800,000 - £500,000 + £600,000 + £560,000

      C   Share capital   £500,000 + £250,000 + £600,000 + £450,000
         Share premium   £800,000 - £250,000 + £600,000 + £1,170,000

      D   Share capital   £500,000 + £250,000 + £300,000 + £350,000
         Share premium   £800,000 - £250,000 + £900,000 + £910,000

10   C

PRACTICE OBJECTIVE TEST: TEST 2

1   D

2   A

3   D   A change of depreciation method is not a change of accounting policy therefore no prior period adjustment is required.

4   A

5   A   A   Turnover 60% × £900,000 = £540,000

		£
Provision for loss		
Total loss £1,200,000 – £900,000 = 300,000		
Recognised		
£540,000 – £720,000		180,000
Further loss to completion		120,000

    C   As A, but with provision for loss offset against debtors.

6   B   3   Obligations under finance leases due within the next twelve months will be shown under Creditors: amounts due within one year.

    4   An asset held under an operating lease is not capitalised by the lessee.

7   D

8   D

9   C   3   The auditor reports to the shareholders not the directors

    4   Compliance tests test that the internal control are operating effectively not substantive tests

10   C   A   –

    B   £100,000 purchase price minus £80,000 profit and loss account

    C   £80,000 profit and loss account minus £50,000 premium on purchase (or £50,000 nominal value minus PCP £20,000)

    D   Amount of premium on purchase

Paper 6

May 2003

Financial Accounting

IFNA

INSTRUCTIONS TO CANDIDATES

You are allowed three hours to answer this question paper.
Answer the ten objective test questions in section A. *Answer the ONE question in section B.* *Answer ONLY TWO questions in section C.*

**DO NOT OPEN THIS PAPER UNTIL YOU ARE READY
TO START UNDER EXAMINATION CONDITIONS**

SECTION A – 20 MARKS

ANSWER *ALL* QUESTIONS

All questions are worth 2 marks each. Each question has only ONE correct answer

1   An investment property is defined by SSAP 19 – *Accounting for Investment Properties* as

     A   an investment in land and / or buildings whether let to third parties or occupied by a company within the group.

     B   a property owned and occupied by a company for its own purposes.

     C   an interest in land and / or buildings which is held for its investment potential.

     D   an investment in land and / or buildings other than leased property.

2   A capital grant received by a company to offset the cost of purchasing a fixed asset should be accounted for as follows:

     (i)   Credit a deferred income account.
     (ii)   Credit the grant to a reserve account.
     (iii)   Release to the profit and loss account over the life of the asset.
     (iv)   Credit the grant to the fixed asset account to show net cost.
     (v)   Credit the full amount to profit and loss account in year of receipt.

     Which one of the following is correct?

     A   (i) and (iii) only
     B   (v) only
     C   (ii) and (iii) only
     D   (iii) and (iv) only

3   SSAP 25 – *Segmental Reporting* requires that turnover and operating profit should be

     A   analysed by class of business and geographic area of sales origin and destination.
     B   analysed by class of business.
     C   analysed by geographic area of sales origin and destination.
     D   analysed by class of business and type of customer.

4   FRS 3 – *Reporting Financial Performance* specifies the definition and treatment of a number of different items.

     Which of the following is NOT specified by FRS 3?

     A   Discontinued activities.
     B   Prior period adjustments.
     C   Exceptional items.
     D   Provisions.

5   The gearing ratio of a company is calculated as

     (i)   equity share capital and reserves;
     (ii)   equity share capital;
     (iii)   non-equity share capital and debt;
     (iv)   total gross assets;
     (v)   total debt.

Which one of the following is correct?

A   (iii) divided by (ii) and (iii)
B   (iii) divided by (i) and (iii)
C   (v) divided by (iv)
D   (v) divided by (ii)

---

6   Which one of the following descriptions most accurately describes "creative accounting"?

A   Creating fictitious assets on the balance sheet to show a stronger financial position.

B   Not applying Companies Act 1985 or Accounting Standards' requirements so as to show a better year-end position.

C   Deliberately falsifying the financial statements to show a stronger financial position.

D   Using loop-holes in the Companies Act 1985 and Accounting Standards' requirements so that the financial statements are biased in the required direction.

Data for questions 7 and 8

B Ltd entered into a three-year contract to build a leisure centre for a local authority. The contract value was £6 million. B Ltd recognises profit on the basis of certified work completed. At the end of the first year, the following figures were extracted from B Ltd's accounting records:

	£000
Certified value of work completed	2,000
Cost of work certified as complete	1,650
Cost of work-in-progress (not included in completed work)	550
Estimated cost of remaining work required to complete the contract	2,750
Cash received from local authority	1,600
Cash paid to creditors for work on the contract	1,300

7   How much profit should B Ltd recognise in its profit and loss account at the end of the first year?

A   £200,000 (loss)
B   £300,000
C   £350,000
D   £400,000

---

8   What values should B Ltd record for this contract as "debtors" and "creditors, amounts falling due within one year"?

	Debtors	Creditors, falling due within one year
A	£400,000	£350,000
B	£400,000	£900,000
C	£600,000	£900,000
D	£700,000	£600,000

---

9   The following balances were extracted from the books of A Ltd:

	31 March 2003 £000
Sales	300
Cost of sales	200
Gross profit	100
Closing stock	15
Trade debtors	36
Trade creditors	28

A Ltd's average working capital cycle for the year ended 31 March 2003 is

A   11·0 days
B   20·1 days
C   34·7 days
D   37·1 days

---

10   R plc redeems 10,000 £1 redeemable preference shares at a premium of 10%. No fresh issue of shares is made to finance the redemption.

Which of the following is the correct set of accounting entries to record this transaction?

	Debit share capital account	Credit capital redemption reserve account	Debit profit and loss account	Credit bank account
A	£10,000	£10,000	£11,000	£11,000
B	£10,000	£11,000	£10,000	£11,000
C	£11,000	£10,000	£10,000	£11,000
D	£10,000	£11,000	£11,000	£10,000

SECTION B – 30 MARKS

THIS QUESTION IS COMPULSORY

2   AZ plc is a quoted manufacturing company. Its finished products are stored in a nearby warehouse until ordered by customers. AZ plc has performed very well in the past, but has been in financial difficulties in recent months and has been reorganising the business to improve performance.

The trial balance for AZ plc at 31 March 2003 was as follows:

	£000	£000
6% preference shares of £1 each		1,000
7% debentures 2007		18,250
Administration expenses	16,020	
Bank and cash	2,250	
Corporation tax	30	
Cost of goods manufactured in the year to 31 March 2003 (excluding depreciation)	94,000	
Creditors		8,120
Debenture interest paid	639	
Debtors	9,930	
Distribution costs	9,060	
Interest received		1,200
Investments at market value	24,000	
Ordinary shares of £1 each, fully paid		20,000
Plant and equipment	30,315	
Profit and loss account at 31 March 2002		9,444
Provision for deferred tax at 31 March 2002		138
Provision for depreciation at 31 March 2002:		
Plant and equipment		6,060
Vehicles		1,670
Provision for doubtful debts at 31 March 2002		600
Restructuring costs	121	
Revaluation reserve		3,125
Sales		124,900
Share issue expenses	70	
Share premium		500
Stock at 31 March 2002	4,852	
Vehicles	3,720	
	195,007	195,007

Additional information provided:

(i)   The fixed assets are being depreciated as follows:

> Plant and equipment 20% per annum straight line
>
> Vehicles 25% per annum reducing balance

Depreciation of plant and equipment is considered to be part of cost of sales while vehicle depreciation should be included under distribution costs.

(ii)   The balance on the corporation tax account is the previous year's corporation tax, underestimated in last year's accounts by £30,000. Corporation tax for the year to 31 March 2003 is estimated at £150,000.

(iii)   A transfer to deferred tax for the year to 31 March 2003 of £11,000 is to be made.

(iv)   The closing stock at 31 March 2003 was £5,180,000. An inspection of finished goods found that a production machine had been set up incorrectly and that several production batches, which had cost £50,000 to manufacture, had the wrong packaging. The goods cannot be sold in this condition but could be repacked at an additional cost of £20,000. They could then be sold for £55,000. The wrongly packaged goods were included in closing stock at their cost of £50,000.

(v)   AZ plc's directors are proposing the payment of the preference dividend and a final ordinary dividend of 5p per share. No interim dividends were declared.

(vi)   The 7% debentures are 10-year loans due for repayment by 31 March 2007. AZ plc incurred no other interest charges in the year to 31 March 2003.

(vii) The provision for doubtful debts is to be adjusted to 5% of the closing debtors' balance.

(viii) The restructuring costs in the trial balance represent the cost of a major fundamental restructuring of the company to improve competitiveness and future profitability.

(ix) As at 31 March 2003, AZ plc was engaged in defending a legal action against the company. Legal advisers have indicated that it is reasonably certain that the outcome of the case will be against the company. The amount of compensation is currently estimated at £25,000.

(x) On 1 October 2002, AZ plc issued 1,000,000 ordinary shares at £1·50 each. All money had been received and correctly accounted for by the year end.

Required:

Prepare the profit and loss account for AZ plc for the year to 31 March 2003 and a balance sheet at that date, in a form suitable for publication and in accordance with all current regulations.

Notes to the financial statements are not required, but all workings must be clearly shown. DO NOT prepare a statement of accounting policies, a statement of total recognised gains and losses or a reconciliation of movements in shareholders' funds.

30 Marks

SECTION C – 50 MARKS

ANSWER *TWO* QUESTIONS ONLY

3   BY Ltd prepares its financial statements to 31 March each year. The following information relates to the year ended 31 March 2003; the financial statements for the year to 31 March 2003 have not yet been completed. There are some transactions regarding tangible fixed assets that need to be clarified.

(a)   Some of the cars used by BY Ltd's sales force needed replacing. Three new cars were acquired on 1 October 2002. The cars were leased from CarLease plc on the following terms:

- a non-cancellable 5-year lease;

- a total of 10 payments, made every six months in arrears;

- each instalment to be £7,200 (£2,400 per car);

- the interest rate implicit in the lease was 3·5% per six-month period;

- the fair value of each car was £20,000. The present value of the lease payments equals the fair value of the cars at the inception of the lease;

- the residual value of each car at the end of the lease is assumed to be zero;

- BY Ltd will pay for all insurance, repairs and maintenance costs.

Required:

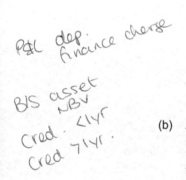

(i)   Explain the meaning of a "finance lease", using the above to illustrate your answer. Identify whether the lease on BY Ltd's cars should be treated as an operating lease or a finance lease.   **8 Marks**

(ii)   Assuming that the lease is to be treated as a finance lease, calculate the figures that will appear in respect of the lease in BY Ltd's profit and loss account for the year ended 31 March 2003 and its balance sheet at that date.   **7 Marks**

(b)   A new type of delivery vehicle, purchased on 1 April 2000 for £20,000, was expected to have a useful economic life of 4 years. It now appears that the original estimate of the useful economic life was too short, and the vehicle is now expected to have a useful economic life of 6 years, from the date of purchase. All delivery vehicles are depreciated using the straight-line method and are assumed to have zero residual value.

Required:

State how BY Ltd should record the delivery vehicle in the profit and loss account for the year ended 31 March 2003 and the balance sheet at that date. Justify your treatment by reference to appropriate Accounting Standards.   **5 Marks**

(c)   A new machine was purchased from a German company during the year to 31 March 2003. The purchase contract provided for payment to be made in UK Pounds. The following payments were detailed in the contract:

	£
Basic cost of the machine	110,000
Upgrades and specific modifications to BY Ltd specifications	22,000
Shipping and transport charges payable in Europe	3,200
Total invoiced cost	135,200
Delivery, handling and installation charges in the UK	900
Total purchase price	136,100

The contract provided for 10% of the invoiced cost to be paid when the contract was signed, 40% when the machine was despatched, and the balance one month after installation. The UK delivery, handling and installation charges were to be paid as incurred in the UK. All UK expenses were paid by 31 March 2003. The contract was signed on 1 January 2003 and the machine was despatched on 1 February 2003. BY Ltd made both payments on the due date. Delivery was made and installation completed on 25 March 2003.

Required:

State how BY Ltd should record the purchase of the machine in the profit and loss account for the year ended 31 March 2003 and the balance sheet at that date. Justify your treatment by reference to appropriate Accounting Standards. **5 Marks**

Total Marks = 25

---

4   Your company, E plc, is considering expansion by acquiring an established business. You, a trainee management accountant, have been co-opted onto a working group whose remit is to identify a suitable company for acquisition.

The two companies under consideration are:

*   X plc, which supplies 30% of E plc's purchases. Acquiring X plc as a subsidiary would give E plc considerable savings through discounts on purchases.

*   Z plc, a company that operates in a related market. No immediate savings have been identified.

The summarised balance sheets and profit and loss accounts for each company at 31 March 2003 are given below.

Summarised balance sheets at 31 March 2003

	X plc £000	Zplc £000
Tangible fixed assets	8,439	7,326
Net current assets	1,263	702
Total assets less current liabilities	9,702	8,028
Creditors due in more than one year:		
10% debentures	(3,800)	(5,000)
	5,902	3,028
Ordinary shares of 20p each	320	
Ordinary shares of £1 each		300
Share premium	2,290	1,800
Revaluation reserve	2,600	0
Profit and loss account	692	928
	5,902	3,028

Summarised profit and loss accounts for the year to 31 March 2003

	X plc £000	Z plc £000
Turnover	7,847	9,340
Cost of sales	(5,689)	(5,960)
Gross profit	2,158	3,380
Expenses:		
Distribution	(354)	(836)
Administration	(611)	(1,162)
Operating profit	1,193	1,382
Interest paid	(380)	(600)
Profit before taxation	813	782
Taxation	(220)	(210)
Profit after taxation	593	572
Ordinary dividend	(320)	(500)
Retained profit	273	72

Average share price for the period was: £5.00   £12.00

Required:

(a)   Calculate the P/E ratio for each company.   **3 Marks**

(b)   Using suitable accounting ratios to support your findings, draft a report to the acquisitions working group identifying the most suitable company for further investigation, assuming:

5 or 6 ratios

*   E plc would acquire 100% of the equity capital;

*   the decision is based entirely on the profitability of each company.

16 Marks

assets met ducres

manage
sales base
location
budgets/forecasts
competitors
staff policy
trains policy

(c) When analysing financial statements and interpreting accounting ratios, it is important to consider "non-financial factors" before making any decisions.

Required:

Explain briefly the main "non-financial factors" which should be considered when deciding whether to acquire a company.   **6 Marks**

Total Marks = 25

---

5 The Accounting Standards Committee, the predecessor of the Accounting Standards Board (ASB), was often criticised for not having developed a conceptual framework of accounting. When the ASB took over, it set about developing a conceptual framework of accounting. In December 1999, the ASB published the Statement of Principles for financial reporting (SoP).

Required:

(a) Explain the four main characteristics that make financial information useful, as outlined in the SoP.   **9 Marks**

(b) The ASB's Foreword to Accounting Standards states "The objective of [the] SoP is to provide a framework for the consistent and logical formulation of individual Accounting Standards".

Required:

Explain how a framework such as the SoP can help with the "consistent and logical formulation of individual Accounting Standards". Use FRS 18 – Accounting Policies to illustrate your answer.

10 Marks

(c) UK financial reporting is based on the principle that financial statements must give a true and fair view. The Companies Act 1985 and the Foreword to Accounting Standards both provide an override clause, which permits companies to use alternative accounting treatments in exceptional *circumstances.*

Required:

Explain the meaning of "true and fair view override" and explain the accounting and / or disclosure requirements that are required when a company uses the override clause.   **6 Marks**

Total Marks = 25

6

(a) Published financial statements include all transactions that took place during the accounting period. Sometimes transactions or events that take place outside of the accounting period are included in the financial statements as well.

Required:

(i) Explain how SSAP 17 – Accounting for Post Balance Sheet Events defines such events and what adjustments (if any) need to be made to the financial statements as a result of such events.   **6 Marks**

(ii) Identify three other Accounting Standards which might require transactions or events occurring in an accounting period to affect the financial statements of an earlier or later period. Give an example for each Standard identified.   **6 Marks**

(b) During April 2003, excessive rain fell in the region where Z plc's main factory and warehouse facilities are situated. At the end of April 2003, the rainfall caused heavy flooding and Z plc's factory and warehouse were standing in two metres of water. The factory plant and equipment were damaged, but can be fully repaired. However, all of Z plc's stock was badly damaged and was written off. Z plc's equipment repairs and stock write-offs were insured and the insurance underwriter has agreed to pay for the repairs and the replacement of the stock. As it will be some time before the factory is able to operate normally again, Z plc has decided to purchase finished goods from outside suppliers during the period that the factory will be closed for repairs. During the period when Z plc is buying in goods instead of manufacturing its own products, its profits will be reduced by a material amount.

Required:

Explain how Z plc should treat this situation in its financial statements for the year to 31 March 2003. **7 Marks**

(c) N plc drilled a new oil well, which started production on 1 March 2003. The licence granting permission to drill the new oil well included a clause that requires N plc to "return the land to the state it was in before drilling commenced". N plc estimates that the oil well will have a 20-year production life. At the end of that time, the oil well will be decommissioned and work carried out to reinstate the land. The cost of this decommissioning work is estimated to be £20 million.

Required:

Explain how N plc should treat the decommissioning costs in its financial statements for the year ended 31 March 2003. **6 Marks**

Total Marks = 25

ANSWERS

DO NOT TURN THIS PAGE UNTIL YOU HAVE COMPLETED THE MOCK EXAM

A PLAN OF ATTACK

As you turned the page to start this exam any one of a number of things could have been going through your mind ranging from the sublime to the ridiculous.

The main thing to do is take a deep breath and do not panic. It's best to sort a plan of attack before the actual exam so that when the invigilator tells you that you can begin and the adrenaline kicks in you are using every minute of the three hours wisely. Make sure you keep your lungs well stocked with a steady supply of oxygen to keep up your energy levels and keep your brain clear, calm and bright!

Your approach

This paper has three sections. The first section contains 10 objective test questions which are compulsory. The second has one compulsory question. The third has four questions and you must answer two of them.

You have a choice.

- Read through and answer Section A before moving on to Section B and Section C

- Go through Section C and select the two questions you will attempt. Then go back and answer the questions in Section A first followed by Section B

- Select the two questions in Section C, answer them and then go back to the other two sections

- Answer the large compulsory question in Section B first and then go back to Sections A and C

You must give yourself a couple of minutes at the start of the exam to go through the questions you are going to do.

Time spent at the start of each question confirming the requirements and producing a plan for the answers is time well spent. Jot down your thoughts using the white spaces on your question paper as you review the questions so you do not lose any key ideas.

Question selection

When selecting the two questions from Section C make sure that you read through all of the requirements. It is painful to answer part (a) of a question and then realise that parts (b) and (c) are beyond you; by then it is too late to change your mind and do another question.

When reviewing the requirements look at how many marks have been allocated to each part. This will give you an idea of how detailed your answer must be.

Highlight or underline the key words in the examiners requirements; this is a positive act that helps to ensure you consciously interpret the requirements.

Doing the exam

Think about your approach. After you've marked your exam spend a few moments reviewing how you tackled the questions.

Did you answer all of the objective test questions in Section A? Even if you don't know an answer, you should guess. Did you allocate your time correctly to the 30 mark question in Section B? Did you answer two questions from Section C?

If you decide on an approach to the exam this will help you to build your confidence. Sitting the two mocks in this kit will enable you to refine your approach.

One possible approach

This is the way I approached this mock exam. It may not suit you. If you can produce the appropriate number of good answers then your approach is equally valid.

My usual preference is to start with some smaller and easier confidence building questions before tackling something more difficult, like a big computational question. I find it useful to finish with a question that has several parts or involves discussing things, which allows me to fit my answer into the time I have left.

Section A

I feel I can really crack this section as there is nothing too scary here. I reckon I can get 7 marks from this section, leaving only 43 to go.

Section C

Question 3. Part (a) requires knowledge of the distinction between operating and finance leases in some detail, not just a basic overview. Parts (b) and (c) are fairly straightforward, but there is no scope for waffle.

Questions 4 is a ratio analysis report. I will always go for this now as I have done a lot of preparation.

Question 5. A nice written question on the *Statement of Principles* with no nasty calculations. I will save this till last.

Question 6 is another question requiring a written answer, this time on events after the balance sheet date and provisions. Main standards involved are SSAP 17, FRS 12 and FRS 15.

Section B

This is quite a meaty question with a list of 10 points. So I keep reminding myself 'Work quickly and accurately – keep it moving'. I hit the bits I am familiar with and take a stab at the parts I am less sure about, rather than agonising over them. I am unlikely to get it all right and set myself a mini target of around 19 to 20 marks, which allows me a little room for error but will keep my mark tally ticking over nicely.

Final question

I will do question 6, which gives me some control over how much I write and yet still present a coherent answer.

Time allocation

Be disciplined. Allocate your time according to the marks available but never go over the time allocation. The last few marks in a question are the hardest to earn.

Be sure to follow the requirements. If four advantages are required, give four. No extra credit will be given for five. Two advantages will only get you half marks.

Answer all of the question. Having a go at every part of all the questions you are required to do will put you in a better position to pass than, say, only doing a few questions. However difficult that last question seems at first there are marks to be earned.

If you have time left at the end of the exam ensure that you have attempted every part of every question you have chosen. If you have, then scan through and ensure you completed any part of an answer you left earlier. Use the full three hours working towards a pass.

270

Marking the exam

When you mark your exam, be honest. Don't be too harsh though. Give yourself credit for the things you did well, but don't kid yourself with 'I would have done that in the real exam'. It may be worth your while making two lists; strengths and weaknesses.

Strengths will be areas of the syllabus you are confident with and also good exam technique (maybe you remembered to lay the memorandum out correctly and draw up a proforma balance sheet).

Weaknesses will be holes in your knowledge and poor exam technique (maybe you ran out of time and couldn't answer all the requirements of the last question).

Making this list will help you focus your last days of revision on the areas which require attention whilst reminding you of the areas you excel in.

SECTION A

1   C

2   A

3   A

4   D

Provisions are covered in FRS 12

5   B

6   D

For accounts to be reliable they must be 'neutral' ie free from systematic bias. Creative accounting involves management trying to show pre determined financial outcomes by taking advantage of loopholes in legislation or regulations.

7   C

Total profit	*£000*
Sales value	6,000
Work completed	(1,650)
WIP	(550)
Remaining work	(2,750)
	1,050

Profit recognised $(1,050 \times \dfrac{2,000}{6,000} = £350,000$

8   B

Debtors	*£000*
Certified value of completed work	2,000
Cash received	(1,600)
	400

Creditors, amounts falling due within one year	
Work certified as complete @ cost	1,650
WIP @ cost	550
Cash paid to creditors	(1,300)
	900

9   B   Stock turnover = $\dfrac{\text{Stock}}{\text{Cost of sales}} \times 365$ days

$= \dfrac{15}{200} \times 365 = 27.4$ days

Debtors turnover = $\dfrac{\text{Debtors}}{\text{Sales}} \times 365$

$$= \frac{36}{300} \times 365 = 43.8 \text{ days}$$

$$\text{Creditors turnover} = \frac{\text{Creditors}}{\text{Cost of sales}} \times 365 \text{ days}$$

$$= \frac{28}{200} \times 365 = 51.1 \text{ days}$$

Working capital cycle = stock turnover + debtors turnover – creditors turnover

= (27.4 + 43.8 – 51.1) days

= 20.1 days

10   A

SECTION B

2

AZ PLC
PROFIT AND LOSS ACCOUNT FOR THE YEAR ENDING 31 MARCH 2003

	£'000	£'000
Turnover		124,900
Cost of sales (W3)		(99,750)
Gross profit		25,150
Administrative expenses (W4)	15,942	
Distribution costs (W4)	9,573	
		(25,515)
Operating profit		(365)
Exceptional item: cost of fundamental restructuring		(121)
Profit/loss on ordinary activities before interest and tax		(486)
Interest payable (18,250 × 7%)	(1,278)	
Income from fixed asset	1,200	
		(78)
Profit on ordinary activities before taxation		(564)
Tax on profit on ordinary activities (W5)		(191)
Profit on ordinary activities after taxation		(755)
Proposed dividends (W7)		(1,060)
Retained loss for the year		(1,815)
Retained profit brought forward		9,444
Retained profit carried forward		7,629
Loss per share		(3.9)p

BALANCE SHEET AS AT 31 MARCH 2003

	£'000	£'000
Fixed assets		
Tangible assets		19,729
Investments (market value)		24,000
		43,729
Current assets		
Stock	5,165	
Debtors (W9)	9,433	
Cash at bank and in bank	2,250	
	16,848	
Creditors: amounts falling due within one year		
Trade creditors	8,120	
Other creditors including taxation	150	
Accrued debenture interest	639	
Proposed dividends	1,060	
	9,969	
Net current assets		6,879
Total assets less current liabilities		50,608
Creditors: amounts falling due after more than one year		
7% debentures 2007		(18,250)
Provisions for liabilities and charges		
Deferred taxation	149	
Other provisions	25	
		(174)
		32,184

Capital and reserves	£'000	£'000
Called up share capital		
Ordinary shares	1,000	
Preference shares	20,000	
		21,000
Reserves		
Share premium account (W11)	430	
Revaluation reserve	3,125	
Retained profits	7,629	
		11,184
		32,184

Workings

1   *Fixed assets*

	P&E £'000	Vehicles £'000	Total £'000
Cost b/f and c/f	30,315	3,720	34,035
Depreciation			
b/f	6,060	1,670	7,730
Charge for year:			
• £30,315 × 20%	6,063		6,063
• (£3,720 – £1,670) × 25%		513	513
	12,123	2,183	14,306
NBV c/f	18,192	1,537	19,729

2   *Stock*

		£'000
Defective batch:		
	Cost of manufacture	50
	Repackaging required	20
		70
	NRV	(55)
	Write off required	15

3   *Cost of sales*

	£'000
Opening stock	4,852
Cost of manufacture excluding depreciation	94,000
Depreciation of P+E	6,063
	104,915
Closing stock (5,180 – 15) (W2)	(5,165)
	99,750

4   *Administration and distribution expenses*

	Administration £'000	Distribution £'000
Per TB	16,020	9,060
Provision for legal claim	25	
Adjustment re doubtful debts	(103)	
Depreciation vehicles		513
	15,942	9,573

5   *Corporation tax*

	£'000
Under estimate from last year	30
Estimate for the current year, carried forward	150
	180
Deferred tax	11
	191

6   *Deferred tax*

	£'000
Brought forward	138
Set aside for year per P+L a/c	11
Carried forward	149

7   *Dividends*

	£'000
Ordinary share (20 million shares × 5p)	1,000
Preference shares (1 million shares × 6p)	60
	1,060

8   *Dividend interest*

	£'000
Due (£18,250,000 × 7%)	1,278
Paid per TB	(639)
Balance carried forward	639

9   *Debtors*

	£'000	£'000
Per TB		9,930
Opening doubtful debts provision	600	
Provision required (£9,930 × 5%)	497	(497)
Write back – to administration (W)	103	
		9,433

10   *Earnings/(loss) per share*

$$\frac{(755)}{(19,000 \times \frac{6}{12}) + (20,000 \times \frac{6}{12})} = \frac{(815)}{19,500} = (3.9)\text{p per share}$$

11   *Share premium account*

	£'000
Opening balance	500
Share issue expenses written off	(70)
	430

BPP
PROFESSIONAL EDUCATION

SECTION C

3   BY Ltd

(a) **New cars**

Examiner's comments. In part (i), most candidates were able to explain the meaning of a finance lease although fewer were able to adequately explain how BY Ltd should treat its lease. Part (ii) was poorly answered. A large proportion of candidates tried answering this part without working out the payments and interest charges first. A significant proportion of those who correctly calculated the interest charges and balances were unable to use the figures calculated to answer the last section of the question.

Note that although the interest rate was given and was expected to be used in the answer, correct calculations using the sum of digits method were given full credit.

Common errors

- Wrongly identifying the lease as an operating lease.
- Incorrectly calculating the finance charges
- Incorrectly using the calculated figures in the profit and loss account and balance sheet.

(i)   *Finance or operating lease*

In terms of SSAP 21, a finance lease is one that **transfers** substantially all the **risks** and **rewards** of ownership of an asset to the lessee.

90% Test

There is a presumption that such a transfer of risks and rewards occurs if at the **inception** of a lease, the **present value** of the **minimum lease payments** including any **initial payment**, amount to substantially all (normally 90% or more) of the fair value of the leased asset.

The minimum lease payments are the minimum payments over the remaining part of the lease team plus any residual amounts guaranteed by the lessee.

The question indicates the present value of the lease payments equals the fair value of the cars at the inception of the lease. Hence the 90% test is satisfied: the leases are finance leases.

Transfer of risks of ownership test

The SSAP 21 definition of finance lease also requires a substantial transfer of the risks and rewards of ownership of the asset to the lessee.

How do the facts stack up against the criteria.

Fact	*Assessment*
• Non-cancellable and for 5 years	If the market has a down turn, BY is saddled with the cars. They cannot be sent back to Car Lease plc
• Residual value is NIL	The lease is effectively for the economic lives of the cars. This is tantamount to ownership of the cars
• BY Ltd to bear costs of insurance, repairs and maintenance	These are a further indication that reinforces the view that BY effectively carries the risks of ownership of the cars.

The above points therefore support the conclusion that the lease should be treated as a finance lease.

(ii)   **Profit and loss account and balance sheet figures**

(The figures for the P+L a/c only indicate 6 months from 1/10/02 to 31/3/03)

Profit and loss account

Finance charge (W1)	£2,100
Depreciation (£60,000 × 20% × 6/12)	£6,000

Balance sheet as at 31 March 2003

	£
Fixed assets – at cost	60,000
Depreciation provision	6,000
Net book value	54,000
Creditors amounts falling due within one year:	
Amounts due under finance leases (54,900 – 44,159)	10,741
Creditors amounts falling due after more than one year:	
Amounts due under finance leases	44,159

Workings

	31.3.03	6 months to 30.9.03	31.3.03
	£	£	£
Balance brought forward	60,000	54,900	49,622
Interest at 3.5%	2,100	1,922	1,737
	62,100	56,822	51,359
Instalment paid	(7,200)	(7,200)	(7,200)
Balance carried forward	54,900	49,622	44,159

(b) **New type delivery vehicle**

> **Examiner's comments.** This was a straight forward question requiring candidates to apply their knowledge of FRS 15. The remaining balance at 1 April 2002 (net book value) had to be calculated first. Then this net book value is used to calculate the new depreciation charge. A significant number of candidates miscalculated the net book value by charging three years depreciation instead of two and a significant proportion also suggested that a prior year adjustment was required.
>
> *Common errors*
>
> • Charging three years depreciation at the original rate.
>
> • Recalculating depreciation over the entire new useful economic life of the asset and calculating a prior year adjustment.

In terms of FRS 15 the current carrying value of the delivery vehicle would be

	£
Cost at 1 April 2000	20,000
Accumulated depreciation (£20,000 × ¼ × 2 years)	(10,000)
Carrying value at 31 March 2002	10,000

Now UEL = 6 yrs. Expired + 2 yrs. ∴ years to go = 4 yrs.

Per FRS 15, this should be accounted for prospectively.

• FRS 15 states that the useful economic life of a tangible fixed asset should be reviewed at the end of each reporting period.

• Where expectations are significantly different from previous estimates, the expected useful economic life should be amended accordingly.

• The adjustment should be done on a prospective basis ie the carrying amount of the asset at the date of the revision should be depreciated over the remaining useful economic life.

279

Hence:

	£
Cost	20,000
Accumulated depreciation	10,000
Opening provision at 31 March 2002	
Charge for current year (10,000 ÷ 4)	2,500
Provision at 31 March 2003	12,500
Net book value at 31 March 2003	7,500

(c) **Initial recognition of machine from Germany**

> **Examiner's comments.** Most candidates recognised that the majority or all of the expenditure should be capitalised. Some candidates incorrectly decided that some of the expenditure should be treated as revenue expenses.
>
> *Common errors*
>
> - Suggesting that some of the expenditure items should be written off and charged as revenue expenses.
> - Incorrectly calculating the amount outstanding at the year end.
> - Assuming delivery was due in the next accounting period.

In terms of FRS 15, a tangible fixed asset should initially be measured at its cost. This should include costs **directly attributable** to bringing the asset into **working condition** for its **intended use**.

For a purchased asset, cost is purchase price, after trade discounts and rebates, plus costs mentioned in the above paragraph.

Directly attributable costs include:

- Direct labour costs of using own employees
- Acquisition costs eg stamp duty, import duties
- Cost of site preparation
- Installation costs
- Professional fees
- Estimated costs of dismantling and site restoration

(*Note.* Administration and general overheads are not directly attributable costs. For tangible fixed assets, costs are capitalised on an incremental/marginal costing basis.)

Hence, the basic cost of the machine, the cost of upgrades and modifications, shipping, transport, delivery, handling and installation should be capitalised by being debited to a plant and equipment account.

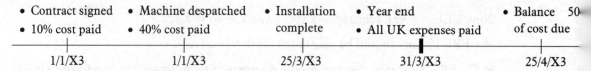

The 50% balance on invoice cost of £67,600 (£135,200 × 50%) should be accrued for and reflected in the balance sheet as at 31 March 20X3 under creditors falling due within one year.

In effect, the transaction would have been as follows

		£	£
DEBIT	Plant and equipment	136,100	
CREDIT	Bank (1st payment – 10%)		13,520
CREDIT	Bank (2nd payment – 40%)		54,080
CREDIT	Bank (Expenses)		900
CREDIT	Accruals (50%)		67,600

As with the company's other fixed assets, depreciation would have to be provided for in accordance with the requirements of FRS 15.

- Written off as an expense to profit and loss account over the useful economic life of the machine

- The charge should reflect the way in which the economic benefits of the machine are consumed by the company.

- However in the year to 31 March 2003 the machine has only been in operation for 6 days and therefore any depreciation charge would be immaterial.

4   (a) Earnings per share

> **Examiner's comments.** Some candidates did not seem to know what the term 'P/E' meant, as a result they calculated a range of unusual ratios.
>
> *Common errors*
>
> - Not noticing that X plc shares were 20p nominal value and therefore using the wrong number of shares in the EPS part of the calculation.
>
> - Using the wrong profit figure.

	X plc £	Z plc £
Profit before tax	593,000	572,000
Number of shares	1,600,000	300,000
EPS (a) ÷ (b)	37 pence	191 pence
Price	500 pence	1,200 pence
Price/earnings ratio	13.5	6.3

(b) Draft report

> **Examiner's comments.** This question was generally not answered well. Interpretation is an important part of the syllabus. There is always an interpretation question of one form or another on this paper. A large proportion of candidates were able to calculate the ratios but were unable to analyse them and suggest reasons why they may be different.
>
> Many of the ratios described were not measures of profitability. Gearing was a common suggestion as were the liquidity ratios, these were not relevant to the question, in fact the information required to calculate the current ratio was not given.
>
> *Common errors*
>
> - Despite the clear requirements of the question, a substantial minority of candidates chose not to concentrate on profitability issues.
>
> - Submitting a list of ratios with no attempt to provide an analysis or to recommend a company for further investigation.
>
> - Providing a commentary on the ratios rather than an analysis.
>
> - ROCE was often calculated incorrectly.

From: Trainee management accountant

To: Acquisitions working group

Subject: Evaluation of X plc and Z plc   Date: XX/XX/XX

Many thanks for co-opting me onto the working group. My draft report on the above companies follows.

(1) *Overall*

1.1 X plc is almost twice as big as Zplc in terms of total net assets, but Z plc's turnover is greater by 19%.

1.2 In addition Z plc's operating profit is greater by 15.8%.

(2) *Trading performance*

2.1 Z plc (36.2%) has a better gross profit margin than X plc (27.5%). This may be because Z plc operates in a more lucrative trading environment or its trading operations and controls are more efficient.

2.2 This raises the question whether there is scope for adding value to X plc by making trading performance improvements after take-over, eg

- Improving sales mix

- Enhancing product quality

- Strengthening stock controls

- Review of purchasing efficiency ie prices paid, discounts received etc.

2.3 In terms of discounts, the effect of acquiring X plc would mean that the cost to the group would be the cost to X plc.

	Say	
Cost of item to X plc	100p	
Normal X plc mark-up	50	50p
X plc selling price	50p	
Discount to E	(10)p	(10)p
Price to E	140p	
Intercompany profit		40p
Z mark-up	30p	
Z selling price	170p	

Hence, on its own, E would earn a 30 pence profit, in this example. As a group including X plc, the profit would be 70 pence.

(3) *Expense structure*

3.1 The distribution and administration expense ratios, as shown in Appendix 2, suggest that Z plc has a higher overhead expense structure as compared to X plc.

3.2 The question is whether:

- Z plc's controls over expenses are more relaxed than X plc's controls, or

- X plc is skimping in its expenditure and therefore giving its customers an inferior service.

3.3 Consideration should therefore be given to whether there is future scope for deriving value by cutting Z plc's expenditure or there is a need to enhance X plc's cost structure.

(4)   *Net profit percentage*

5.1   Z plc's asset turnover ratio of 1.16 is significantly higher than that of X plc's ratio.

5.2   However, if the revaluation reserve is adjusted back against X plc's assets, we get a revised ratio of 1.10 which is similar to that of Z plc.

5.3   Revaluation of X plc's fixed assets also means that its profit and loss account has to suffer an extra depreciation charge (Rough estimate £2,600 × 20% = £520). This would significantly improve X plc's profitability.

5.4   Accumulated depreciation figures are not provided so it is not possible to discern the overall age of the fixed assets of the companies.

5.5   In circumstances where the NBV indicates that fixed assets are heavily written down, this may suggest the need for further investment. On the other hand, it might also suggest some scope for improving operational efficiency. The quality of a company's fixed assets can significantly affect its efficiency and profitability.

(6)   *Return on capital employed*

6.1   The unadjusted ROCE figures suggest that Z plc (17.2%) gives a better return to shareholders than X plc (12.3%).

6.2   However, if adjustments are made the impact of revaluation of X plc's assets, X plc's ROCE would be 24.1% and significantly better than that of Z plc.

6.3   The problem here is the importance of comparing like with like. We need to know what revaluation might need to be made to Z plc's assets.

(7)   *Conclusion*

7.1   A preliminary analysis suggests that Z plc is a better performer in terms of the profitability shown in the accounts. Although its net profit percentage is slightly lower than that of X plc, there may be scope for some cost cutting by Z plc.

7.2   My recommendation, is therefore to pursue further investigation into the possibility of acquiring Z plc.

APPENDIX 1

	X plc	*Z plc*	*Difference*	*Percentage*
Total assets less current liabilities	9,702	8,028	1,674	*20.1%
Turnover	7,847	9,340	1,493	*19.0%
Operating profit	1,193	1,382	189	*15.8%

* = Percentage difference over the smaller figure.

APPENDIX 2

	X plc	Z plc
Gross margin		
2,158/7,847	27.5%	
3,380/9,340		36.2%
Distribution expenses		
354/7,847	4.5%	
836/9,340		8.9%
Admin expenses		
611/7,847	7.8%	
1,162/9,340		12.4%
Net profit percentage		
1,193/7,847	15.2%	
1,382/9,340		14.8%
Asset turnover		
7,847/9,702	0.81	
9,340/8,028		1.16
7,847/(9,702 – 2,600) Adjusted	1.10	
ROCE		
1,193/9,702	12.3%	
1,382/8,028		17.2%
(1,193 + 520)/(9,702 – 2,600)	24.1%	

(c) **Non-financial factors**

> **Examiner's comments.** Most candidates were able to identify a wide range of non-financial factors although some candidates also included financial factors as well.
>
> *Common errors*
>
> - Including finance related factors.
> - Not giving sufficient explanation for each factor.

These can include both internal and external factors, when considering an acquisition.

Internal

- Qualifications, calibre and experience of management
- Skills and motivation of staff
- Effectiveness of internal control systems
- Quality of IT systems and fixed assets
- Effectiveness of teamwork, communication and knowledge sharing
- Streamlined organisational structure
- Flexible working practices
- Relevance of business strategy

External

- Factors in the economic environment
- Corporate image/brand image
- Customer relationships/reputation for quality of service/products
- Scope and quality of business networks
- Location of various business units
- Relations with competitors
- Positioning within market/industry
- Nature of market/industry sector
- Impact of globalisation
- Impact of future trends

5   (a) **Characteristics of useful information**

In terms of the ASB's Statement of Principles, the qualitative characteristics that make information useful are relevance, reliability, comparability and understandability.

However, for information to be useful, it must also be material. The **materiality test** asks whether the **information** involved is of **such significance** as to **require** its **inclusion** in the financial statements. It exerts a **quality threshold** on financial information.

Relevance

(i)   Information is **relevant** if it possess **certain qualities**

- Ability to **influence economic decisions** of users
- Is sufficiently **timely** to influence the decision
- Has **predictive** or **confirmatory** value, or both

Eg the FRS 3 requirement for separate analyses of the results of discontinued operations can be said to improve the predictive value of a set of financial statements.

Reliability

(ii) Financial information is reliable if:

- It can be depended upon by users to **represent faithfully** what it either purports to represent or could reasonably be expected to represent, and therefore reflects the **substance of the transactions** and other events that have taken place

- It is **free** from deliberate or systematic **bias** (ie it is **neutral**)

- It is **free** from **material error**

- It is **complete** within the bounds of **materiality**

- Under conditions of **uncertainty**, it has been **prudently prepared**

If financial statements are not neutral they cannot be reliable. Tension often exists between neutrality and prudence. This should be reconciled by finding a balance that ensures that the deliberate and systematic understatement of assets and gains, and overstatement of liabilities and losses, does not occur.

Sometimes, there are circumstances when choices have to be made between treatments that are relevant and reliable but mutually exclusive. The option selected should be the one that results in the relevance of the information package as a whole being maximised – in other words, the one that is reliable and would be of most use in taking economic decisions.

Comparability

Similarities and differences can be discerned and evaluated:

- Enables identification of **trends** in financial position and performance **over time** for an entity

- Helps compare **financial performance** between entities

- Achieved through **consistency** and **disclosure**

Understandability

The significance of the information can be perceived and depends on various factors

- How transactions are **characterised, aggregated** and **classified**

- Way in which information is **presented**

- Capability of user – assumed **reasonably knowledgeable** and diligent

(b) **Role of SoP**

Examiner's comments. This part was not always completed by candidates. Those that did attempt the question often missed the point of the question and did not relate FRS 18 to the SoP.

Common errors

Not answering the question asked:

- General answer on the advantages of a conceptual framework with no attempt to relate the answer to the question.

- No reference to FRS 18.

- General explanation of FRS 18 requirements with no attempt to relate them to the question.

The Statement of Principles for Financial Reporting sets out the principles that the ASB believes should underlie the preparation and presentation of general purpose financial statements.

The primary purpose of articulating such principles is to provide a coherent frame of reference to be used by the ASB in the development and review of accounting standards and by others who interact with the Board during the standard-setting process.

A framework such as the SoP can help with the consistent and logical formulation of individual accounting standards for the following reasons

- General **principles** are **clearly laid out** so that an *ad hoc* or piecemeal basis that responds to issues as they arise is avoided

- Standards are likely to be **up-to-date** with **modern developments** and business practices

- There is a **reduction** in the **need to debate fundamental** issues each time a standard is addressed

- It provides a **framework** for the **future development of financial reporting standards**

Generally, it provides various parties such as financial statement users, preparers and auditors with a picture of the direction from which the ASB is coming when it goes about developing standards.

FRS 18 *Accounting policies* was developed and issued to replace SSAP 2 *Disclosure of accounting policies*. It builds on the concepts outlined in SSAP 2 (issued almost 30 years ago) and attempts to align them with the ASB *Statement of Principles*. FRS 18 can be said to provide a 'bridge' between the ideas and concepts envisaged by the *Statement of Principles* and enshrined in SSAP 2 for a long time in the past.

A key point about FRS 18 is that it defines accruals in terms of whether there is a valid liability to be carried forward into the following accounting period rather than in terms of the concept of item matching i.e. FRS 18 enshrines the ASB balance sheet driven approach towards the recognition of assets and liabilities.

Together with the definitions of assets and liabilities set out in FRS 5, *Reporting the Substance of Transactions*, FRS 18 in effect provides a discipline within which the old SSAP 2 matching process can operate.

The SoP sets out the characteristics of useful financial information, namely relevance, reliability and comparability. Under FRS 18, these characteristics become accounting policy objectives which underpin the application of the two ' pervasive concepts' of the accruals basis and the going concern assumption. In terms of FRS 18, the prudence and consistency concepts have been relegated to being 'desirable features.

(c) **True and fair override**

Examiner's comments. Candidates generally knew the meaning of the override clause and were able to explain the disclosure requirements.

Common error

- Too much emphasis on one part of the question.

There may be 'special' or 'exceptional' circumstances where compliance with an accounting standard, UITF abstract or the Companies Act is inconsistent with the requirement to give a true and fair view. In such cases, the directors may depart from the standard, abstract or legislation to the extent necessary to give a true and fair view. This is called the true and fair override.

Recent accounting standards have been very carefully drafted so as to minimise the need to do something different.

Hence both the Companies Act and FRS 18 require certain disclosures to be made when a company resorts to using the true and fair override.

(a) A statement that there has been a departure from the requirements of companies legislation, an accounting standard or UITF abstract, and that the departure is necessary to give a true and fair view.

(b) A description of the treatment normally required and also a description of the treatment actually used.

(c) An explanation of why the prescribed treatment would not give a true and fair view.

(d) Its effect: a description of how the position shown in the accounts is different as a result of the departure, with quantification if possible, or an explanation of the circumstances.

The disclosures required should either be included in or cross referenced to the note required about compliance with accounting standards, particulars of any material departure from those standards and the reasons for it (Paragraph 36A Sch4).

6   (a)   (i)   **PBSE definition and any required adjustments**

SSAP 17 defines a **post balance sheet event** as those events, both favourable and unfavourable, which occur between the **balance sheet date** and the date on which the financial statements are **approved** by the board of **directors**.

Events occurring after the balance sheet date may be classified into **two categories** i.e. *adjusting events* and *non-adjusting events*.

Adjusting events: These provide **additional evidence** of **conditions existing** at the **balance sheet date**. They require **changes** in amounts to be included in **financial statements** e.g.

- A valuation of property that provides evidence of an impairment in value.
- Notice of insolvency of a debtor
- Details of net realisable value of stocks
- Discovery of errors or frauds which indicate that the financial statements were incorrect

Non-adjusting events: These arise after the balance sheet date and concern conditions which did not exist at the time. Therefore, they do not result in changes in financial statements, e.g.

- Losses of fixed assets by fire or flood
- Declines in value of property and investments occurring after year-end.
- Changes in foreign exchange rates
- Closing of a significant part of trading activities not actually anticipated at balance sheet date.

There may be situations where non-adjusting events may be of such **materiality** that their **disclosure** is required by way of **note** to ensure that the financial statements are not misleading.

In these circumstances, the note should include

(1) The nature of the event

(2) An estimate of the financial impact

(3) When it is not practicable to make an estimate, a statement explaining this situation

(ii)   **Other accounting standards**

Here are a few examples

(1) **FRS 15/FRS 10.** A fixed asset is acquired in one year. However, consumption of economic benefits in subsequent years require depreciation or amortisation to be written off.

(2) **SSAP 13.** Development expenditure, to the extent that it is recoverable, is deferred to be set off against revenue in a future period.

(3) **FRS 12.** An event has occurred, but the obligation payable is uncertain as to amount or timing, eg. legal case not yet determined by the courts.

(4) **FRS 19.** Ensures that the future tax consequences of past transactions and events are recognised as liabilities in the financial statements.

(b) **Storm damage**

The damage occurred after the year end and clearly does affect conditions existing at balance sheet date.

The event is hence *prima facia* a non-adjusting event. However, SSAP 17 does require non-adjusting events to be disclosed if they are material.

The question tells us that the loss of stock and damage to fixed assets are covered by insurance. However, it appears that the risk in respect of consequential losses has not been covered by the insurance.

Hence there will be no loss in respect of the flood damaged stock and fixed assets require no adjustment or disclosure.

However, the cost of the finished goods bought-in from outside suppliers will have to be suffered by the company and have a material impact on profits. The circumstances of the flood and these costs must be disclosed by way of a note to the accounts.

(c) **Decommissioning costs**

FRS 15 specifies that cost of a tangible fixed asset should include the estimated costs of dismantling and removing the asset and restoring the site, to the extent that it is recognised as a provision under FRS 12.

In terms of FRS 12, any future obligations arising out of past events should be recognised immediately. Hence the cost of decommissioning the oil well should be recognised in the accounts for the year ended 31 March 20X3.

However, the £20 million is payable in some 20 years time. Hence the amount to be capitalised at 31 March 20X3 will be the £20 million discounted over 20 years to present value.

Notes

- The present value of the decommissioning cost will be amortised over the life of the oil well

- However, the unwinding of the discount over the 20 years will be charged as a financial cost and not depreciation.

Intermediate

MOCK EXAM 2

Paper 6

November 2003

Financial Accounting

IFNA

INSTRUCTIONS TO CANDIDATES

You are allowed three hours to answer this question paper.

Answer the ten objective test questions in section A

Answer the ONE question in section B.

Answer ONLY TWO questions in section C.

**DO NOT OPEN THIS PAPER UNTIL YOU ARE READY
TO START UNDER EXAMINATION CONDITIONS**

SECTION A – 20 MARKS

ANSWER *ALL* QUESTIONS

All questions are worth 2 marks each. Each question has only ONE correct answer

1   A sub-committee of the Accounting Standards Board (ASB) is known as the UITF.

What does the UITF stand for?

A   Urgent International Task Force
B   Undecided Issues Task Forum
C   Urgent Issues Task Force
D   Urgent Issues Task Forum

2   The ASB's *Statement of Principles* (SoP) lists the qualitative characteristics of the financial statements.

Which THREE of the following are NOT included in the main qualitative characteristics listed by the SoP?

(i)	Comparability	(v)	Understandability
(ii)	Relevance	(vi)	Matching
(iii)	Prudence	(vii)	Consistency
(iv)	Reliability		

A   (i), (iii) and (vii)

B   (i), (ii) and (v)

C   (iii), (vi) and (vii)

D   (iii), (iv) and (vi)

3   Which of the following is NOT regarded as a related party of a company by FRS 8 *Related party disclosures*?

A   Directors of the company.
B   A bank providing a loan to the company.
C   The company's employee pension fund.
D   A close relative of a director of the company.

4   SSAP 17 *Post balance sheet events* classifies post balance sheet events as adjusting and non-adjusting.

Which of the following is an adjusting event?

A   One month after the year end, a customer lodged a claim for £1,000,000 compensation. The customer claimed to have suffered permanent mental damage as a result of the fright she had when one of the company's products malfunctioned and exploded. The outcome of the court case cannot be predicted at this stage.
B   There was a dispute with the workers and all production ceased one week after the year end.
C   A fire destroyed all of the company's stock in its finished goods warehouse two weeks after the year end.
D   Stock valued at the year end at £20,000 was sold one month later for £15,000.

5   B plc, a listed company, has 5,000,000 issued ordinary shares with a par value of 20 pence each. There were no movements of issued share capital during the year. B plc had the following results for the year ended 30 April 2003:

	£'000
Profit before taxation	400
Taxation	100
Profit after taxation	300
Dividends paid	200
Retained profit	100

The quoted price of B plc shares on 30 April 2003 was £1.50.

B plc's P/E ratio on this date was

A   5
B   15
C   18.75
D   25

6   X Ltd signed a finance agreement on 1 October 2002. The lease provided for five annual payments, in arrears, of £20,000. The fair value of the asset was agreed at £80,000.

Using the sum of digits method, how much should be charged to the profit and loss account for the finance cost in the year to 30 September 2003?

A   £4,000
B   £6,667
C   £8,000
D   £20,000

7   D Ltd purchased a fixed asset on 1 April 2000 for £200,000. The asset attracted writing down allowances at 25% on the reducing balance. Depreciation was 10% on the straight-line basis. Assume corporation tax is at 30%.

The deferred tax balance for this asset at 31 March 2003 is

A   £9,000
B   £16,688
C   £27,000
D   £55,625

8   C Ltd started work on a contract to build a dam for a hydro-electric scheme. The work commenced on 24 August 2001 and is scheduled to take four years to complete. C Ltd recognises profit on the basis of the certified percentage of work completed. The contract price is £10 million.

An analysis of C Ltd's records provided the following information:

Year to 30 September	2002	2003
Percentage of work completed and certified in year	30%	25%
	£'000	£'000
Total cost incurred during the year	2,900	1,700
Estimated cost of remaining work to complete contract	6,000	3,900
Total payments made for the cost incurred during the year	2,500	2,000

How much profit should C Ltd recognise in its profit and loss account for the years ended

	30 September 2002 £'000	30 September 2003 £'000
A	100	375
B	330	375
C	330	495
D	500	825

9   F Ltd's year end is June. F Ltd purchased an asset for £50,000 on 1 July 2000.

Depreciation was provided at the rate of 20% per annum on the straight-line basis. There was no forecast residual value.

On 1 July 2002, the asset was revalued to £60,000 and then depreciated on a straight-line basis over its remaining useful economic life which was unchanged. On 1 July 2003, the asset was sold for £35,000.

In addition to the entries in the fixed asset account and provision for depreciation account, which TWO of the following statements correctly record the entries required on disposal of the asset?

   (i)   Debit profit and loss account with a loss on disposal of £5,000.

   (ii)   Credit profit and loss account with a gain on disposal of £25,000.

   (iii)   Transfer £60,000 from revaluation reserve to profit and loss reserve as a movement on reserves.

   (iv)   Transfer £30,000 from revaluation reserve to profit and loss reserve as a movement on reserves.

   (v)   Transfer £30,000 from revaluation reserve to profit and loss account.

   (vi)   Transfer £60,000 from revaluation reserve to profit and loss account.

A   (i) and (iv)
B   (ii) and (iii)
C   (i) and (v)
D   (ii) and (vi)

10   S plc announced a rights issue of 1 for every 5 shares currently held, at a price of £2 each. S plc currently has 2,000,000 £1 ordinary shares with a quoted market price of £2.50 each. Directly attributable costs amounted to £25,000.

Assuming all rights are taken up and all money paid in full, how much will be credited to the share premium account for the rights issue?

A   £200,000
B   £308,333
C   £375,000
D   £400,000

Total Marks = 20

SECTION B – 30 MARKS

THIS QUESTION IS COMPULSORY

---

2   Hi plc, listed on its local stock exchange, is a retail organisation operating several retail outlets countrywide. A reorganisation of the company was started in 2002 because of a significant reduction in profits. This reorganisation was completed during the current financial year.

The trial balance for Hi plc at 30 September 2003 was as follows:

	£'000	£'000
10% debentures 2010		1,000
Administrative expenses	615	
Bank and cash	959	
Buildings	11,200	
Cash received on disposal of equipment		11
Cost of goods sold	3,591	
Debenture interest paid – half year to 31 March 2003	50	
Debtors	852	
Distribution costs	314	
Equipment and fixtures	2,625	
Fixed asset investments at market value 30 September 2002	492	
Interim dividend paid	800	
Investment income received		37
Ordinary shares of £1 each, fully paid		4,000
Profit and loss account at 30 September 2002		1,390
Provision for deferred tax		256
Provision for reorganisation expenses at 30 September 2002		1,010
Provisions for depreciation at 30 September 2002:		
Buildings		1,404
Equipment and fixtures		1,741
Reorganisation expenses	900	
Revaluation reserve		172
Sales		9,415
Share premium		2,388
Stock at 30 September 2003	822	
Trade creditors		396
	23,220	23,220

Additional information provided:

(i)   The reorganisation expenses relate to a comprehensive restructuring and reorganisation of the company that began in 2002. Hi plc's financial statements for 2002 include a provision for reorganisation expenses of £1,010,000. All costs had been incurred by the year end, but an invoice for £65,000, received on 2 October 2003, remained unpaid and is not included in the trial balance figures. No further restructuring and reorganisation costs are expected to occur and the provision is no longer required.

(ii)   Fixed asset investments are carried in the financial statements at market value. The market value of the fixed asset investments at 30 September 2003 was £522,000. There were no movements in the investments held during the year.

(iii)   On 1 November 2003, Hi plc was informed that one of its debtors, X Ltd, had ceased trading. The liquidators advised Hi plc that it was very unlikely to receive payment of any of the £45,000 due from X Ltd at 30 September 2003.

(iv)   One of Hi plc's customers is suing the company for damages as a consequence of a faulty product. Legal advisers are currently advising that the probability of Hi plc being found liable is 75%. The amount payable is estimated to be the full amount claimed of £100,000.

(v)   The corporation tax for the year ended 30 September 2003 is estimated at £1,180,000 and the deferred tax provision needs to be increased to £281,000.

(vi)   A final dividend of 20p per share is being proposed by the directors.

(vii) During the year, Hi plc disposed of old equipment for £11,000. The original cost of this equipment was £210,000 and accumulated depreciation at 30 September 2002 was £205,000 Hi plc's accounting policy is to charge no depreciation in the year of disposal.

(viii) Depreciation is charged using the straight-line basis on fixed assets as follows:

Buildings	3%
Equipment and fixtures	20%

(ix) On 1 April 2003, Hi plc made a rights issue of 1 new share for 4 existing shares, at a price of £3. The fair value immediately before the rights issue was £4.25 per share. All the rights were taken up and all money paid by 30 September 2003.

Required:

(a) Prepare the profit and loss account for Hi plc for the year to 30 September 2003 and a balance sheet at that date, in a form suitable for publication and in accordance with all current regulations.

> Notes to the financial statements are NOT required, but all workings must be clearly shown. DO NOT prepare a statement of accounting policies or a statement of total recognised gains and losses.

20 Marks

(b) Prepare a reconciliation of movements in shareholders' funds for Hi plc for the year ended 30 September 2003. **5 Marks**

(c) Calculate Hi plc's earnings per share for the year ended 30 September 2003. **5 Marks**

Total Marks = 30

SECTION C

ANSWER ***TWO*** QUESTIONS ONLY

3   (a)   A Ltd purchased a site on the edge of a city and built a large new retail site there. A Ltd has now transferred its retail business from the city centre site to the new site. The former retail unit, on the city centre site, is surplus to requirements and A Ltd is trying to sell it. At 31 October 2003, a buyer had not been found. A Ltd's accounting policy is to carry property in its financial statements at current value.

At 31 October 2003, the property values were:

BALANCE SHEETS AT 30 SEPTEMBER 20X2

New retail outlet	£'000
Cost of land plus construction cost	900
Existing use valuation at 31 October 2003	1,000
Open market valuation at 31 October 2003	1,200

Former retail unit	
Valuation at 31 October 2003	400
Existing valuation at 31 October 2003	600
Open market valuation at 31 October 2003	1,200

Required:

State, with reasons, the valuation that A Ltd should use in its financial statements at 31 October 2003 in respect of each of these properties.   **5 Marks**

(b)   C plc owns a number of buildings, factories, offices and warehouses. C plc's accounting policy is not to revalue any fixed assets; all fixed assets are carried at depreciated historical cost.

A firm of independent valuers carried out a valuation of all the buildings on 30 June 2003. The results for three properties are given in the table below; all other properties were broadly similar in value to their net book values.

	Net book value	*Open market value*	*Existing use value*
	£'000	£'000	£'000
Factory	2,300	1,400	1,600
Office	1,000	1,500	1,800
Warehouse	1,500	2,000	1,750
Totals	4,800	4,900	5,150

C plc's directors do not intend changing the carrying values of any of the buildings as their total open market value and existing use value are both greater than total net book value.

C plc's external auditors have indicated that they are unhappy with the directors' proposed treatment of the buildings.

Required:

(i)   Explain why C plc's external auditors may be unhappy with the proposal to leave the value of the three buildings at £4,800,000 at 30 June 2003. Your explanation should refer to relevant Accounting Standards.   **7 Marks**

(ii)   Calculate the figures that should appear in respect of the three buildings in C plc's financial statements for the year ended 30 June 2003. Ignore depreciation.

   3 Marks

(iii)   Explain the action that the external auditors could take if the directors still intend to pursue their view and use the current net book value of the three buildings (£4,800,000) in the financial statements at 30 June 2003.

   3 Marks

(iv)   After the external auditiors have done everything they can to dissuade them, the directors still intend to publish the company's financial statements using the current net book value of the three buildings (£4,800,000). Explain the role of the Financial Reporting Review Panel (FRRP) and how it might relate to this situation.   **7 Marks**

   Total Marks= 25

4   The following are the financial statements of B Ltd for the period 1 October 2001 to 30 September 2003:

Balance sheets at 30 September

	2003		2002	
	£'000	£'000	£'000	£'000
Fixed assets				
Intangible assets		550		470
Tangible assets		3,260		1,630
Investments		400		260
		4,210		2,360
Current assets				
Stock	515		360	
Debtors	1,000		950	
Investments	315		100	
Bank	650		370	
	2,480		1,780	
Creditors amounts falling due within one year				
Trade creditors	784		773	
Taxation	140		74	
Proposed dividend	320		200	
Bank loans and overdrafts	950		528	
	2,194		1,575	
Net current assets		286		205
Total assets less current liabilities		4,496		2,565
Creditors amounts falling due after more than one year				
10% debentures 2003/2006		251		979
		4,245		1,586
Capital and reserves				
Ordinary shares of £1 each		325		150
Share premium		2,300		900
Revaluation reserve		1,339		350
Profit and loss account		281		186
		4,245		1,586

Profit and loss accounts for the year to 30 September

	2003		2002	
	£'000	£'000	£'000	£'000
Turnover		3,920		3,730
Cost of sales		(2,743)		(2,703)
Gross profit		1,177		1,027
Administrative expenses	(308)		(290)	
Distribution costs	(184)	(492)	(157)	(447)
Operating profit		685		580
Interest receivable	31		24	
Interest payable	(191)	(160)	(170)	(146)
Profit before tax		525		434
Taxation		(110)		(71)
Profit after tax		415		363
Proposed dividend		(320)		(200)
Retained profit		95		163

On 1 October 2002, the company made a new issue of ordinary shares at £9 per share. Part of the issue proceeds was used to purchase new equipment which became operational from 1 June 2003.

As the trainee management accountant, you have been asked to draft a briefing paper for the company Chairman to use to respond to possible questions from the shareholders regarding the performance of B Ltd between 2002 and 2003.

Required:

Prepare the briefing paper specified above:

Your paper should cover the following aspects of performance:

(i)	Profitability	**13 Marks**
(ii)	Liquidity and efficiency	**5 Marks**
(iii)	Financial structure	**7 Marks**

Total Marks = 25

5   (a)   Z plc acquired the business and assets of Q, a sole trader, on 31 October 2002.

The fair value of the assets acquired from Q were:

	£'000
Intangible fixed assets	
Brand X – brand name	220
Tangible fixed assets	
Plant and equipment	268
Stock	5
	493
Cash paid to Q	523

Z plc spent the following amounts creating and promoting the brand name:

Year to 31 October 2000	£100,000
Year to 31 October 2001	£90,000
Year to 31 October 2002	£80,000

Z plc's accounting policy on recognised intangible fixed assets is that goodwill and brand names are amortised over 10 years.

On 31 October 2003, Z plc's brand names were valued by an independent valuer as follows:

Brand X at £250,000

Brand Z at £300,000

The directors of Z plc have been very impressed with the increase in profits from Q's former business. They are certain that the goodwill has increased since they acquired Q's business. Z plc's directors have estimated that the goodwill is worth £45,000 at 31 October 2003.

Required:

Explain how Z plc should treat:

(i)   the brand names;   **9 Marks**

(ii)   goodwill;   **6 Marks**

in its financial statements for the years ended 31 October 2002 and 2003. Your explanation should include reference to relevant Accounting Standards.

(b)   Y Ltd provides packaging products to mail order and internet retailers. Y Ltd is the market leader in its sector and is trying to keep ahead of the competition by researching new packaging products. Y Ltd is about to launch a new type of packaging on to the market. The new product is expected to be commercially viable and Y Ltd has sufficient resources for the foreseeable future.

Y Ltd has developed this product from original research started three years ago. The research and development had three phases

- Phase 1 – July 2000 to May 2001 – pure research into possible new types of material. Carried out by a local university department at a cost of £75,000.

- Phase 2 – June 2001 to April 2002 – consultancy fees incurred for the investigation of the commercial possibilities of the newly discovered material. Fees incurred £192,000.

- Phase 3 – June 2002 to May 2003 – costs of developing the product and preparing for product launch, £223,000.

The second phase, investigating the commercial possibilities of the newly discovered material, attracted a 50% government grant. All conditions attached to the grant were fully complied with during the year ended 30 May 2002.

Required:

Explain how Y Ltd should treat the research and development costs and government grant in its financial statements for the years ended 31 May 2001, 2002 and 2003. Your explanation should include reference to relevant Accounting Standards. **10 Marks**

Total Marks = 25

6   The financial statements of YZ are given below.

Balance sheets at	30 September 2003		30 September 2002	
	£'000	£'000	£'000	£'000
Tangible fixed assets		634		510
Current assets				
Stock	420		460	
Debtors	390		320	
Interest receivable	4		9	
Investments	50		0	
Bank	75		0	
Cash	7		5	
	946		794	
Creditors amounts falling due within one year				
Bank overdraft	0		70	
Trade creditors	550		400	
Corporation tax	100		90	
Dividends	30		0	
Interest payable	6		33	
	686		593	
Net current assets		260		201
Total assets less current liabilities		894		711
Creditors amounts falling due after more than one year				
10% debentures		0		40
5% debentures		329		349
		565		322
Capital and reserves				
Ordinary shares £0.50 each		363		300
Share premium account		89		92
Revaluation reserve		50		0
Profit and loss account		63		(70)
		565		322

Profit and loss account for the year to 30 September 2003

	£'000	£'000
Turnover		2,900
Cost of sales		(1,734)
Gross profit		1,166
Administrative expenses	(342)	
Distribution costs	(520)	(862)
Operating profit		304
Interest receivable	5	
Interest payable	(19)	(14)
Profit before tax		290
Taxation		(104)
Profit after tax		186
Dividends		(53)
Retained profit		133

Additional information

(1)   On October 2002, YZ Ltd issued 60,000 £0.50 ordinary shares at a premium of 100%. The proceeds were used to finance the purchase and cancellation of all its 10% debentures and some of its 5% debentures, both at par. A bonus issue of one for ten shares held was made on 1 November 2002; all shares in issue qualified for the bonus.

(2)   The current asset investment was a 30 day government bond.

(3)   Tangible fixed assets include certain properties which were revalued last year.

(4)   Tangible fixed assets disposed of in the year had a net book value of £75,000; cash received on disposal was £98,000.

(5)   Depreciation charged for the year was £87,000.

Required:

(a)   Prepare the following for YZ Ltd for the year ended 30 September 2003, in accordance with FRS 1 *Cash flow statements*:

    (i)   a reconciliation of operating profit to net cash inflow from operating activities;   **4 Marks**

    (ii)   a cash flow statement;   **14 Marks**

    (iii)   an analysis of changes in net debt.   **3 Marks**

(b)   Briefly explain the usefulness of cash flow information to shareholders.   **4 Marks**

    Total Marks = 25

ANSWERS

DO NOT TURN THIS PAGE UNTIL YOU
HAVE COMPLETED THE MOCK EXAM

A PLAN OF ATTACK

As you turned the page to start this exam any one of a number of things could have been going through your mind ranging from the sublime to the ridiculous.

The main thing to do is take a deep breath and do not panic. It's best to sort a plan of attack before the actual exam so that when the invigilator tells you that you can begin and the adrenaline kicks in you are using every minute of the three hours wisely.

Your approach

This paper has three sections. The first section contains 10 multiple choice questions which are compulsory. The second has one compulsory question. The third has four questions and you must answer two of them.

You have a choice.

- Read through and answer Section A before moving on to Section B and Section C

- Go through Section C and select the two questions you will attempt. Then go back and answer the questions in Section A first followed by Section B

- Select the two questions in Section C, answer them and then go back to the other two sections

- Answer the large compulsory question in Section B first and then go back to Sections A and C

You must give yourself a couple of minutes at the start of the exam to go through the questions you are going to do.

Time spent at the start of each question confirming the requirements and producing a plan for the answers is time well spent.

Question selection

When selecting the two questions from Section C make sure that you read through all of the requirements. It is painful to answer part (a) of a question and then realise that parts (b) and (c) are beyond you; by then it is too late to change your mind and do another question.

When reviewing the requirements look at how many marks have been allocated to each part. This will give you an idea of how detailed your answer must be.

Doing the exam

Think about your approach. After you've marked your exam spend a few moments reviewing how you tackled the questions.

Did you answer all of the multiple choice questions in Section A? Even if you don't know an answer, you should guess. Did you allocate your time correctly to the 30 mark question in Section B? Did you answer two questions from Section C?

If you decide on an approach to the exam this will help you to build your confidence. Sitting the two mocks in this kit will enable you to refine your approach.

One possible approach

This is the way I approached this mock exam. It may not suit you. If you can produce four good answers then your approach is equally valid.

Section A

It seems very sensible to me to ease my way into the exam by tackling the objective questions first. I would have a go at the non-computational ones first and then do the ones involving calculations. Long term contract calculations are difficult, so I might park these on one side until the end of exam so as not to get myself behind in time or get too frustrated early on in the exam. I put an o/s mark next to it so I do not forget it!

Section C

Question 4. I would do this next as I like ratio analysis questions because I can usually say something commercially sensible. This will help me build my confidence and help me to accumulate marks.

Question 3. This is a little obscure so I may want to give this one a miss.

Question 4. Share capital transactions can be tricky and I do not have a lot of experience of doing them in real life. Again I will avoid doing this question.

Question 5. This requires detailed knowledge of FRS 10 and SSAP 13 – I will only try this if I feel confident.

Question 6. Cash flow statements are a relatively easy and practical area. Remember to leave time for the five mark discussion element.

Section B

Having built up some confidence and some good marks, I will now have a go at the big 30 mark compulsory question. I will work through the profit and loss account and balance sheet in order, leaving out anything I cannot deal with, such as the provision problem.

Time allocation

Be disciplined. Allocate your time according to the marks available but never go over the time allocation. The last few marks in a question are the hardest to earn.

Be sure to follow the requirements. If four advantages are required, give four. No extra credit will be given for five. Two advantages will only get you half marks.

Answer all of the question. Having a go at every part of all the questions you are required to do will put you in a better position to pass than, say, only doing some questions. However difficult that last question seems at first there are marks to be earned.

If you have time left at the end of the exam ensure that you have attempted every part of every question. If you have, then scan through and ensure you completed any part of an answer you left earlier. Use the full three hours working towards a pass.

Marking the exam

When you mark your exam, be honest. Don't be too harsh though. Give yourself credit for the things you did well, but don't kid yourself with 'I would have done that in the real exam'. It may be worth your while making two lists; strengths and weaknesses.

Strengths will be areas of the syllabus you are confident with and also good exam technique (maybe you remembered to lay the memorandum out correctly and draw up a proforma balance sheet).

Weaknesses will be holes in your knowledge and poor exam technique (maybe you ran out of time and couldn't answer all the requirements of the last question).

Making this list will help you focus your last days of revision on the areas which require attention whilst reminding you of the areas you excel in.

SECTION A

1   C

2   C   Qualitative characteristics:

- Relevance
- Reliability
- Understandability
- Comparability

3   B   FRS 8 paragraph 4 specifically excludes 'providers of finance in control of their business in that regard.'

4   D   The subsequent sale provides evidence of the net realisable value of the stock as at year end.

5   D   EPS $= \dfrac{£300,000}{5 \text{ million shares}} = 6p$

   PE ratio $= \dfrac{150}{6} = 25X$

6   B $£20,000 \times \dfrac{5}{5+4+3+2+1}$

   $= 20,000 \times \dfrac{5}{15}$

   $= £6,667$

7   B

WDA	£	Capital Allowance
Cost 1.4 × 0	200,000	
WDA 25%	50,000	50,000
WDV 31.3 × 1	150,000	
WDA 25%	(37,500)	37,500
WDV 31.3 × 2	112,500	
WDA 25%	(28,125)	28,125
WDV 31.3 × 3	84,375	
Capital allowances claimed		115,625
Depreciation w/off		
3 yrs @ 10% straight line		60,000
Accelerated allowances		55,625
CT rate		× 30%
		16,688

8   C

	2002	2003
	£'000	£'000
Costs to date	2,900	4,600
Costs to complete	6,000	3,900
Estimates total cost	8,900	8,500
Projected profit	1,100	1,500
Contract price	10,000	10,001
Completed	30%	55%
Cumulative profit	330	825
P & L credit	330	495

9   A

	£	*Revaluation reserve*
Cost 1/7 × 0	50,000	
Depreciation to 1/7 × 2		
20% × 2 yrs	20,000	
Book value 1/7 × 2	30,000	
Revaluation increase	30,000	30,000
New carrying value 1/7 × 3	60,000	
Depreciation	20,000	
Net book value at 1/7	40,000	
Disposal	35,000	
Loss on disposal	5,000	

10   C $\dfrac{2,000,000}{5}$ = 400,000 shares

	£
Issue price	2
Nominal value	1
Premium	1

	£
∴ Total premium	400,000
Less Issue costs	25,000
Net to share premium	375,000

SECTION B

2   (a)

> **Pass marks.** Please note that this question does not requires Notes to the Accountants. Read the question carefully to determine whether they are required or not.

HI PLC
PROFIT AND LOSS ACCOUNT FOR THE YEAR ENDING 30 SEPTEMBER 2003

	£'000	£'000
Turnover		9,415
Cost of sales (3,591 + 819)		(4,410)
Gross profit		5,005
Administrative expenses (W1)	760	
Distribution costs	314	
		(1,074)
Operating profit		3,931
Exceptional item: Net surplus on cost of fundamental restructuring written back		45
Profit on disposal of fixed asset (W10)		6
Profit/loss on ordinary activities before interest and tax		3,982
Interest payable (W3)	(100)	
Income from fixed asset	37	
		(63)
Profit on ordinary activities before taxation		3,919
Tax on profit on ordinary activities (1,180 + 25) (W8)		(1,205)
Profit on ordinary activities after taxation		2,714
Dividends paid and proposed (W4)		(1,600)
Retained profit for the year		1,114
Retained profit brought forward		1,390
		2,504
Earnings per share		73.4p

BALANCE SHEET AS AT 30 SEPTEMBER 2003

	£'000	£'000
Fixed assets		
Tangible assets (W2)		9,856
Investments (market value) (W9)		522
		10,378
Current assets		
Stock	822	
Debtors (852 – 45)	807	
Cash at bank and in bank	959	
	2,588	
Creditors: amounts falling due within one year		
Trade creditors	396	
Other creditors including taxation (1,180 + 65 + 100)	1,345	
Accrued debenture interest (W3)	50	
Proposed dividends (W4)	800	
	2,591	
Net current assets/liabilities		(3)
Total assets lees current liabilities		10,375
Creditors: amounts falling due after more than one year		
10% debentures 2010		(1,000)
Provisions for liabilities and charges		
Deferred taxation (W6)	281	
Other provisions	-	(281)
		9,094

Capital and reserves

	£'000	£'000
Called up share capital		
Ordinary shares of £1 each, fully paid		4,000
Reserves		
Share premium account	2,388	
Revaluation reserve (172 + 30)	202	
Retained profits	2,504	
		5,094
		9,094

> **Pass marks.** Where you do not need to provide notes to the financial statements, you may need to make your decisions clear via your workings.

1   *Administrative expenses*

	£'000
As per TB	615
Bad debt written off - X Ltd *	45
Provision for legal claim re faulty product **	100
	7,60

*   Adjusting event – provides additional evidence of conditions existing at balance sheet date.

**   The obligation appears to be probable rather than possible. Hence treated as a provision rather than a liability.

2   *Fixed assets*

	Buildings £'000	Plant & Equipment £'000	Total £'000
Cost			
Opening balance	11,200	2,625	13,825
Additions		-	-
Disposals		(210)	(210)
Closing balance	11,200	2,415	13,615
Accumulated depreciation			
Opening balance	1,404	1,741	3,145
On disposals		(205)	(205)
Charge for year			
• £11,200 × 3%	336		
• £2,415 × 20%		483	
			819
Closing balance	1,740	2,019	3,759
Net bank value			9,856

Note. Where the question does not require notes, it may be worth setting up the table for cost and depreciation. This could help you to squeeze out the missing figures in a structured manner.

3   *Debenture interest*

	£'000
Per TB – ½ year	50
Accruals – further ½ year	50
P&L charge for year	100

4   *Dividends*

Interim dividend paid	800
Proposed final – 4,000 × 20p	800
	1,600

5   *Share capital*

	* Factor	Shares	£'000
Opening balance	4	3,200	3,200
Rights issue – 1 for 4	1	800	800
Closing balance	5	4,000	4,000

★   The opening balance is arrived at by working backwards. A 1 for 4 rights issue will give shareholders 5 shares, which corresponds to the £4 million share capital in the trial balance. Hence the opening balance is

£4 million × $^4/_5$ = £3.2 million

6   *Deferred taxation*

	£'000
As per TB	256
Amount set aside for year	25
Amount required for balance sheet	281

7   *Earnings per share*

		£'000
Before issue:		
Fair value per share	£4.25	
Number of shares	× 3,200	
		13,600
Received from exercise of rights:		
Exercise price	£3.00	
Number of shares	× 800	
		2,400
Total 'value'		16,000
Number of shares after rights issue		÷ 4,000
Theoretical ex-rights value per share		£4.00
Adjustment factor		£4.25
		£4.00

Number of shares (denominator):

$$(3,200 \times \frac{425}{400} \times {}^6/_{12}) + (4,000 \times {}^6/_{12})$$

$$= 1,700 + 2,000$$

$$= 3,700 \text{ shares}$$

$$EPS = \frac{2,714}{3,700} = 73.4 \text{ pence}$$

8   *Reorganisation expenses*

	Provision	P&L a/c
	£'000	£'000
As per TB	(1,010)	900
Invoice received	65	
	945	
Written back	(945)	(945)

9   *Fixed asset investments*

	£'000
Opening valuation	492
Mark-to-market adjustment	30
Closing valuation	522

Note. The ASC believed that 'marking-to-market' does not comply with the requirements of the companies act and has to be justified on the basis of a true and fair override. However, the DTI does not support the view that this can be a generic practice because the true and fair override has to be applied on a case by case basis.

10   *Disposals account*

	£'000
Cost of asset sale	210
Depreciation thereon	205
Book value	5
Proceeds	11
Profit on disposal	6

(b)   HI PLC

RECONCILIATION OF MOVEMENTS IN SHAREHOLDERS FUNDS FOR THE YEAR ENDED 30 SEPTEMBER 2003

	£'000
Profit for the financial year	2,714
Other recognised gains and losses relating to the year	30
	2,744
Dividends paid and proposed	(1,600)
New share issued	800
Share premium on new shares issued	1,600
Net addition to shareholders' funds	3,544
Opening shareholders funds	5,550
Closing shareholders funds	9,094

(c)   **EPS**

EPS = 73.4p [W7, part (a)]

SECTION C

3

> **Pass marks.** This is a very full suggested solution provided as a basis for revising the key learning points.

(a) **Financial statement figures**

    (i)   *New retail outlet*

- In terms of FRS 15, A Ltd has the **choice** of carrying its tangible fixed assets at **valuation**. If such a policy is adopted, it should be **consistently applied** to all tangible fixed assets of the **same class**.

- A retail outlet is a **non-specialised property** and should therefore be valued on the basis of **existing use value**. However, where the open market value is materially different from existing use value, the open market value and reasons for the difference should be disclosed in the notes to the accounts. Hence, under the revaluation route, the property would be shown at its existing use valuation of £1,000,000 but an appropriate note to the accounts included, disclosing and explaining its difference from the open market value of £1,200,000.

    (ii)   *Former retail unit*

- This now falls into the 'surplus to requirements' category and should therefore be valued at **open market value less expected direct selling costs**, if **material**. The unit should therefore be shown in the balance sheet at £1,200,000 less estimated direct selling costs.

- Although a buyer has not yet been found, it is assumed there are no indications of **impairment** and that being a city centre site, the property will indeed be sold.

(b) (i)   *Valuation of three buildings*

If events or changes in circumstances indicate that the carrying amount of a fixed asset may not be recoverable, an **impairment review** should be carried out.

FRS 11 specifies that a significant decline in market value is an indication of impairment. Hence, the factory should be reviewed for impairment.

FRS 11 specifies the process for conducting an impairment review.

- The impairment review will consist of a comparison of the carrying amount of the fixed asset or goodwill with its recoverable amount (the higher of net realisable value, if known, and value in use).

- To the extent that the carrying amount exceeds the recoverable amount, the fixed assets or goodwill is impaired and should be written down.

- The impairment loss should be recognised in the profit and loss account unless it arises on a previously revalued fixed asset.

Therefore the external auditor would expect the factory to be written down to its recoverable amount with a charge to the profit and loss account.

    (ii)   **Financial statement figures**

For the office and warehouse, the carrying amount (NBV) is lower than the **recoverable amount** and hence these should be included at their net book values at 30 June 20X3 ie £1,000,000 and £1,500,000 respectively.

For the factory the recoverable amount is the higher of:

- open market value £1,400,000

- Existing use value £1,600,000

ie £1,600,000

The **recoverable amount** of £1,600,000 is lower than NBV of £2,300,000 so the factory should be shown in the accounts at £1,600,000.

(iii) **External audit available actions**

The auditors could refuse to issue an unqualified audit report.

There is a **disagreement** regarding the treatment of tangible fixed assets, amounting to a £700,000 **overstatement**. We are not provided with a full set of accounts, so we cannot categorically state whether this amount is **material or fundamental**. There are therefore three courses open to the auditors.

- **Amount is not material:** Unqualified audit report could be issued

- **Amount is material but not fundamental** Auditors would issue an 'except for' opinion highlighting the particular issue of disagreement

- **Amount is fundamental** Auditors would give an adverse opinion stating that the accounts do not give a true and fair view.

(iv) **Financial Reporting Review Panel**

The role of the Review Panel is to examine material departures from the accounting requirements of the Companies Act 1985, including **applicable accounting standards**.

The Panel is concerned with an examination of **material departures** from accounting standards with a view to considering whether the accounts in question nevertheless meet the **statutory requirement** to give a **true and fair view**. While such a departure does not necessarily mean that a company's accounts fail the true and fair test it will raise the question.

The Panel normally aims to discharge its tasks by seeking **voluntary agreement** with the directors of a company on any **necessary revisions** to the accounts in question. But if that **approach fails** and the Panel believes that revision of the accounts is necessary it will seek :

(1)   A **declaration from the court** that the **annual accounts** of the company concerned do not comply with the requirements of the Companies Act 1985,

(2)   An **order** requiring the directors of the company to **prepare revised accounts**. If the court grants such an order it may also require the directors to meet the **costs** of the proceedings and of revising the accounts.

Where accounts are revised at the instance of the Panel, either voluntarily or by order of the court, but the company's auditor had **not qualified** his **audit report** on the defective accounts the Panel will draw this **fact** to the **attention of the auditor's professional body**.

4

> **Pass marks**: This is a very practical question. Company chairpersons usually prepare detailed briefing notes to deal with practical questions when meeting shareholders.
>
> The question provided very little detailed data behind the numbers, the suggested solution hence uses typical reasons to interpret the ratios computed. This became a question that asks for a **briefing document rather than an analysis** of financial information.

(a)

B Limited

Shareholders meeting re: Financial Statements 10 October 2001 to 30 September 2003

BRIEFING REPORT

1 Profitability

1.1 The company continues to trade successfully with turnover going up by 5.1% from 2002 to 2003.

1.2 We have improved gross margin from 27.5% in 2002 to 30.0% in 2003. This has been achieved by reducing cost of sales through improvements in operating efficiency. Sales performance has been increased through a focus on selling more profitable products rather than pushing up selling prices.

1.3 Administration and distribution expenses appear to have increased by 10.1% year on year, but the absolute amounts involved are relatively small. In percentage terms, administration expenses as a percentage of turnover has increased from 7.8% to 7.9%.

Internal controls over spending remain strong

1.4 The happy combination of successful trading and sound cost control has enabled us to improve operating profit on turnover from 15.5% in 2002 to 17.5% for 2003.

1.5 Profit before tax has gone up by £91,000 in 2003, representing a 21.0% increase over 2002.

1.6 The dividend for the year 2003 is £320,000 as compared to £200,000 in 2002, an increase in the magnitude of 60.0%. This is influenced by the increased shares in issue from 150,000 in 2002 to 325,000 in 2003. In congruence, retained profits for 2003 have gone down to £95,000 as compared to £163,000 for 2002.

1.7 Although the absolute value of the dividends has increased significantly between the two years, the dividend per share has not gone up (2003; 98p. 2002; 133p). This is because the number of shares in issue has gone up by 216.7%.

1.8 Although earnings have gone up by 14.3% over the two years, the number of shares in issue have increased by 216.7%. This helps to explain why EPS has gone down from 242p in 2002 to 127p in 2003.

1.9 ROCE has decreased from 22.6% in 2002 to 15.2% in 2003. Again, this is owing primarily to the large volume of shares issued in 2003, increasing capital employed significantly.

2.0 Asset turnover has decreased to 0.87 times in 2003 from 1.45 times in 2002. Again, this is a consequence of a disproportionate increase in capital employed resulting from the issue of 175,000 shares at £9 each during 2003.

2.1 The share issue proceeds were used in part to purchase new equipment but this did not become operational until the last four months of the year. In subsequent years we should see the full benefits of this new machinery.

316

2 Liquidity and efficiency

2.1 The current ratio, quick ratio, debtors turnover and trade creditors turnover figures calculated in Appendix II, indicate that the company maintains a steady course in its efficient management of its working capital.

2.2 An aspect where there has been a change from 2002 to 2003 is stock turnover. This metric has gone up from 48.6 days in 2002 to 68.5 days in 2003. This is (probably) because the company is trying to improve it's customer service by increasing stock levels so as to avoid stock-out situations which cause customer dissatisfaction.

2.3 Thus overall analysis of how the proceeds of the share issue have been put to use, suggests that some of it has gone into increasing stock levels by £155,000 (43.1%).

3 Financial structure

3.1 Generally, the key event impacting on the company's financial structure is the additional £1,575,000 sale of 175,000 shares at £9 per share, and how this has been utilised.

The liability in respect of debentures has gone down by £728,000 from £979,000 in 2002 to £251,000 in 2003. It therefore seems that a significant part of the share issue proceeds has been used to pay off long term debt. As a result the debt equity ratio has improved dramatically, being reduced to 0.06 in 2003 from 0.2 in 2002. The injection of capital; has partly been used to improve the company's long-term financial stability.

3.2 The carrying value of fixed assets has increased by £1,630,000 during the year. Part of this has been achieved via the revaluation reserve, which has gone up by £989,000. However, some £641,000 of the share issue proceeds has been channelled into fixed asset additions .

(No adjustment made for depreciation; figure not provided by question)

3.3 Reduction of debt has helped to improve interest cover from 3.97 times in 2002 to 4.28 times in 2003. Again, this is a pleasing indicator of long term financial stability.

Signed

Trainee Management Accountant

APPENDIX I

YEAR ON YEAR CHANGES

Profit and loss account	*20X3* *£'000*	*20X2* *£'000*	*Difference* *£'000*	*Percentage*
Turnover	3,920	3,730	190	5.1%
Administrative and distribution expense	492	447	45	10.1%
Profit before tax	525	434	91	21.0%
Dividends	320	200	120	60.0%
Retained profit for year	95	163	(68)	41.7%
Earnings	415	363	52	14.3%
Balance sheet	*£'000*	*£'000*	*£'000*	
Tangible fixed assets	3,260	1,630	1,630	100.0%
Stocks	515	360	155	43.1%
Debentures	251	979	(728)	74.4%
Share capital + premium	2,625	1,050	1,575	150.0%
Revaluation reserve	1,339	350	989	282.0%

Note: Where two years figures are provided in respect of a company, it may be worthwhile to reviewing the accounts line-by-lie to spot any significant changes

APPENDIX II

Profitability

	20X3	20X2
Gross margin		
1,177/3,920	30.0%	
1,027/3,730		27.5%
Admin expense		
308/3,920	7.9%	
290/3,730		7.8%
Distribution		
184/3,920	4.7%	
157/3,730		4.2%
Operating profit		
685/3,920	17.5%	
580/3,730		15.5%
Earnings per share		
415/325	127p	
363/150		242p
Dividend per share		
320/325	98p	
200/150		133p
ROCE		
685/4,496	15.2%	
580/2,565		22.6%
Asset turnover		
3,920/4,496	0.87x	
3,730/2,565		1.45x

Liquidity and efficiency

	20X3	20X2
Current ratio		
2,480/2,194	1.13	
1,780/1,575		1.13
Quick ratio		
(2480–515)/2,194	0.90	
(1780–360)/1,575		0.90
Stock turnover		
515/2,743×365	68.5 days	
360/2,703×365		48.6 days
Debtors turnover		
1,000/3,920×365	93.1 days	
950/3,730×365		93.0 days
Trade creditors turnover		
784/2,743*×365	104.3 days	
773/2,703*×365		104.4 days

* cost of sales used: purchases not given

319

Financial structure

	20X3	20X2
Debt equity ratio	0.06	
251/4,245		0.62
979/1,586		
Interest cover		
685/160★★	4.28X	
580/164★★		3.97X

★★ Net figures used

5   (a)   **Treatment of intangibles**

(i)   *Intangible assets – Brand X*

Where an intangible asset is acquired as part of the acquisition of a business FRS 10 specifies that the treatment depends on whether its value can be **measured reliably** on its **initial recognition**.

- If its value can be measured reliably, it should initially be recorded at its **fair value**. (The fair value should not create or increase any negative goodwill arising on the acquisition unless the asset has a readily ascertainable market value.)

- If the value of the asset cannot be measured reliably, the intangible asset must be subsumed within the amount of the purchase price attributed to goodwill.

Brand X acquired from Q has an identifiable fair value of £220,000 and should be initially recognised in the accounting records of Z plc on 31 October 2002 at this value. It does not create any negative goodwill.

In terms of FRS 10, the amount capitalised should be amortised on a systematic basis over the useful economic life of the brand, ie over the 10 yrs stated in the question.

Hence Z plc's balance sheet would include under Intangible Fixed Assets:

	31.10.03	31.10.02
	£'000	£'000
'Brands' at cost	220	220
Accumulated depreciation	44	22
Net book value	176	198

It is possible that amortisation would not start until year ending 31 October 2003 as the purchase took place on the last day of the previous year.

FRS 10 allows revaluation of intangibles to market value, subject to this policy being applied to all other capitalised intangible assets of the same class; so this is an alternative treatment that might be applied.

Internally developed intangibles

FRS 10 allows companies to capitalise non-purchased ('internally-developed') intangibles but only if they have a 'readily ascertainable market value'. This is an important definition that requires that:

- The asset belongs to a group of **homogenous assets** (ie they are all of the same kind) that are **equivalent in all material respects**.

- There is an **active market** for that group of assets, evidenced by frequent transactions.

Examples given by FRS 10 of intangibles that may meet these conditions include certain operating licenses, franchises and quotas.

FRS 10 also suggests **certain intangibles** that are **not equivalent in all material aspects**, are indeed **unique** and so do not have readily identifiable market values.

- Brands

- Publishing titles

- Patented drugs

- Engineering design patents

Hence, FRS 10 effectively precludes the recognition of most internally developed intangibles in financial accounts. Hence the amounts spent on creating and promoting Brand Z should not be capitalised, but instead, written off to the profit and loss account in the period of incurrence.

(ii)   *Goodwill*

	£'000
Cash paid to Q	523
Fair value of assets acquired	493
Positive goodwill	30

Where the fair value of consideration paid for an acquired entity exceeds the aggregate of fair values of the identifiable assets and liabilities taken out, positive goodwill arises.

In terms of FRS 10, **positive purchased goodwill** should be **capitalised** and classified as an asset on the balance sheet.

(**Internally generated goodwill should not be capitalised**. This requirement is the same as in the old SSAP 22.)

Hence an intangible fixed asset, goodwill of £30,000 should be raised in the accounting records of Z plc on 31 October 2002.

In terms of FRS 10, this goodwill should be amortised on a systematic basis over its useful economic life of 10 years.

Hence Z plc's balance sheet would include

	31.10.03	*31.10.02*
	£'000	£'000
Goodwill at cost	30	30
Accumulated depreciation	(6)	(3)
Net book value	24	27

As with Brand X it is possible that amortisation would not start until 2003 as the purchase took place on the last day of the previous year.

FRS 10 does **not allow** for the **capitalisation** of **internally generated goodwill**. Hence any goodwill arising subsequent to the acquisition of the business of Q, cannot be recognised in the accounts.

(b)   **Treatment of RD costs and grant – 2001, 2002 & 2003**

Year end 31 May 2001

SSAP 13 suggests that expenditure on **pure research** does **not benefit any particular accounting period** over another period and hence should be **written off** in the **year of incurrence**. Hence the money spent in Phase 1 sponsoring a local university department, in the amount of £75,000, should be written off to the profit and loss account for the year ended 31 May 2001.

Year end 31 May 2002

SSAP 13 specifically **excludes market research** from its examples of activities that might be classified as research and development within the ambit of SSAP 13. The treatment of the Phase 2 expenditure on market research would therefore be governed by the rules set out in FRS 18 regarding the **accruals basis of accounting**.

Hence, whether any market research expenditure, incurred in any period, should be carried forward, will depend on whether it satisfies the **definition of an asset**, ie is there a right or other access to **future economic benefits** controlled by the entity as a result of past transactions or events (*Note.* This contrasts with the old styled definition of accruals *'concept'* enshrined in SSAP 13 whereby 'revenues and costs are accrued, matched and dealt with in the period to which they relate.')

On the basis of the above, the element of Phase 2 consultancy fees incurred in respect of the year to 31 May 2002 does not qualify as an asset to be carried forward and hence should be written off to profit and loss account.

With regard to the grant, SSAP 4 specifies that where these should be recognised in the profit and loss account so as to 'match' them with the expenditure towards which they are intended to contribute.

Note. SSAP 4 was developed pre-Statement of Principles, hence still refers to item matching.

As discussed above, the Phase 2 consultancy fees should be written off to profit and loss account in the year they are incurred.

Year end 31 May 2003

We are told that this expenditure includes both development costs as well as product launch preparation costs.

The product launch preparation costs are **normal marketing costs** and do not fall into the scope of SSAP 13. They should be expensed or accrued for in forms of the **accruals basis of accounting** set out in **FRS 18**. We will need a split between the development costs and the launch preparation costs.

SSAP 13 allows development costs to be capitalised provided certain conditions are satisfied.

(i)   There must be a **separately** defined development project, with project **expenses** clearly identifiable.

(ii)   The expected outcome of the project must have been assessed, and there should be reasonable certainty that it is:

- **Commercially** viable, having regard to market conditions, competition, public opinion and consumer and environmental legislation

- **Technically** feasible

(iii)   The **overall profits** from the developed product or system should reasonably be expected to cover the past and future development costs.

(iv)   The company should have adequate **resources** to complete the development project.

Amortisation should begin with the commencement of production, and should then be written off on a systematic basis over the period in which the product is expected to be sold. If the accounting policy of deferral of development expenditure is adopted it should be consistently applied to all projects that meet the criteria.

However, deferred development expenditure should be reviewed at the end of every accounting period. If the conditions which justified the deferral of the expenditure no longer apply or are considered doubtful, the deferred expenditure, to the extent that it is now considered to be irrecoverable, should be written off.

6

(a) YZ LIMITED

CASH FLOW STATEMENT FOR THE YEAR ENDED 30 SEPTEMBER 2003

Reconciliation of operating profit to net cash inflow from operating activities

	£'000
Operating profit	304
Depreciation charges (87 – 23)	64
Decrease in stocks	40
Increase in debtors	(70)
Increase in creditors	150
Net cash inflow from operating activities	488

CASH FLOW STATEMENT

	£'000
Net cash inflow from operating activities	488
Returns on investments and servicing of finance (note 1)	(36)
Taxation	(94)
Capital expenditure (note 1)	(138)
	220
Equity dividends paid	(23)
	197
Management of liquid resources (note 1)	(50)
Financing (note 1)	-
Increase in cash	147

Reconciliation of net cash flow to movement in net debt (note 2)

	£'000	£'000
Increase in cash in the period	147	
Cash to repurchase debenture	60	
Cash used to increase liquid resources	50	
Change in net debt*		257
Net debt at 1.10.X2		(454)
Net funds at 30.9.X3		197

The reconciliation of operating profit to net cash flows from operating activities can be shown in a note.

NOTES TO THE CASH FLOW STATEMENT

1   *Gross cash flows*

	£'000	£'000
Returns on investments and servicing of finance		
Interest received	10	
Interest paid	(46)	
		36
Capital expenditure		
Payments to acquire tangible fixed assets	(236)	
Receipts from sales of tangible fixed assets	98	
		(138)
Management of liquid resources		
Purchase of government bonds		(50)
Financing		
Issue of ordinary share capital	60	
Repurchase of debenture loan	(60)	
		-

Note. These gross cash flows can be shown on the face of the cash flow statement, but it may sometimes be neater to show them as a note like this.

2   *Analysis of changes in net debt*

	1.10.02 £'000	Cash flows £'000	30.9.03 £'000
Cash in hand, at bank	5	77	82
Overdrafts	(70)	70	-
		147	
Debt due after 1 year	(389)	60	(329)
Current asset investments	-	50	50
Total	(454)	257	197

Workings

1   *Fixed assets*

Carrying value

	£'000		£'000
Balance b/f	510	Tfr to disposals	75
Revaluation	50	Depreciation	87
Additions	236	Balance c/f	634
	796		796

Carrying value

	£'000		£'000
NBV	75	Proceeds	98
P&L a/c	23	Depreciation	87
	98		98

2

	Balance 1.10.X2	P&L figure	Balance 30.9.X3	Cash flow
Interest receivable	9	5	(4)	(10)
Corporation tax	(90)	(104)	100	94
Dividends	-	(53)	30	20
Interest payable	(33)	(19)	6	46

( ) = Items appearing on credit side of a T account.

(b) **Usefulness of cash flow statements**

Cash is an important concept. **The survival of a business depends on its ability to generate cash to meet its liabilities.**

Cash flow statements are useful because they:

(1) Report their cash generation and cash absorption for a period by highlighting the significant components of cash flow in a way that facilitates **comparison** of the cash flow performance of **different businesses.**

(2) Provide information that assists in the assessment of their **liquidity, solvency** and **financial adaptability.**

The profit and loss account and balance sheet show the results of operations and the financial position of a company. Part of that financial position is the increase/decrease in cash over the year.

The cash flow statement in FRS 1 shows the summary of cash movements on the face of the statement under a number of standard headings.

This can be seen in the statement for YZ Ltd. The cash inflow from operating activities can be seen as can its expenditure on tax, interest and dividends.

The cash flow statement shows its shareholders how the money they have pumped into the company by way of fresh share capital has been utilised in reducing debenture debt and thereby helping to improve the company's financial stability, by reducing its debt equity ratio from 120.8% in 2002 to 58.2% in 2003.

Use of these standard headings allows the user to see at a quick glance how cash has been generated/expended by different components of the business.

Pass marks. Liquidity, solvency and financial adaptability are key words to bring into most discursive questions about cash flow statements. Also, try to link your comments to a few specific observations in the statement you have prepared. This ensures that you do not give the impression you have just learnt the points by rote!

See overleaf for information on other
BPP products and how to order

CIMA Order

To BPP Professional Education, Aldine Place, London W12 8AW

Tel: 020 8740 2211 Fax: 020 8740 1184

email: publishing@bpp.com

Order online www.bpp.com website: www.bpp.com

Mr/Mrs/Ms (Full name) _____

Daytime delivery address _____

_____ Postcode _____

Daytime Tel _____ Email _____ Date of exam (month/year) _____

Occasionally we may wish to email you relevant offers and information about courses and products. Please tick to opt into this service. ☐

POSTAGE & PACKING

Study Texts

	First	Each extra	Online
UK	£5.00	£2.00	£2.00
Europe*	£6.00	£4.00	£4.00
Rest of world	£20.00	£10.00	£10.00

Kits

	First	Each extra	Online
UK	£5.00	£2.00	£2.00
Europe*	£6.00	£4.00	£4.00
Rest of world	£20.00	£10.00	£10.00

Passcards/Success Tapes/MCQ Cards/CDs

	First	Each extra	Online
UK	£2.00	£1.00	£1.00
Europe*	£3.00	£2.00	£2.00
Rest of world	£8.00	£8.00	£8.00

Grand Total (incl. Postage) £ ☐☐☐☐

I enclose a cheque for ____ (Cheques to *BPP Professional Education*)

Or charge to Visa/Mastercard/Switch

Card Number ☐☐☐☐☐☐☐☐☐☐☐☐☐

Expiry date ____ Start Date ____

Issue Number (Switch Only) ____

Signature _____

Order table

	7/03 Texts £20.95	1/04 Kits £10.95	1/04 Passcards £6.95	Success Tapes £12.95	Success CDs £14.95	Virtual Campus	7/03 i-Pass £24.95	7/03 i-Learn £34.95	5/03 MCQ cards £5.95
FOUNDATION									
1 Financial Accounting Fundamentals	£20.95	£10.95	£6.95	£12.95	£14.95	£50	£24.95	£34.95	£5.95
2 Management Accounting Fundamentals	£20.95	£10.95	£6.95	£12.95	£14.95	£50	£24.95	£34.95	£5.95
3A Economics for Business	£20.95	£10.95	£6.95	£12.95	£14.95	£50	£24.95	£34.95	£5.95
3B Business Law	£20.95	£10.95	£6.95	£12.95	£14.95	£50	£24.95	£34.95	£5.95
3C Business Mathematics	£20.95	£10.95	£6.95	£12.95	£14.95	£50	£24.95	£34.95	£5.95
INTERMEDIATE									
4 Finance	£20.95	£10.95	£6.95	£12.95	£14.95	£90	£24.95	£34.95	£5.95
5 Business Tax (FA 2003) (10/03)	£20.95	£10.95	£6.95	£12.95	£14.95	£90	£24.95	£34.95	£5.95
6 Financial Accounting	£20.95	£10.95	£6.95	£12.95	£14.95	£90	£24.95	£34.95	£5.95
6i Financial Accounting International	£20.95	£10.95	£6.95				£24.95	£34.95	£5.95
7 Financial Reporting	£20.95	£10.95	£6.95	£12.95	£14.95	£90	£24.95	£34.95	£5.95
7i Financial Reporting International	£20.95	£10.95	£6.95				£24.95	£34.95	£5.95
8 Management Accounting - Performance Management	£20.95	£10.95	£6.95	£12.95	£14.95	£90	£24.95	£34.95	£5.95
9 Management Accounting - Decision Making	£20.95	£10.95	£6.95	£12.95	£14.95	£90	£24.95	£34.95	£5.95
10 Systems and Project Management	£20.95	£10.95	£6.95	£12.95	£14.95	£90	£24.95	£34.95	£5.95
11 Organisational Management	£20.95	£10.95	£6.95	£12.95	£14.95	£90	£24.95	£34.95	£5.95
FINAL									
12 Management Accounting - Business Strategy	£20.95	£10.95	£6.95	£12.95	£14.95		£24.95		
13 Management Accounting - Financial Strategy	£20.95	£10.95	£6.95	£12.95	£14.95		£24.95		
14 Management Accounting - Information Strategy	£20.95	£10.95	£6.95	£12.95	£14.95		£24.95		
15 Case Study (1) Workbook	£20.95			£12.95	£14.95				
(2) Toolkit	£20.95 (For 5/04: available 3/04. For 11/04: available 9/04)								
Learning to Learn Accountancy (7/02)	£9.95								

Total ☐

A signature will be required. Orders to all EU addresses should be delivered within 6 working days. All other orders to overseas addresses should be delivered

REVIEW FORM & FREE PRIZE DRAW

All original review forms from the entire BPP range, completed with genuine comments, will be entered into one of two draws on 31 July 2004 and 31 January 2005. The names on the first four forms picked out on each occasion will be sent a cheque for £50.

Name: _____ **Address**: _____

_____

_____

How have you used this Kit?
(Tick one box only)

☐ Self study (book only)

☐ On a course: college (please state)_____

_____

☐ With 'correspondence' package

☐ Other _____

Why did you decide to purchase this Kit?
(Tick one box only)

☐ Have used the complementary Study Text

☐ Have used other BPP products in the past

☐ Recommendation by friend/colleague

☐ Recommendation by a lecturer at college

☐ Saw advertising in journals

☐ Saw website

☐ Other _____

During the past six months do you recall seeing/receiving any of the following?
(Tick as many boxes as are relevant)

☐ Our advertisement in *CIMA Insider*

☐ Our advertisement in *Financial Management*

☐ Our advertisement in *Pass*

☐ Our brochure with a letter through the post

☐ Our website

Which (if any) aspects of our advertising do you find useful?
(Tick as many boxes as are relevant)

☐ Prices and publication dates of new editions

☐ Information on product content

☐ Facility to order books off-the-page

☐ None of the above

When did you sit the exam? _____

Which of the following BPP products have you used for this paper?

☐ Study Text ☐ MCQ Cards ☑ Kit ☐ Passcards ☐ Success Tape ☐ Breakthrough Video ☐ i-Products

Your ratings, comments and suggestions would be appreciated on the following areas of this Kit.

	Very useful	Useful	Not useful
Effective revision and revision plan	☐	☐	☐
Exam guidance	☐	☐	☐
Background (Websites and mindmaps)	☐	☐	☐
Preparation questions	☐	☐	☐
Exam standard questions	☐	☐	☐
'Pass marks' section in answers	☐	☐	☐
Content and structure of answers	☐	☐	☐
Mock exams	☐	☐	☐
'Plan of attack'	☐	☐	☐
Mock exam answers	☐	☐	☐

	Excellent	Good	Adequate	Poor
Overall opinion of this Kit	☐	☐	☐	☐

Do you intend to continue using BPP products?   ☐ Yes ☐ No

Please note any further comments and suggestions/errors on the reverse of this page. The BPP author of this edition can be e-mailed at: philfontbin@bpp.com

Please return this form to: Nick Weller, CIMA range manager, BPP Professional Education, FREEPOST, London, W12 8BR

REVIEW FORM & FREE PRIZE DRAW (continued)

Please note any further comments and suggestions/errors below.

FREE PRIZE DRAW RULES

1   Closing date for 31 July 2004 draw is 30 June 2004. Closing date for 31 January 2005 draw is 31 December 2004.

2   Restricted to entries with UK and Eire addresses only. BPP employees, their families and business associates are excluded.

3   No purchase necessary. Entry forms are available upon request from BPP Professional Education. No more than one entry per title, per person. Draw restricted to persons aged 16 and over.

4   Winners will be notified by post and receive their cheques not later than 6 weeks after the relevant draw date.

5   The decision of the promoter in all matters is final and binding. No correspondence will be entered into.